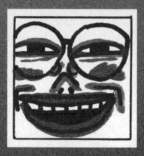

PRODUCTION REPORT SERIES 2: NAMES
I DON'T GIVE TOO MUCH THOUGHT TO THE
CHARACTER NAMES. I FLIP THROUGH THE
DICTIONARY AND COMBINE KANJI I LIKE.
YUSUKE'S NAME IS PRACTICALLY A JOKE,
AND KUWABARA'S NAME IS A COMBINATION
OF TWO BASEBALL PLAYERS. KURAMA AND
HIEI'S NAMES WERE ALSO SPURS OF THE
MOMENT. "YOSHIHIRO TOGASHI" IS MY REAL
NAME, THOUGH (NOT A PEN NAME). IF I
EVER GET MARRIED AND HAVE KIDS, MAYBE
I'LL GIVE THEM OBSCENE NAMES, TOO.
HEH HEH HEH.

—*YOSHIHIRO TOGASHI, 1991*

Born in 1966, Yoshihiro Togashi won
the prestigious Tezuka Award for new
manga artists at the age of 20. He
debuted in Japan's WEEKLY SHONEN JUMP
magazine in 1988 with the romantic
comedy manga **Tende Showaru Cupid**.
His hit comic **YuYu Hakusho** ran in
WEEKLY SHONEN JUMP from 1990 to
1994. Togashi's other manga include
I'm Not Afraid of Wolves!, **Level E**,
and **Hunter x Hunter**.

YUYU HAKUSHO VOL. 7
The SHONEN JUMP Graphic Novel Edition

This graphic novel contains material that was originally published
in English in **SHONEN JUMP** #26-30.

STORY AND ART BY
YOSHIHIRO TOGASHI

English Adaptation/Gary Leach
Translation/Lillian Olsen
Touch-Up Art & Lettering/Kathryn Renta
Graphics & Cover Design/Courtney Utt
Editor/Michelle Pangilinan

Managing Editor/Elizabeth Kawasaki
Director of Production/Noboru Watanabe
Vice President of Publishing/Alvin Lu
Vice President & Editor in Chief/Yumi Hoashi
Sr. Director of Acquisitions/Rika Inouye
Vice President of Sales & Marketing/Liza Coppola
Publisher/Hyoe Narita

YUYU HAKUSHO © 1992 YOSHIHIRO TOGASHI. All rights
reserved. First published in Japan in 1992 by SHUEISHA Inc., Tokyo.
English translation rights in the United States of America and Canada
arranged by SHUEISHA Inc. The stories, characters, and incidents
mentioned in this publication are entirely fictional.

No portion of this book may be reproduced or transmitted in any form
or by any means without written permission from the copyright holders.

Printed in the U.S.A.

Published by VIZ, LLC
P.O. Box 77010 • San Francisco, CA 94107

SHONEN JUMP Graphic Novel Edition
10 9 8 7 6 5 4 3 2 1
First printing, May 2005

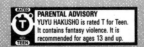

PARENTAL ADVISORY
YUYU HAKUSHO is rated T for Teen.
It contains fantasy violence. It is
recommended for ages 13 and up.

THE WORLD'S
MOST POPULAR MANGA

www.viz.com

www.shonenjump.com

SHONEN JUMP GRAPHIC NOVEL

YuYu HAKUSHO™

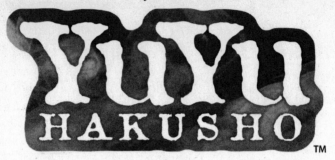

Vol.7

Knife-Edge Death Match

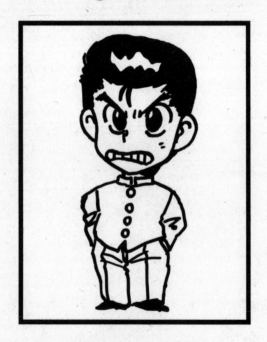

STORY AND ART BY

YOSHIHIRO TOGASHI

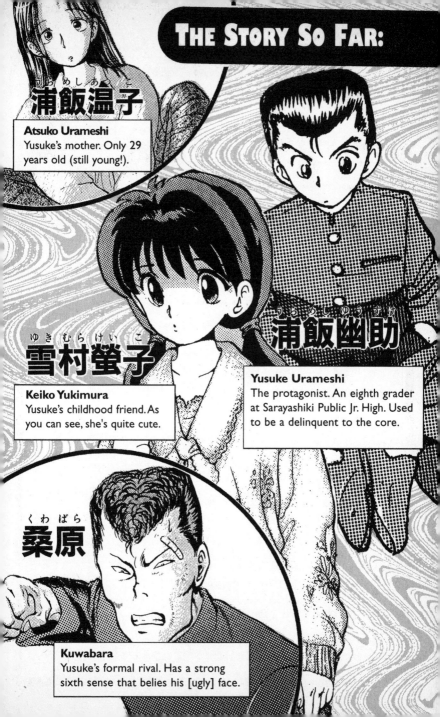

THE STORY SO FAR:

浦飯温子
うらめしあつこ

Atsuko Urameshi
Yusuke's mother. Only 29 years old (still young!).

浦飯幽助
うらめしゆうすけ

Yusuke Urameshi
The protagonist. An eighth grader at Sarayashiki Public Jr. High. Used to be a delinquent to the core.

雪村螢子
ゆきむらけいこ

Keiko Yukimura
Yusuke's childhood friend. As you can see, she's quite cute.

桑原
くわばら

Kuwabara
Yusuke's formal rival. Has a strong sixth sense that belies his [ugly] face.

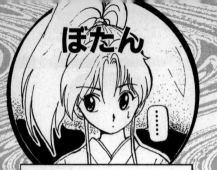

ぼたん

Botan
Guide to the Underworld.
Yusuke's guardian of sorts.

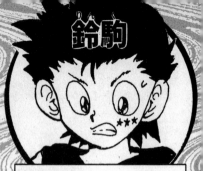

鈴駒

Rinku
Vanguard of the Jolly Devil Six.

T his is the story of the hapless Yusuke Urameshi... He got into a car accident trying to save a kid and became a ghost. King Enma gave him a number of ordeals, and now he's back to life. He became an Underworld Detective to track down the most wanted demons.

The Black Book Club caught wind of Yusuke and company's prowess after they defeated the Four Beasts, and forced them to compete in the Dark Tournament. For the first match, Yusuke's team went against the Jolly Devil Six, and Kuwabara and his opponent knocked each other out...!

CONTENTS

Chapter 56   Blood-Stained Flowers!!...........................7

Chapter 57   The Fearsome Hell of Blazing Heat!!.....27

Chapter 58   Drunken Master: Chu!!...........................49

Chapter 59   A Close Game!!..67

Chapter 60   Knife-Edge Sudden Death!!.....................87

Chapter 61   The Top Eight Line-Up!!...........................109

Chapter 62   The Second Round Begins!!.....................129

Chapter 63   The Despicable Blood-Slaver Node.......149

Special Bonus
Episode: YuYu Hakusho Tales: Two Shot................169

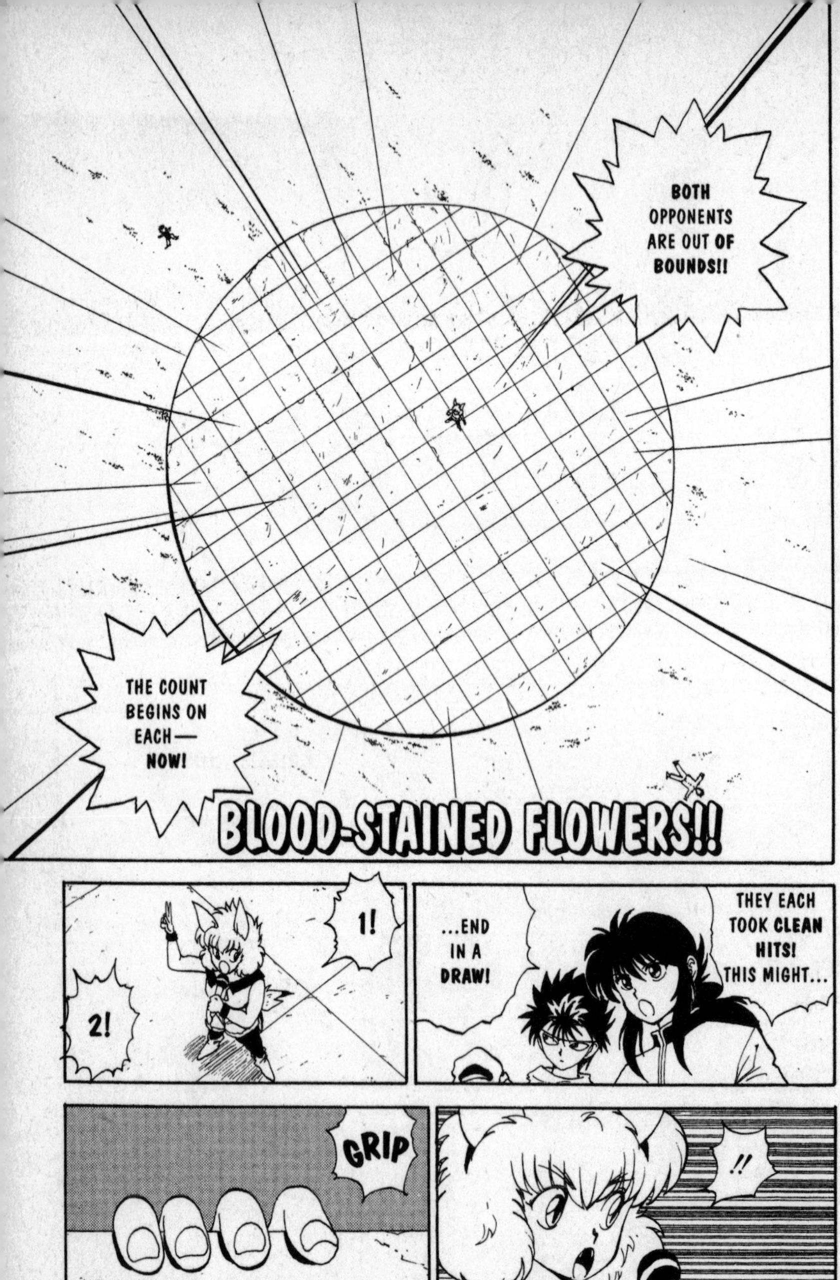
BOTH OPPONENTS ARE OUT OF BOUNDS!!
THE COUNT BEGINS ON EACH— NOW!
BLOOD-STAINED FLOWERS!!
THEY EACH TOOK CLEAN HITS! THIS MIGHT...
...END IN A DRAW!
1!
2!
!!
GRIP

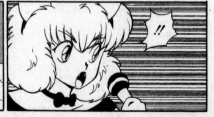

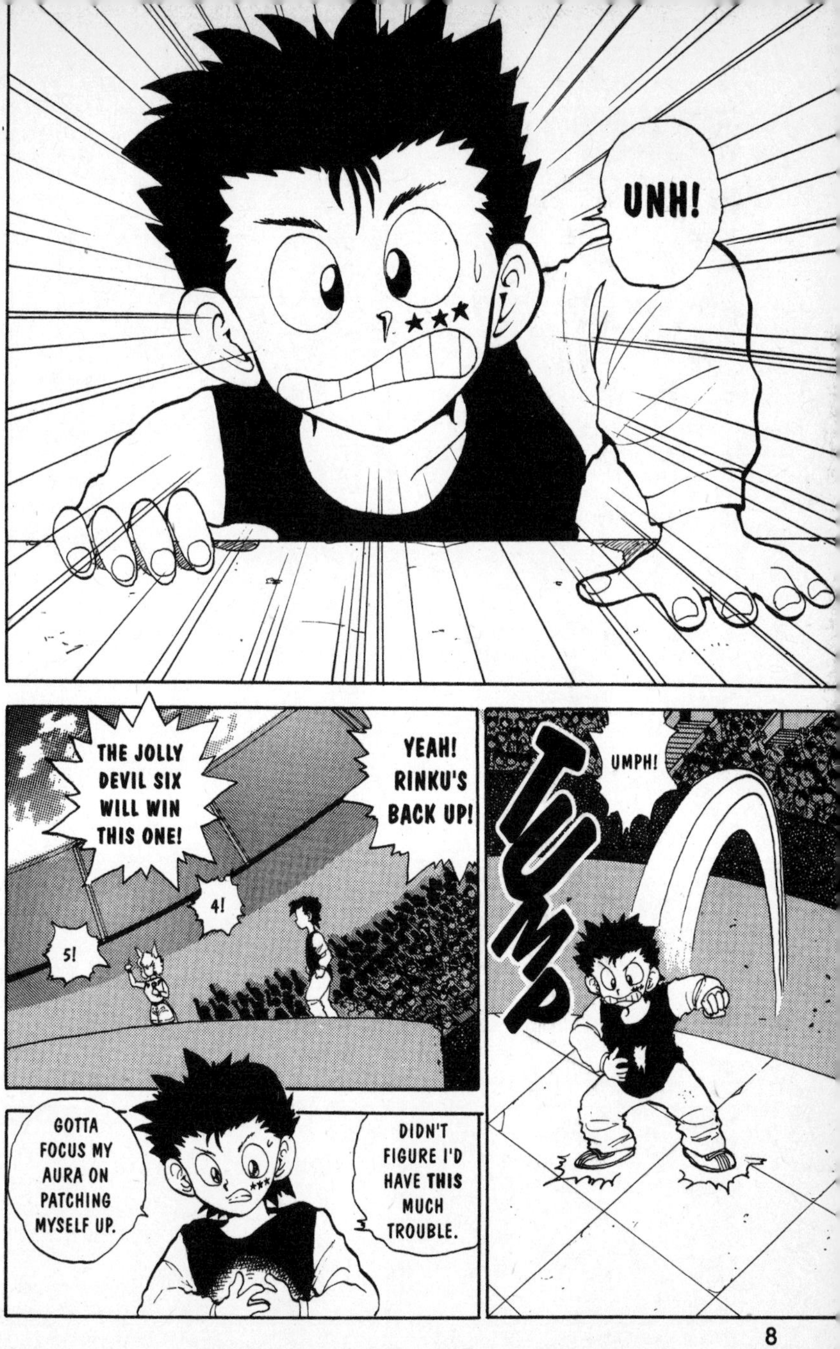
UNH!
UMPH!
TUMP
YEAH! RINKU'S BACK UP!
THE JOLLY DEVIL SIX WILL WIN THIS ONE!
4!
5!
DIDN'T FIGURE I'D HAVE THIS MUCH TROUBLE.
GOTTA FOCUS MY AURA ON PATCHING MYSELF UP.

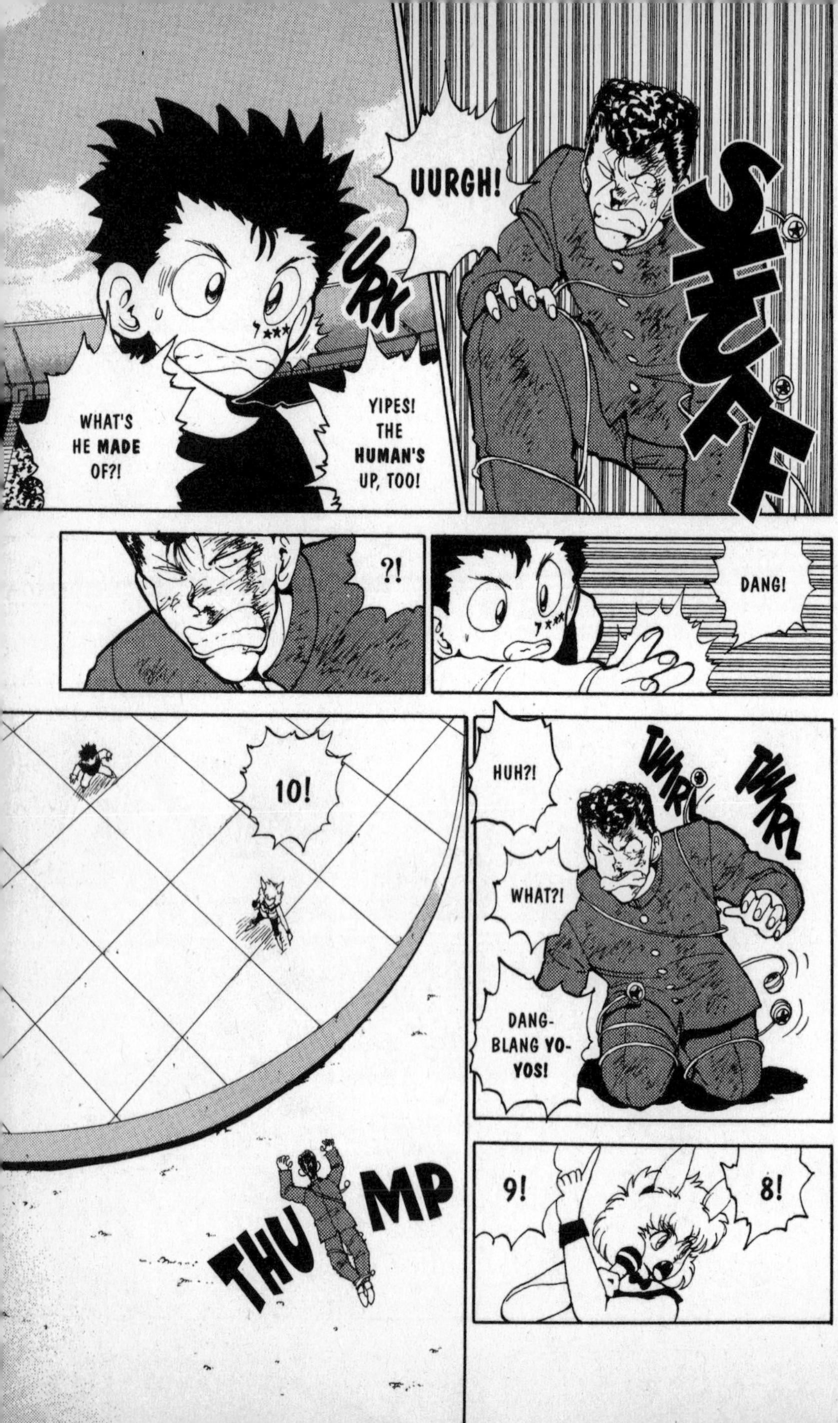
UURGH!
SHUFF
URK
YIPES! THE HUMAN'S UP, TOO!
WHAT'S HE MADE OF?!
DANG!
?!
TWIRL
TWIRL
HUH?!
WHAT?!
DANG-BLANG YO-YOS!
8!
9!
10!
THUMP

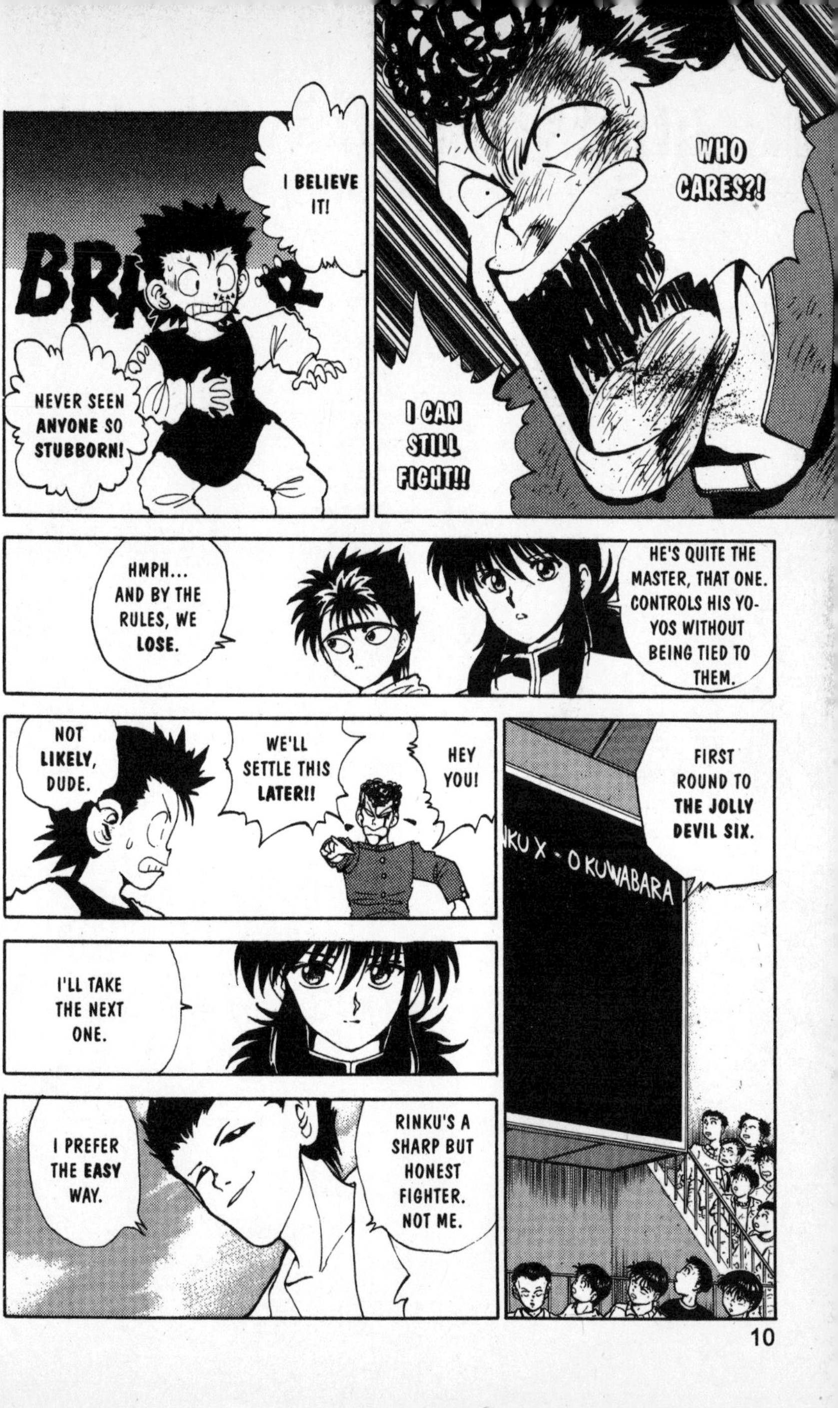
WHO CARES?!
I CAN STILL FIGHT!!
I BELIEVE IT!
NEVER SEEN ANYONE SO STUBBORN!
HE'S QUITE THE MASTER, THAT ONE. CONTROLS HIS YO-YOS WITHOUT BEING TIED TO THEM.
HMPH... AND BY THE RULES, WE LOSE.
FIRST ROUND TO THE JOLLY DEVIL SIX.
NKU X - O KUWABARA
HEY YOU!
WE'LL SETTLE THIS LATER!!
NOT LIKELY, DUDE.
I'LL TAKE THE NEXT ONE.
RINKU'S A SHARP BUT HONEST FIGHTER. NOT ME.
I PREFER THE EASY WAY.

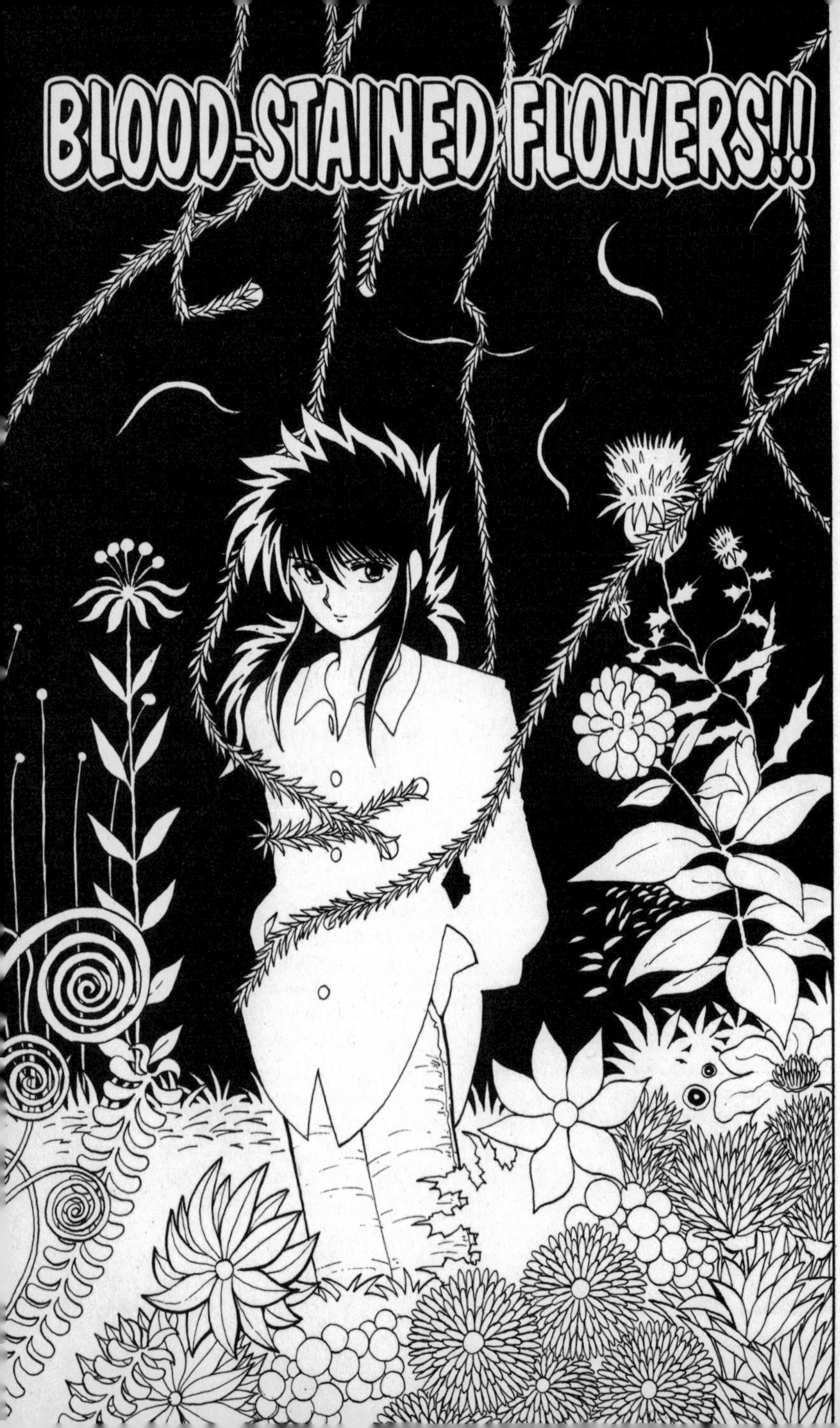
BLOOD-STAINED FLOWERS!!

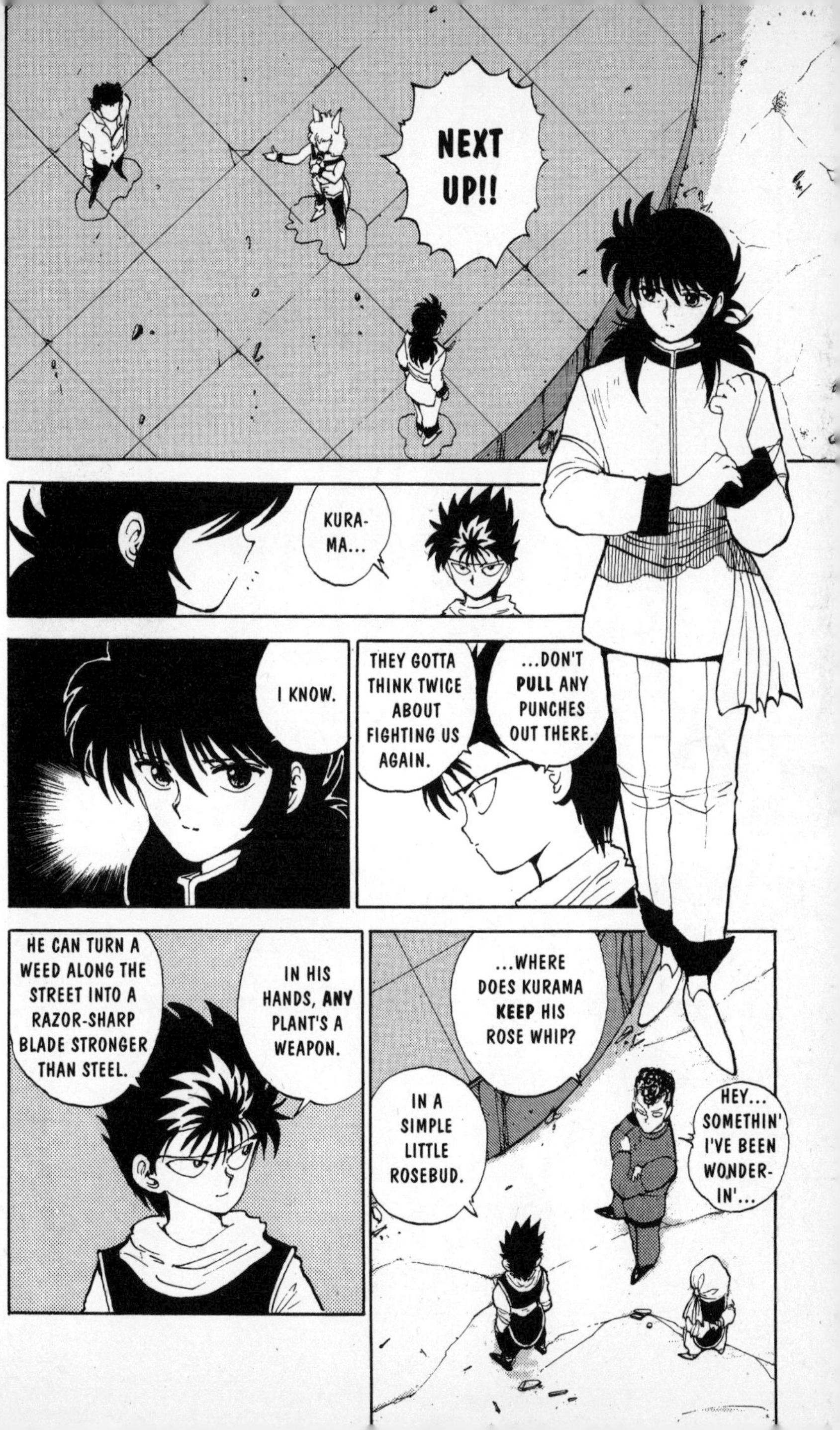
NEXT UP!!
KURA-MA...
...DON'T PULL ANY PUNCHES OUT THERE.
THEY GOTTA THINK TWICE ABOUT FIGHTING US AGAIN.
I KNOW.
HEY... SOMETHIN' I'VE BEEN WONDER-IN'...
...WHERE DOES KURAMA KEEP HIS ROSE WHIP?
IN A SIMPLE LITTLE ROSEBUD.
IN HIS HANDS, ANY PLANT'S A WEAPON.
HE CAN TURN A WEED ALONG THE STREET INTO A RAZOR-SHARP BLADE STRONGER THAN STEEL.

READ THIS WAY

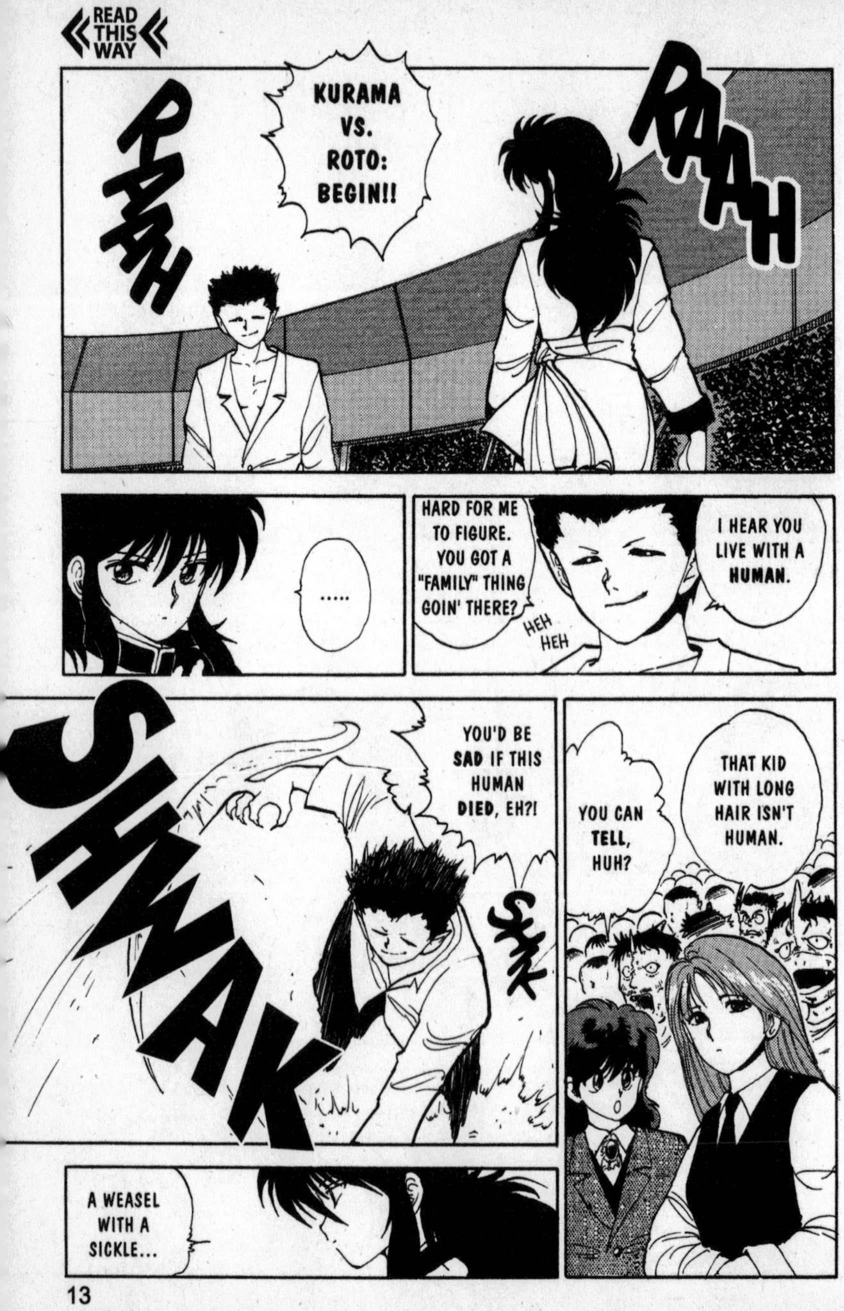
RAAAH
KURAMA VS. ROTO: BEGIN!!
RAAAH
I HEAR YOU LIVE WITH A HUMAN.
HARD FOR ME TO FIGURE. YOU GOT A "FAMILY" THING GOIN' THERE?
HEH HEH
......
THAT KID WITH LONG HAIR ISN'T HUMAN.
YOU CAN TELL, HUH?
YOU'D BE SAD IF THIS HUMAN DIED, EH?!
SHK
SHWAK
A WEASEL WITH A SICKLE...

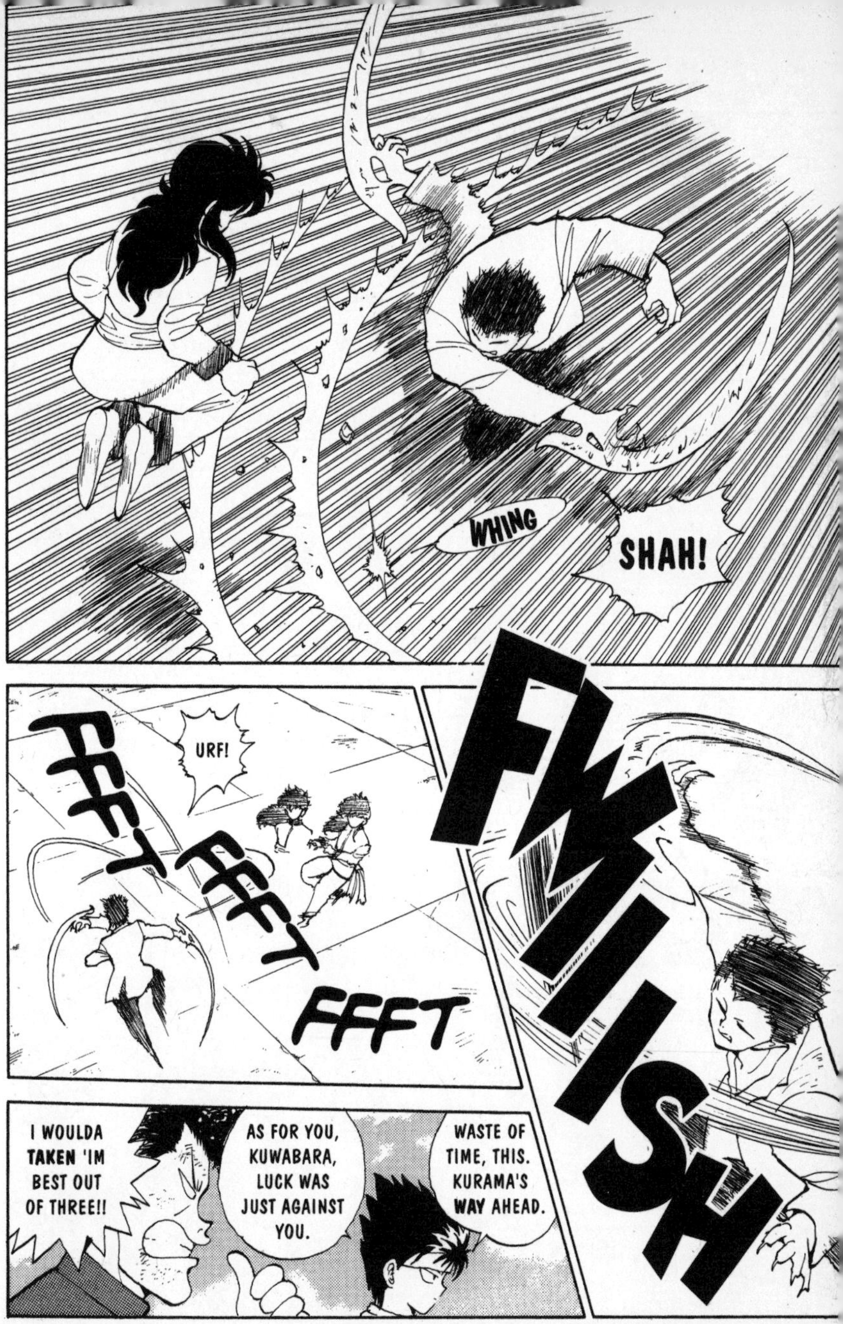
WHING
SHAH!
FWIISH
URF!
FFFT
FFFT
FFFT
WASTE OF TIME, THIS. KURAMA'S WAY AHEAD.
AS FOR YOU, KUWABARA, LUCK WAS JUST AGAINST YOU.
I WOULDA TAKEN 'IM BEST OUT OF THREE!!

READ THIS WAY

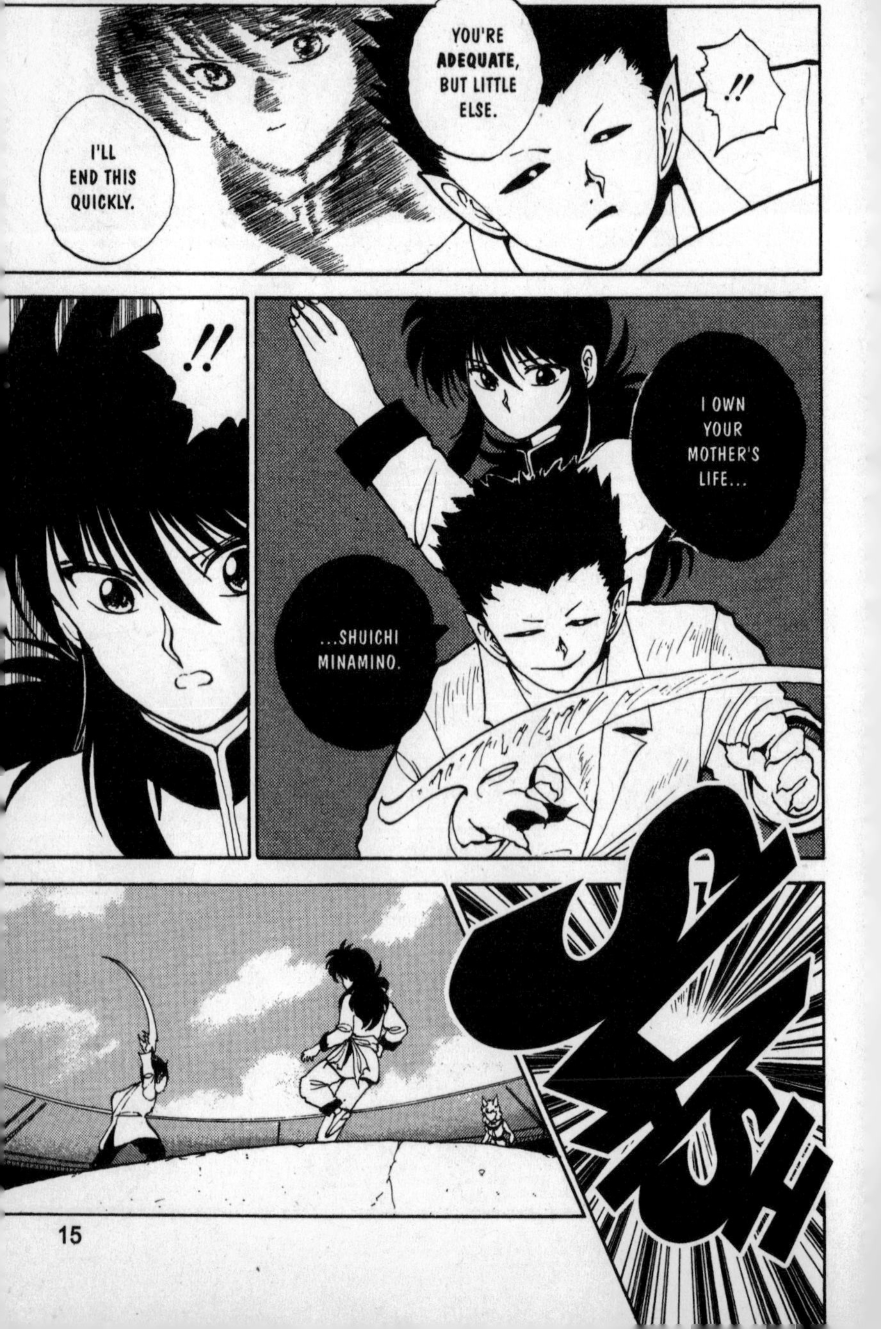

!!
YOU'RE ADEQUATE, BUT LITTLE ELSE.
I'LL END THIS QUICKLY.
I OWN YOUR MOTHER'S LIFE...
...SHUICHI MINAMINO.
!!

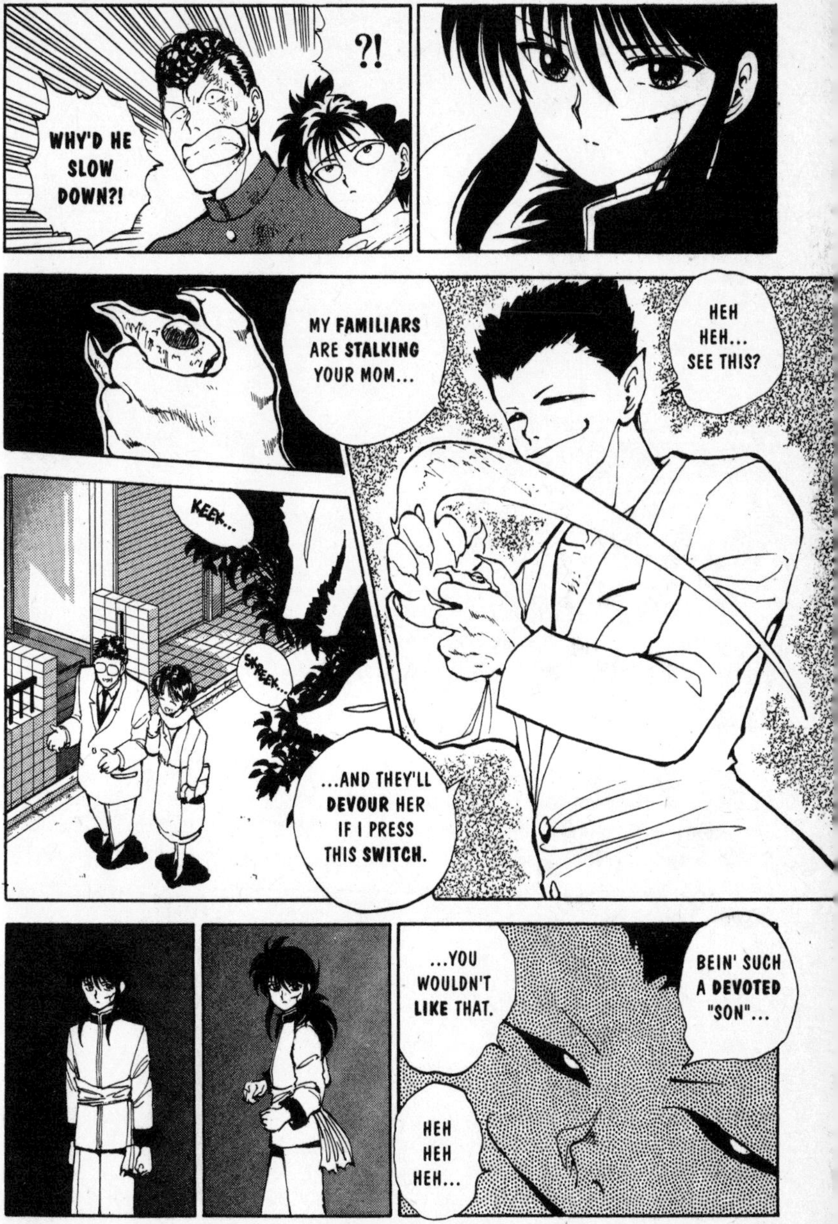
?!
WHY'D HE SLOW DOWN?!
HEH HEH... SEE THIS?
MY FAMILIARS ARE STALKING YOUR MOM...
KEEK...
SKREEK...
...AND THEY'LL DEVOUR HER IF I PRESS THIS SWITCH.
BEIN' SUCH A DEVOTED "SON"...
...YOU WOULDN'T LIKE THAT.
HEH HEH HEH...

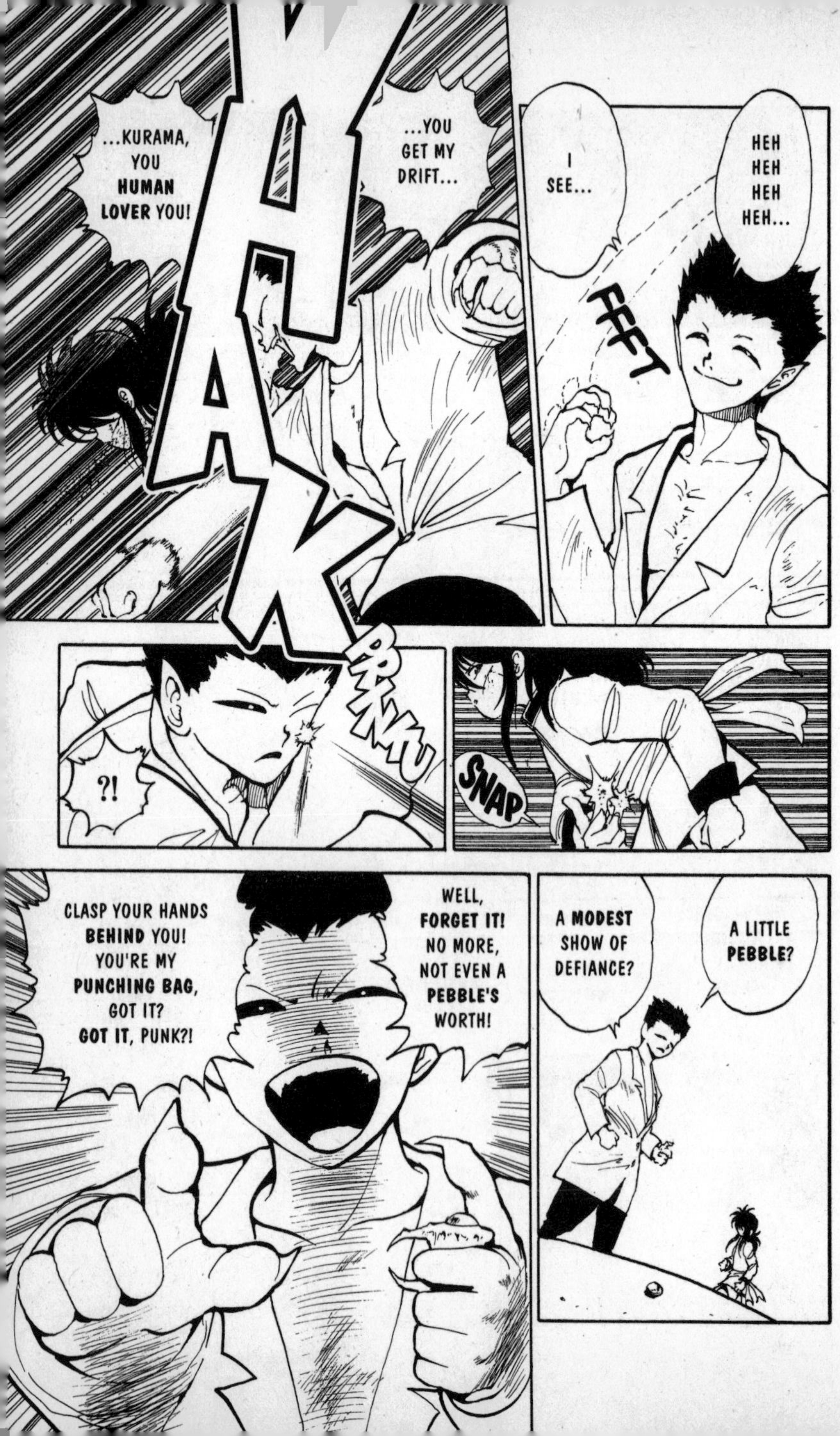
HEH HEH HEH HEH...
I SEE...
FFFT
...YOU GET MY DRIFT...
...KURAMA, YOU HUMAN LOVER YOU!
HAK
SNAP
?!
A LITTLE PEBBLE?
A MODEST SHOW OF DEFIANCE?
WELL, FORGET IT! NO MORE, NOT EVEN A PEBBLE'S WORTH!
CLASP YOUR HANDS BEHIND YOU! YOU'RE MY PUNCHING BAG, GOT IT? GOT IT, PUNK?!

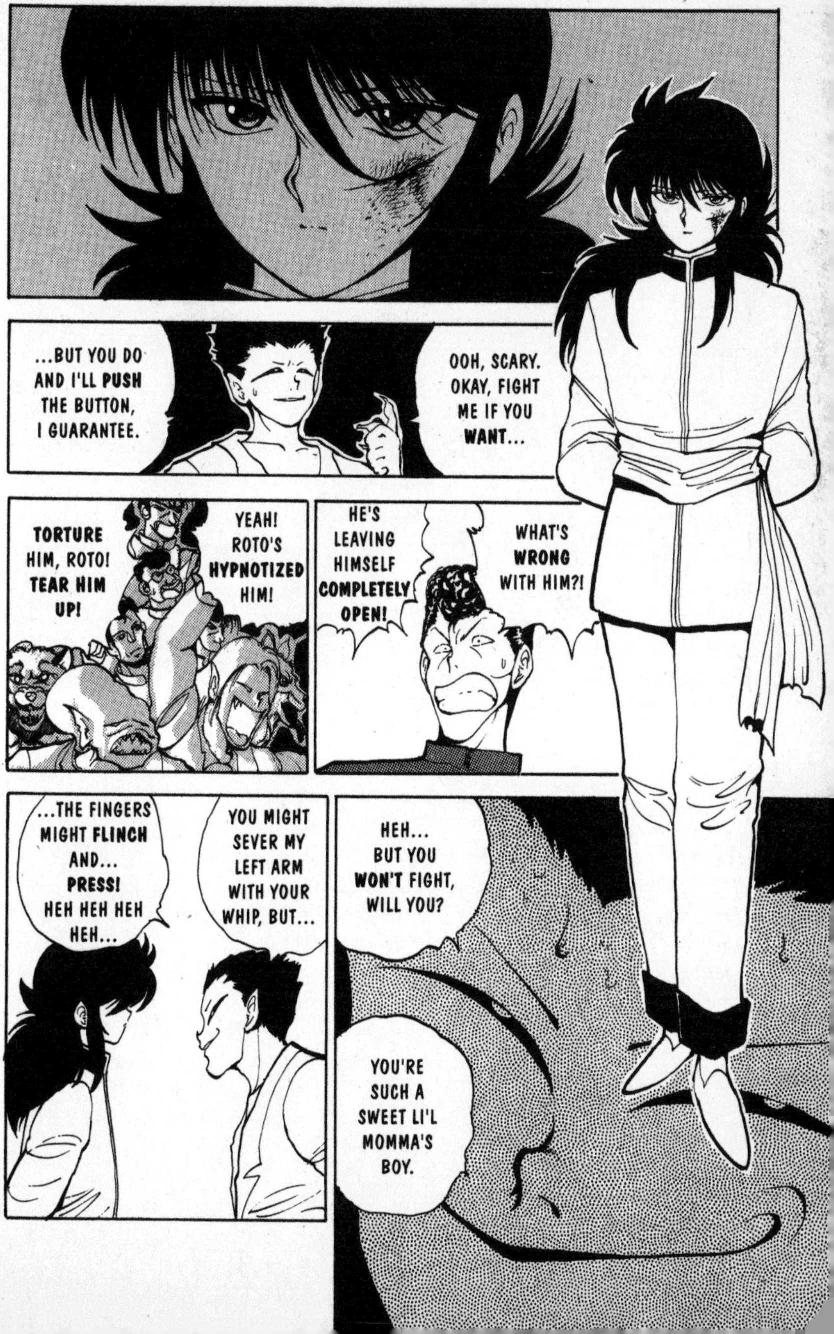
OOH, SCARY. OKAY, FIGHT ME IF YOU WANT...
...BUT YOU DO AND I'LL PUSH THE BUTTON, I GUARANTEE.
WHAT'S WRONG WITH HIM?!
HE'S LEAVING HIMSELF COMPLETELY OPEN!
YEAH! ROTO'S HYPNOTIZED HIM!
TORTURE HIM, ROTO! TEAR HIM UP!
HEH... BUT YOU WON'T FIGHT, WILL YOU?
YOU'RE SUCH A SWEET LI'L MOMMA'S BOY.
YOU MIGHT SEVER MY LEFT ARM WITH YOUR WHIP, BUT...
...THE FINGERS MIGHT FLINCH AND... PRESS! HEH HEH HEH HEH...

READ THIS WAY

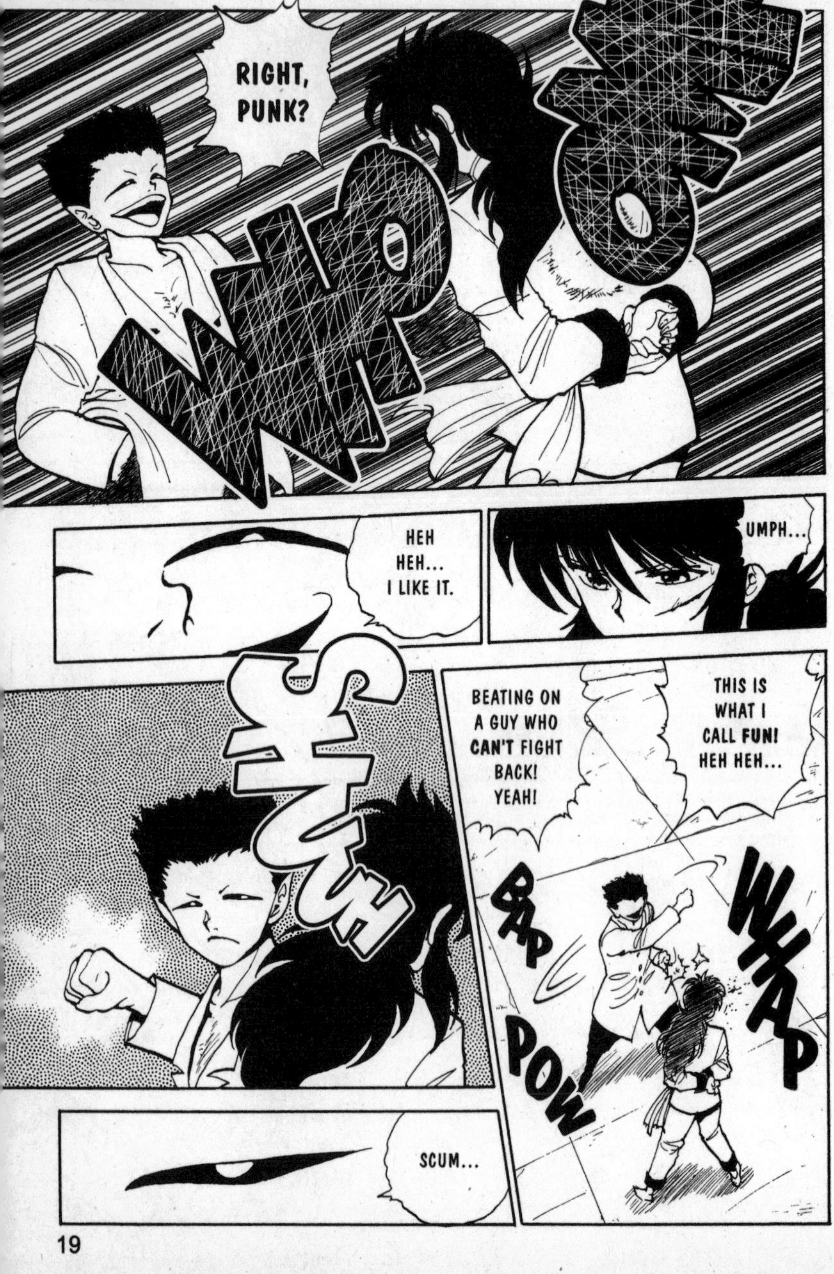
RIGHT, PUNK?
UMPH...
HEH HEH... I LIKE IT.
THIS IS WHAT I CALL **FUN!** HEH HEH...
BEATING ON A GUY WHO **CAN'T** FIGHT BACK! YEAH!
WHAP
BAP
POW
SCUM...

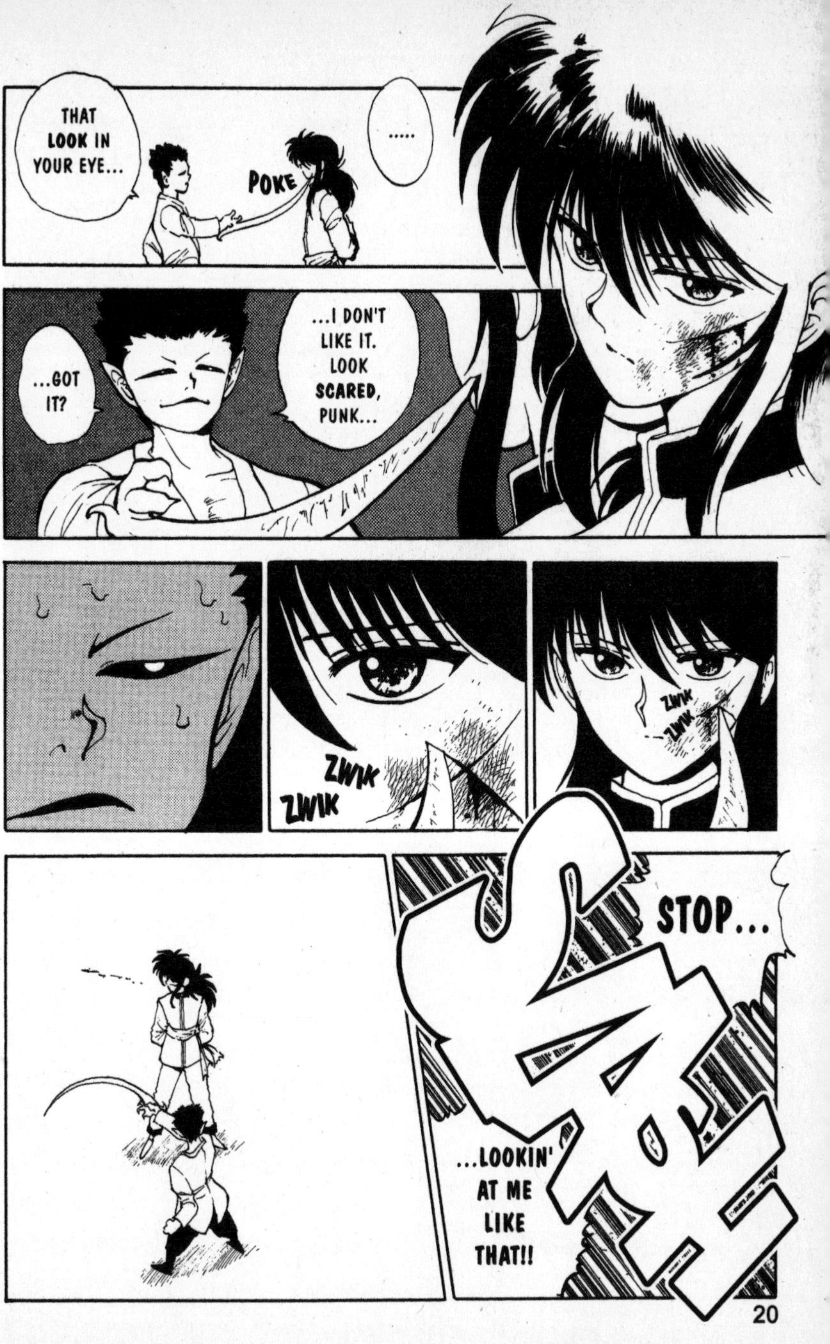
.....
THAT LOOK IN YOUR EYE...
POKE
...I DON'T LIKE IT. LOOK SCARED, PUNK...
...GOT IT?
ZWIK
ZWIK
ZWIK
ZWIK
STOP...
...LOOKIN' AT ME LIKE THAT!!

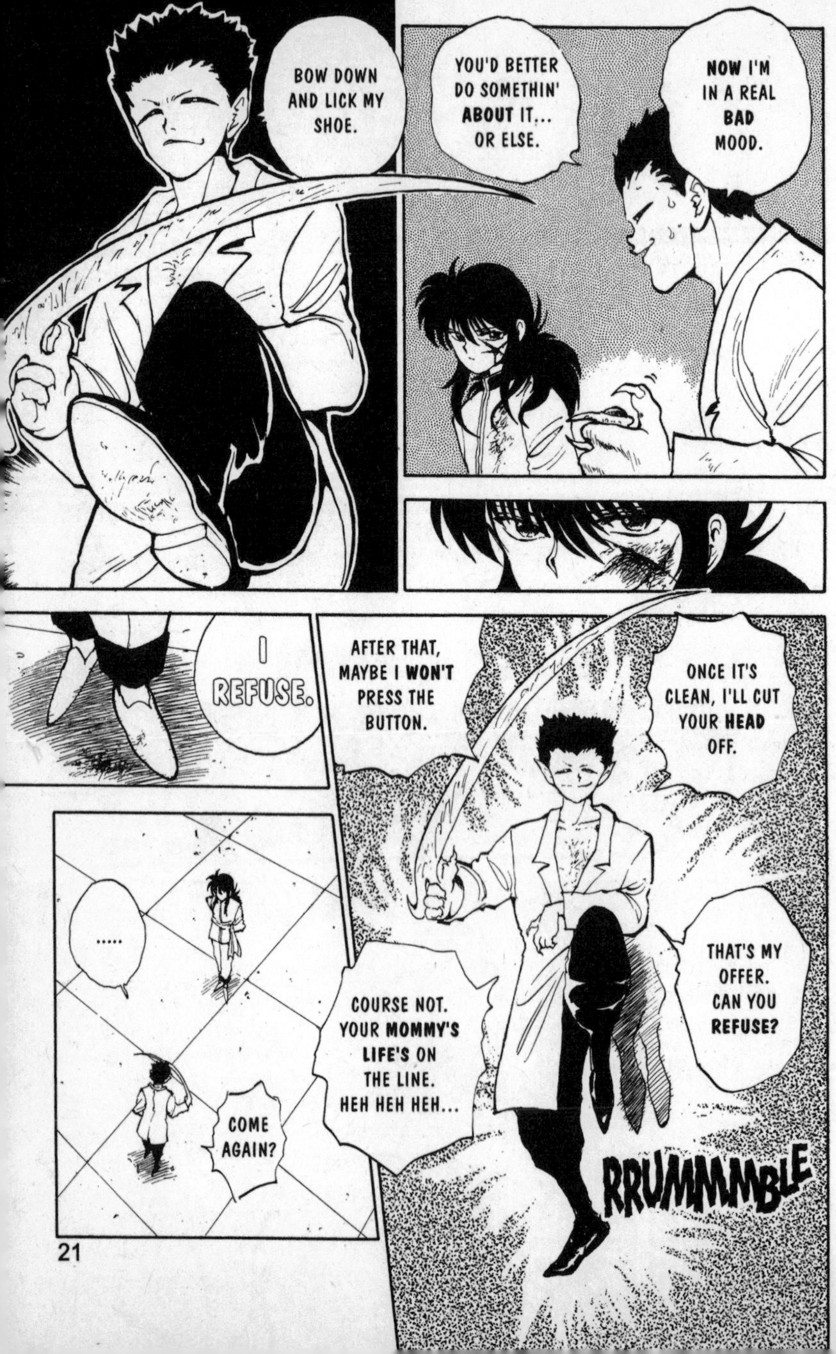
NOW I'M IN A REAL BAD MOOD.
YOU'D BETTER DO SOMETHIN' ABOUT IT... OR ELSE.
BOW DOWN AND LICK MY SHOE.
ONCE IT'S CLEAN, I'LL CUT YOUR HEAD OFF.
AFTER THAT, MAYBE I WON'T PRESS THE BUTTON.
THAT'S MY OFFER. CAN YOU REFUSE?
COURSE NOT. YOUR MOMMY'S LIFE'S ON THE LINE. HEH HEH HEH...
RRUMMMBLE
I REFUSE.
.....
COME AGAIN?

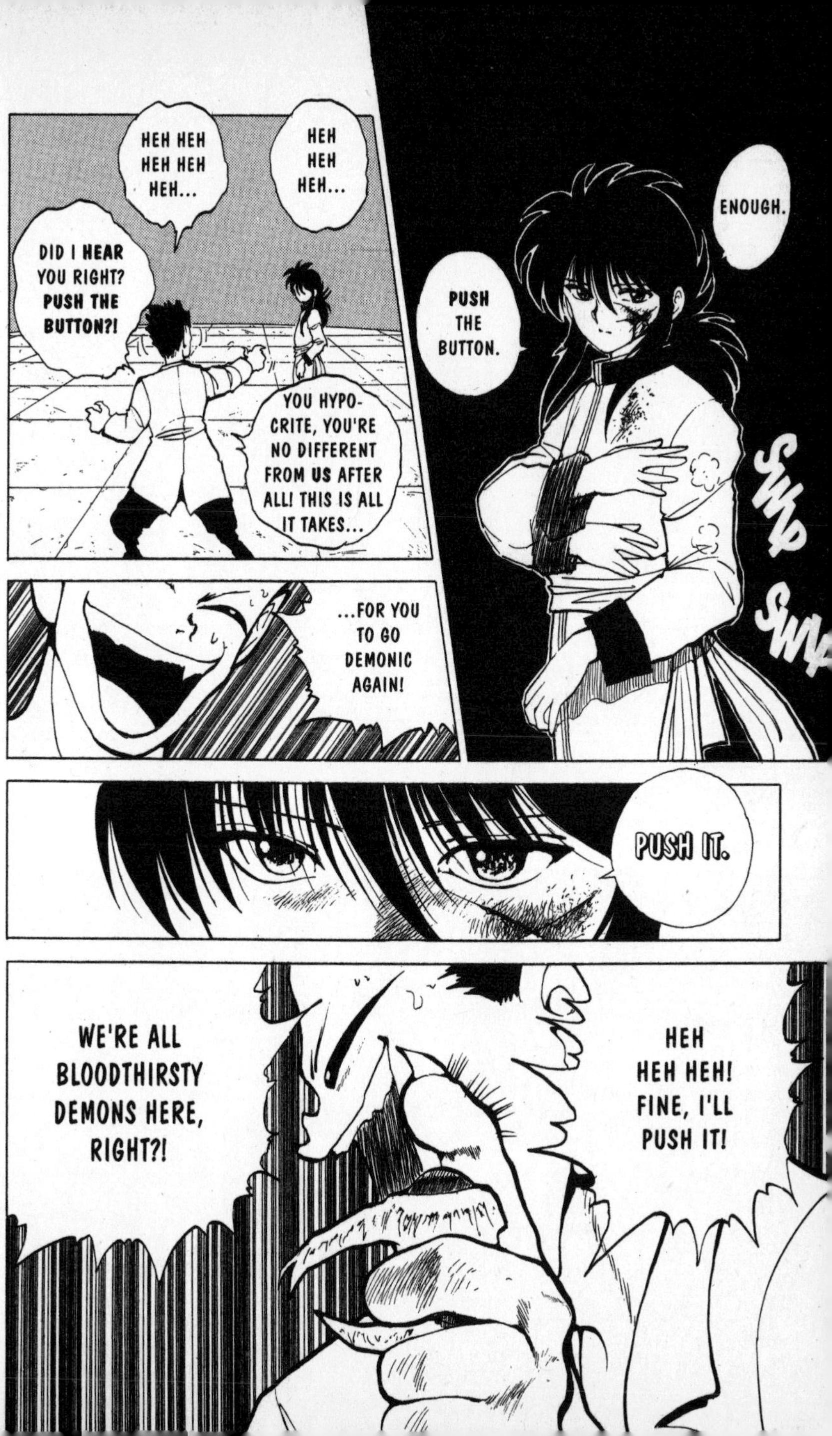
ENOUGH.
PUSH THE BUTTON.
SWIP SWIP
HEH HEH HEH...
HEH HEH HEH HEH HEH...
DID I HEAR YOU RIGHT? PUSH THE BUTTON?!
YOU HYPOCRITE, YOU'RE NO DIFFERENT FROM US AFTER ALL! THIS IS ALL IT TAKES...
...FOR YOU TO GO DEMONIC AGAIN!
PUSH IT.
HEH HEH HEH! FINE, I'LL PUSH IT!
WE'RE ALL BLOODTHIRSTY DEMONS HERE, RIGHT?!

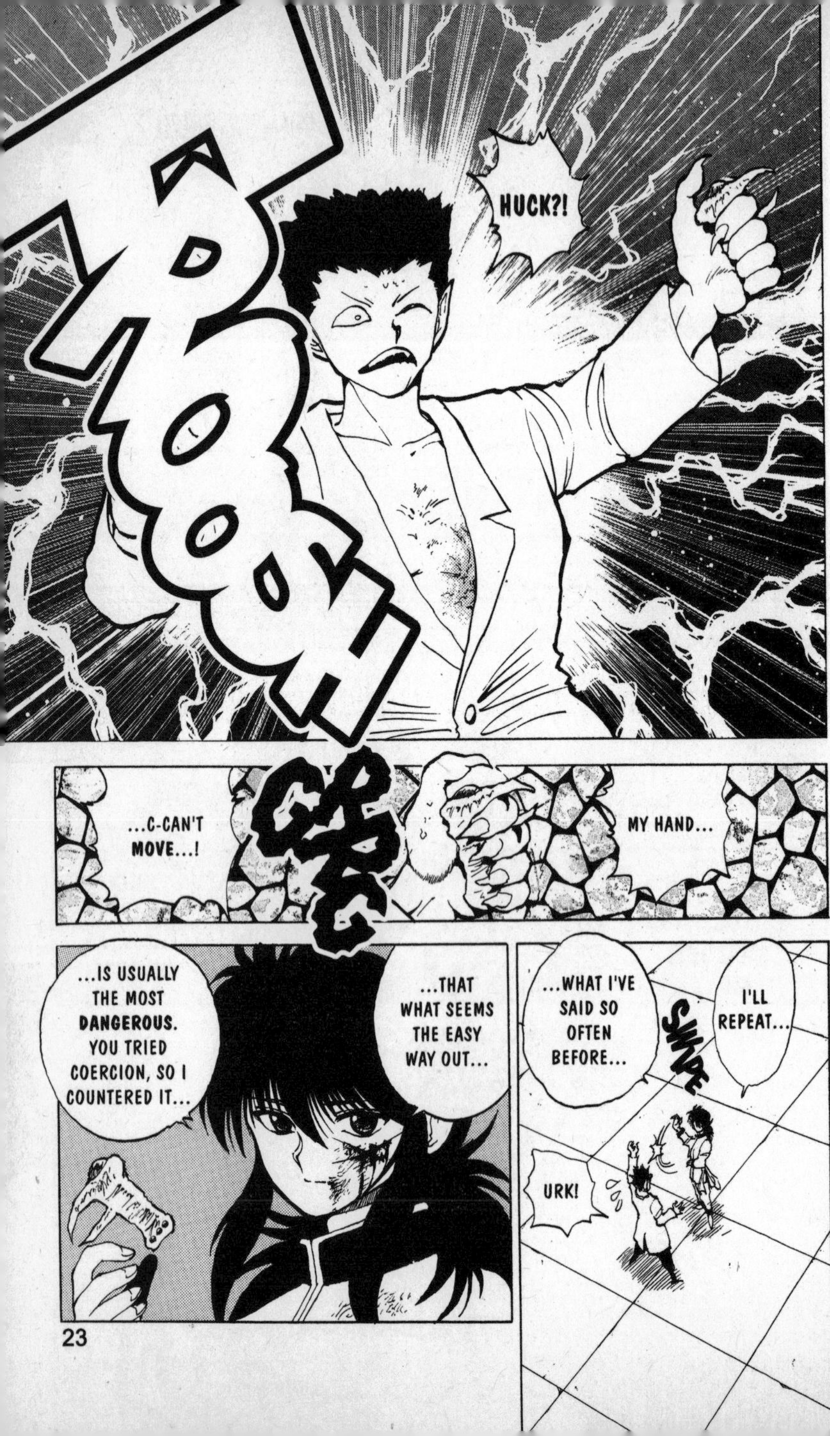
HUCK?!
MY HAND...
...C-CAN'T MOVE...!
I'LL REPEAT...
...WHAT I'VE SAID SO OFTEN BEFORE...
URK!
...THAT WHAT SEEMS THE EASY WAY OUT...
...IS USUALLY THE MOST **DANGEROUS**. YOU TRIED COERCION, SO I COUNTERED IT...

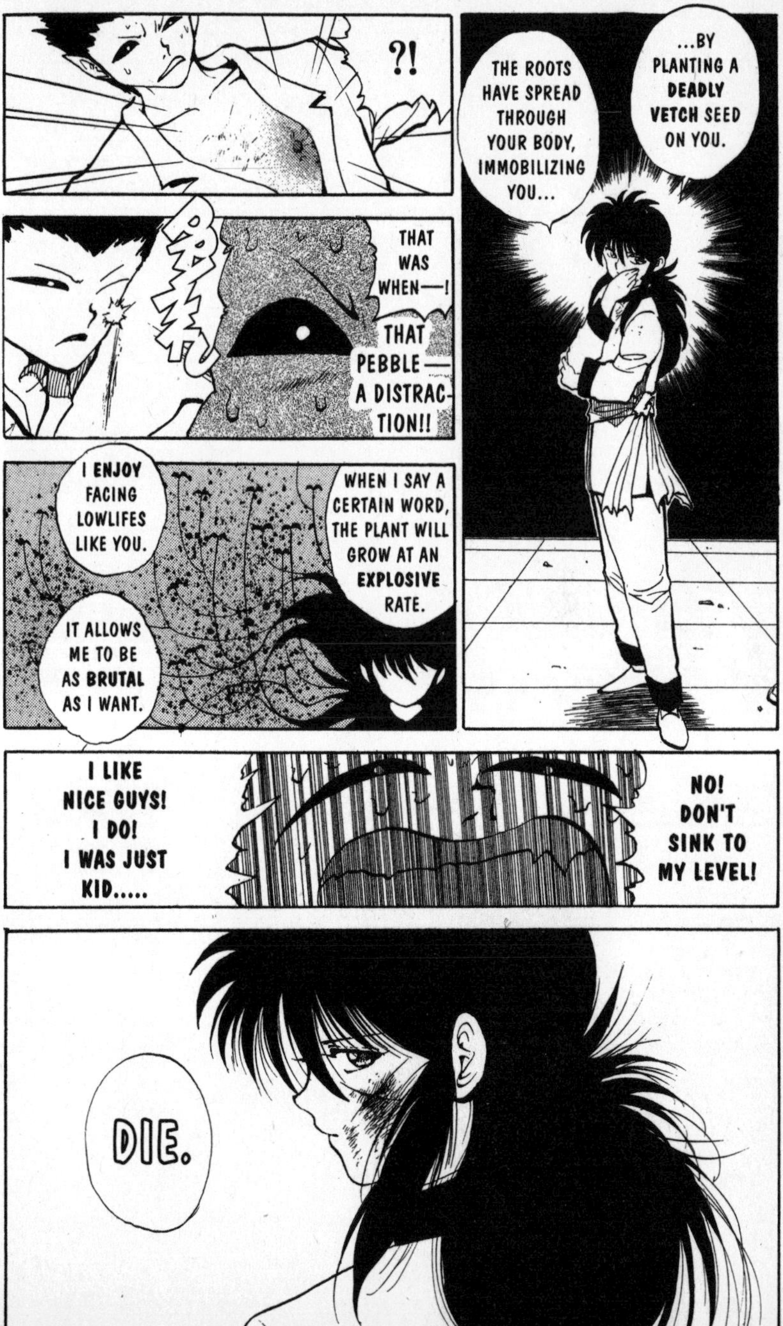
...BY PLANTING A DEADLY VETCH SEED ON YOU.
THE ROOTS HAVE SPREAD THROUGH YOUR BODY, IMMOBILIZING YOU...
?!
THAT WAS WHEN—!
THAT PEBBLE— A DISTRACTION!!
WHEN I SAY A CERTAIN WORD, THE PLANT WILL GROW AT AN EXPLOSIVE RATE.
I ENJOY FACING LOWLIFES LIKE YOU.
IT ALLOWS ME TO BE AS BRUTAL AS I WANT.
NO! DON'T SINK TO MY LEVEL!
I LIKE NICE GUYS! I DO! I WAS JUST KID.....
DIE.

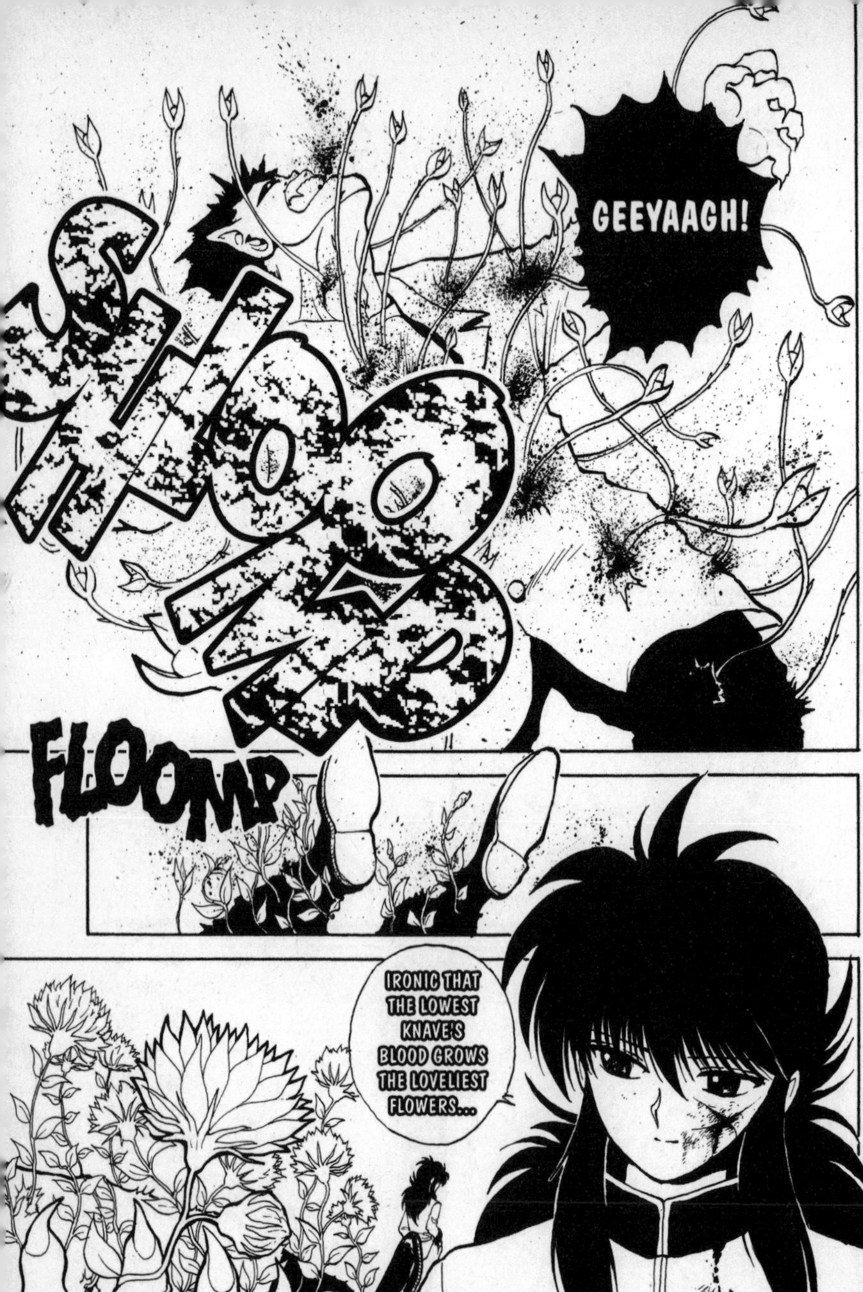
GEEYAAGH!
FLOOMP
IRONIC THAT THE LOWEST KNAVE'S BLOOD GROWS THE LOVELIEST FLOWERS...

MY RAMBLING DIARY

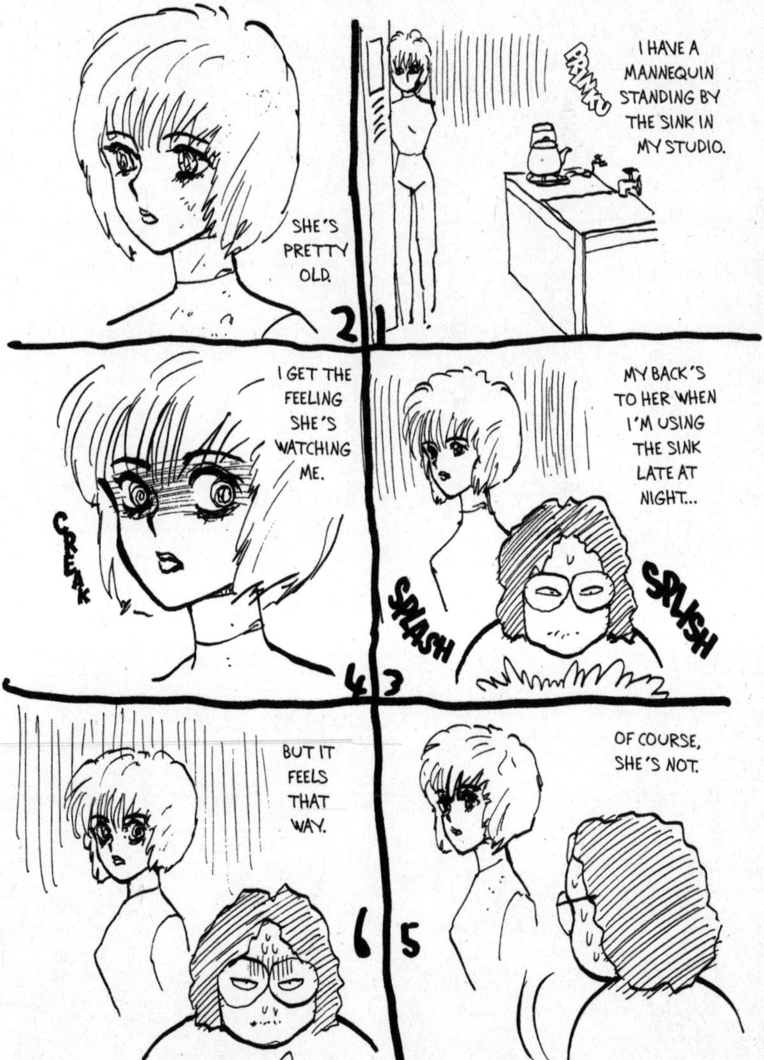
I HAVE A MANNEQUIN STANDING BY THE SINK IN MY STUDIO.
DRINKU
1
SHE'S PRETTY OLD.
2
MY BACK'S TO HER WHEN I'M USING THE SINK LATE AT NIGHT...
SPLISH
SPLASH
3
I GET THE FEELING SHE'S WATCHING ME.
CREAK
4
OF COURSE, SHE'S NOT.
5
BUT IT FEELS THAT WAY.
6

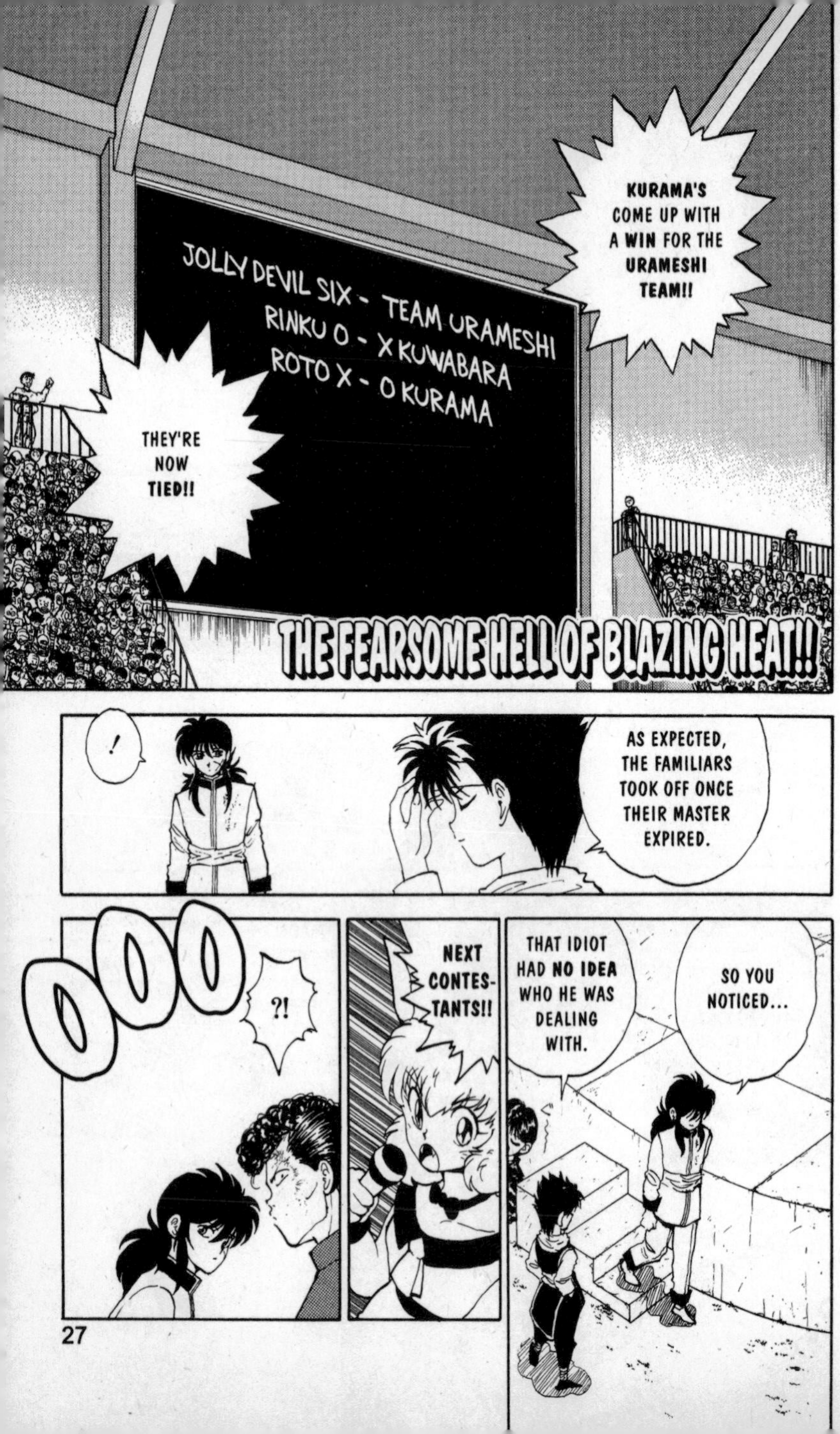
KURAMA'S COME UP WITH A WIN FOR THE URAMESHI TEAM!!
JOLLY DEVIL SIX - TEAM URAMESHI
RINKU O - X KUWABARA
ROTO X - O KURAMA
THEY'RE NOW TIED!!
THE FEARSOME HELL OF BLAZING HEAT!!
AS EXPECTED, THE FAMILIARS TOOK OFF ONCE THEIR MASTER EXPIRED.
!
SO YOU NOTICED...
THAT IDIOT HAD **NO IDEA** WHO HE WAS DEALING WITH.
NEXT CONTES-TANTS!!
?!
OOO

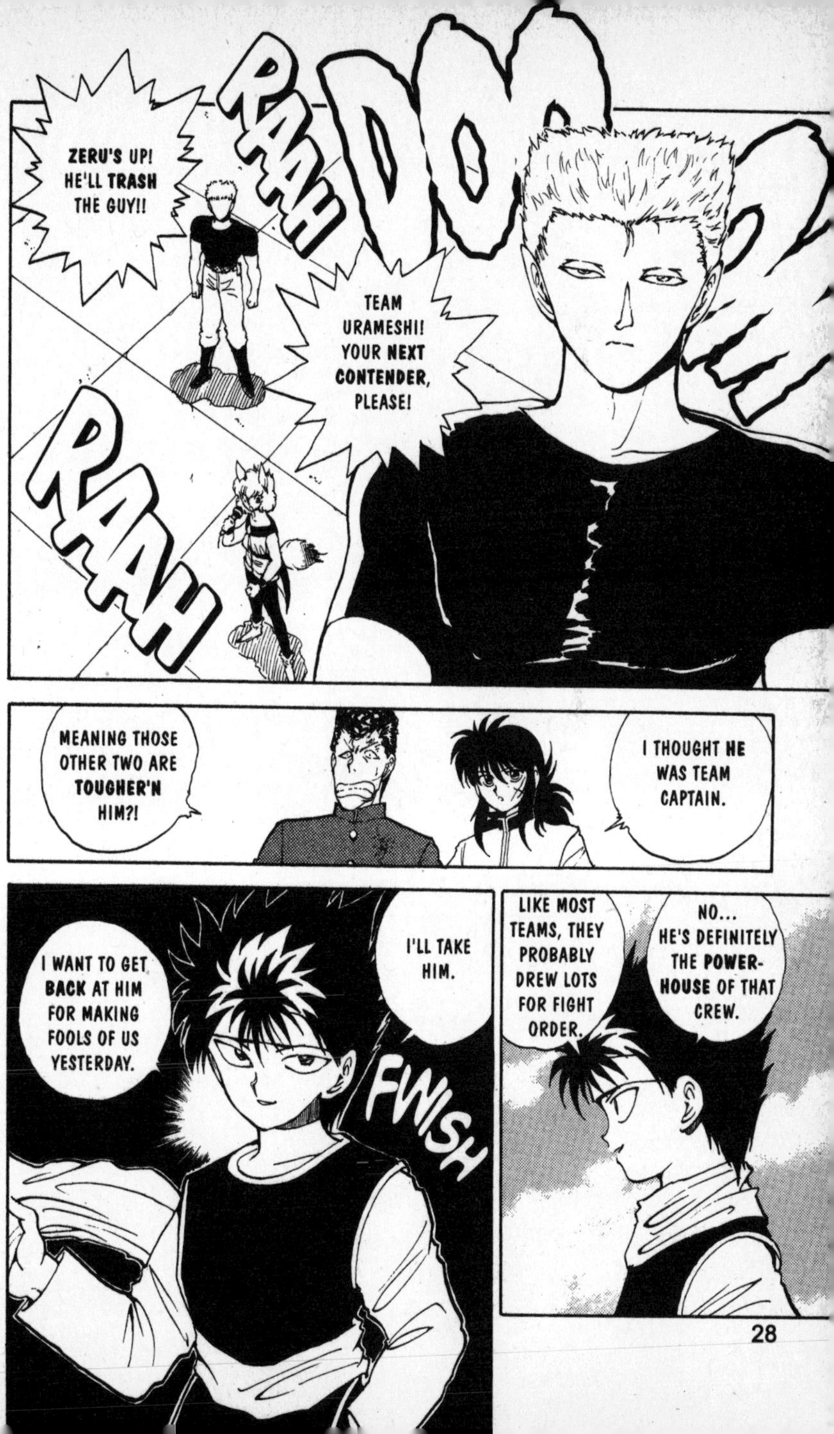
RAAH
TEAM URAMESHI! YOUR NEXT CONTENDER, PLEASE!
ZERU'S UP! HE'LL TRASH THE GUY!!
RAAH
I THOUGHT HE WAS TEAM CAPTAIN.
MEANING THOSE OTHER TWO ARE TOUGHER'N HIM?!
NO... HE'S DEFINITELY THE POWER-HOUSE OF THAT CREW.
LIKE MOST TEAMS, THEY PROBABLY DREW LOTS FOR FIGHT ORDER.
I'LL TAKE HIM.
FWISH
I WANT TO GET BACK AT HIM FOR MAKING FOOLS OF US YESTERDAY.

THE FEARSOME HELL OF BLAZING HEAT!!

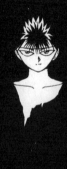

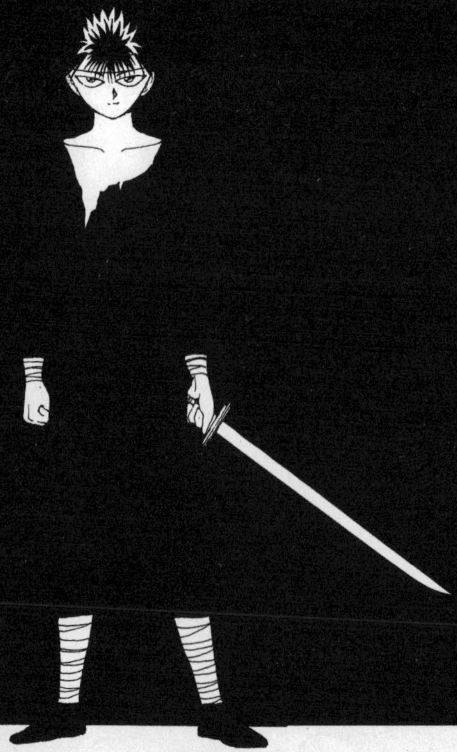

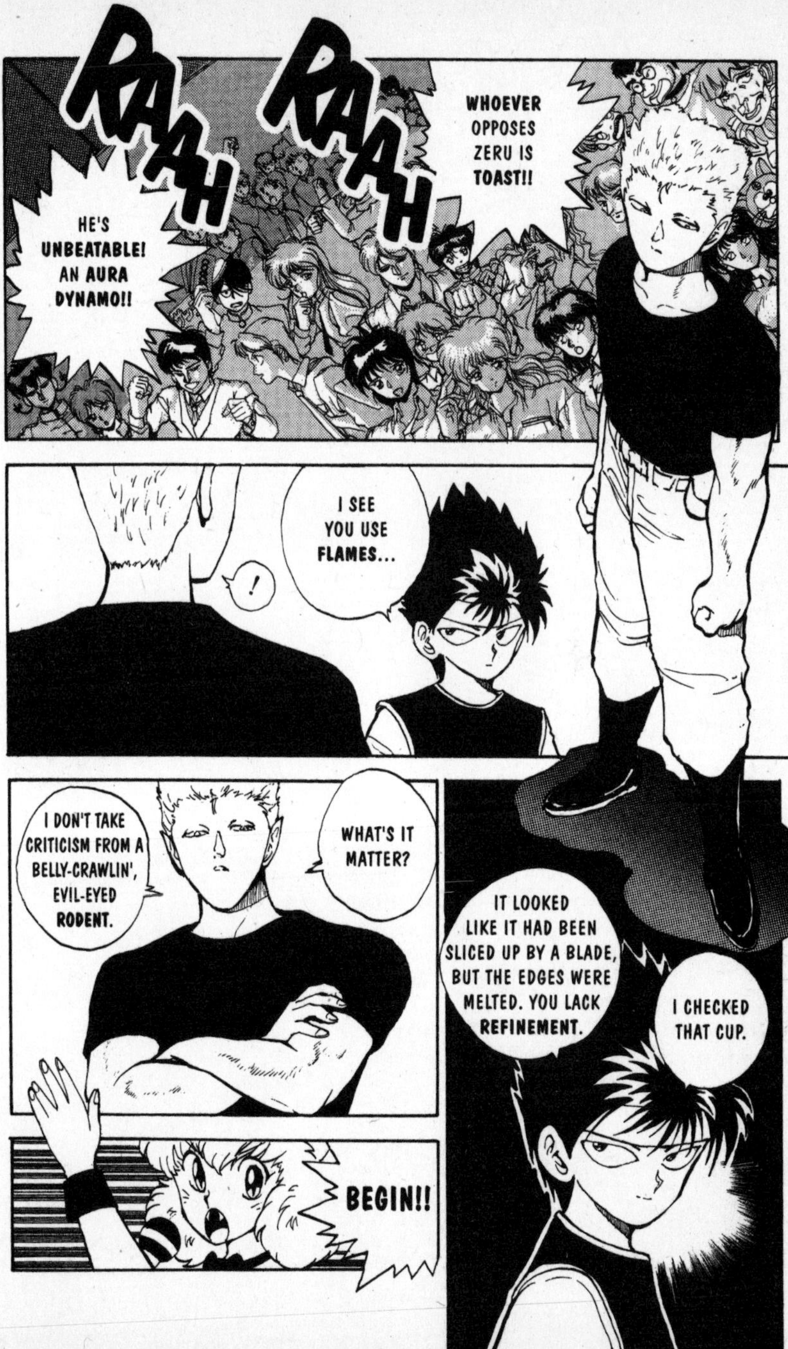
WHOEVER OPPOSES ZERU IS TOAST!!
RAAAH
RAAAH
HE'S UNBEATABLE! AN AURA DYNAMO!!
I SEE YOU USE FLAMES...
!
I CHECKED THAT CUP.
IT LOOKED LIKE IT HAD BEEN SLICED UP BY A BLADE, BUT THE EDGES WERE MELTED. YOU LACK REFINEMENT.
WHAT'S IT MATTER?
I DON'T TAKE CRITICISM FROM A BELLY-CRAWLIN', EVIL-EYED RODENT.
BEGIN!!

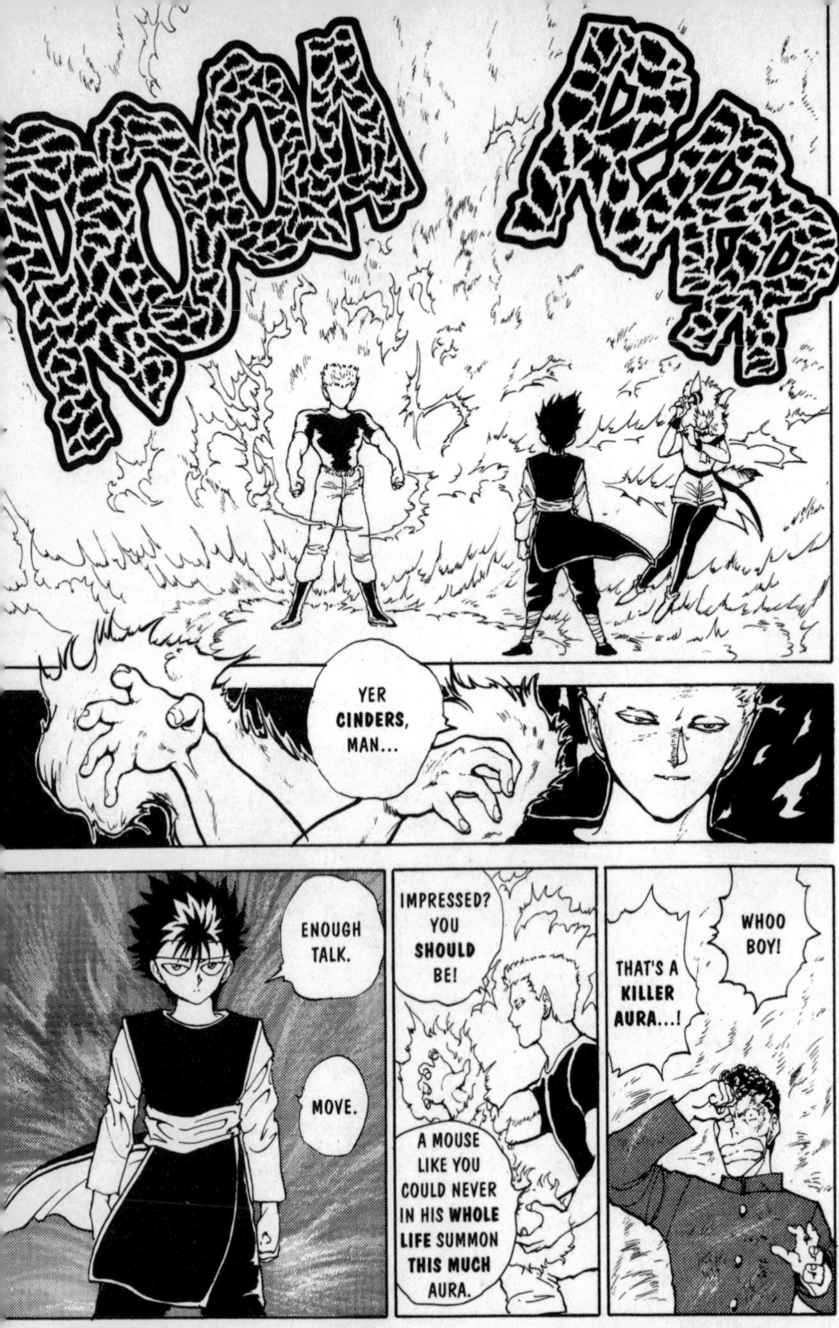
YER CINDERS, MAN...
WHOO BOY!
THAT'S A KILLER AURA...!
IMPRESSED? YOU SHOULD BE!
A MOUSE LIKE YOU COULD NEVER IN HIS WHOLE LIFE SUMMON THIS MUCH AURA.
ENOUGH TALK.
MOVE.

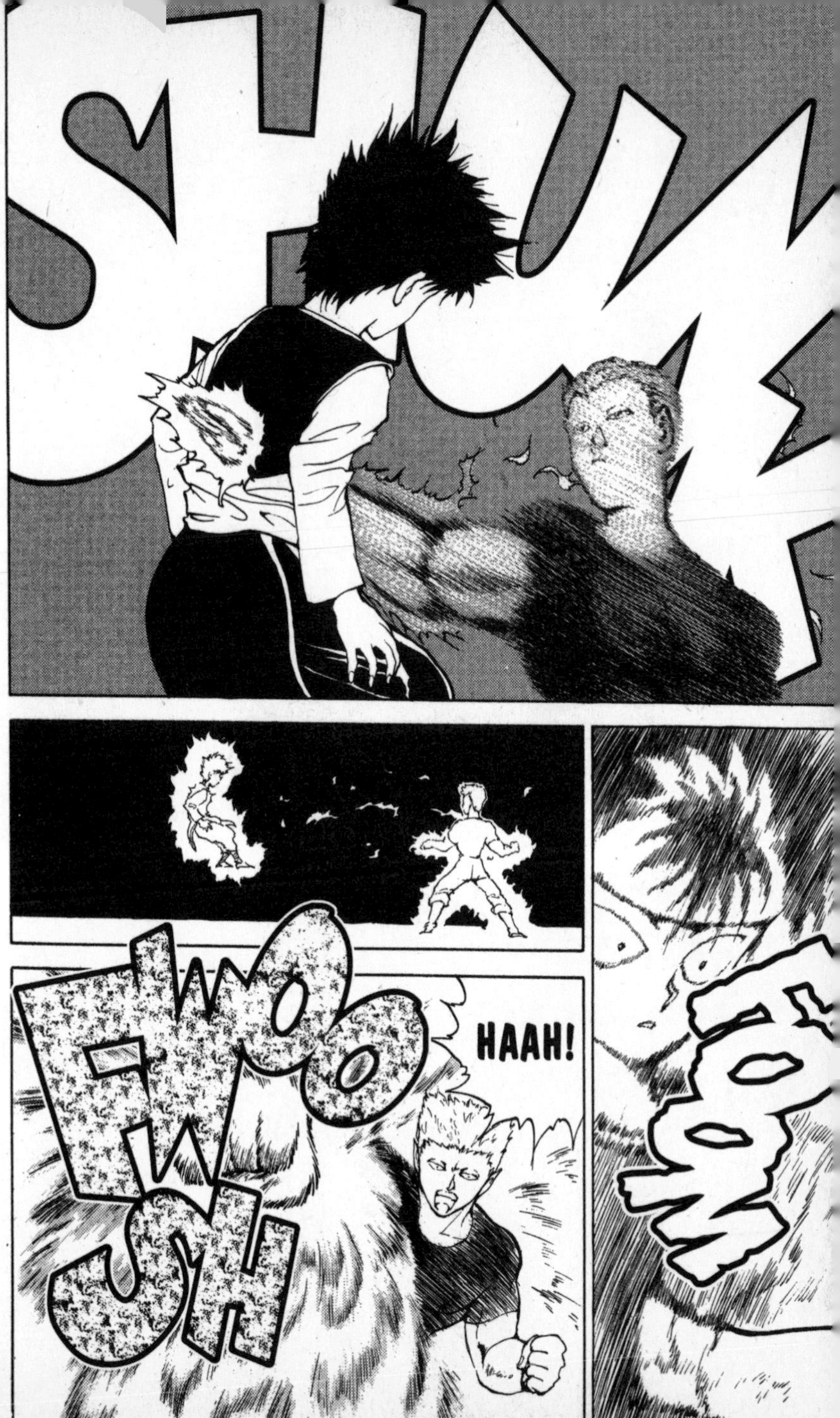
FOOM
FWOOSH
HAAH!

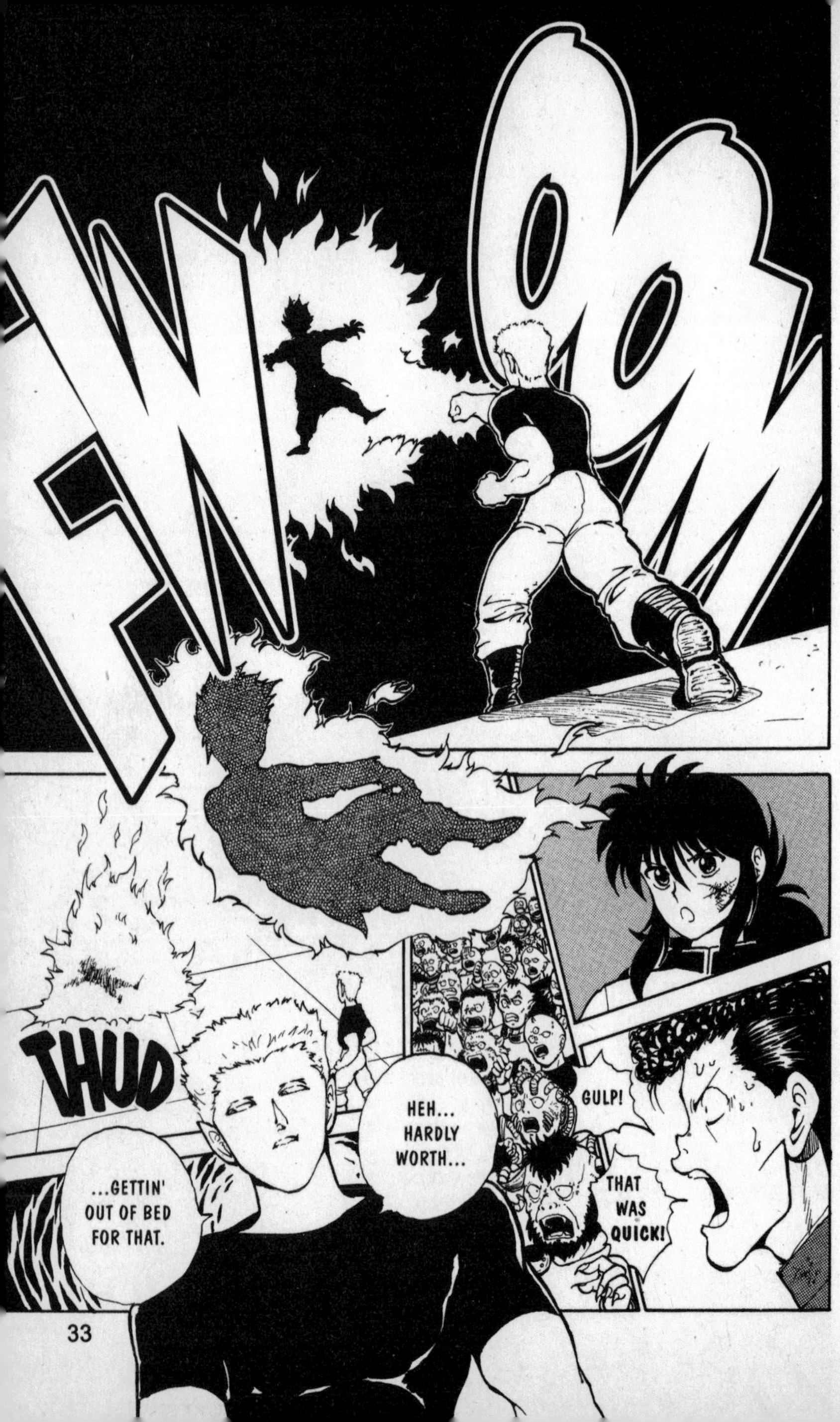
GULP!
THAT WAS QUICK!
THUD
HEH... HARDLY WORTH...
...GETTIN' OUT OF BED FOR THAT.

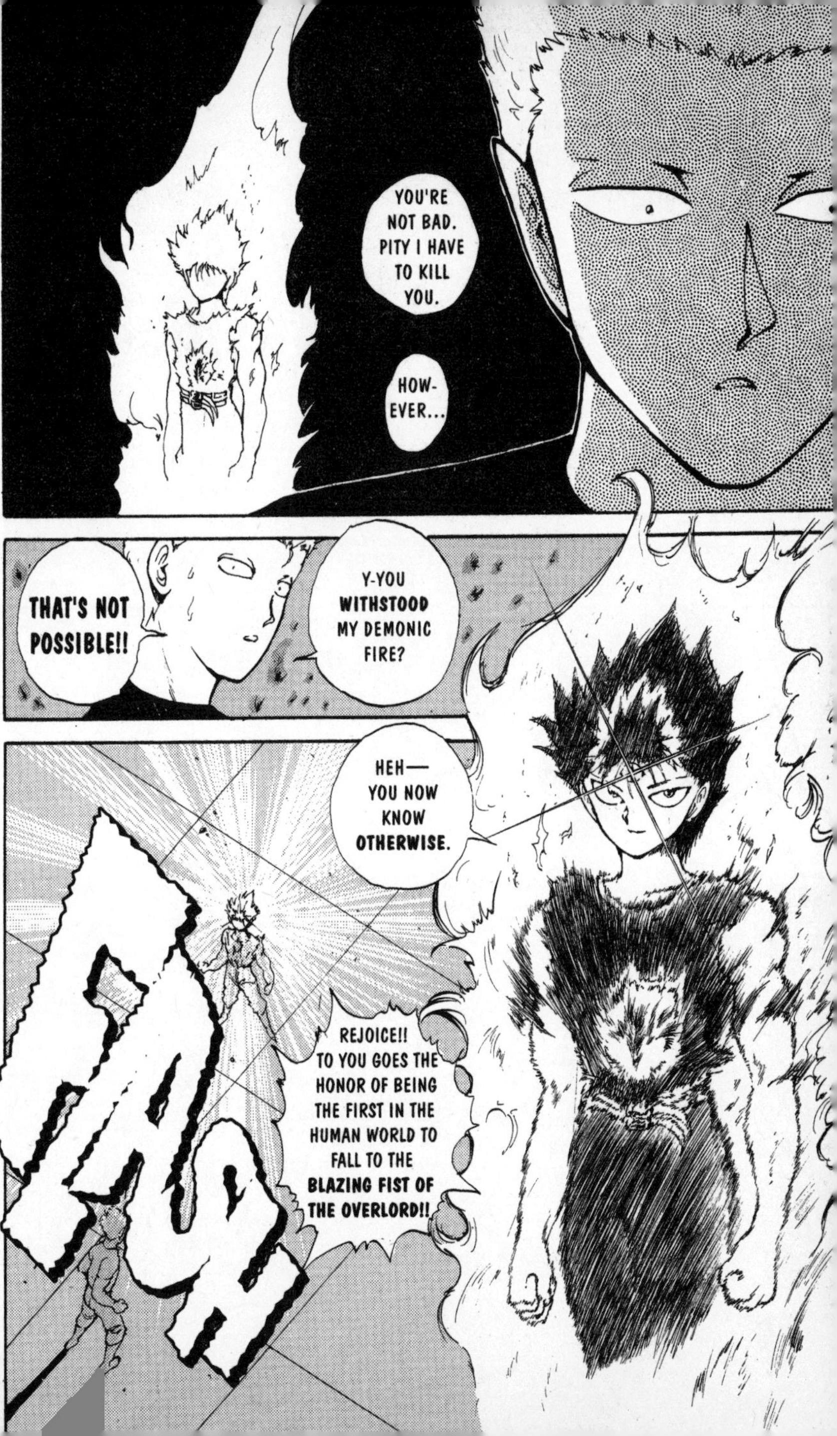
YOU'RE NOT BAD. PITY I HAVE TO KILL YOU.
HOW-EVER...
Y-YOU **WITHSTOOD** MY DEMONIC FIRE?
THAT'S NOT POSSIBLE!!
HEH— YOU NOW KNOW **OTHERWISE.**
REJOICE!! TO YOU GOES THE HONOR OF BEING THE FIRST IN THE HUMAN WORLD TO FALL TO THE **BLAZING FIST OF THE OVERLORD!!**

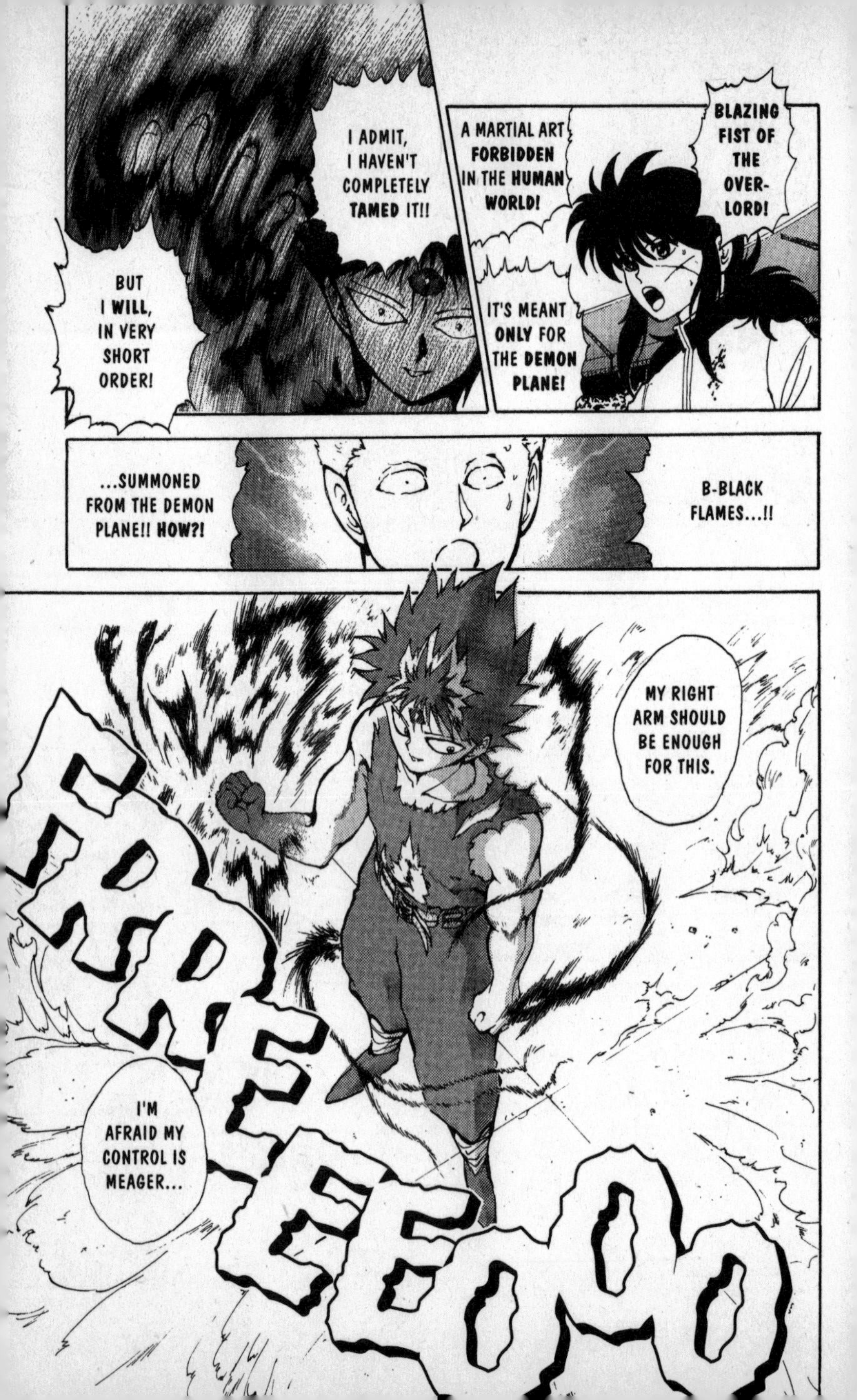
BLAZING FIST OF THE OVER-LORD!
A MARTIAL ART FORBIDDEN IN THE HUMAN WORLD!
IT'S MEANT ONLY FOR THE DEMON PLANE!
I ADMIT, I HAVEN'T COMPLETELY TAMED IT!!
BUT I WILL, IN VERY SHORT ORDER!
B-BLACK FLAMES...!!
...SUMMONED FROM THE DEMON PLANE!! HOW?!
MY RIGHT ARM SHOULD BE ENOUGH FOR THIS.
I'M AFRAID MY CONTROL IS MEAGER...

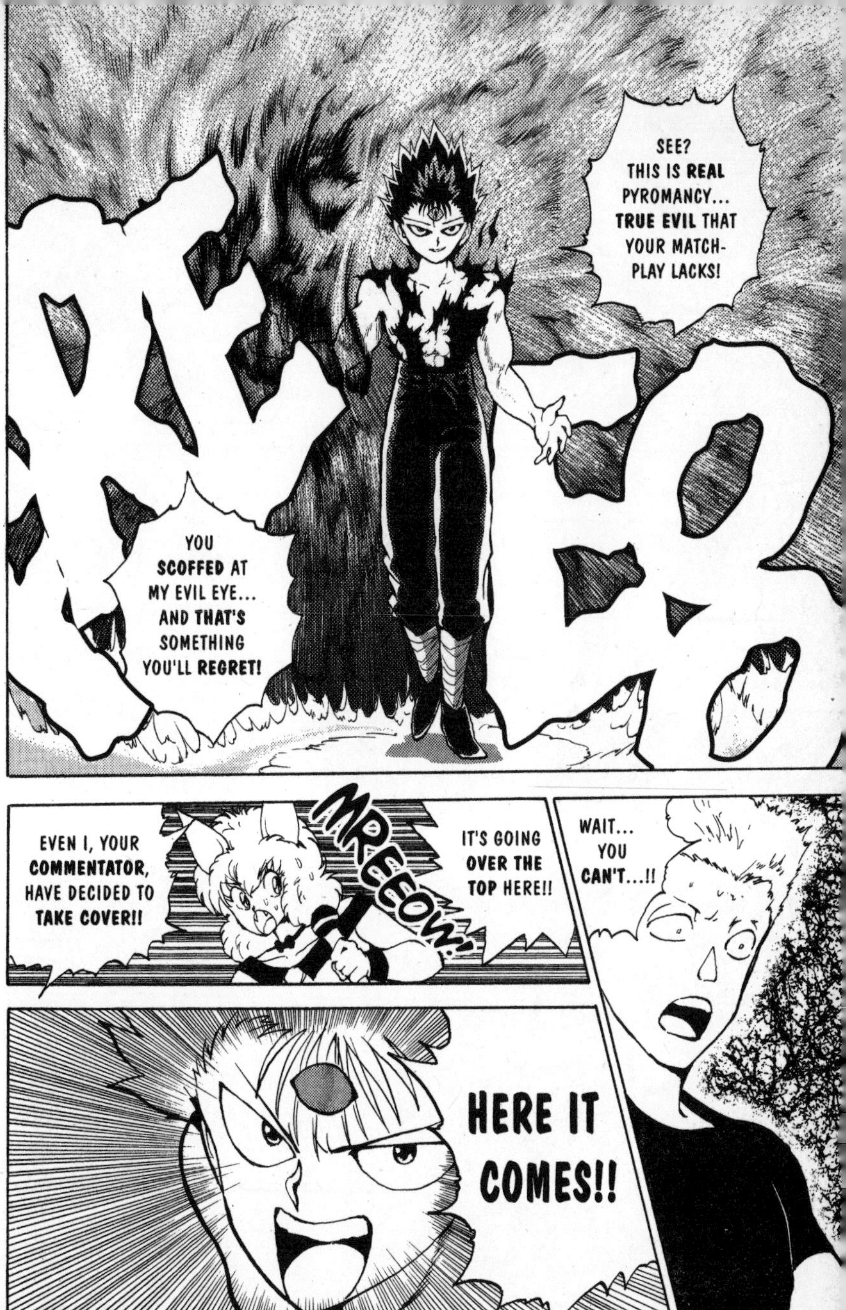
SEE? THIS IS REAL PYROMANCY... TRUE EVIL THAT YOUR MATCH-PLAY LACKS!
YOU SCOFFED AT MY EVIL EYE... AND THAT'S SOMETHING YOU'LL REGRET!
WAIT... YOU CAN'T...!!
IT'S GOING OVER THE TOP HERE!!
MREEOW!
EVEN I, YOUR COMMENTATOR, HAVE DECIDED TO TAKE COVER!!
HERE IT COMES!!

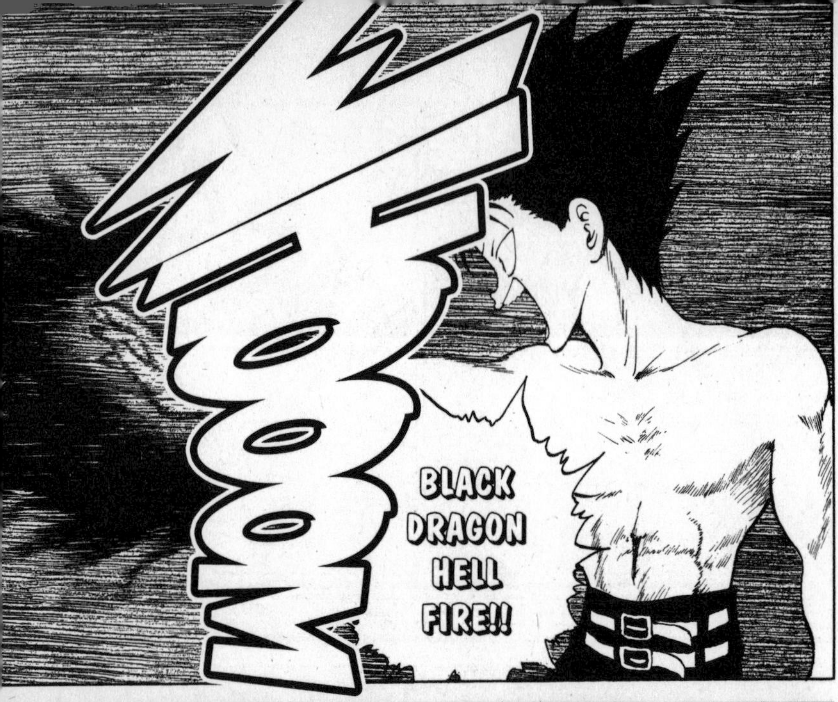
WOOOM
BLACK DRAGON HELL FIRE!!
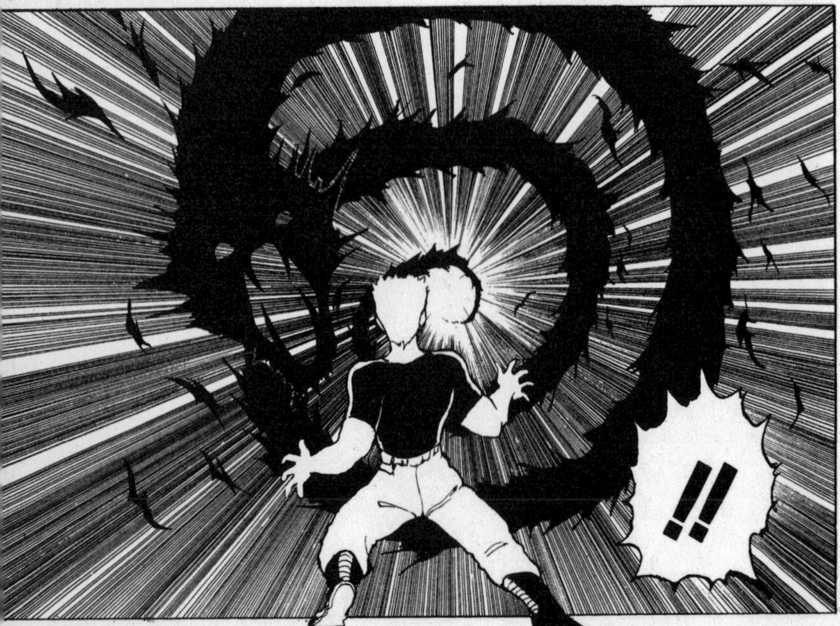
!!

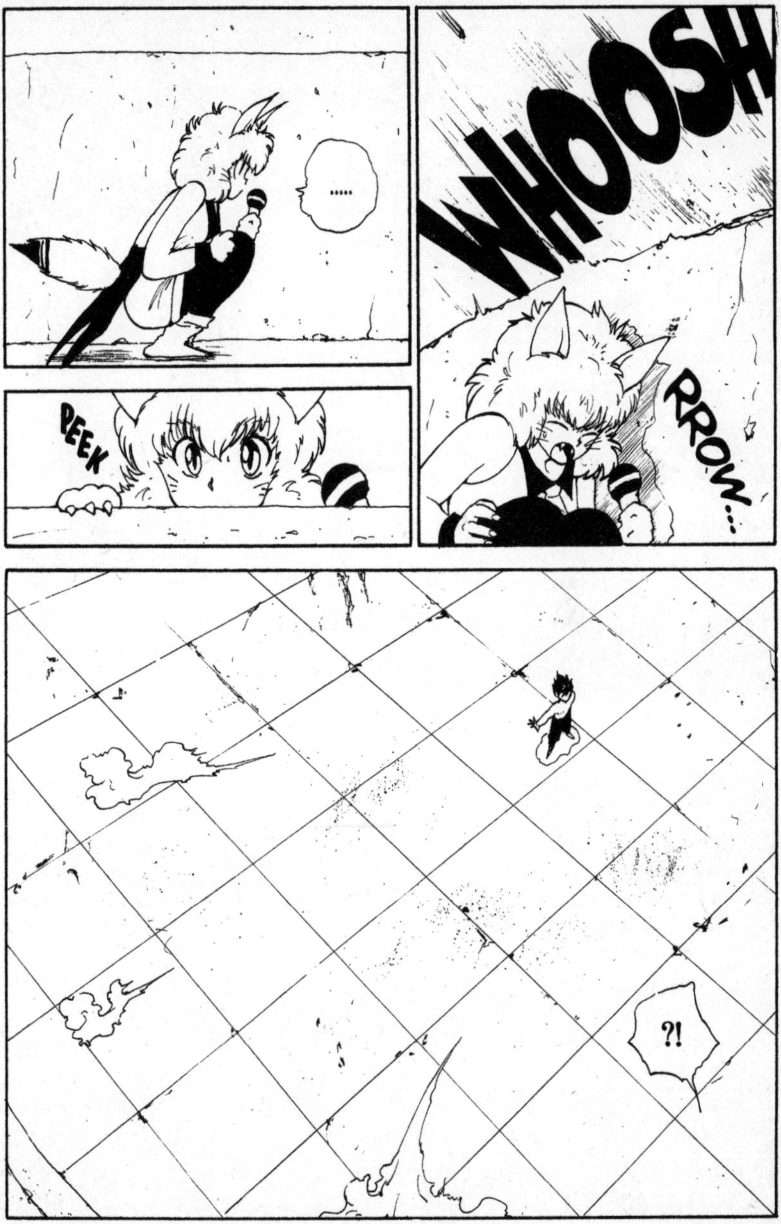
WHOOSH
RROW...
......
PEEK
?!

READ THIS WAY

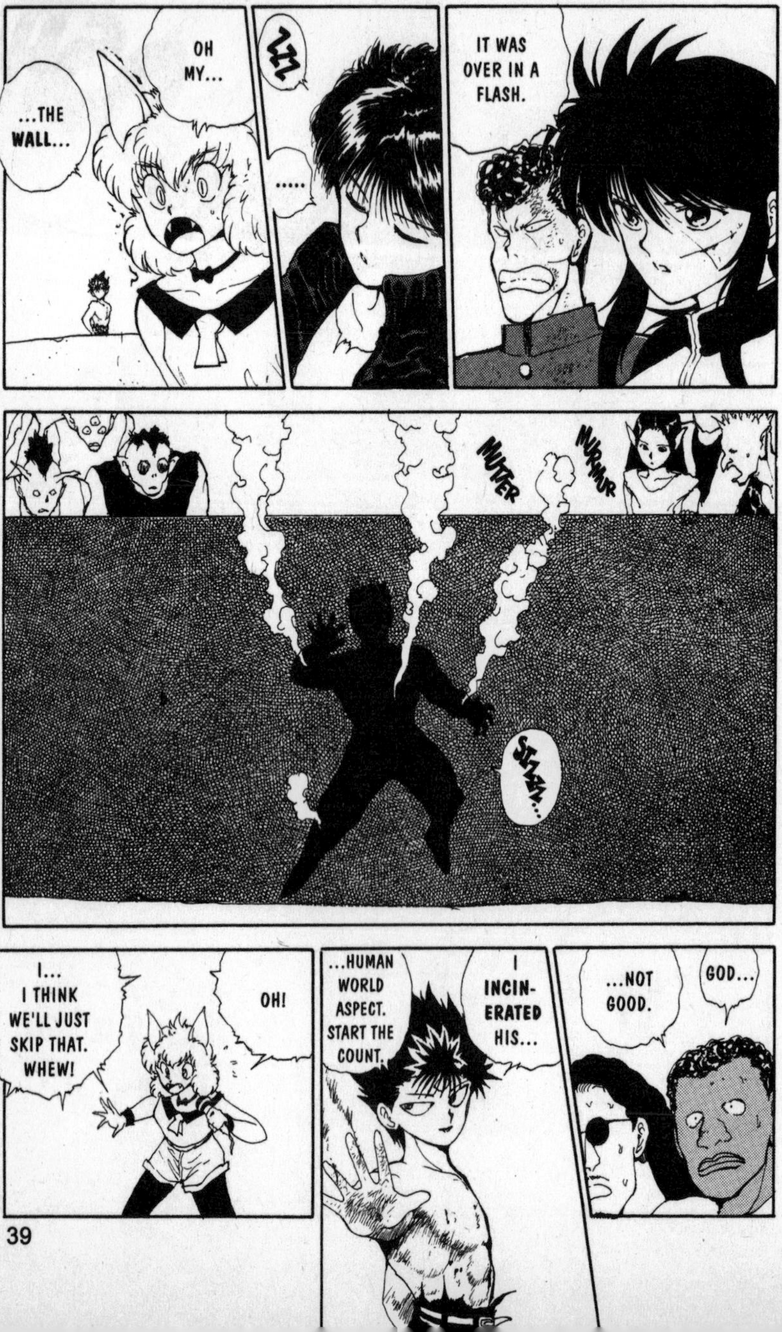
IT WAS OVER IN A FLASH.
.....
OH MY...
...THE WALL...
MURMUR
MUTTER
GOD...
...NOT GOOD.
I INCIN-ERATED HIS...
...HUMAN WORLD ASPECT. START THE COUNT.
OH!
I... I THINK WE'LL JUST SKIP THAT. WHEW!

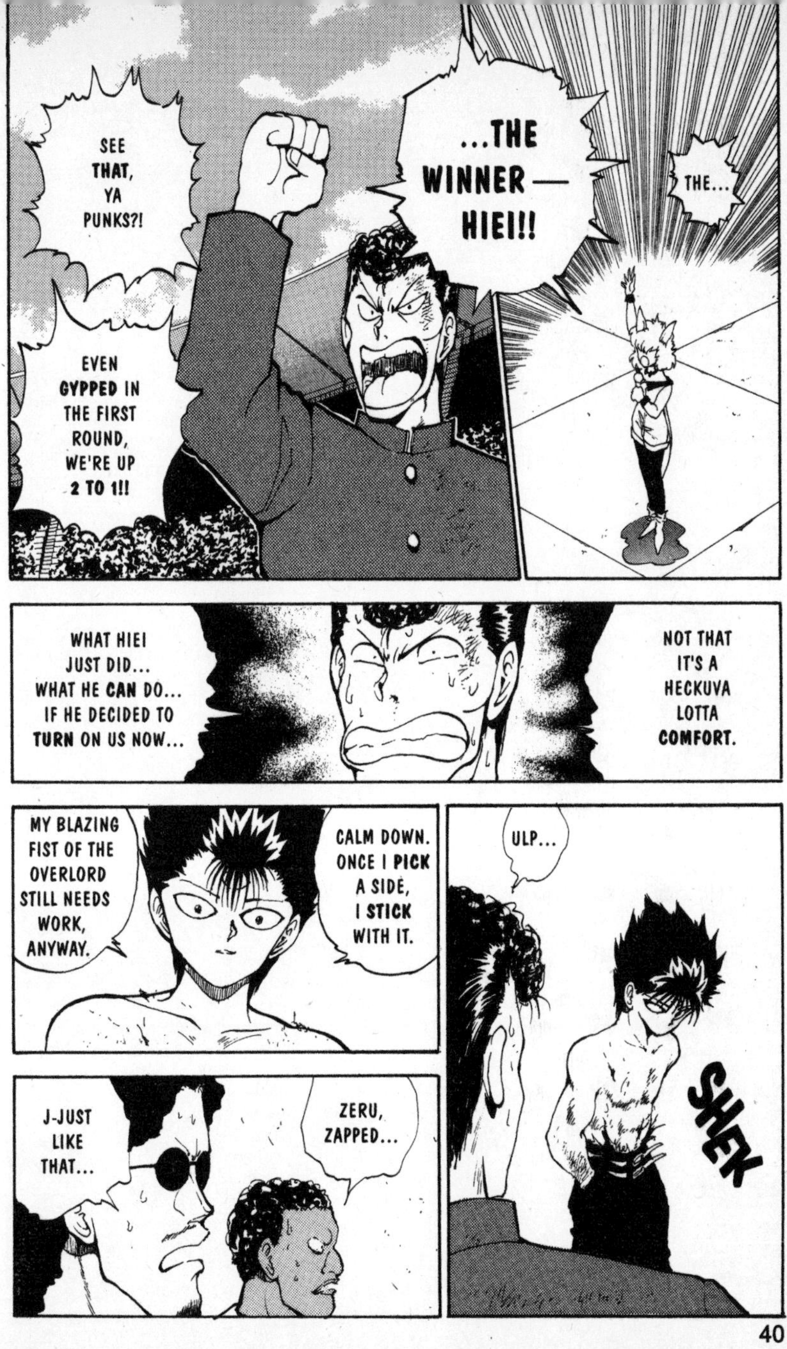
THE...
...THE WINNER—HIEI!!
SEE THAT, YA PUNKS?!
EVEN GYPPED IN THE FIRST ROUND, WE'RE UP 2 TO 1!!
NOT THAT IT'S A HECKUVA LOTTA COMFORT.
WHAT HIEI JUST DID... WHAT HE CAN DO... IF HE DECIDED TO TURN ON US NOW...
ULP...
SHEK
CALM DOWN. ONCE I PICK A SIDE, I STICK WITH IT.
MY BLAZING FIST OF THE OVERLORD STILL NEEDS WORK, ANYWAY.
ZERU, ZAPPED...
J-JUST LIKE THAT...

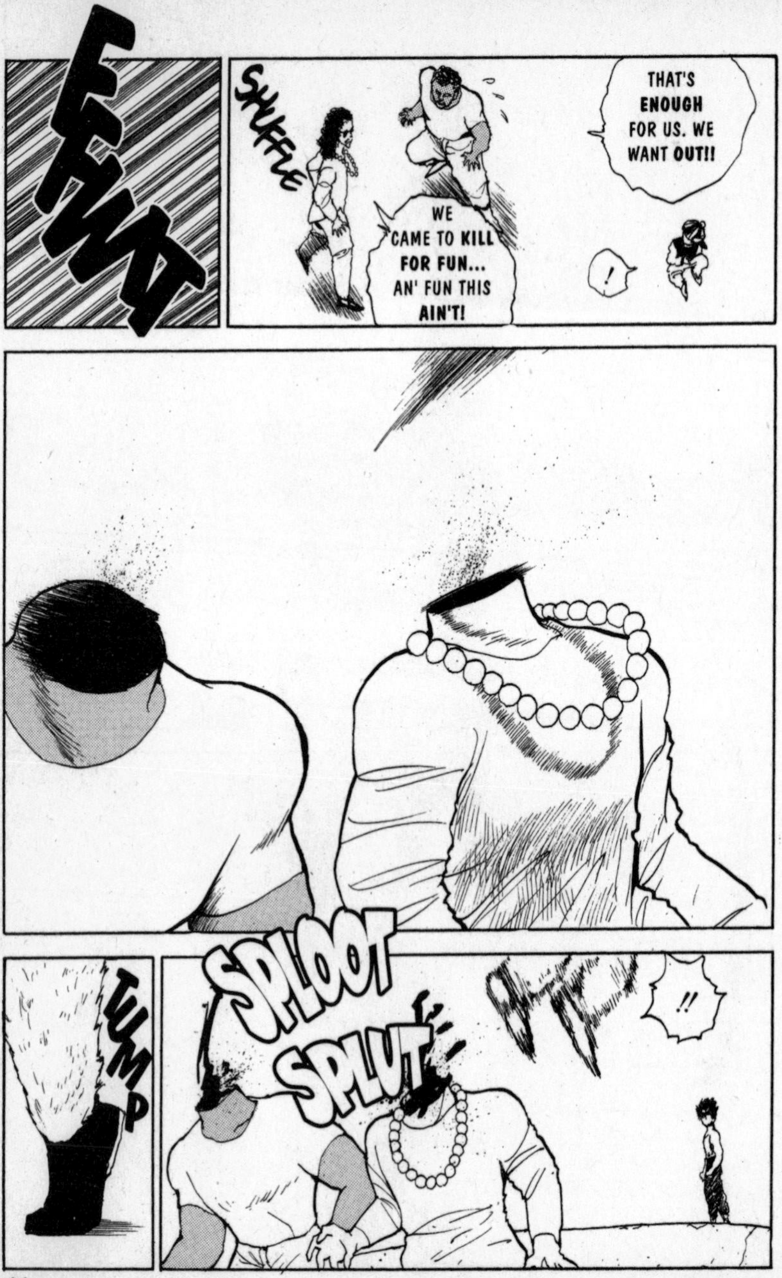
THAT'S ENOUGH FOR US. WE WANT OUT!!
!
WE CAME TO KILL FOR FUN... AN' FUN THIS AIN'T!
SHUFFLE
FFWT
!!
SPLOOT
SPLUT
TUMP

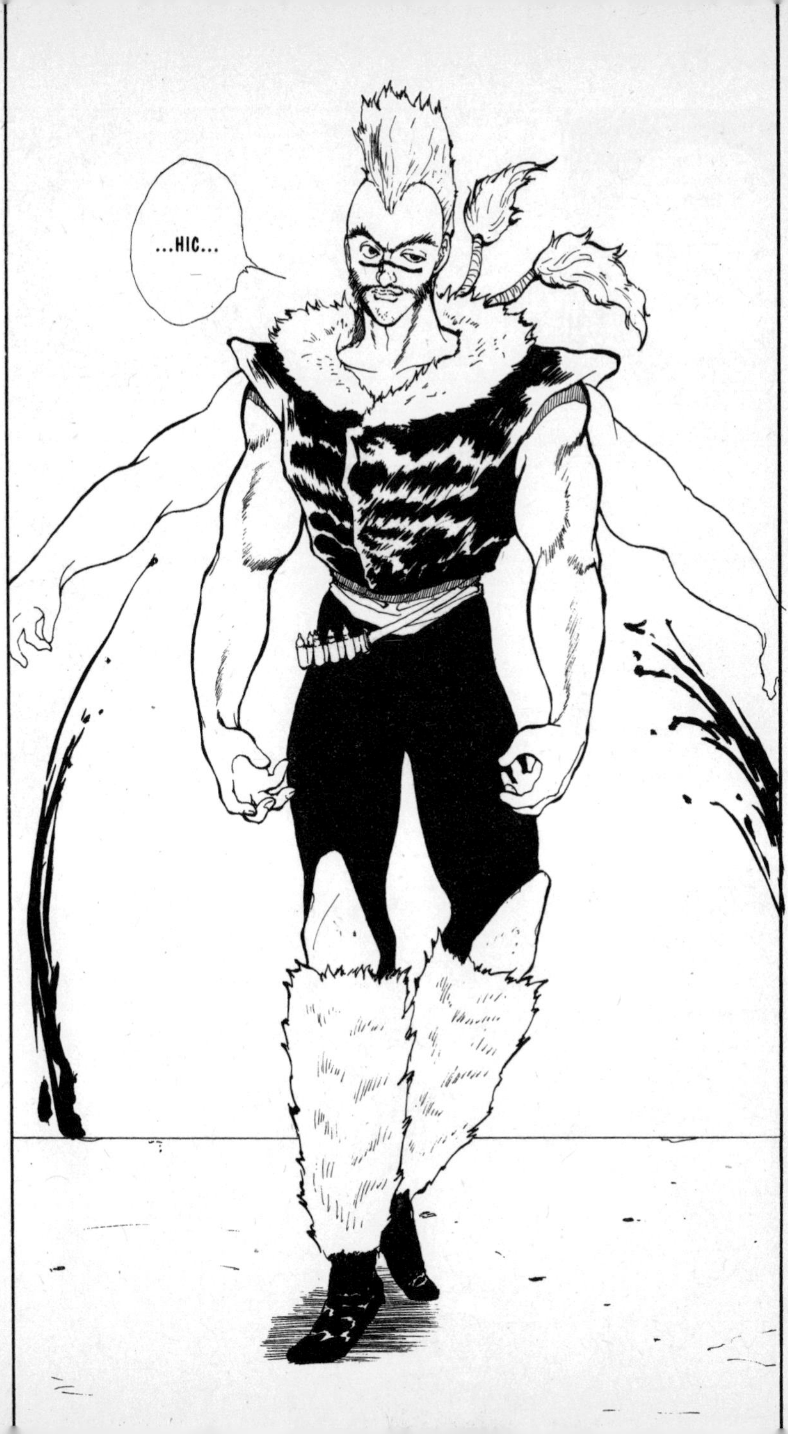
...HIC...

READ THIS WAY

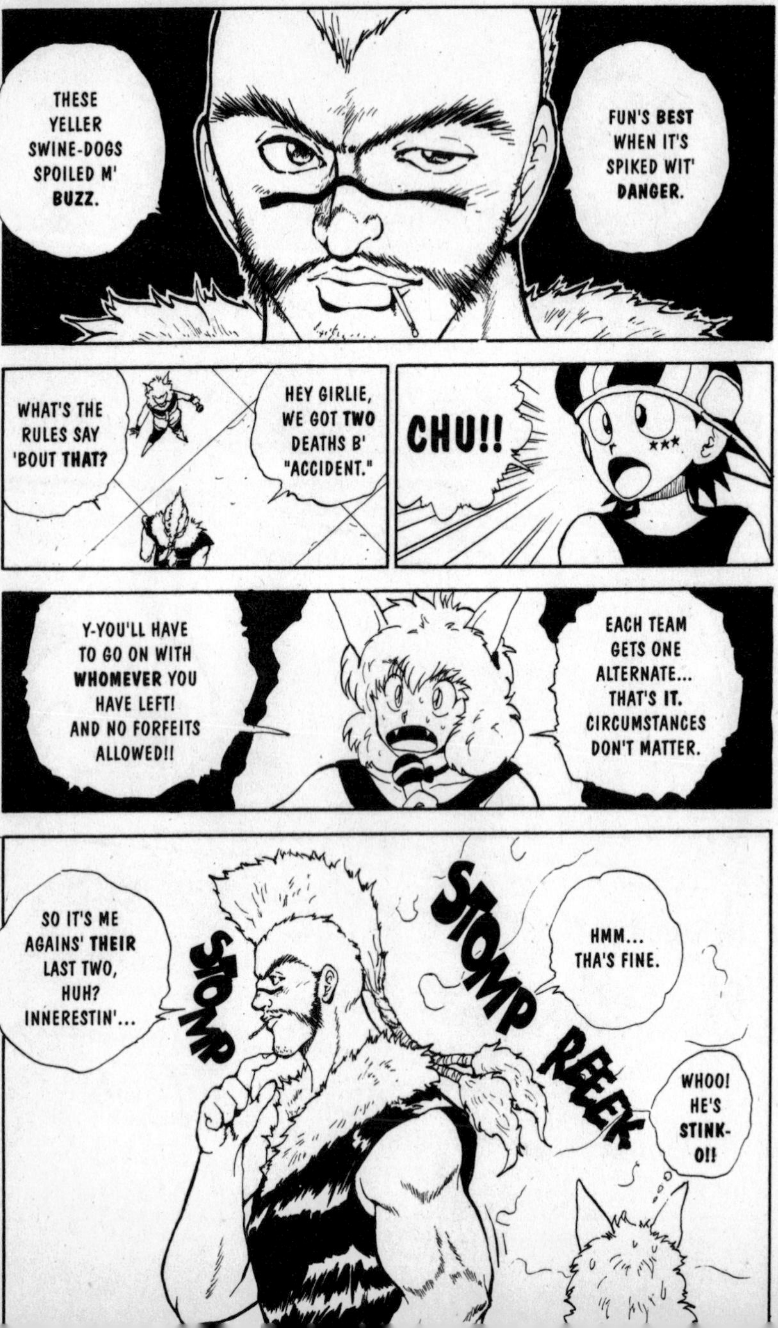
FUN'S BEST WHEN IT'S SPIKED WIT' DANGER.
THESE YELLER SWINE-DOGS SPOILED M' BUZZ.
CHU!!
HEY GIRLIE, WE GOT TWO DEATHS B' "ACCIDENT."
WHAT'S THE RULES SAY 'BOUT THAT?
EACH TEAM GETS ONE ALTERNATE... THAT'S IT. CIRCUMSTANCES DON'T MATTER.
Y-YOU'LL HAVE TO GO ON WITH WHOMEVER YOU HAVE LEFT! AND NO FORFEITS ALLOWED!!
STOMP
HMM... THA'S FINE.
SO IT'S ME AGAINS' THEIR LAST TWO, HUH? INNERESTIN'...
STOMP
REEEK
WHOO! HE'S STINK-O!!

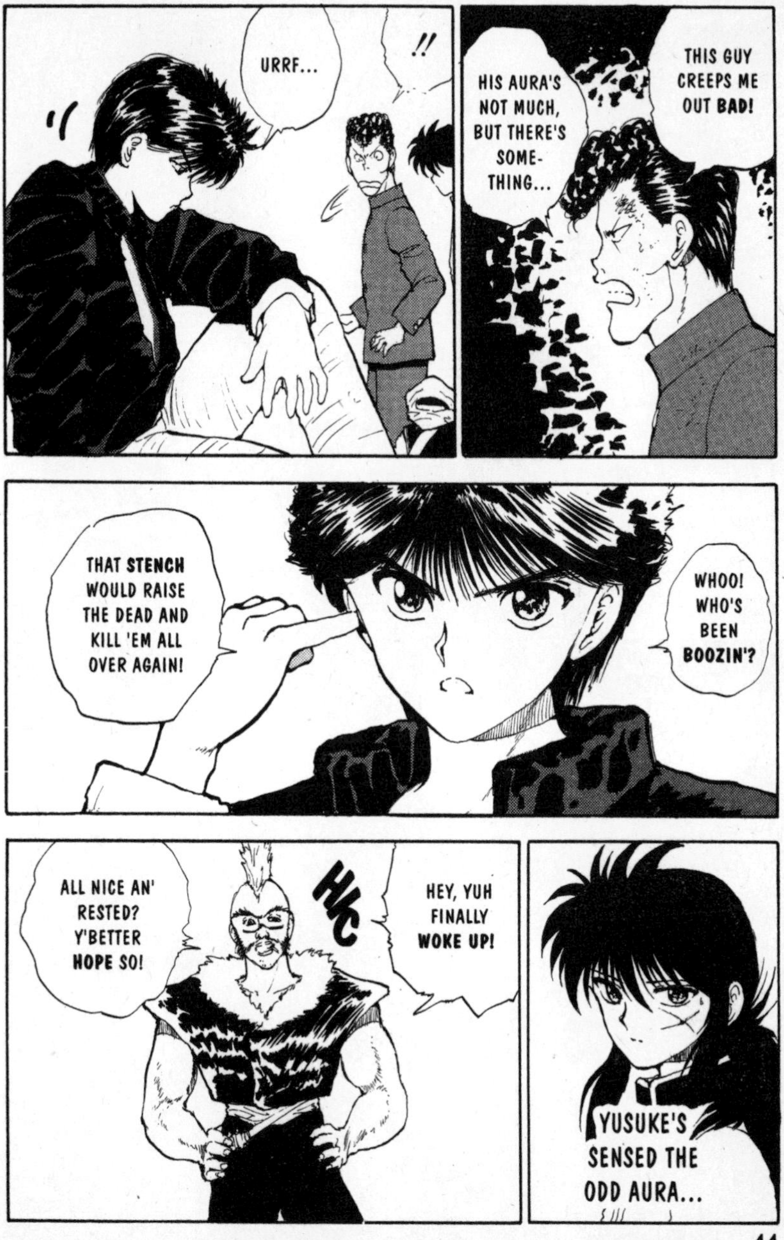
THIS GUY CREEPS ME OUT BAD!
HIS AURA'S NOT MUCH, BUT THERE'S SOME-THING...
!!
URRF...
WHOO! WHO'S BEEN BOOZIN'?
THAT STENCH WOULD RAISE THE DEAD AND KILL 'EM ALL OVER AGAIN!
YUSUKE'S SENSED THE ODD AURA...
HEY, YUH FINALLY WOKE UP!
HIC
ALL NICE AN' RESTED? Y'BETTER HOPE SO!

READ THIS WAY

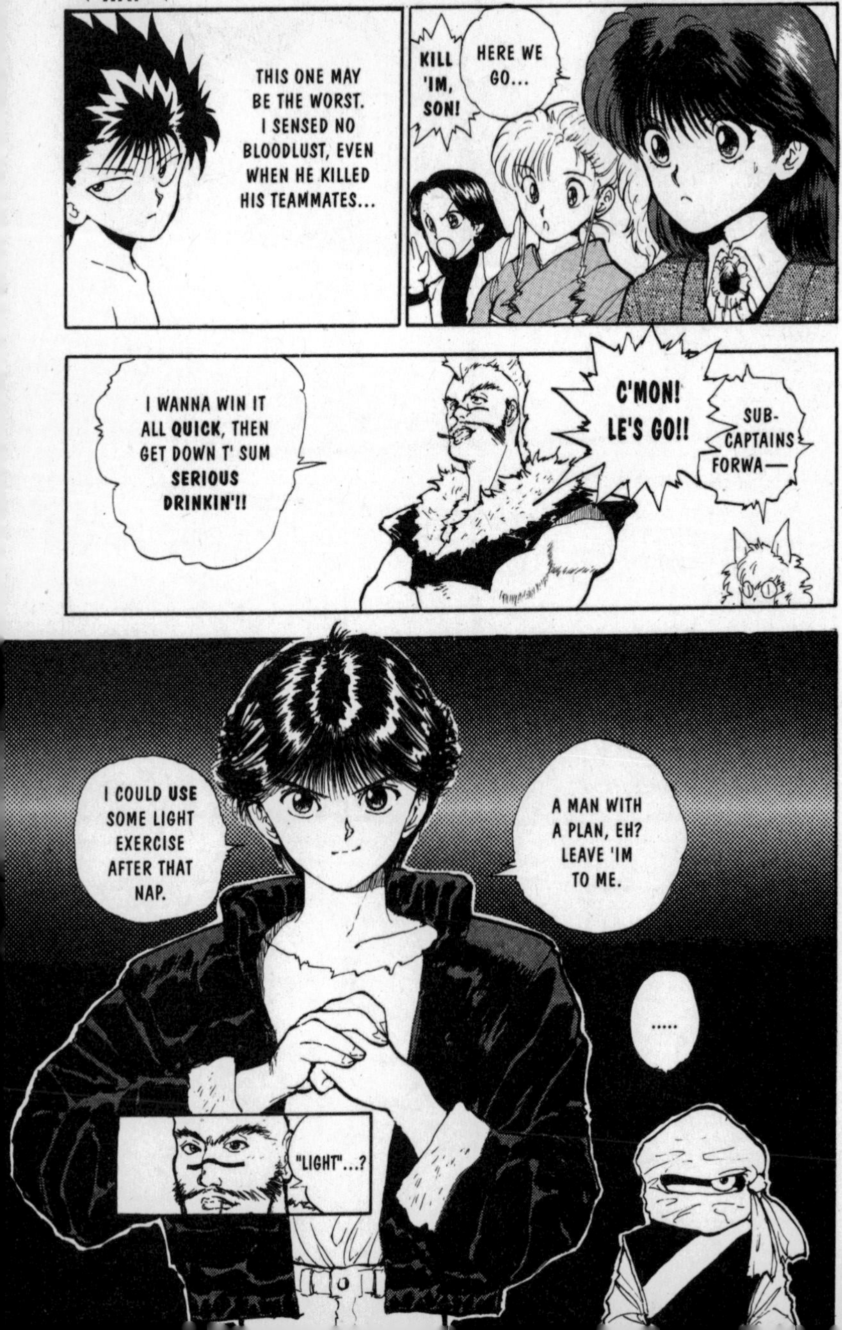

HERE WE GO...
KILL 'IM, SON!
THIS ONE MAY BE THE WORST. I SENSED NO BLOODLUST, EVEN WHEN HE KILLED HIS TEAMMATES...
SUB-CAPTAINS FORWA—
C'MON! LE'S GO!!
I WANNA WIN IT ALL QUICK, THEN GET DOWN T' SUM SERIOUS DRINKIN'!!
A MAN WITH A PLAN, EH? LEAVE 'IM TO ME.
I COULD USE SOME LIGHT EXERCISE AFTER THAT NAP.
......
"LIGHT"...?

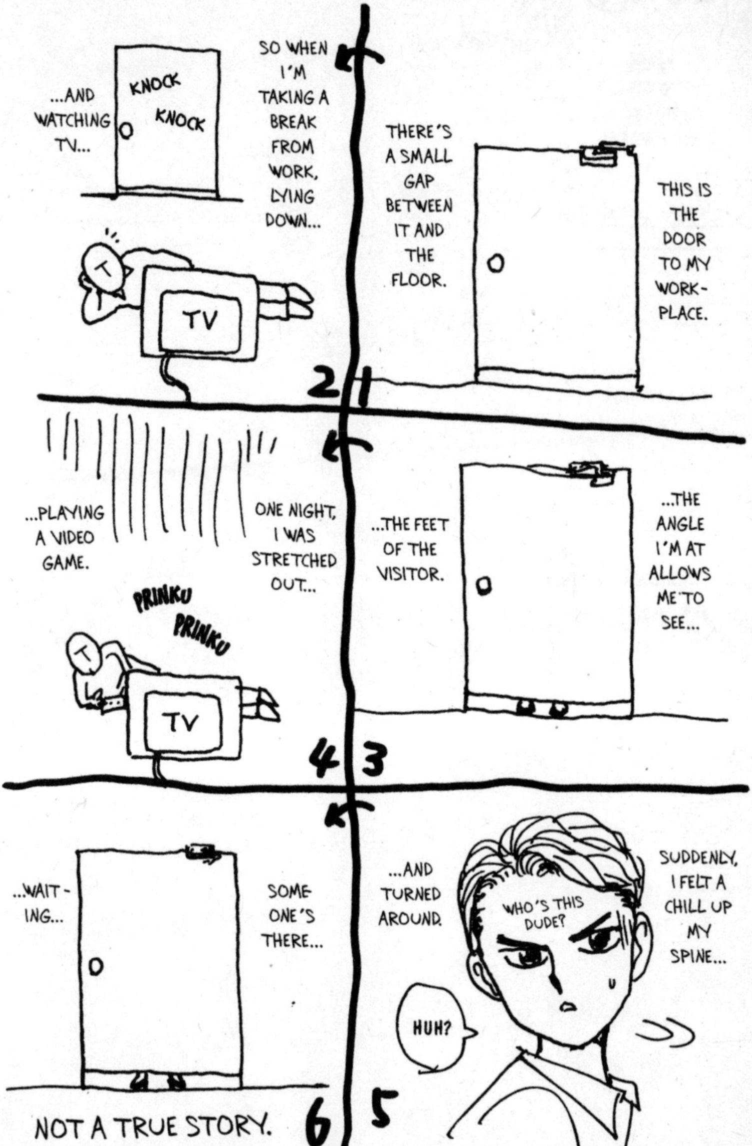
THIS IS THE DOOR TO MY WORK-PLACE.
THERE'S A SMALL GAP BETWEEN IT AND THE FLOOR.
SO WHEN I'M TAKING A BREAK FROM WORK, LYING DOWN...
...AND WATCHING TV...
KNOCK
KNOCK
TV
...THE ANGLE I'M AT ALLOWS ME TO SEE...
...THE FEET OF THE VISITOR.
ONE NIGHT, I WAS STRETCHED OUT...
...PLAYING A VIDEO GAME.
PRINKU
PRINKU
TV
SUDDENLY, I FELT A CHILL UP MY SPINE...
...AND TURNED AROUND.
WHO'S THIS DUDE?
HUH?
SOME-ONE'S THERE...
...WAIT-ING...
NOT A TRUE STORY.

DRUNKEN MASTER: CHU!!

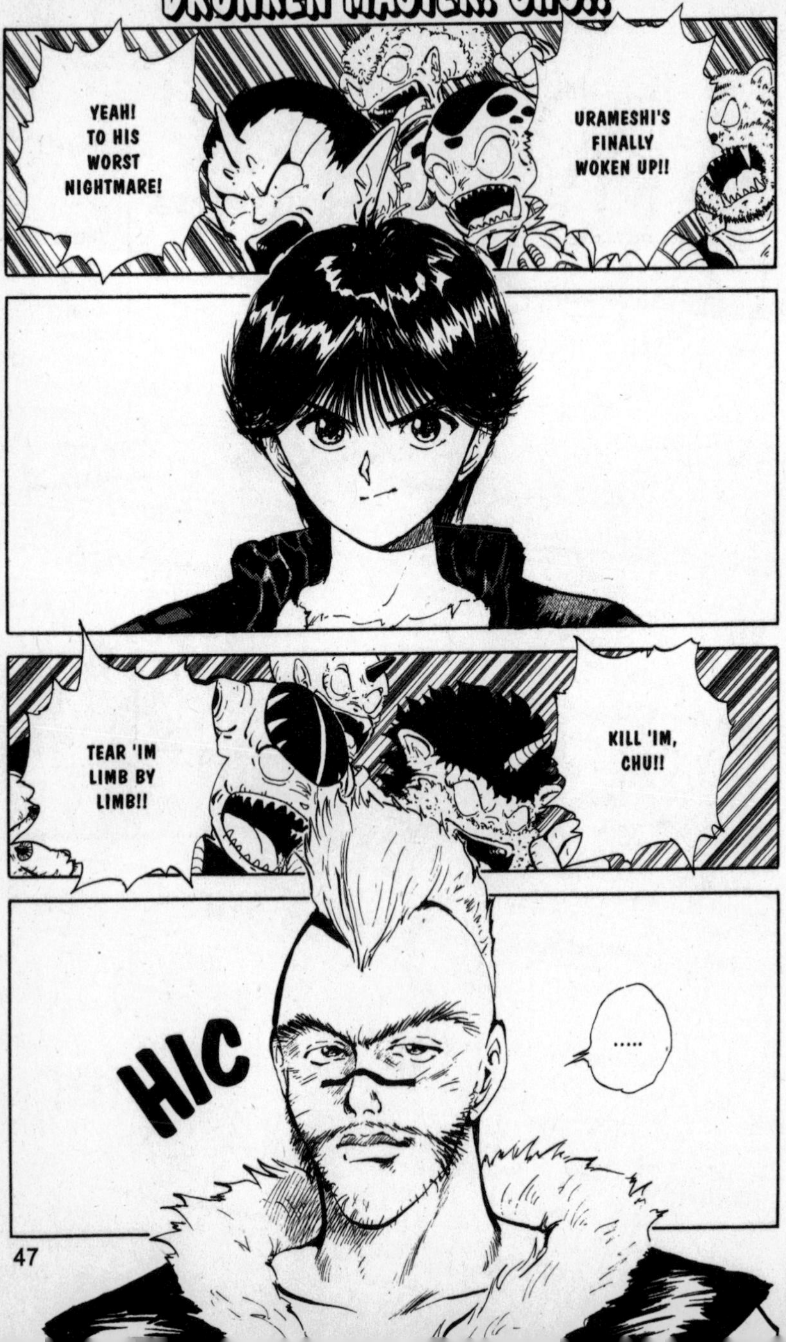
URAMESHI'S FINALLY WOKEN UP!!
YEAH! TO HIS WORST NIGHTMARE!
KILL 'IM, CHU!!
TEAR 'IM LIMB BY LIMB!!
.....
HIC

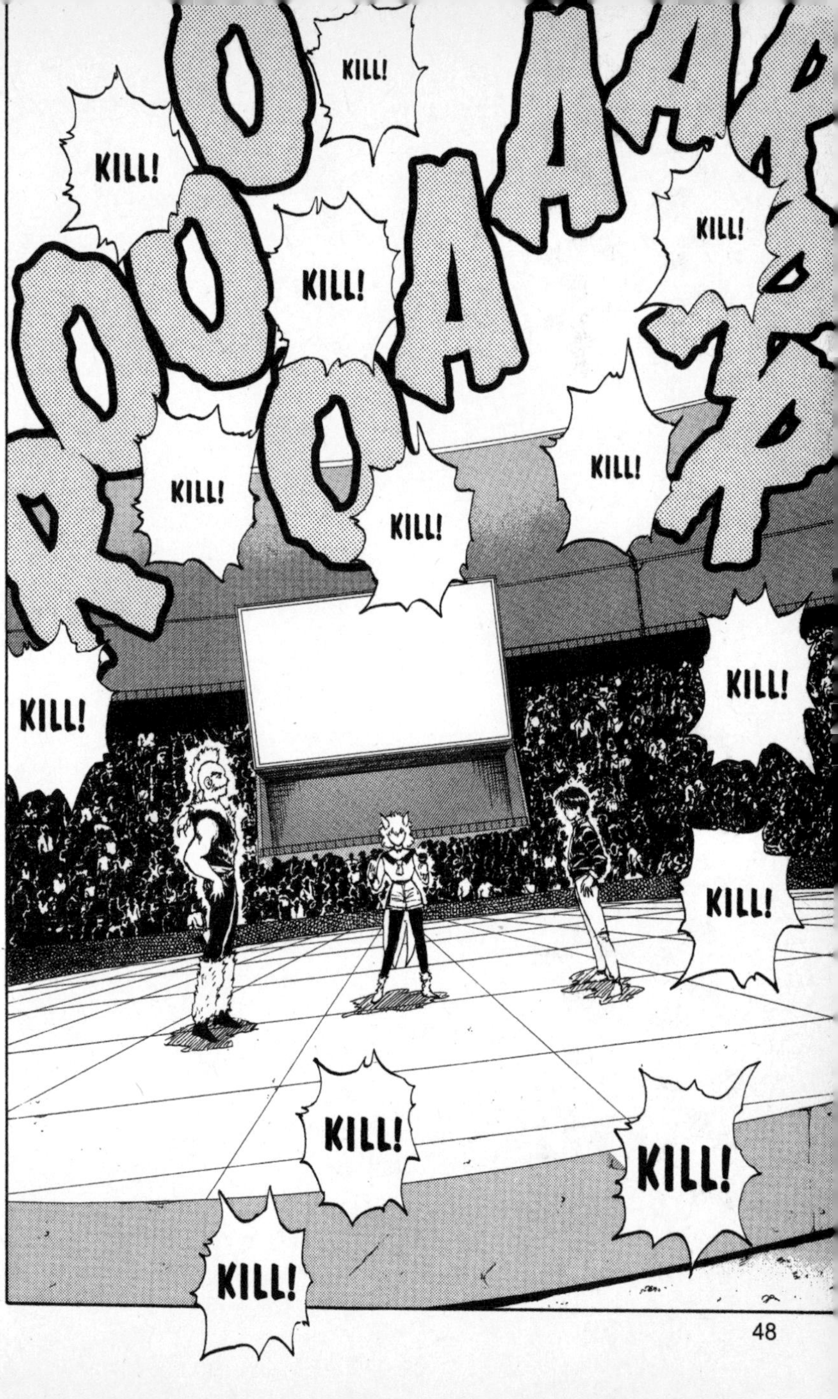
ROOOOAAAR
KILL!
KILL!
KILL!
KILL!
KILL!
KILL!
KILL!
KILL!
KILL!
KILL!
KILL!
KILL!
KILL!

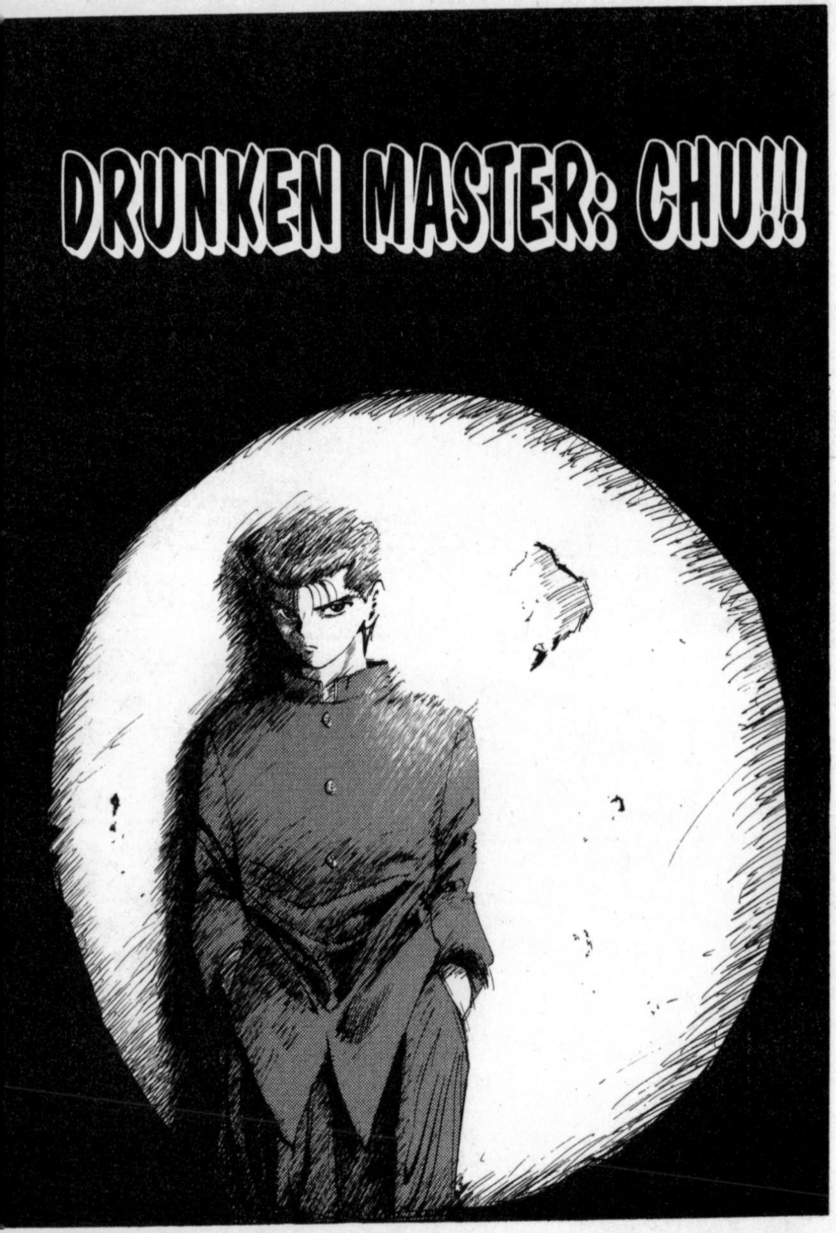
DRUNKEN MASTER: CHU!!

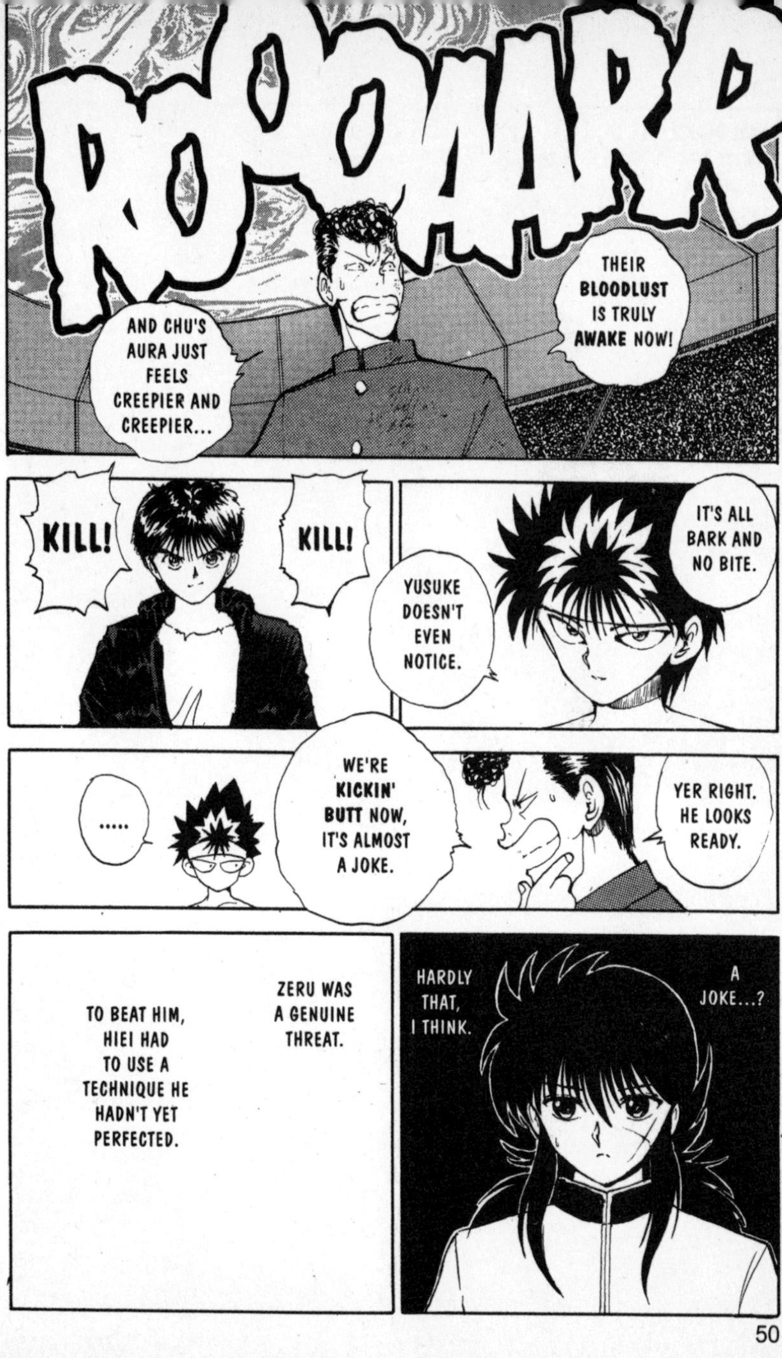
ROOARR
THEIR BLOODLUST IS TRULY AWAKE NOW!
AND CHU'S AURA JUST FEELS CREEPIER AND CREEPIER...
IT'S ALL BARK AND NO BITE.
YUSUKE DOESN'T EVEN NOTICE.
KILL!
KILL!
YER RIGHT. HE LOOKS READY.
WE'RE KICKIN' BUTT NOW, IT'S ALMOST A JOKE.
.....
A JOKE...?
HARDLY THAT, I THINK.
ZERU WAS A GENUINE THREAT.
TO BEAT HIM, HIEI HAD TO USE A TECHNIQUE HE HADN'T YET PERFECTED.

READ THIS WAY

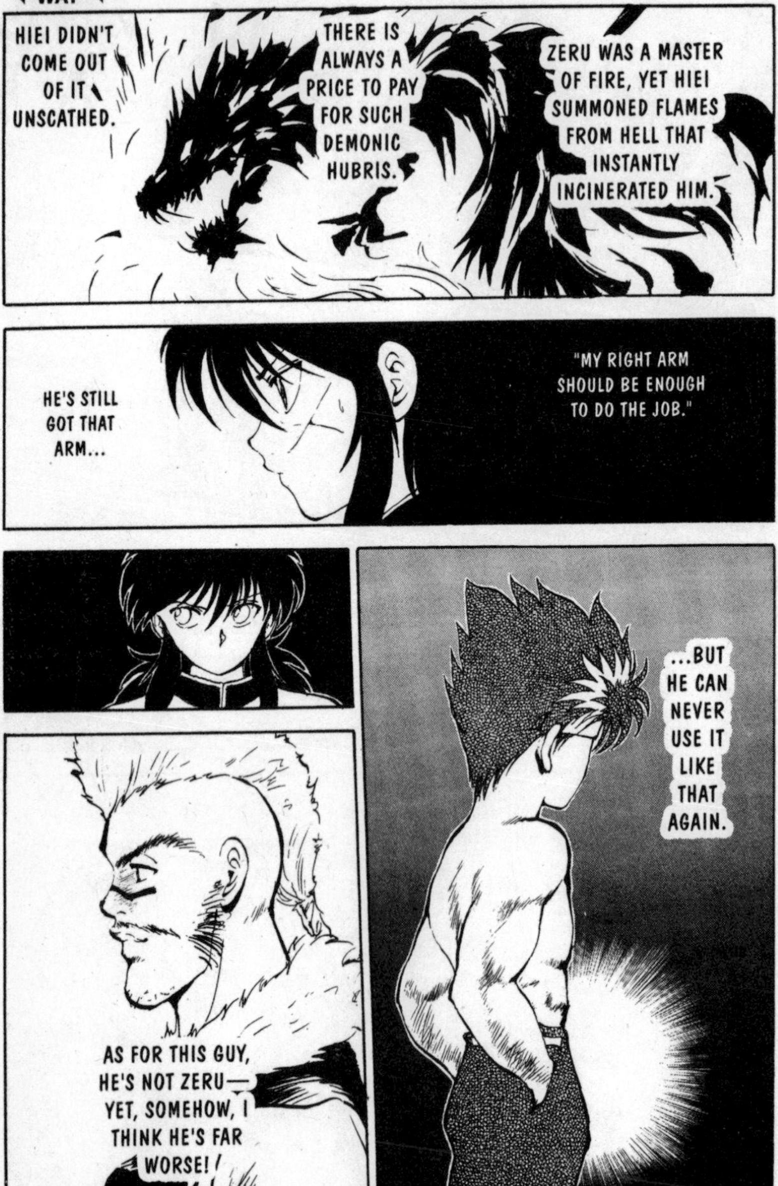

ZERU WAS A MASTER OF FIRE, YET HIEI SUMMONED FLAMES FROM HELL THAT INSTANTLY INCINERATED HIM.
THERE IS ALWAYS A PRICE TO PAY FOR SUCH DEMONIC HUBRIS.
HIEI DIDN'T COME OUT OF IT UNSCATHED.
"MY RIGHT ARM SHOULD BE ENOUGH TO DO THE JOB."
HE'S STILL GOT THAT ARM...
...BUT HE CAN NEVER USE IT LIKE THAT AGAIN.
AS FOR THIS GUY, HE'S NOT ZERU— YET, SOMEHOW, I THINK HE'S FAR WORSE!

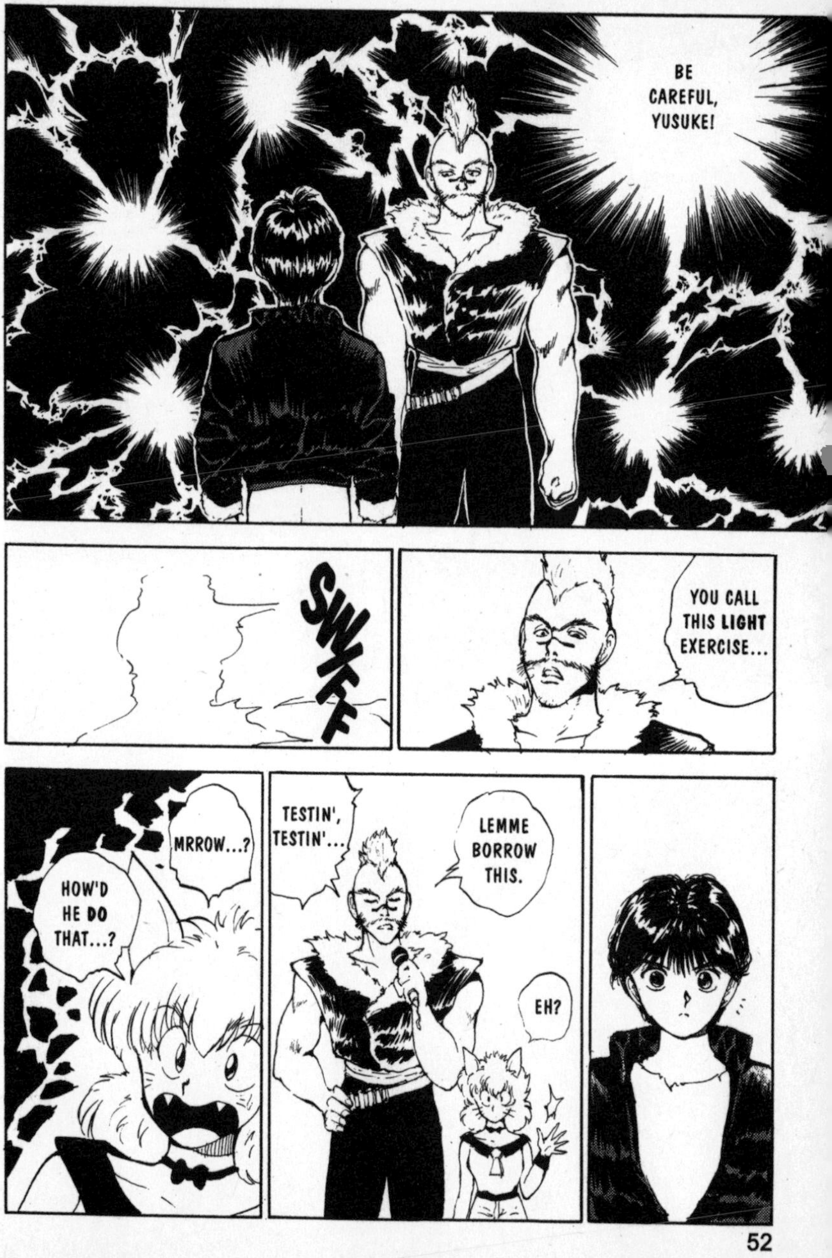
BE CAREFUL, YUSUKE!
YOU CALL THIS LIGHT EXERCISE...
SWFF
LEMME BORROW THIS.
TESTIN', TESTIN'...
EH?
MRROW...?
HOW'D HE DO THAT...?

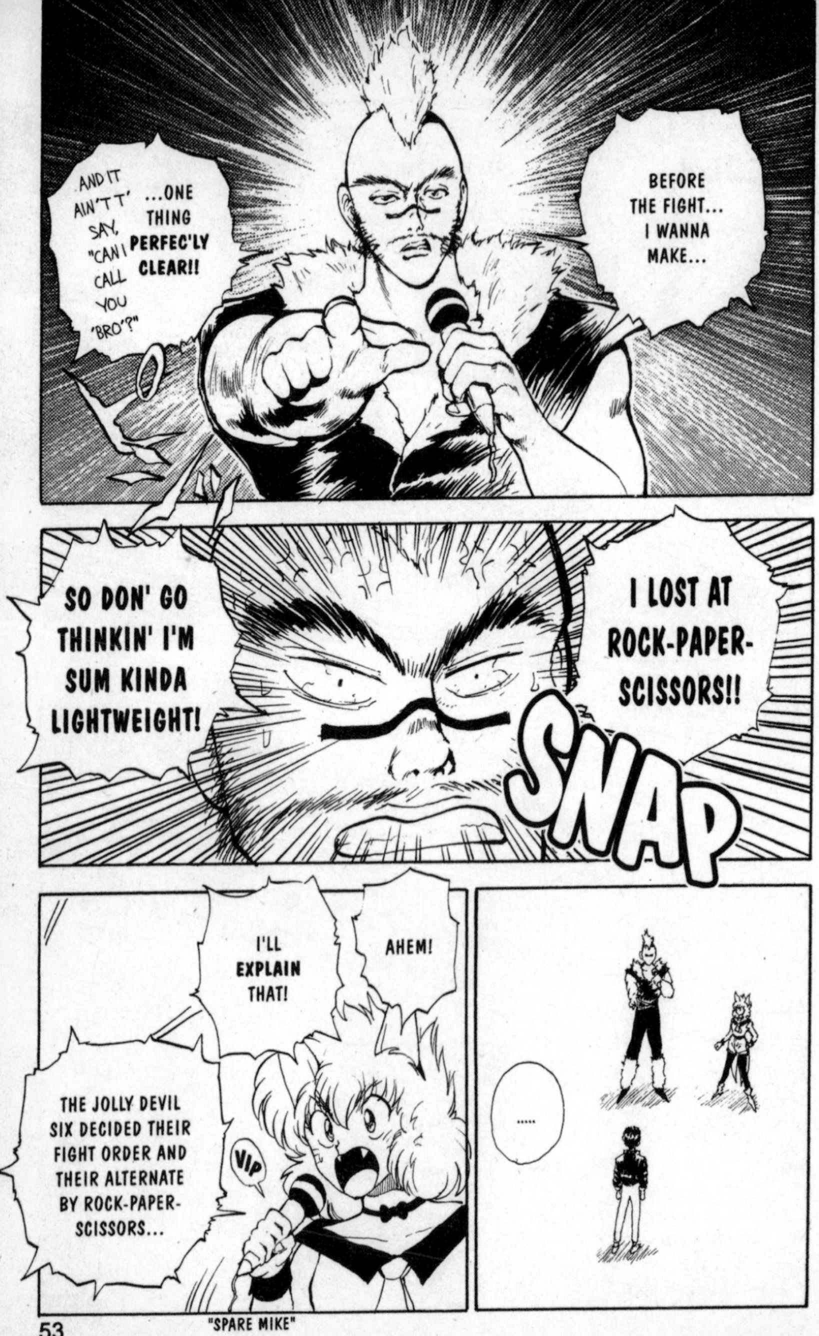
BEFORE THE FIGHT... I WANNA MAKE...
...ONE THING PERFEC'LY CLEAR!!
AND IT AIN'T T' SAY, "CAN I CALL YOU 'BRO'?"
I LOST AT ROCK-PAPER-SCISSORS!!
SNAP
SO DON' GO THINKIN' I'M SUM KINDA LIGHTWEIGHT!
.....
AHEM!
I'LL EXPLAIN THAT!
THE JOLLY DEVIL SIX DECIDED THEIR FIGHT ORDER AND THEIR ALTERNATE BY ROCK-PAPER-SCISSORS...
VIP

"SPARE MIKE"

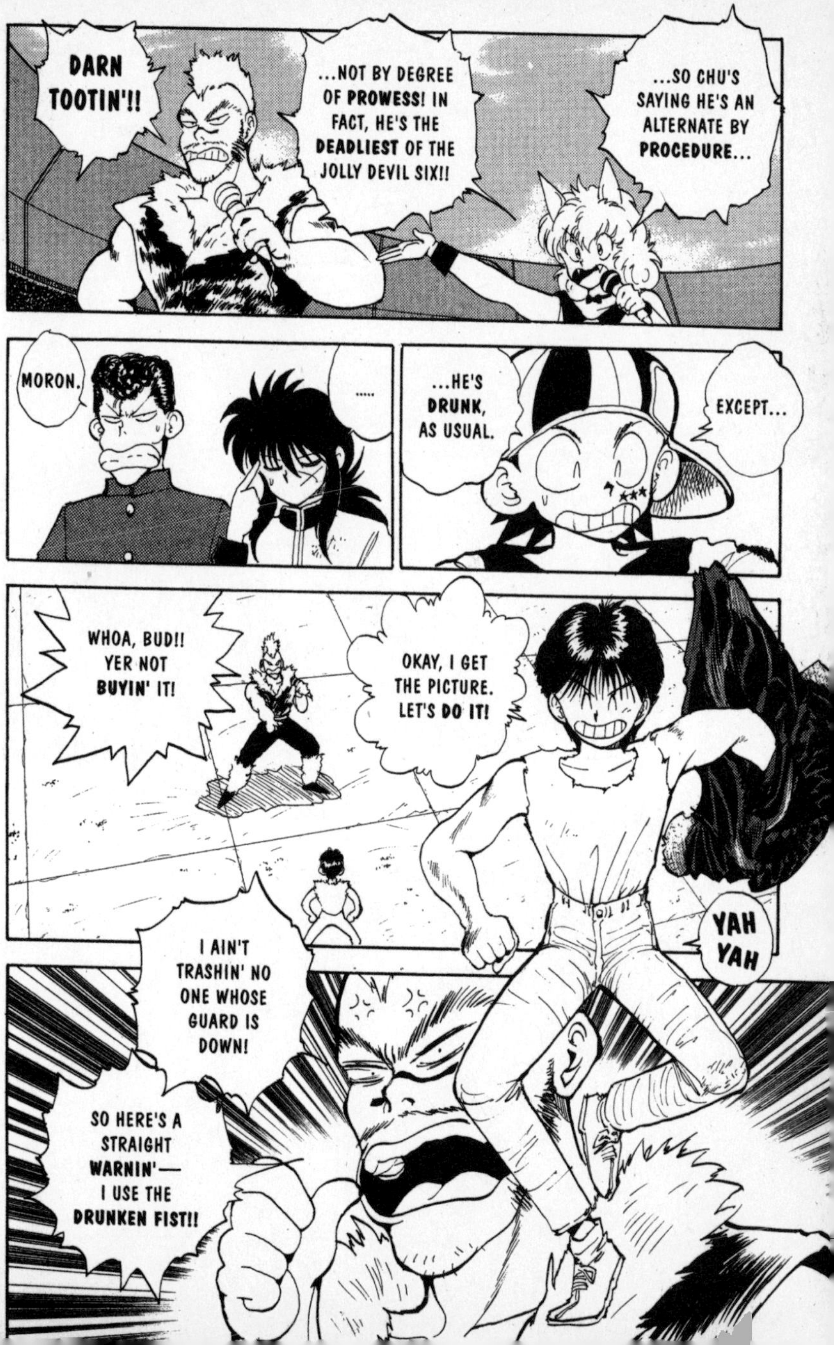
...SO CHU'S SAYING HE'S AN ALTERNATE BY PROCEDURE...
...NOT BY DEGREE OF PROWESS! IN FACT, HE'S THE DEADLIEST OF THE JOLLY DEVIL SIX!!
DARN TOOTIN'!!
EXCEPT...
...HE'S DRUNK, AS USUAL.
.....
MORON.
OKAY, I GET THE PICTURE. LET'S DO IT!
WHOA, BUD!! YER NOT BUYIN' IT!
YAH YAH
I AIN'T TRASHIN' NO ONE WHOSE GUARD IS DOWN!
SO HERE'S A STRAIGHT WARNIN'— I USE THE DRUNKEN FIST!!

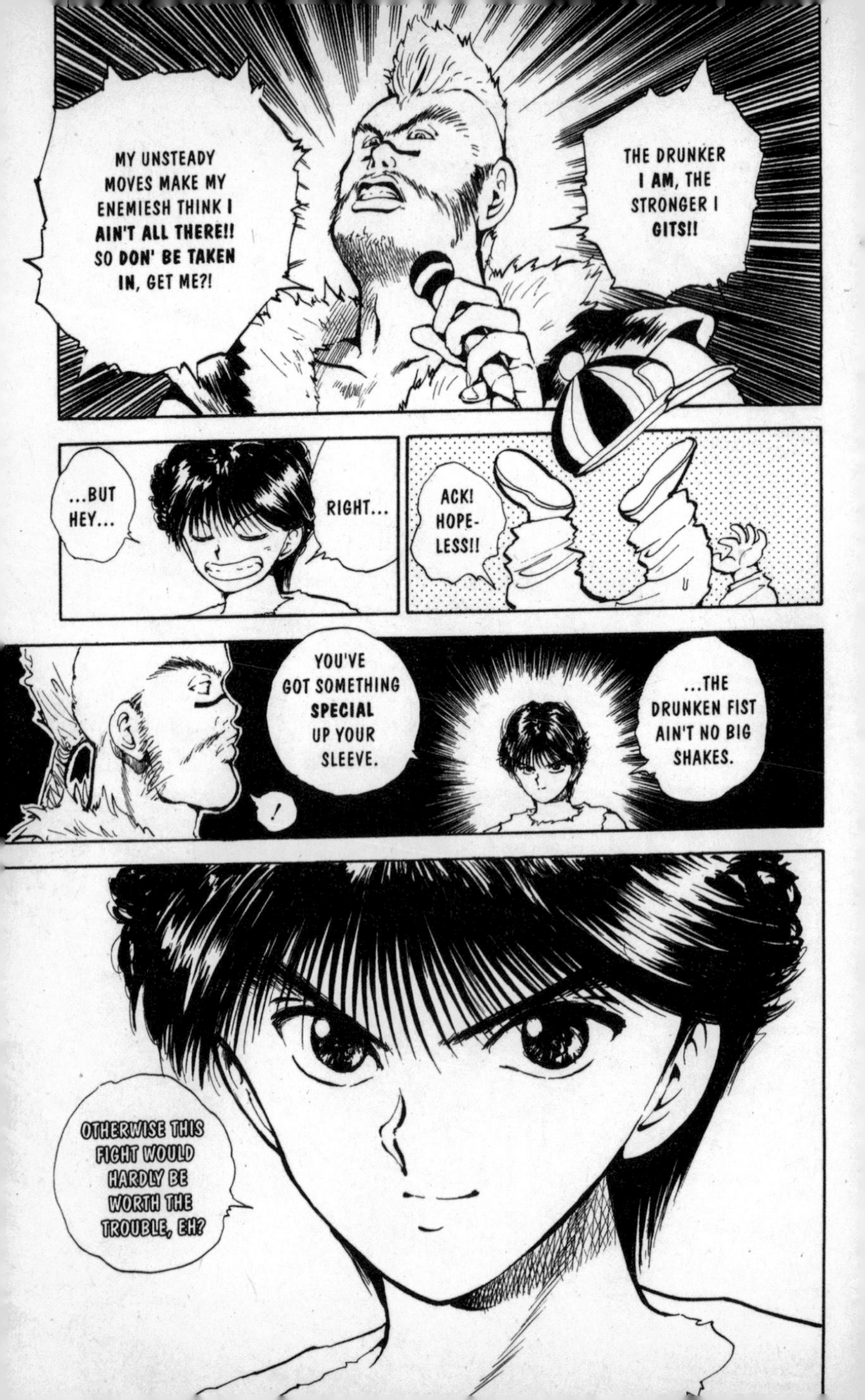
THE DRUNKER I AM, THE STRONGER I GITS!!
MY UNSTEADY MOVES MAKE MY ENEMIESH THINK I AIN'T ALL THERE!! SO DON' BE TAKEN IN, GET ME?!
ACK! HOPE-LESS!!
RIGHT...
...BUT HEY...
...THE DRUNKEN FIST AIN'T NO BIG SHAKES.
YOU'VE GOT SOMETHING SPECIAL UP YOUR SLEEVE.
!
OTHERWISE THIS FIGHT WOULD HARDLY BE WORTH THE TROUBLE, EH?

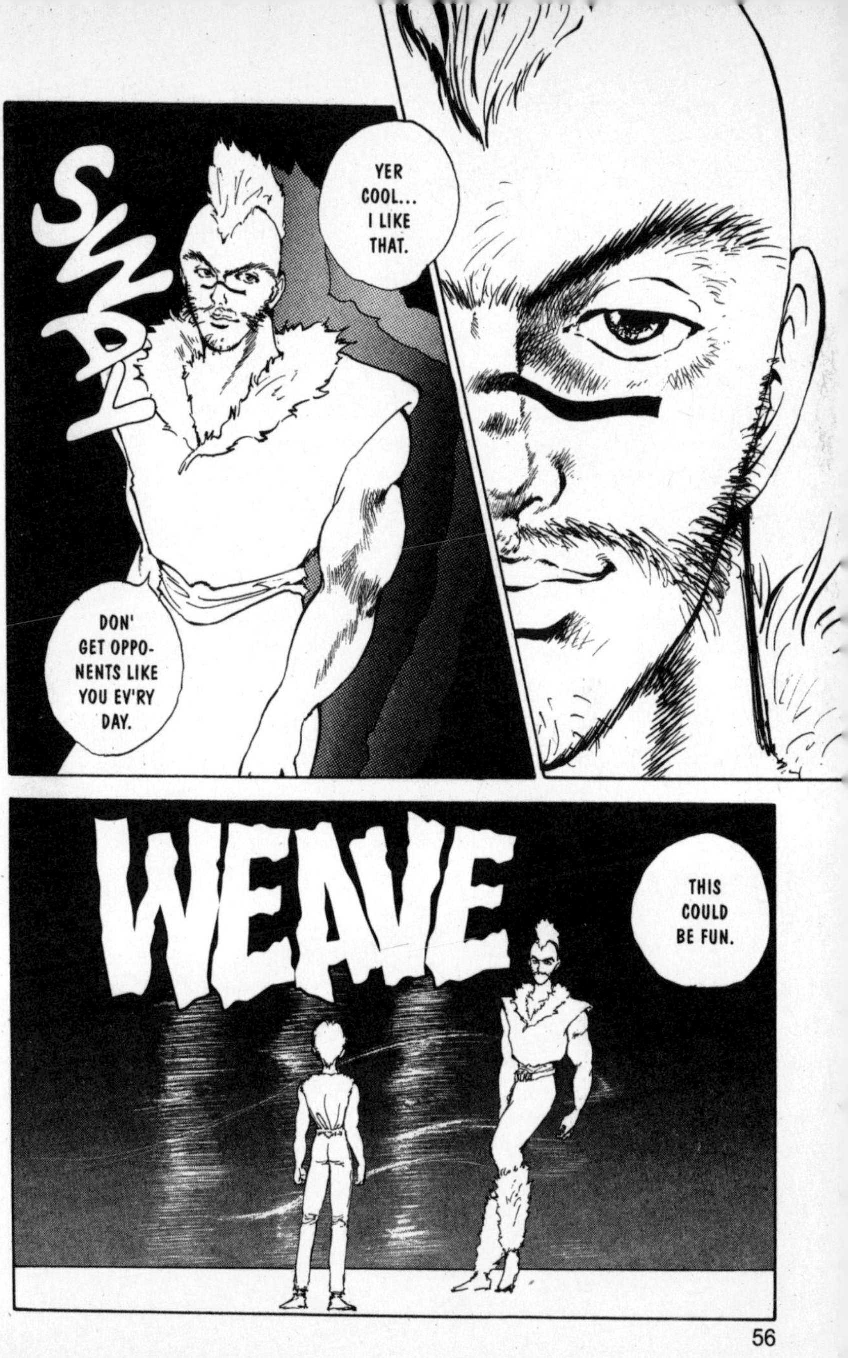
SWAY
YER COOL... I LIKE THAT.
DON' GET OPPO-NENTS LIKE YOU EV'RY DAY.
WEAVE
THIS COULD BE FUN.

READ THIS WAY

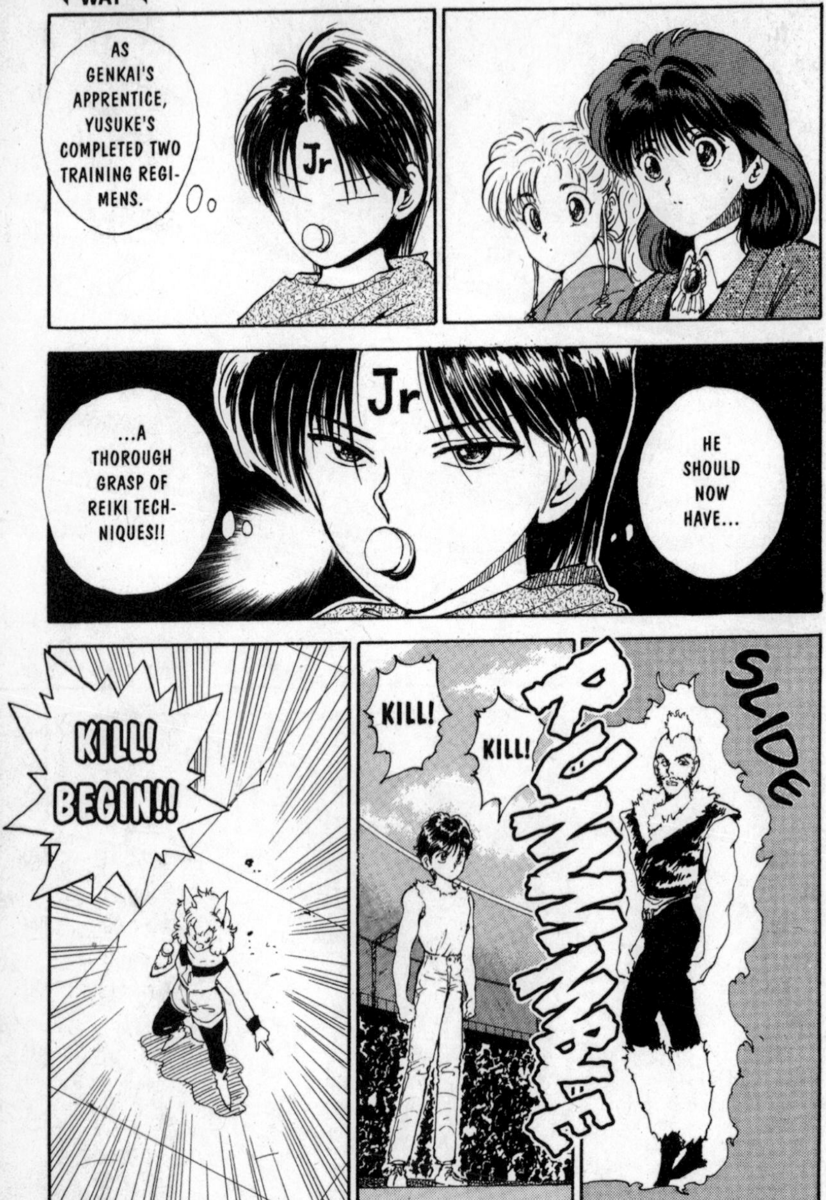
AS GENKAI'S APPRENTICE, YUSUKE'S COMPLETED TWO TRAINING REGIMENS.
HE SHOULD NOW HAVE...
...A THOROUGH GRASP OF REIKI TECHNIQUES!!
SLIDE
RUMMMBLE
KILL!
KILL!
KILL! BEGIN!!

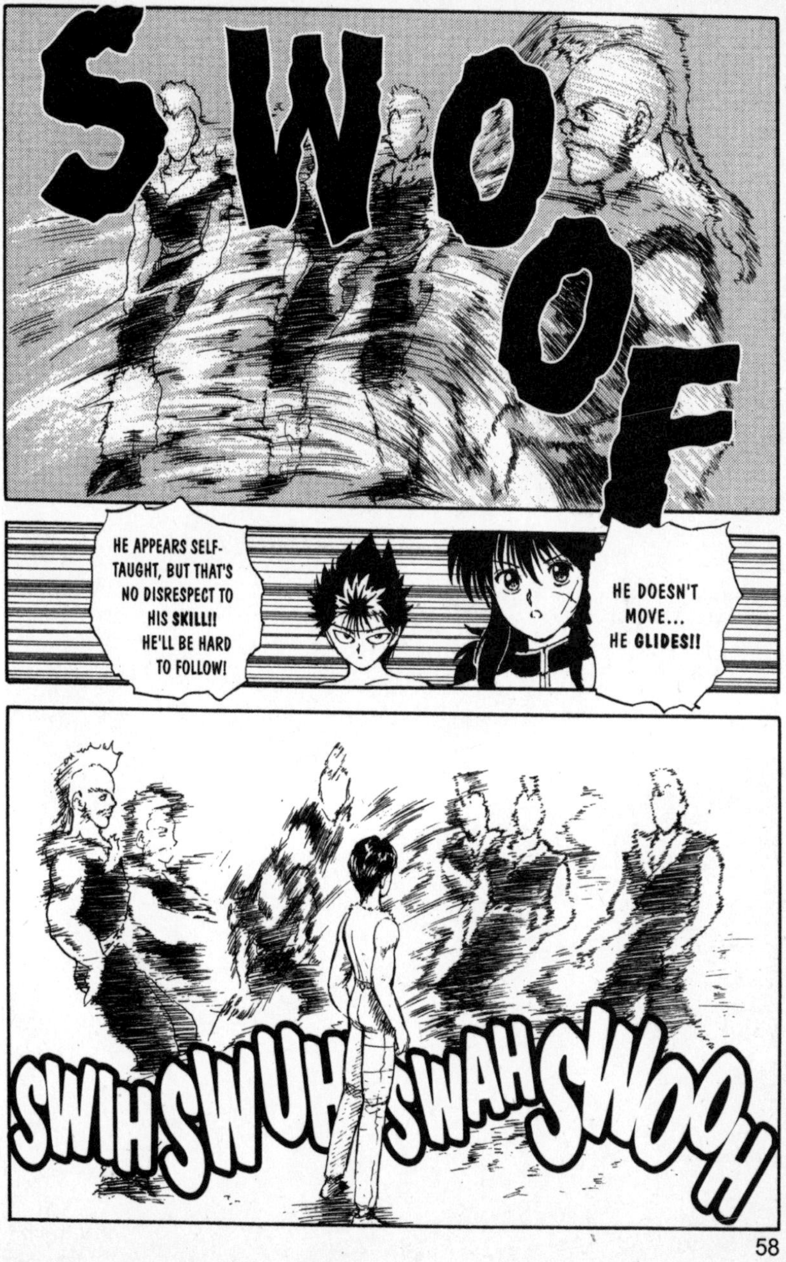
SWOOF
HE DOESN'T MOVE... HE GLIDES!!
HE APPEARS SELF-TAUGHT, BUT THAT'S NO DISRESPECT TO HIS SKILL!! HE'LL BE HARD TO FOLLOW!
SWIH SWUH SWAH SWOOH

READ THIS WAY

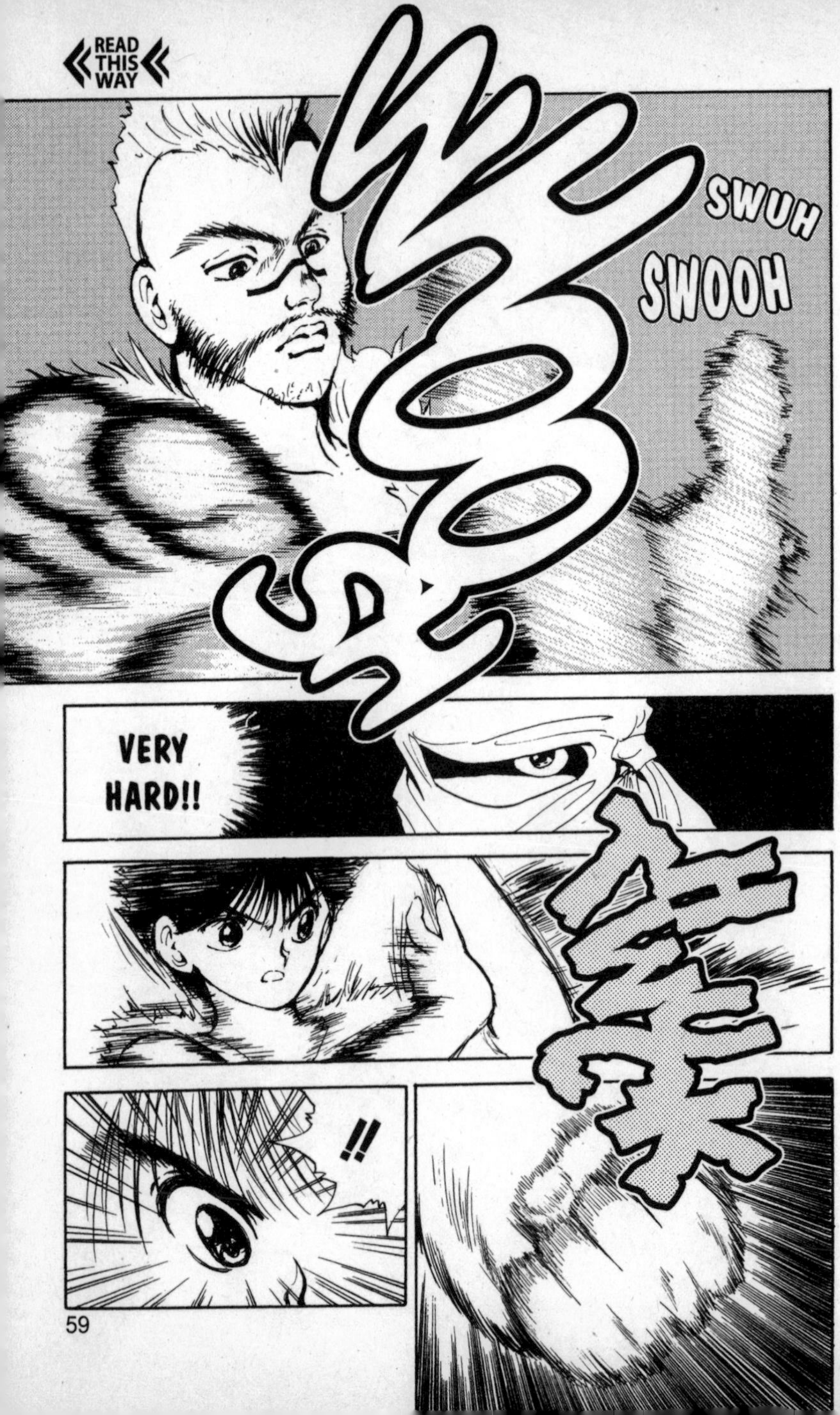
SWUH
SWOOH
VERY HARD!!
!!

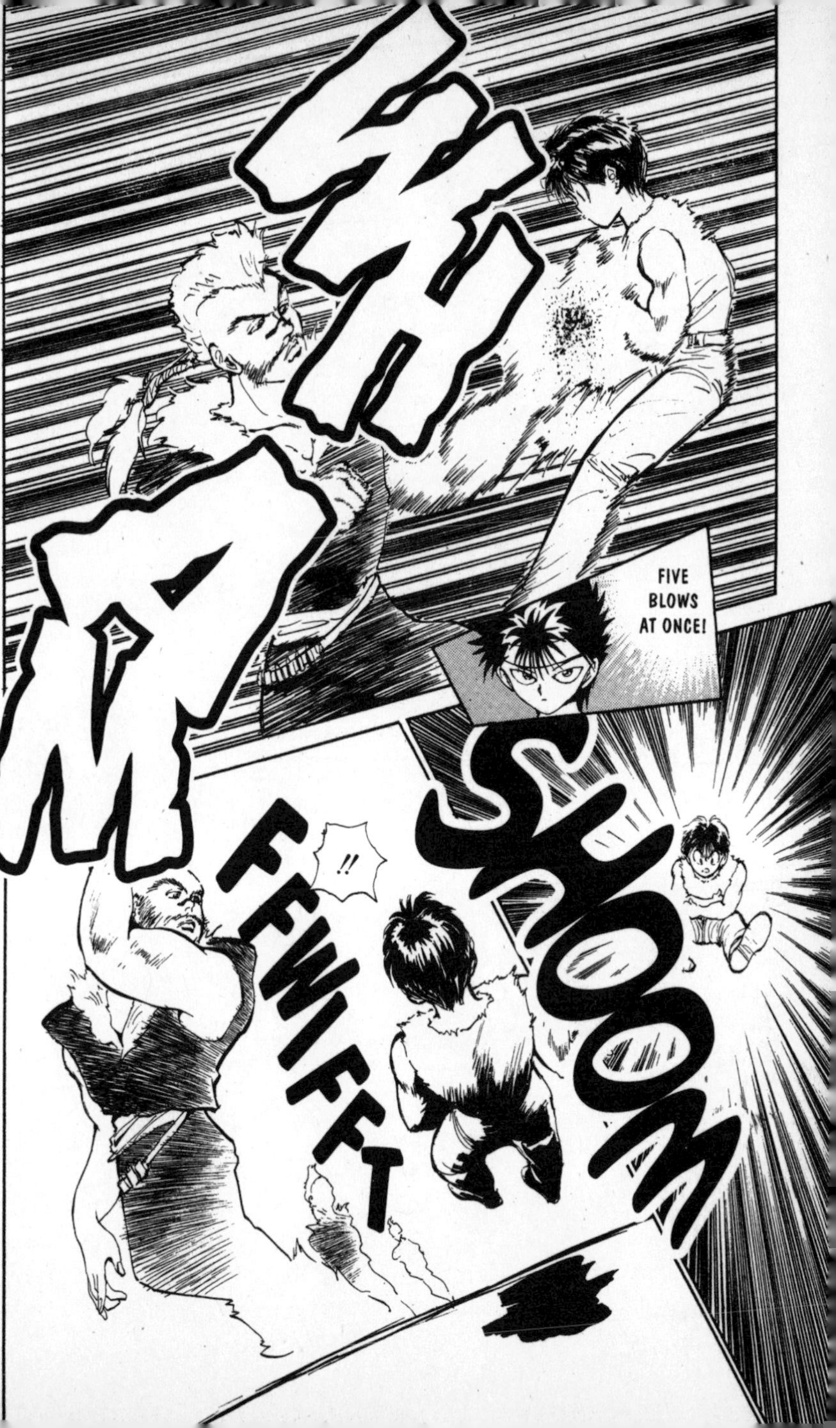
FIVE BLOWS AT ONCE!
SHOOM
!!
FFWIFFT

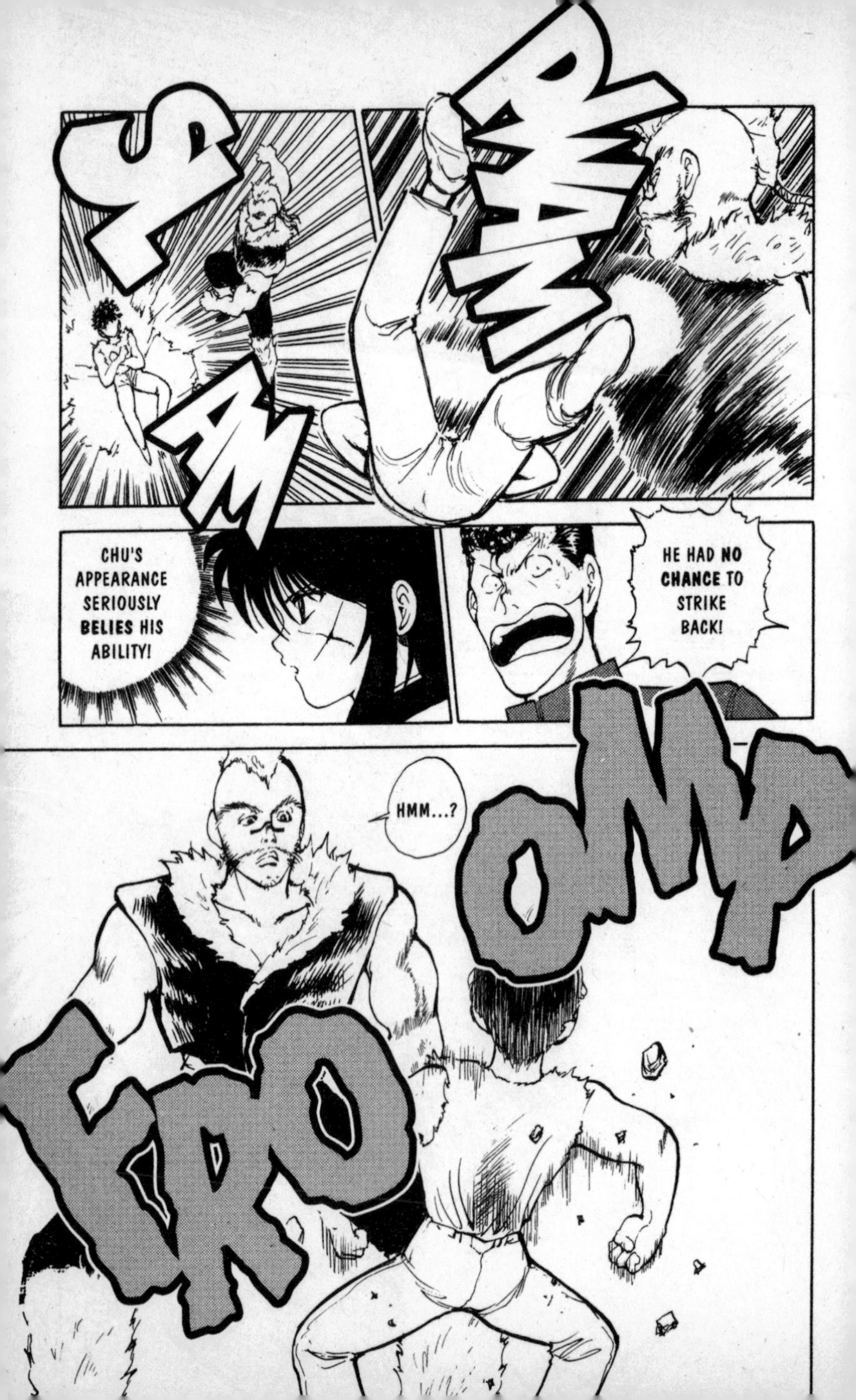
DWAM
SPAM
HE HAD NO CHANCE TO STRIKE BACK!
CHU'S APPEARANCE SERIOUSLY BELIES HIS ABILITY!
HMM...?
KROOMP

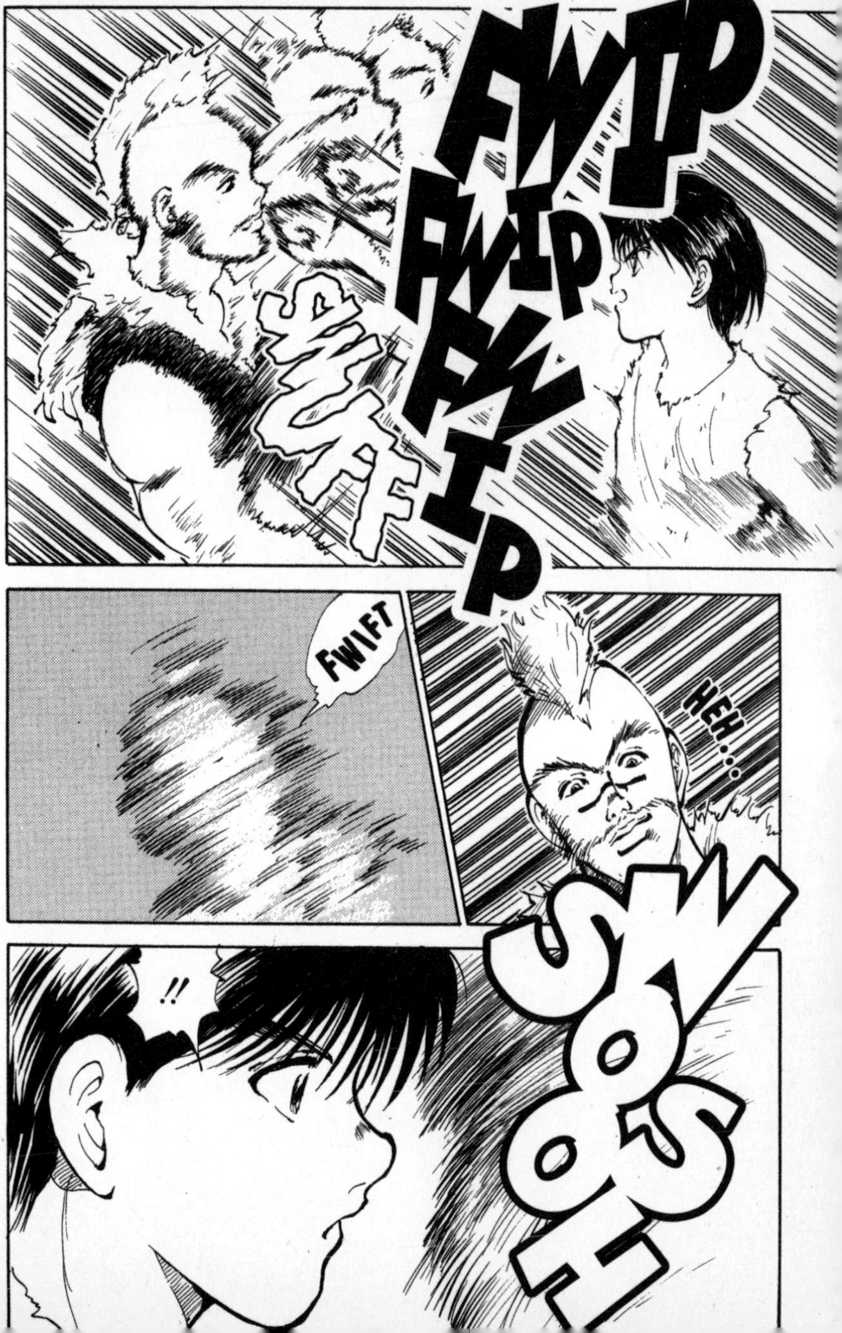
FWIP
FWIP
FWIP
HEH...
FWIFT
SWOOSH
!!

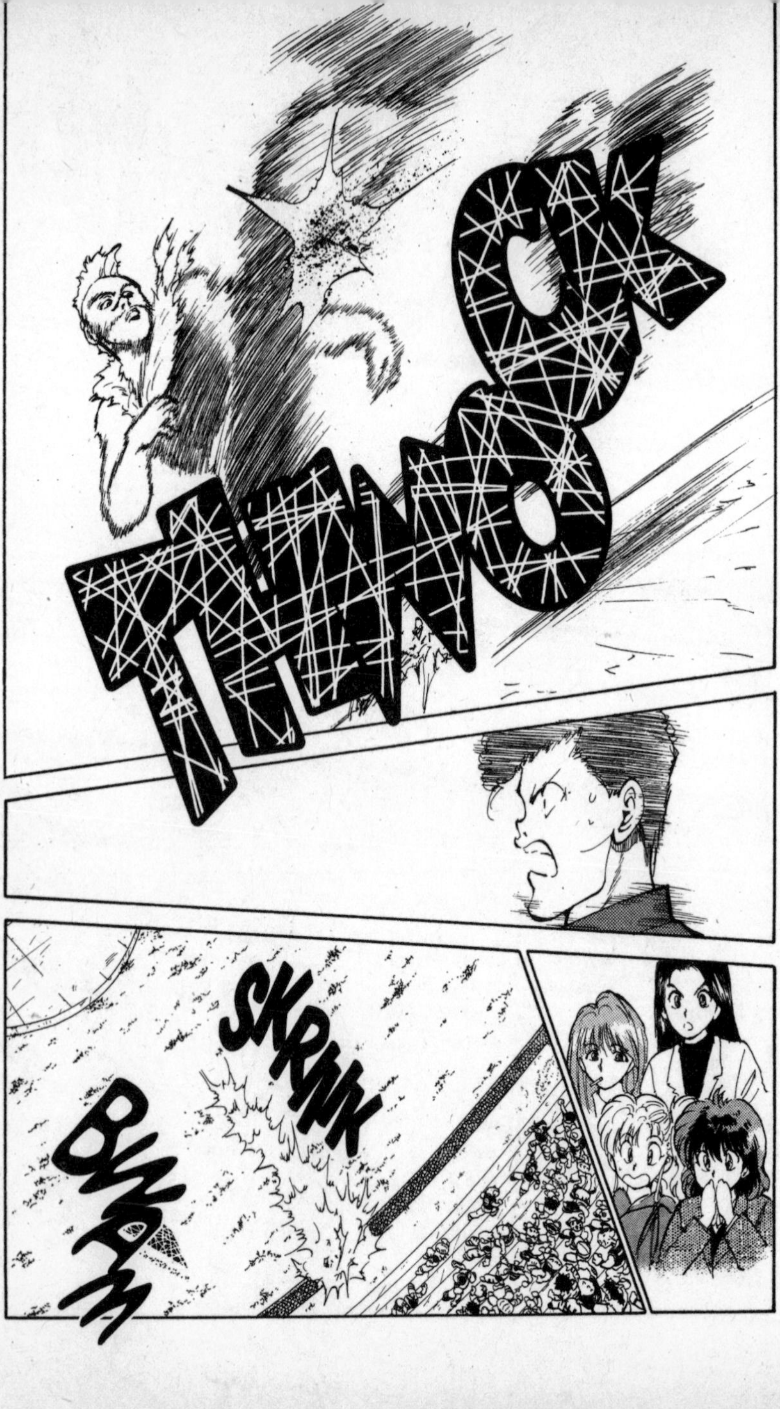
THWOCK
SKRUNK
BWAM

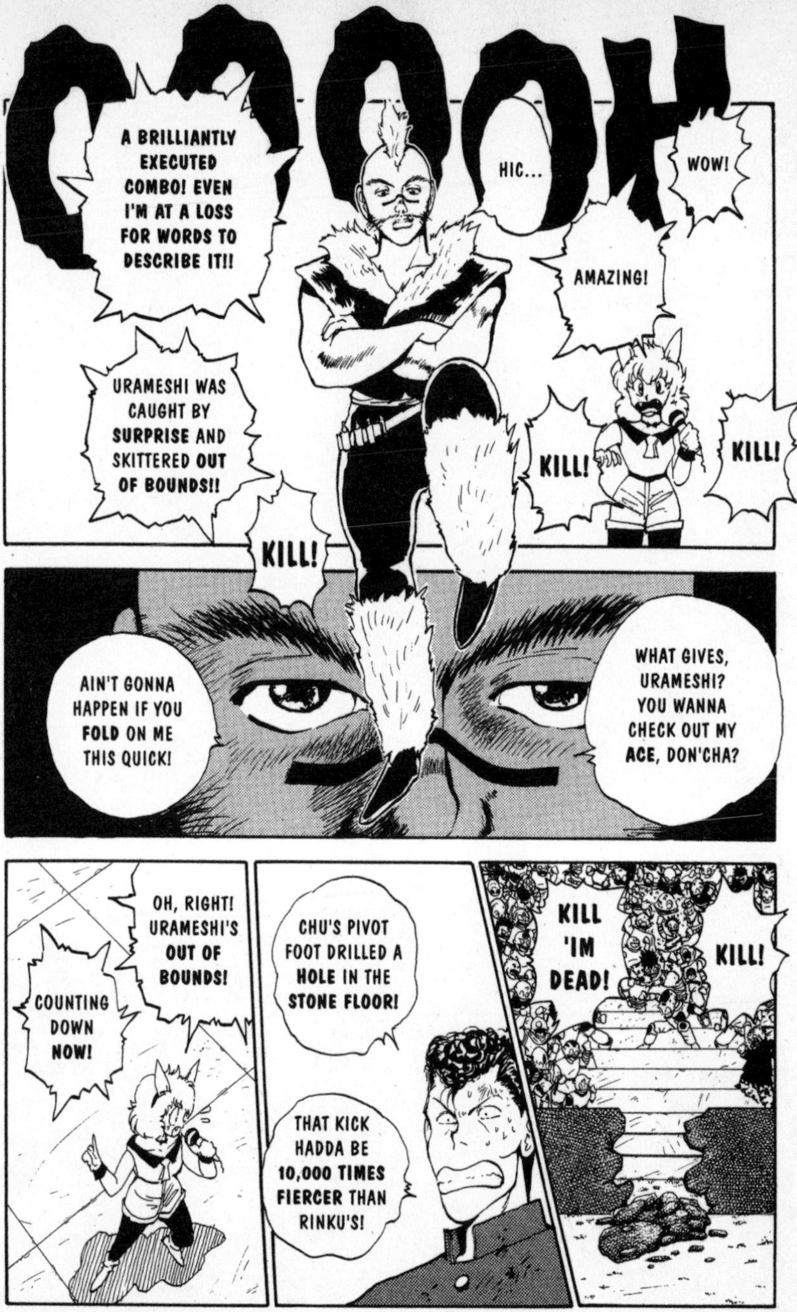

WOW!
HIC...
OOOOH
A BRILLIANTLY EXECUTED COMBO! EVEN I'M AT A LOSS FOR WORDS TO DESCRIBE IT!!
AMAZING!
KILL!
KILL!
URAMESHI WAS CAUGHT BY SURPRISE AND SKITTERED OUT OF BOUNDS!!
KILL!
WHAT GIVES, URAMESHI? YOU WANNA CHECK OUT MY ACE, DON'CHA?
AIN'T GONNA HAPPEN IF YOU FOLD ON ME THIS QUICK!
KILL!
KILL 'IM DEAD!
CHU'S PIVOT FOOT DRILLED A HOLE IN THE STONE FLOOR!
THAT KICK HADDA BE 10,000 TIMES FIERCER THAN RINKU'S!
OH, RIGHT! URAMESHI'S OUT OF BOUNDS!
COUNTING DOWN NOW!

READ THIS WAY

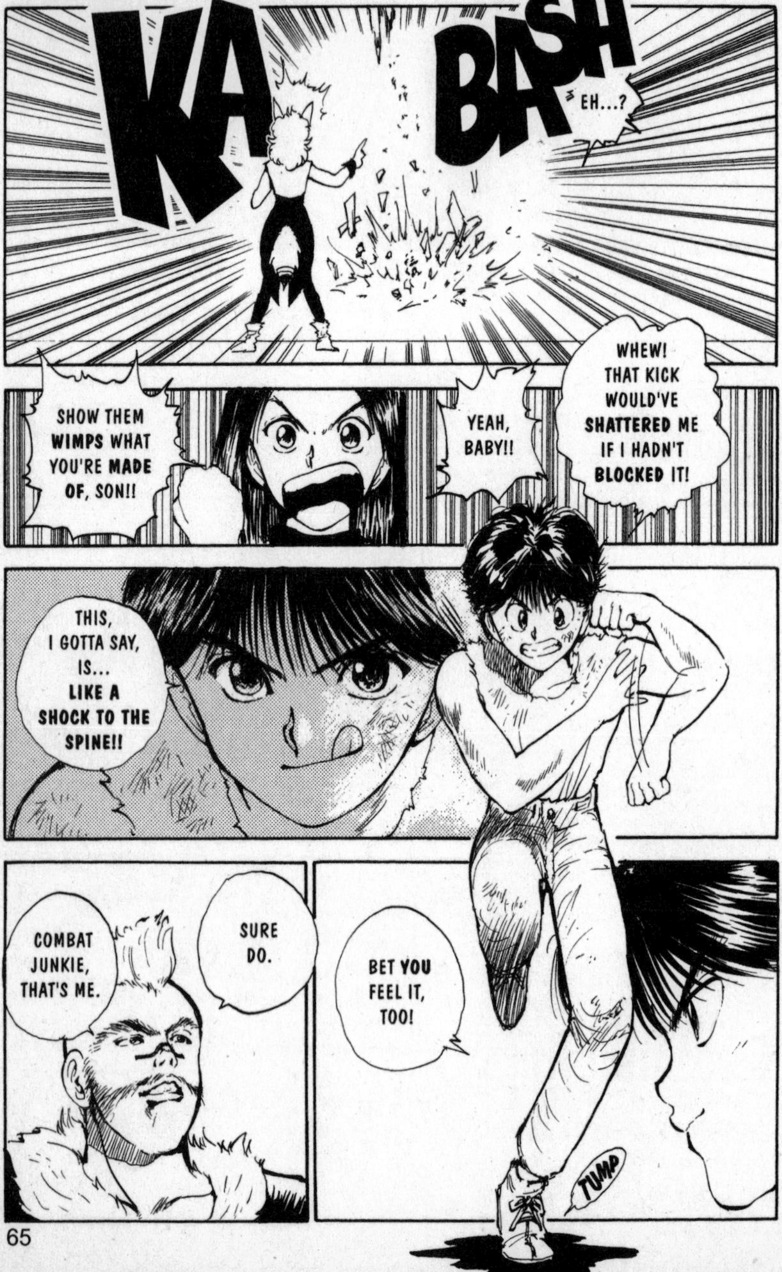

KA BASH
EH...?
WHEW! THAT KICK WOULD'VE SHATTERED ME IF I HADN'T BLOCKED IT!
YEAH, BABY!!
SHOW THEM WIMPS WHAT YOU'RE MADE OF, SON!!
THIS, I GOTTA SAY, IS... LIKE A SHOCK TO THE SPINE!!
BET YOU FEEL IT, TOO!
TUMP
SURE DO.
COMBAT JUNKIE, THAT'S ME.

TRUE STORY! THIS ISN'T FUNNY.
IT REALLY HAPPENED.

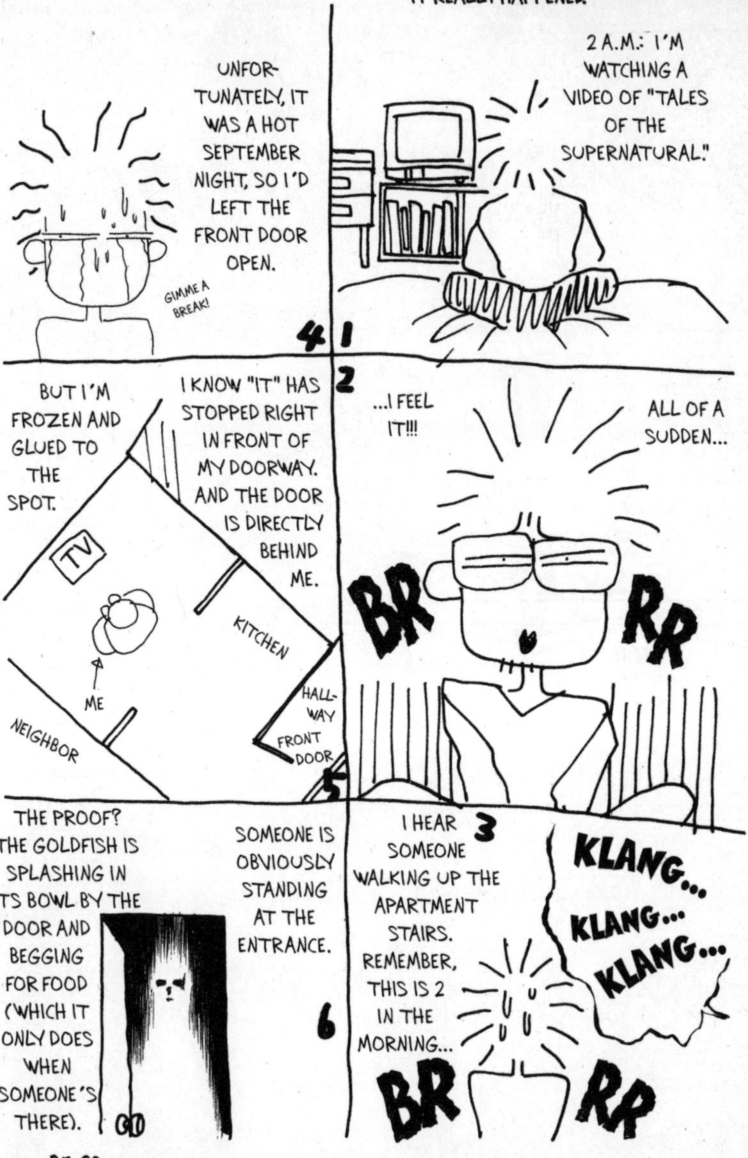
2 A.M.: I'M WATCHING A VIDEO OF "TALES OF THE SUPERNATURAL."
ALL OF A SUDDEN...
...I FEEL IT!!!
BR RR
I HEAR SOMEONE WALKING UP THE APARTMENT STAIRS. REMEMBER, THIS IS 2 IN THE MORNING...
KLANG... KLANG... KLANG...
BR RR
UNFORTUNATELY, IT WAS A HOT SEPTEMBER NIGHT, SO I'D LEFT THE FRONT DOOR OPEN.
GIMME A BREAK!
I KNOW "IT" HAS STOPPED RIGHT IN FRONT OF MY DOORWAY. AND THE DOOR IS DIRECTLY BEHIND ME.
BUT I'M FROZEN AND GLUED TO THE SPOT.
TV
KITCHEN
ME
NEIGHBOR
HALLWAY
FRONT DOOR
SOMEONE IS OBVIOUSLY STANDING AT THE ENTRANCE.
THE PROOF? THE GOLDFISH IS SPLASHING IN ITS BOWL BY THE DOOR AND BEGGING FOR FOOD (WHICH IT ONLY DOES WHEN SOMEONE'S THERE).

TO BE CONTINUED...

READ THIS WAY

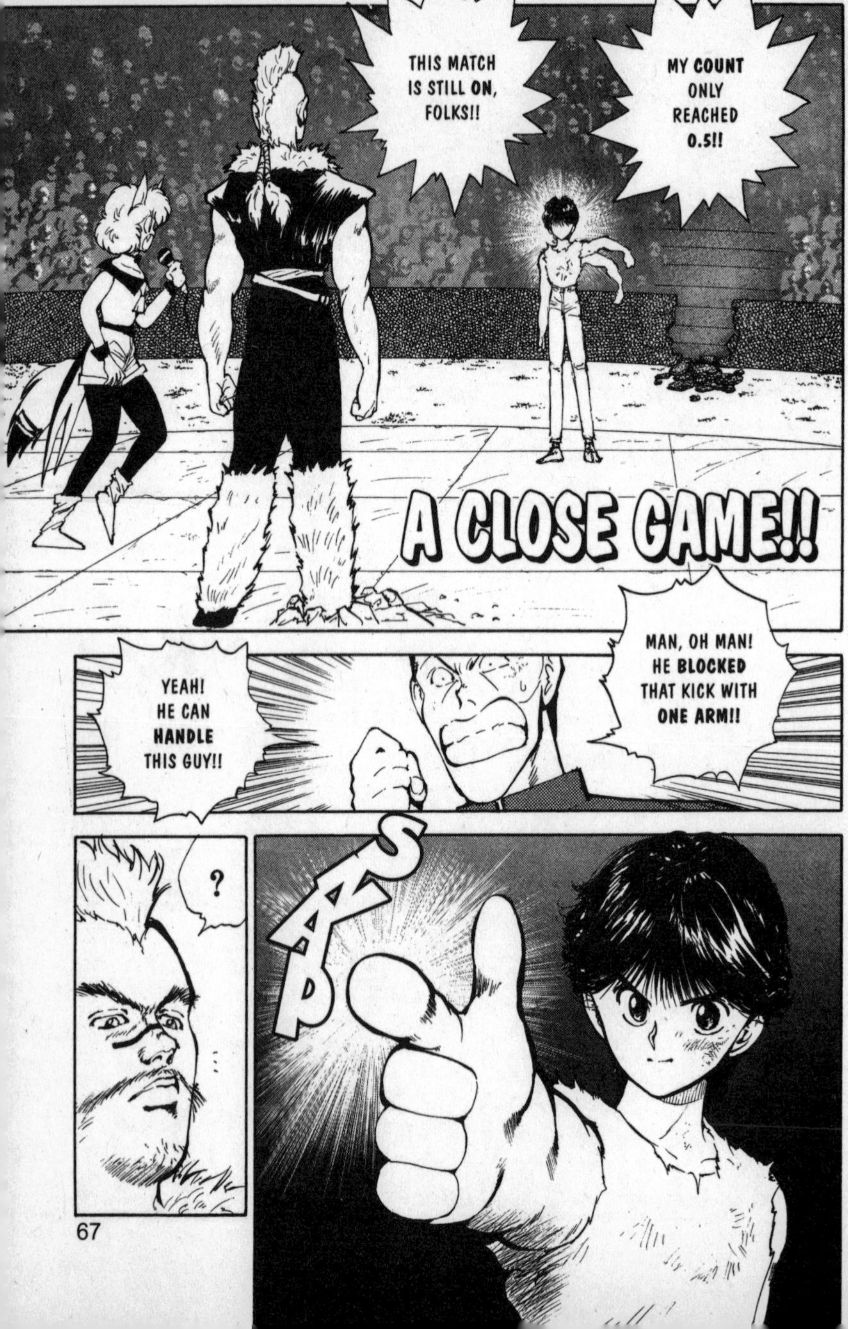

MY COUNT ONLY REACHED 0.5!!
THIS MATCH IS STILL ON, FOLKS!!
A CLOSE GAME!!
MAN, OH MAN! HE BLOCKED THAT KICK WITH ONE ARM!!
YEAH! HE CAN HANDLE THIS GUY!!
SNAP
?

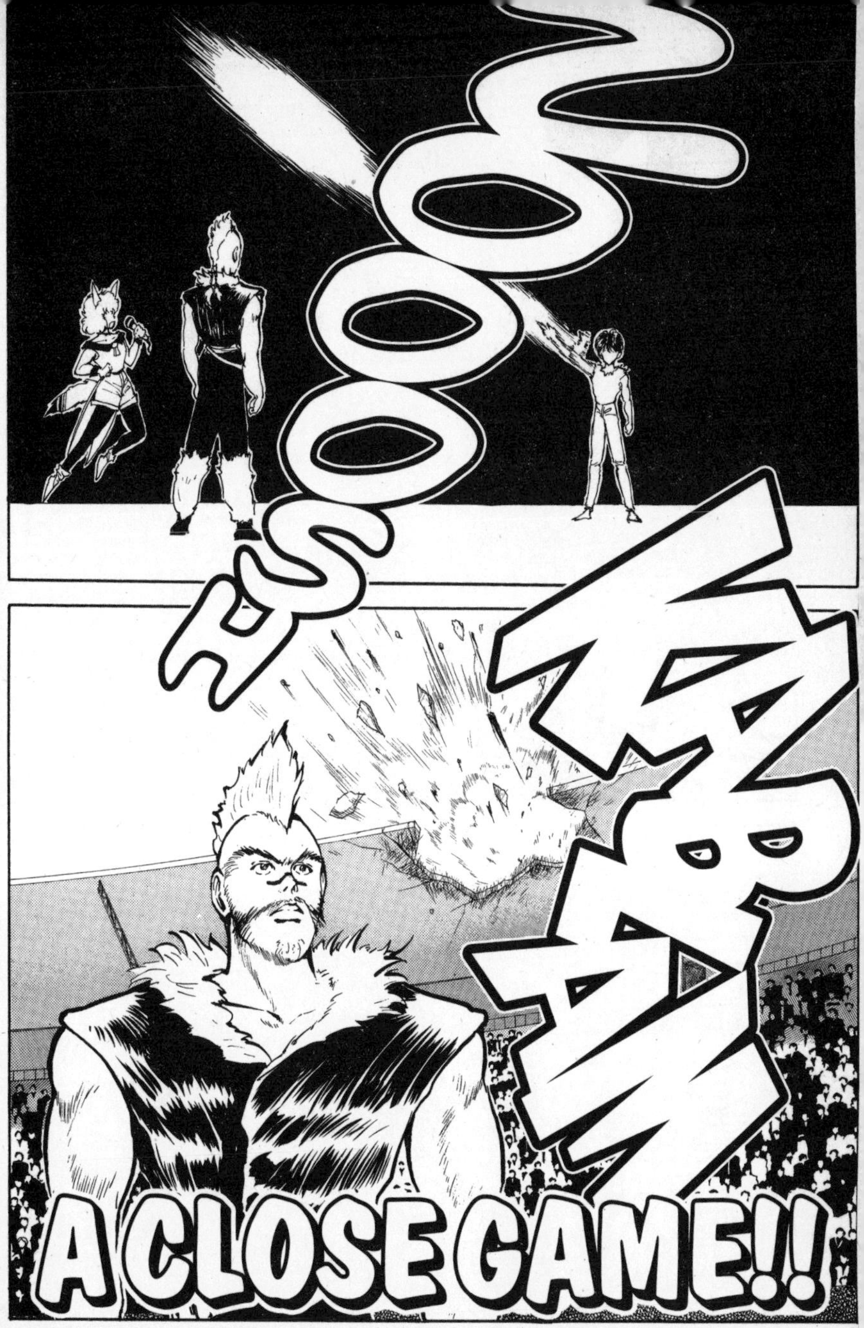
WOOOOSH
KABAM
A CLOSE GAME!!

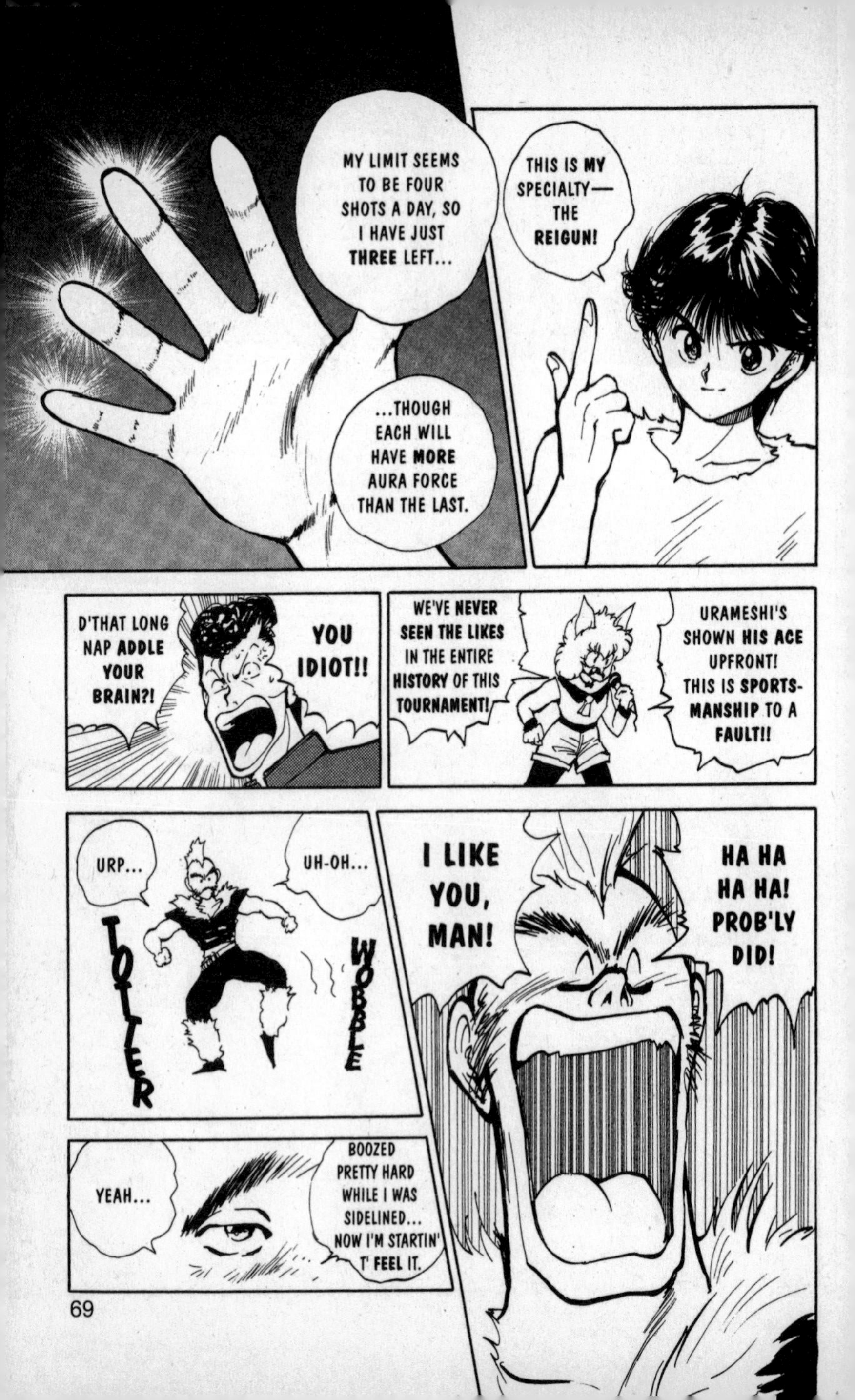
THIS IS MY SPECIALTY— THE REIGUN!
MY LIMIT SEEMS TO BE FOUR SHOTS A DAY, SO I HAVE JUST THREE LEFT...
...THOUGH EACH WILL HAVE MORE AURA FORCE THAN THE LAST.
URAMESHI'S SHOWN HIS ACE UPFRONT! THIS IS SPORTS-MANSHIP TO A FAULT!!
WE'VE NEVER SEEN THE LIKES IN THE ENTIRE HISTORY OF THIS TOURNAMENT!
YOU IDIOT!!
D'THAT LONG NAP ADDLE YOUR BRAIN?!
HA HA HA HA! PROB'LY DID!
I LIKE YOU, MAN!
UH-OH...
URP...
WOBBLE
TOTTER
BOOZED PRETTY HARD WHILE I WAS SIDELINED... NOW I'M STARTIN' T' FEEL IT.
YEAH...

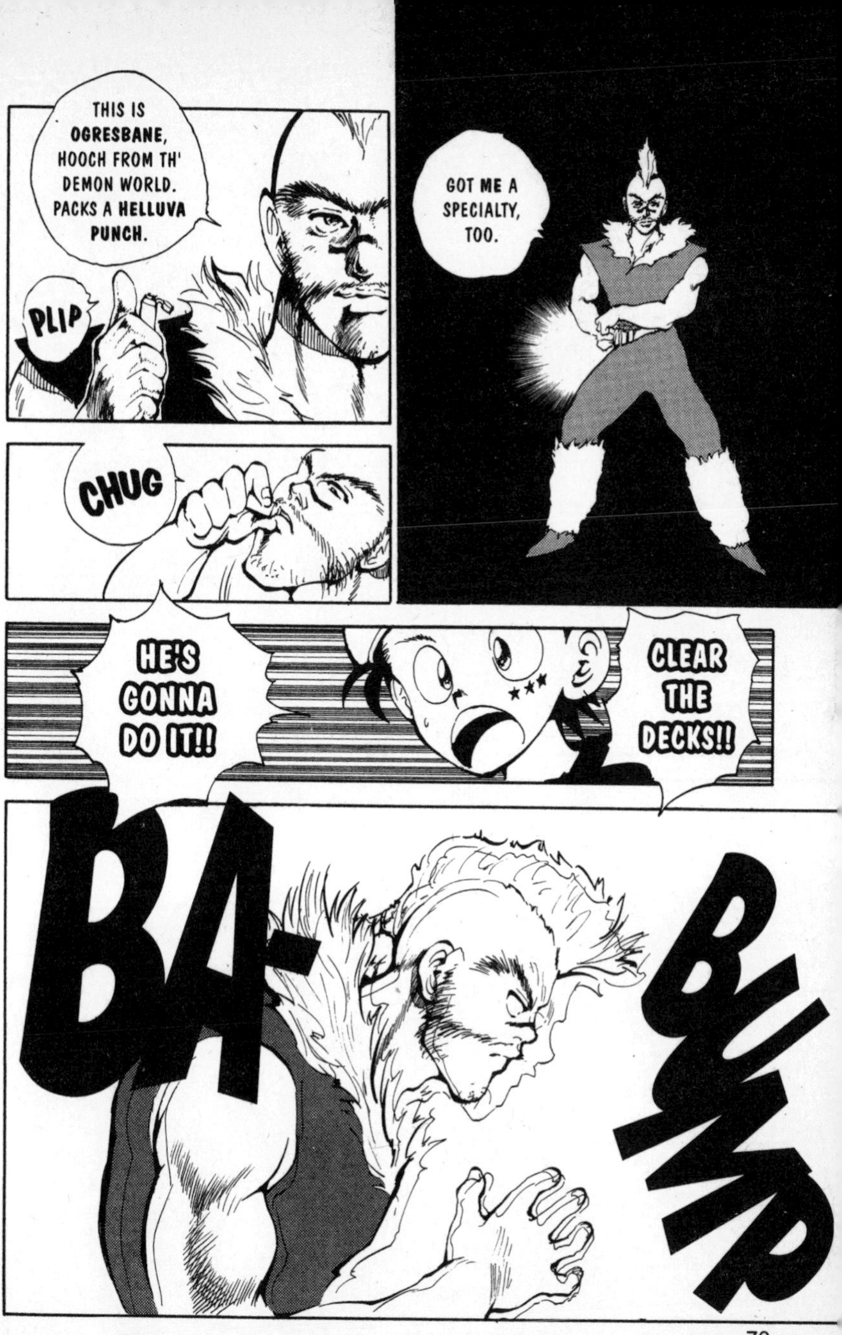

GOT ME A SPECIALTY, TOO.
THIS IS OGRESBANE, HOOCH FROM TH' DEMON WORLD. PACKS A HELLUVA PUNCH.
PLIP
CHUG
CLEAR THE DECKS!!
HE'S GONNA DO IT!!
BA-BUMP

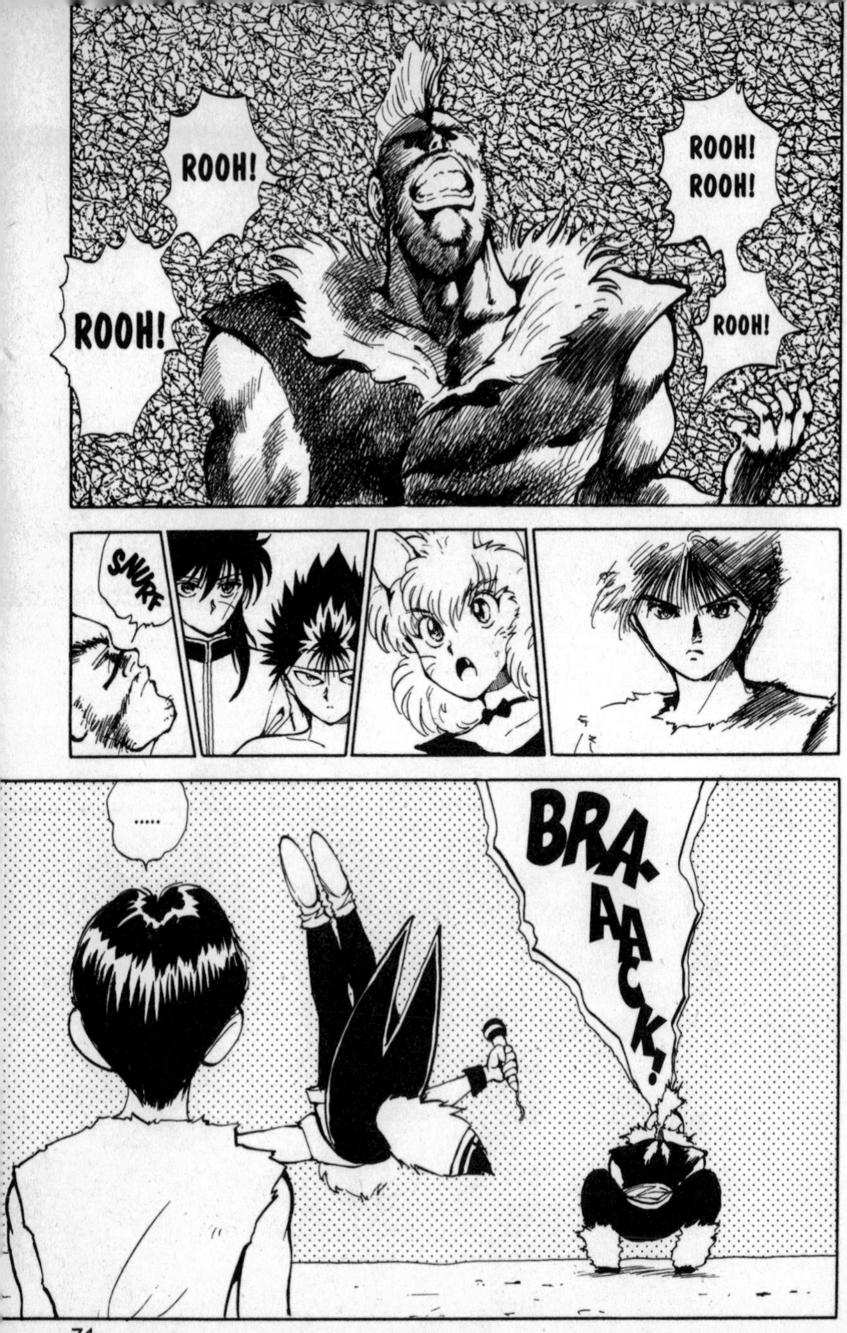
ROOH!
ROOH!
ROOH!
ROOH!
ROOH!
SNURF
BRA-AACK!
......

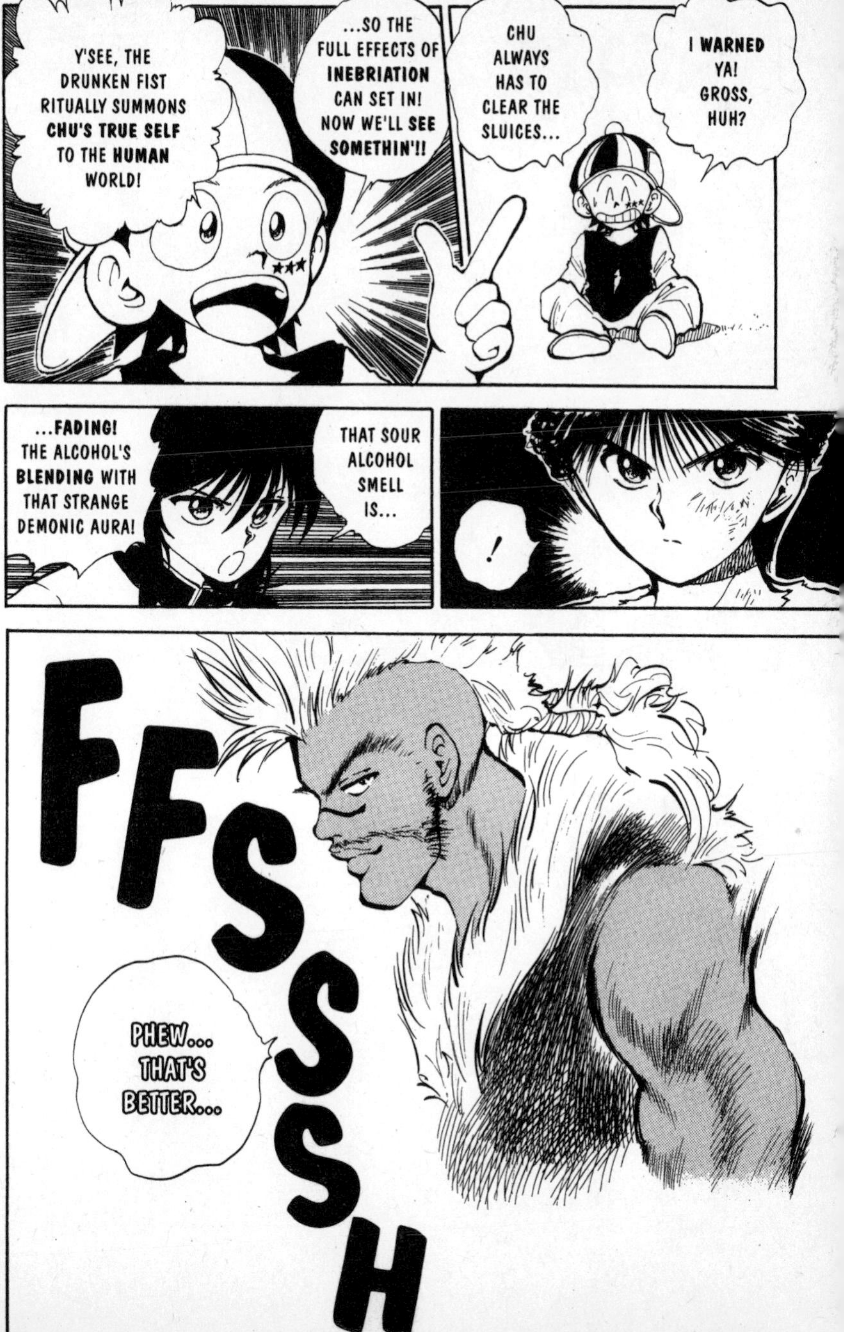
I WARNED YA! GROSS, HUH?
CHU ALWAYS HAS TO CLEAR THE SLUICES...
...SO THE FULL EFFECTS OF INEBRIATION CAN SET IN! NOW WE'LL SEE SOMETHIN'!!
Y'SEE, THE DRUNKEN FIST RITUALLY SUMMONS CHU'S TRUE SELF TO THE HUMAN WORLD!
!
THAT SOUR ALCOHOL SMELL IS...
...FADING! THE ALCOHOL'S BLENDING WITH THAT STRANGE DEMONIC AURA!
FFSSSH
PHEW... THAT'S BETTER...

READ THIS WAY

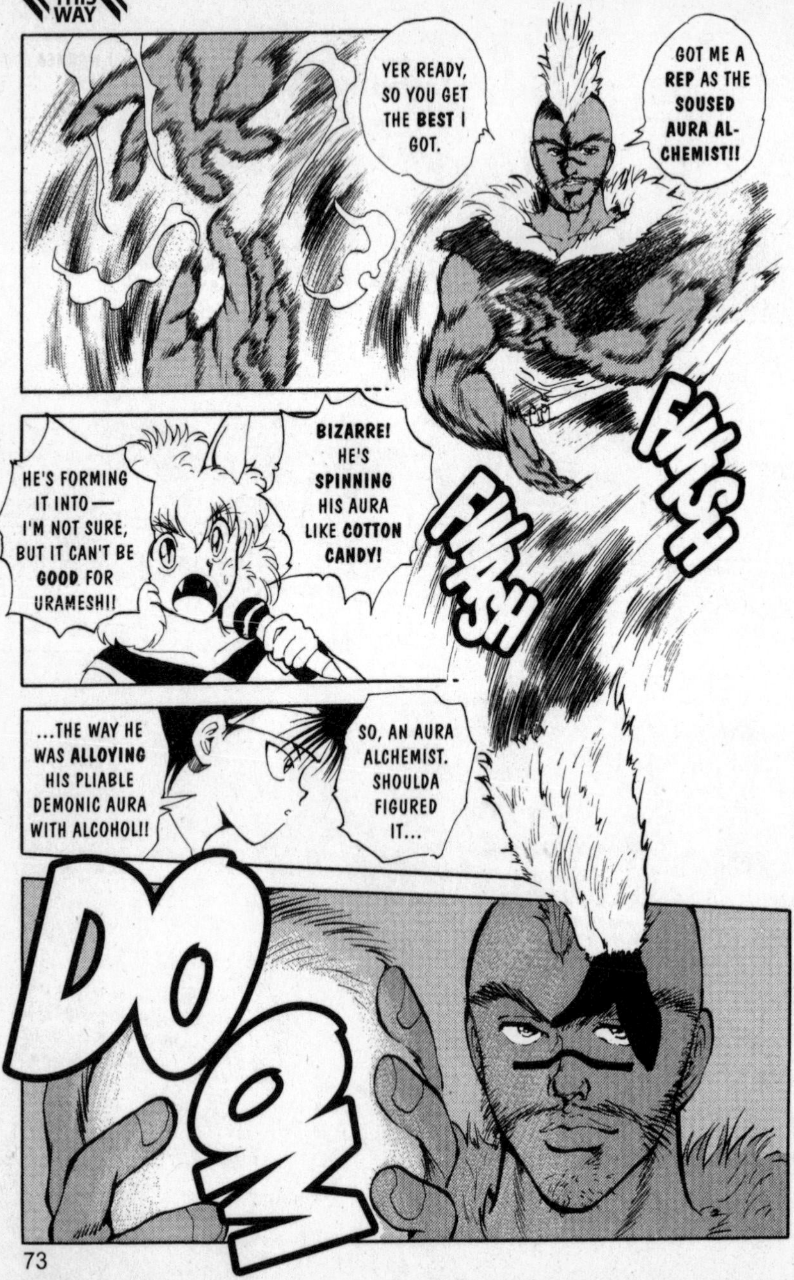

GOT ME A REP AS THE SOUSED AURA AL-CHEMIST!!
YER READY, SO YOU GET THE BEST I GOT.
FWASH
FWASH
BIZARRE! HE'S SPINNING HIS AURA LIKE COTTON CANDY!
HE'S FORMING IT INTO— I'M NOT SURE, BUT IT CAN'T BE GOOD FOR URAMESHI!!
SO, AN AURA ALCHEMIST. SHOULDA FIGURED IT...
...THE WAY HE WAS ALLOYING HIS PLIABLE DEMONIC AURA WITH ALCOHOL!!
DOOM

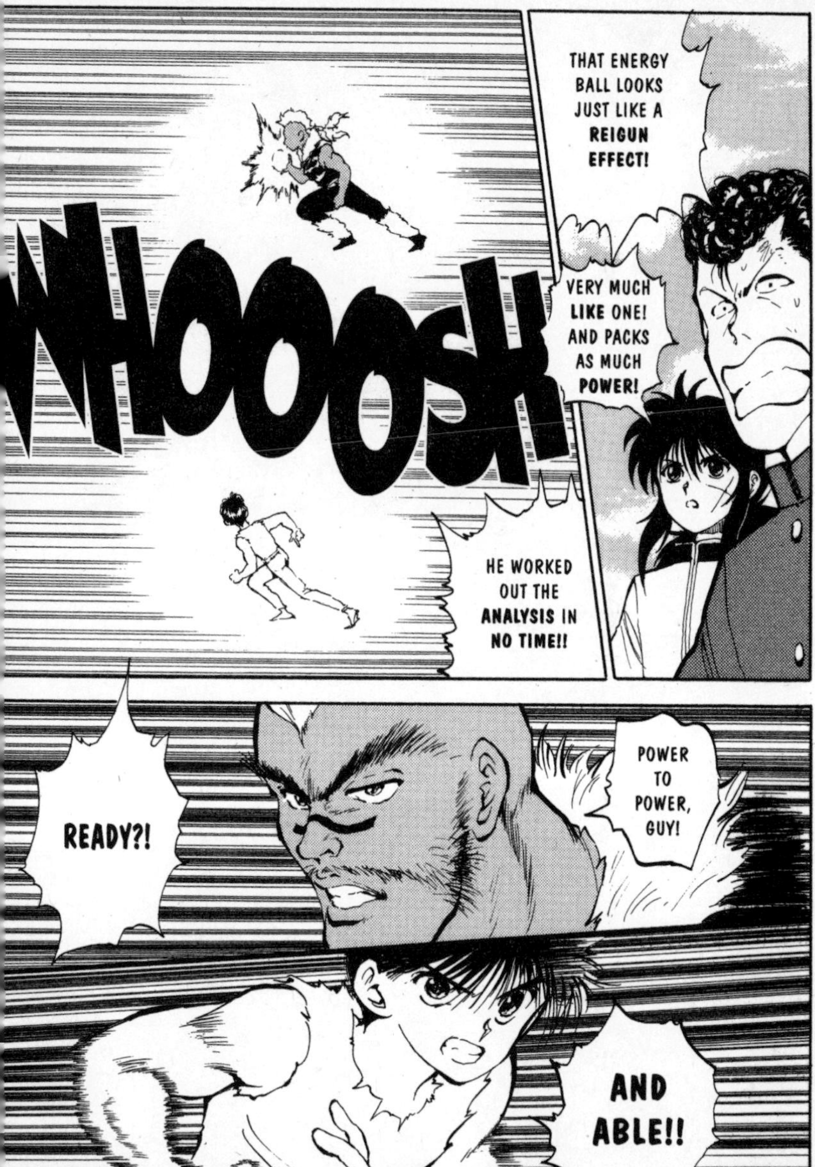
THAT ENERGY BALL LOOKS JUST LIKE A **REIGUN EFFECT!**
VERY MUCH **LIKE** ONE! AND PACKS AS MUCH **POWER!**
WHOOOSH!
HE WORKED OUT THE **ANALYSIS** IN **NO TIME!!**
POWER TO POWER, GUY!
READY?!
AND ABLE!!

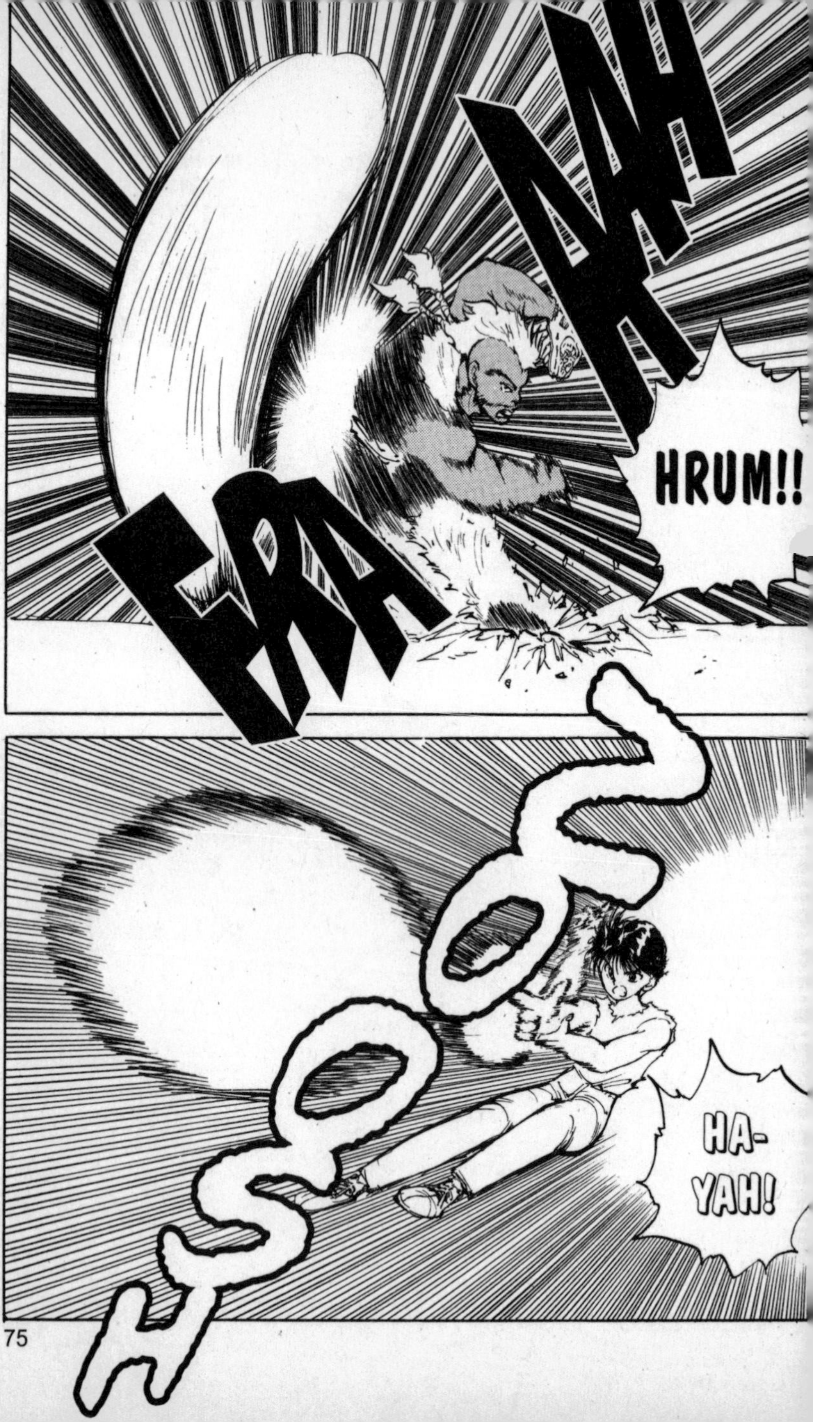
FPAAAH
HRUM!!
HA-YAH!

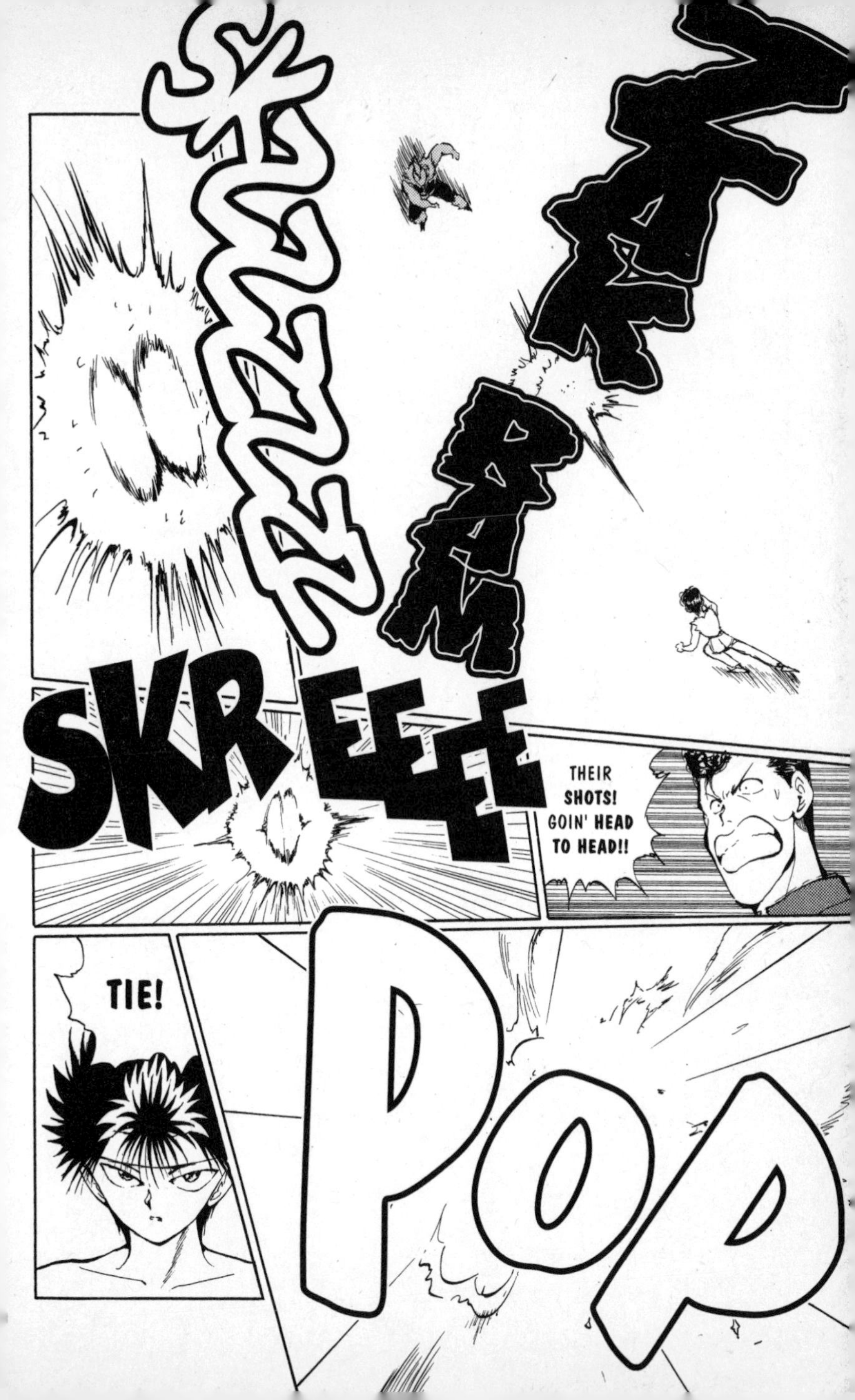
BAM
THEIR SHOTS! GOIN' HEAD TO HEAD!!
SKREEEE
POP
TIE!

READ THIS WAY

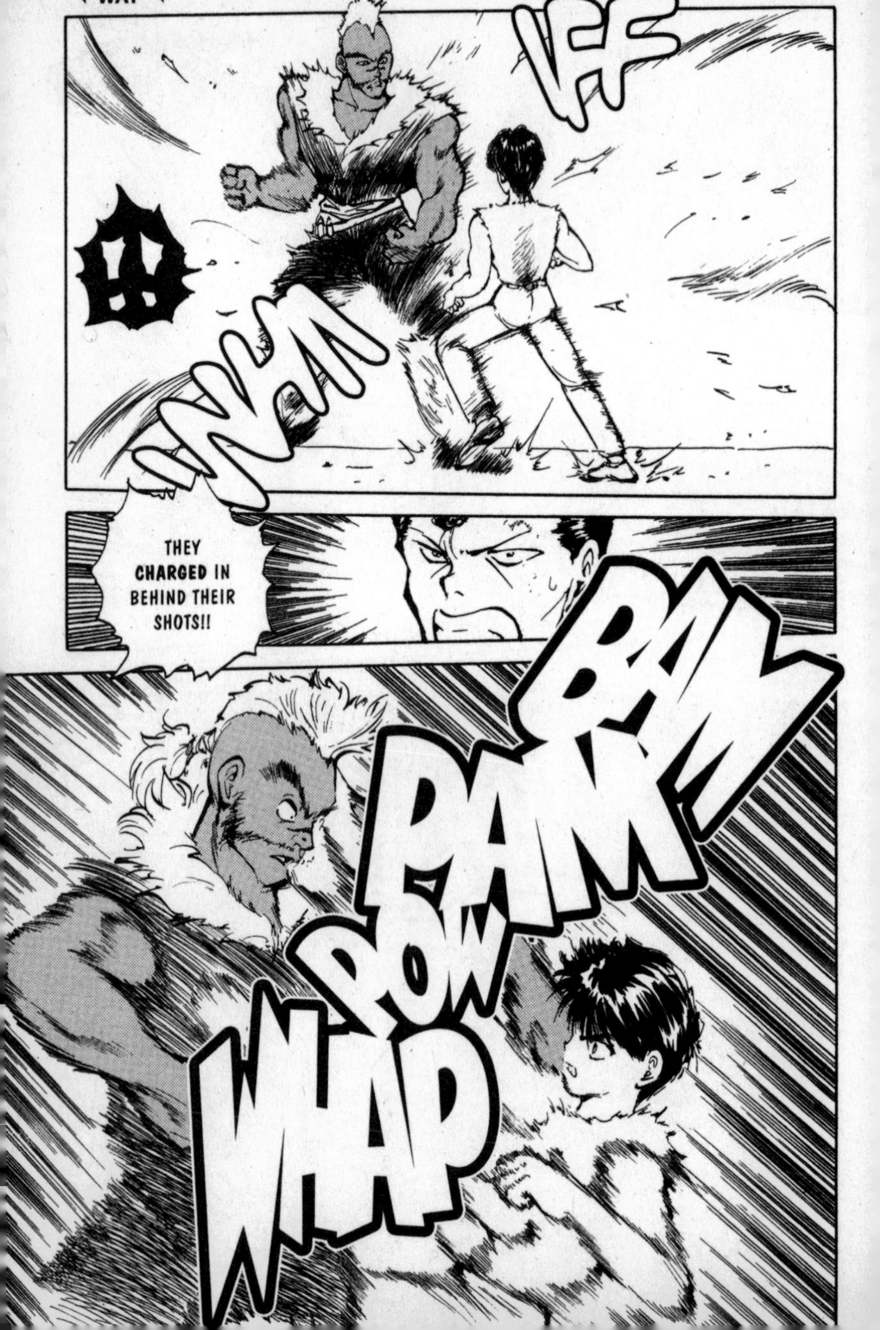
FF
!!
WHAM
THEY CHARGED IN BEHIND THEIR SHOTS!!
BAM
BAM
POW
WHAP

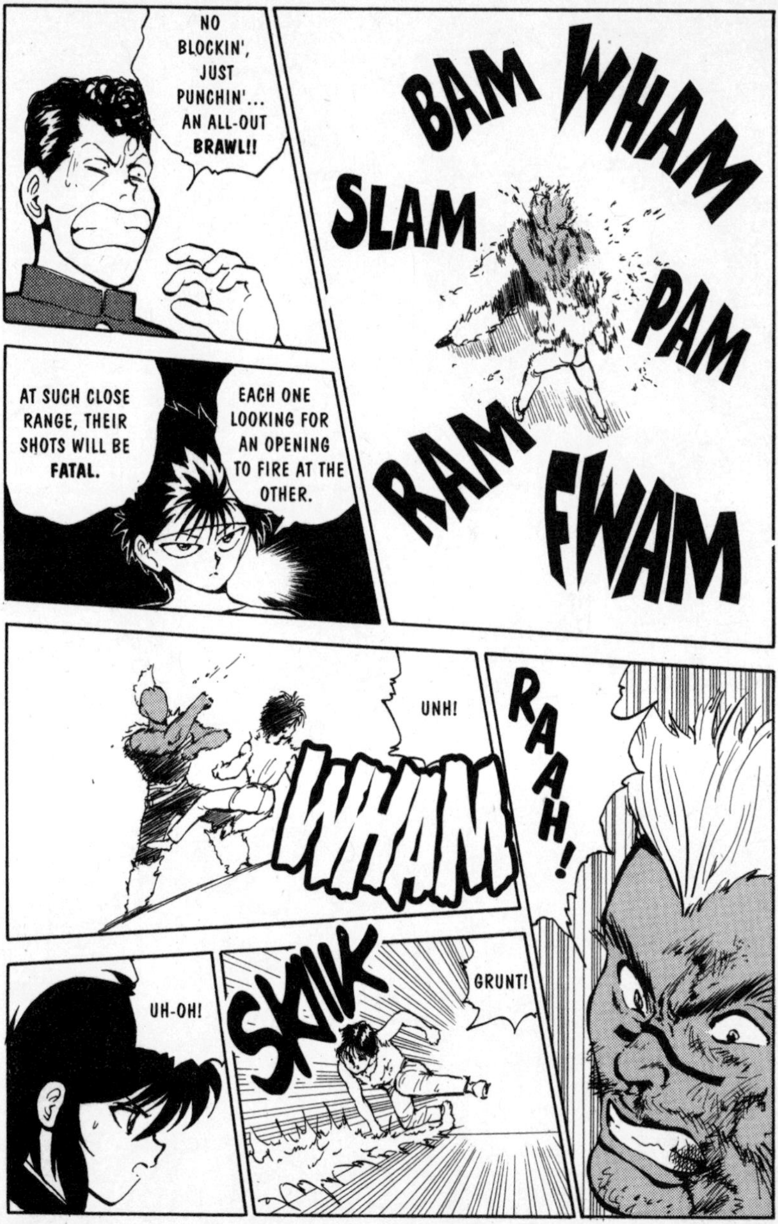
WHAM
BAM
SLAM
PAM
FWAM
RAM
NO BLOCKIN', JUST PUNCHIN'... AN ALL-OUT BRAWL!!
EACH ONE LOOKING FOR AN OPENING TO FIRE AT THE OTHER.
AT SUCH CLOSE RANGE, THEIR SHOTS WILL BE FATAL.
RAAAH!
UNH!
WHAM
GRUNT!
SKIIK
UH-OH!

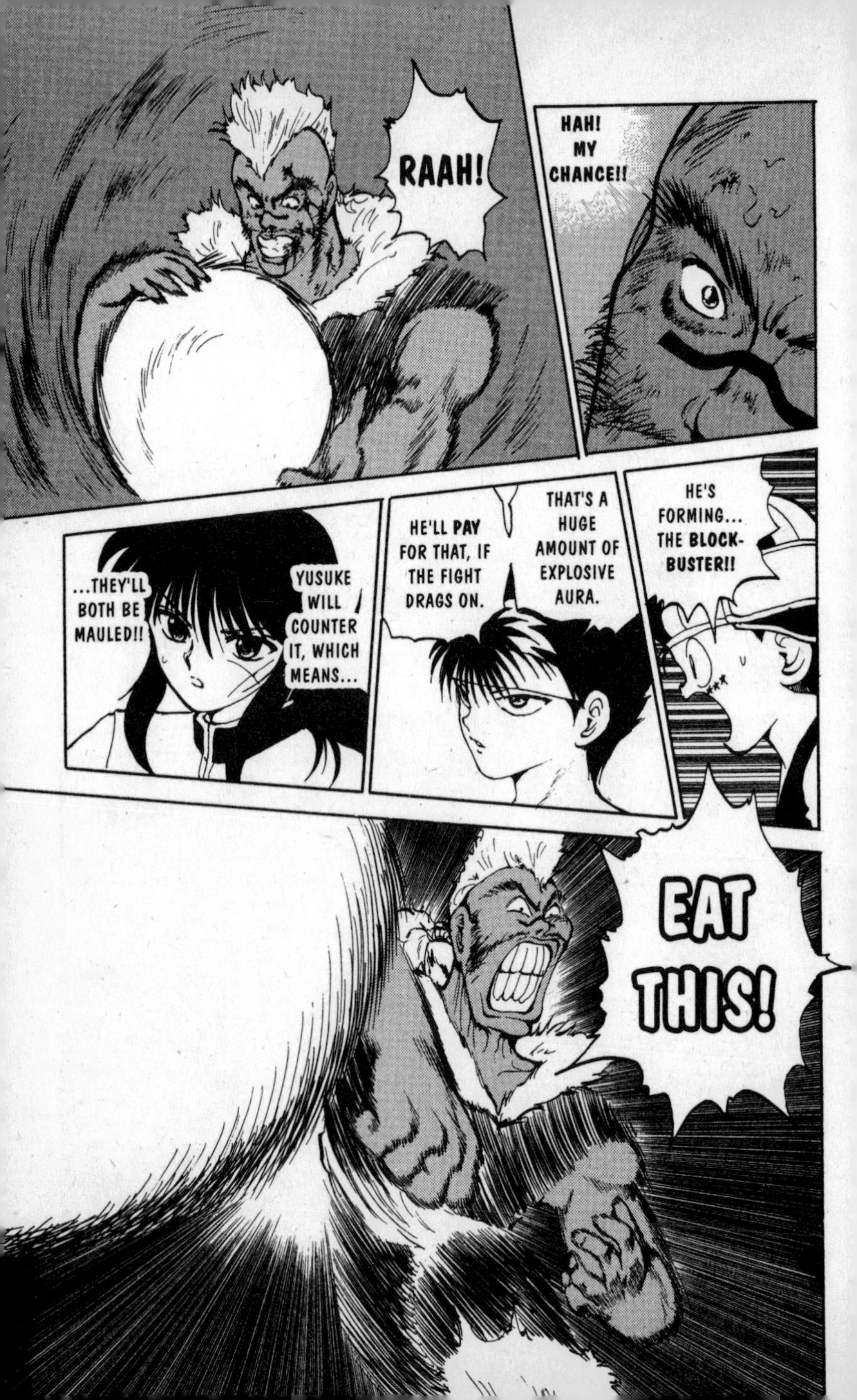
HAH! MY CHANCE!!
RAAH!
HE'S FORMING... THE BLOCK-BUSTER!!
THAT'S A HUGE AMOUNT OF EXPLOSIVE AURA.
HE'LL PAY FOR THAT, IF THE FIGHT DRAGS ON.
YUSUKE WILL COUNTER IT, WHICH MEANS...
...THEY'LL BOTH BE MAULED!!
EAT THIS!

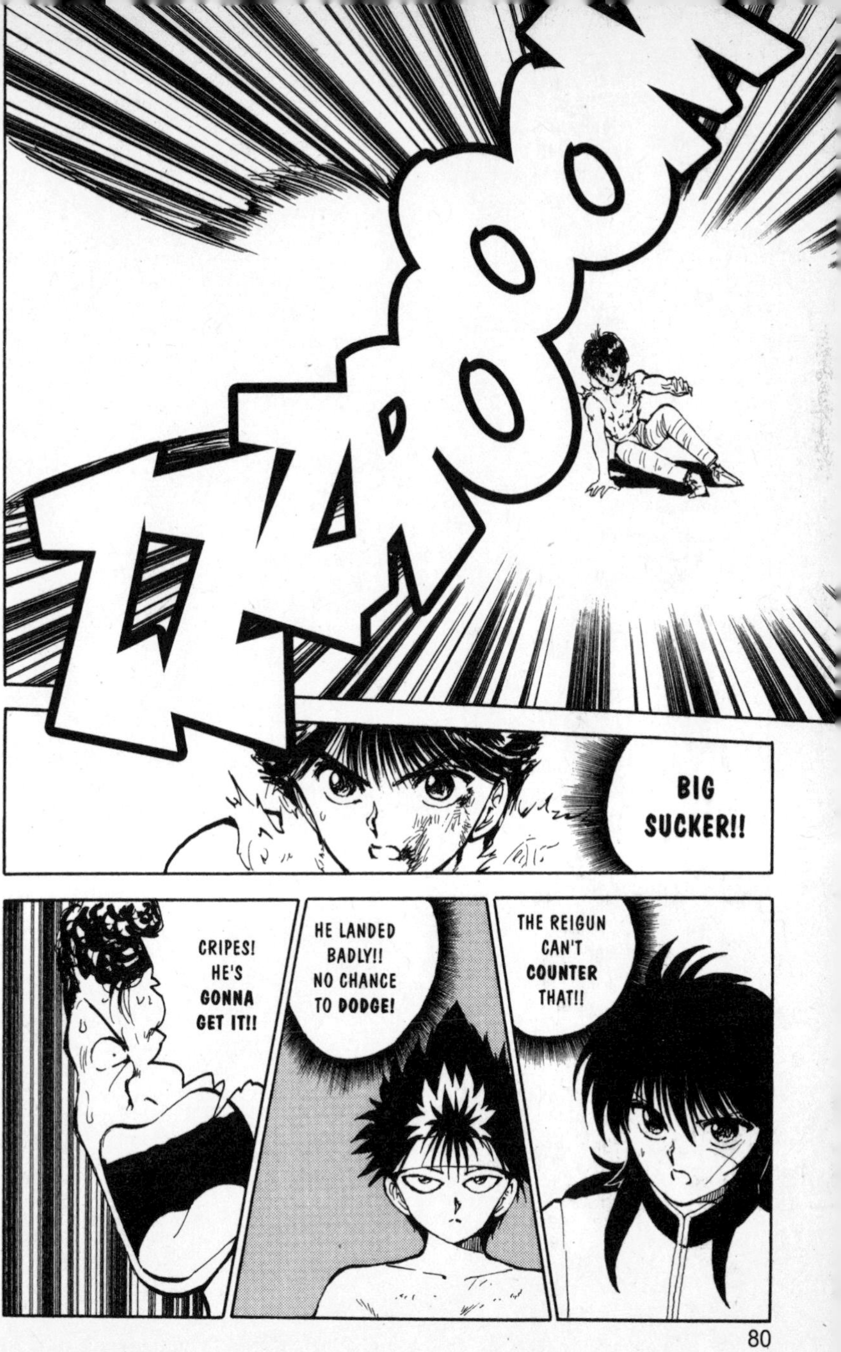
ZZZBOOOM
BIG SUCKER!!
THE REIGUN CAN'T COUNTER THAT!!
HE LANDED BADLY!! NO CHANCE TO DODGE!
CRIPES! HE'S GONNA GET IT!!

READ THIS WAY

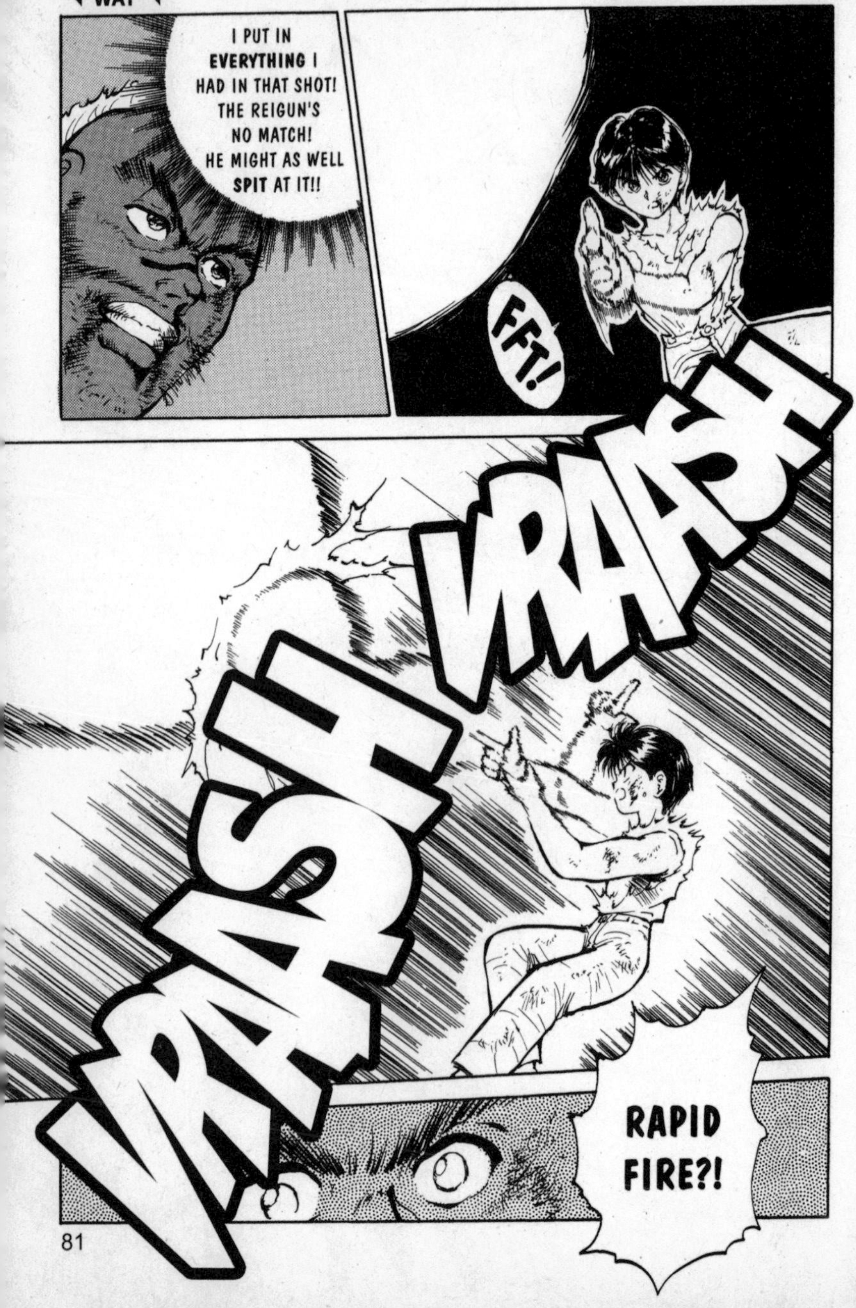
FFT!
I PUT IN EVERYTHING I HAD IN THAT SHOT! THE REIGUN'S NO MATCH! HE MIGHT AS WELL SPIT AT IT!!
VRAASH
VRAASH
RAPID FIRE?!

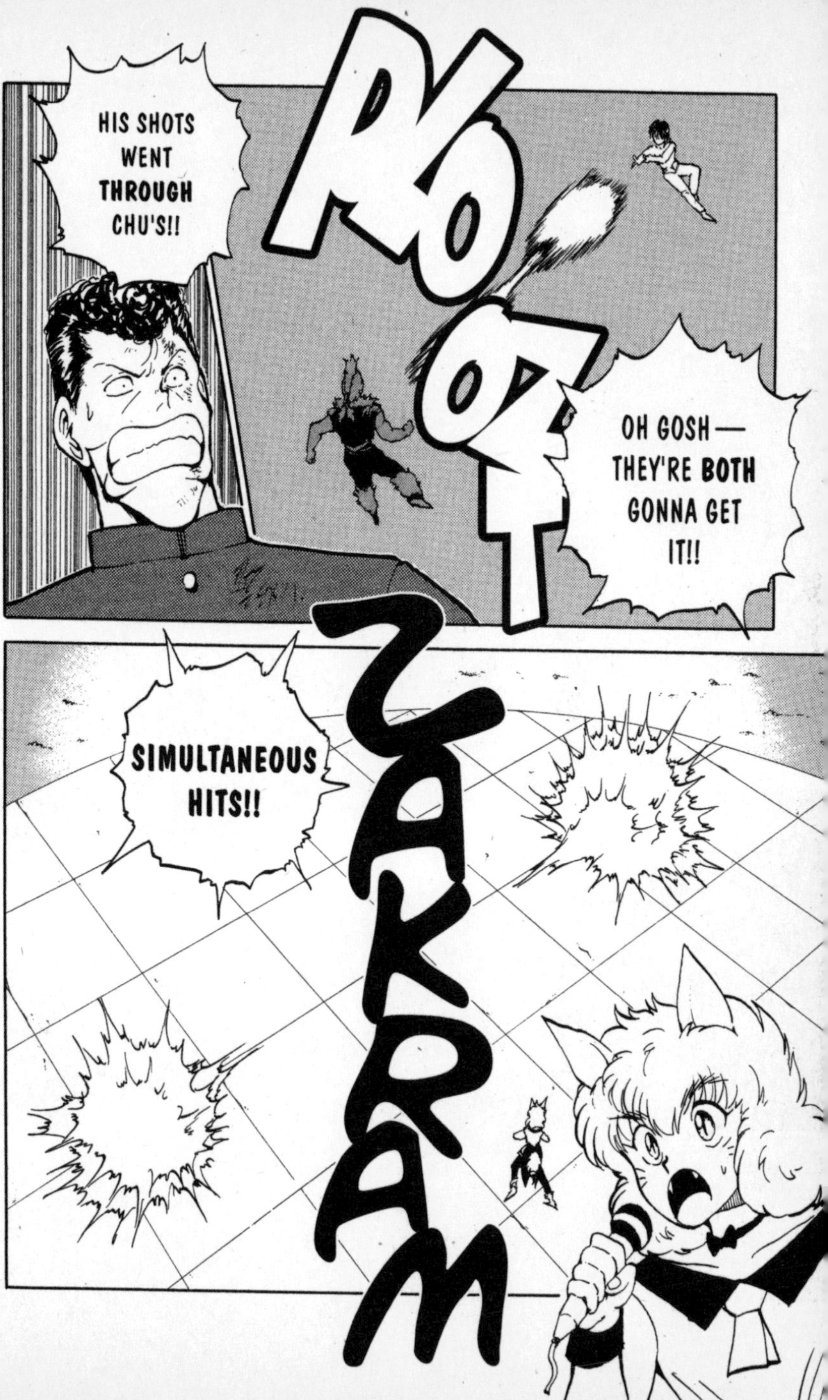
OH GOSH— THEY'RE BOTH GONNA GET IT!!
POOT
HIS SHOTS WENT THROUGH CHU'S!!
ZAKRAM
SIMULTANEOUS HITS!!

READ THIS WAY

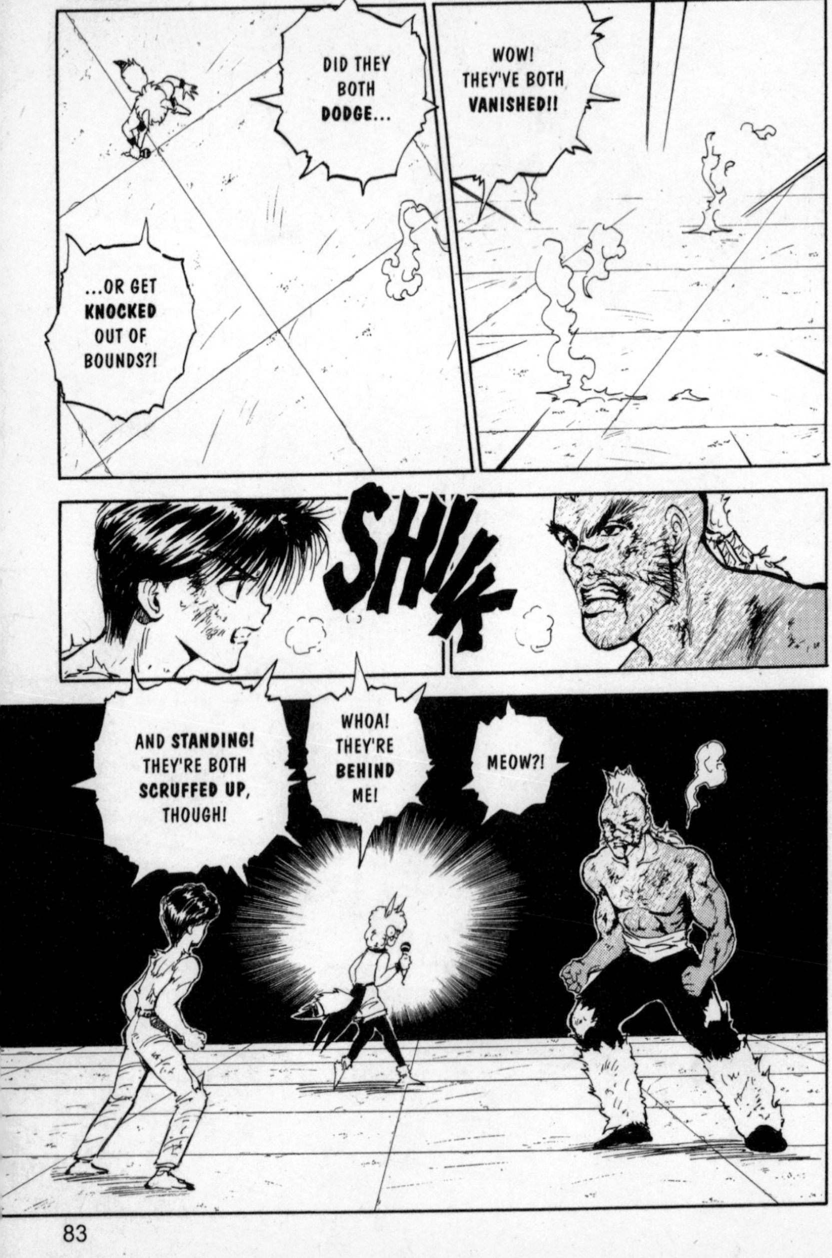
WOW! THEY'VE BOTH VANISHED!!
DID THEY BOTH DODGE...
...OR GET KNOCKED OUT OF BOUNDS?!
SHIIK
MEOW?!
WHOA! THEY'RE BEHIND ME!
AND STANDING! THEY'RE BOTH SCRUFFED UP, THOUGH!

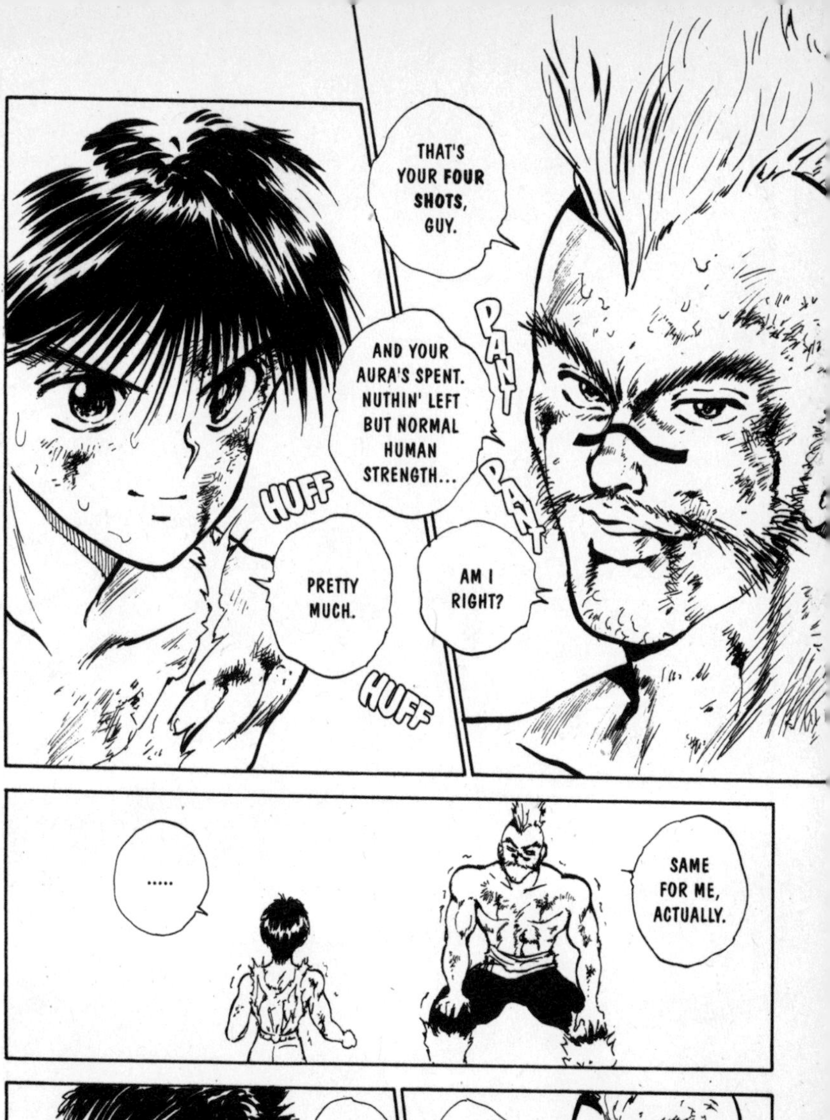
THAT'S YOUR FOUR SHOTS, GUY.
AND YOUR AURA'S SPENT. NUTHIN' LEFT BUT NORMAL HUMAN STRENGTH...
PANT
PANT
AM I RIGHT?
HUFF
PRETTY MUCH.
HUFF
SAME FOR ME, ACTUALLY.
......
HEH...
HEH...

READ THIS WAY

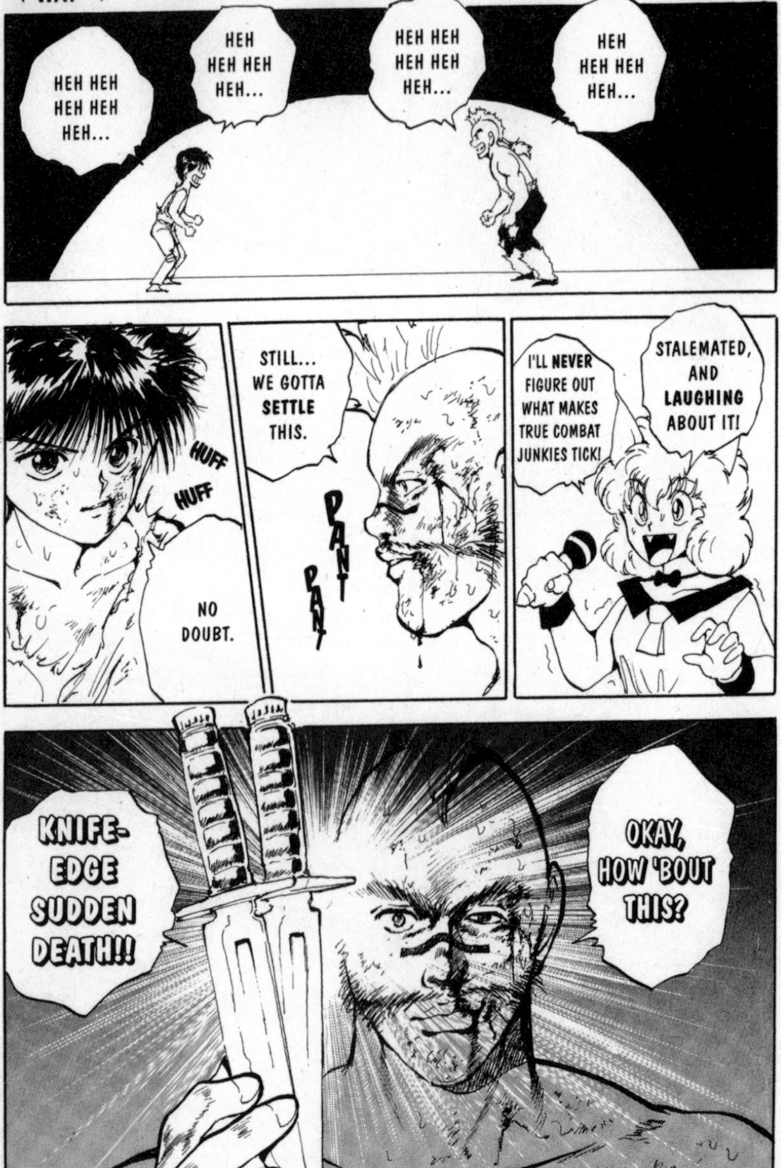
HEH HEH HEH HEH...
HEH HEH HEH HEH HEH...
HEH HEH HEH HEH...
HEH HEH HEH HEH HEH...
STALEMATED, AND LAUGHING ABOUT IT!
I'LL NEVER FIGURE OUT WHAT MAKES TRUE COMBAT JUNKIES TICK!
STILL... WE GOTTA SETTLE THIS.
PANT
PANT
HUFF
HUFF
NO DOUBT.
OKAY, HOW 'BOUT THIS?
KNIFE-EDGE SUDDEN DEATH!!

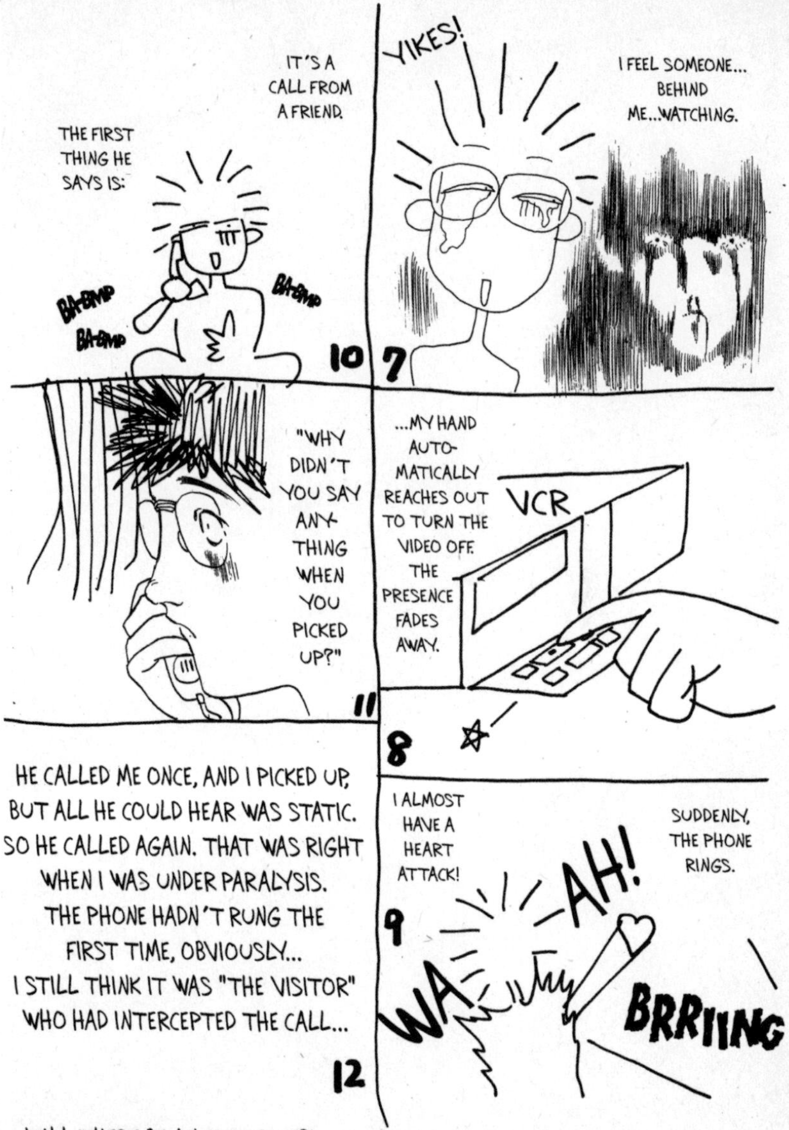
YIKES!
I FEEL SOMEONE... BEHIND ME...WATCHING.
7
...MY HAND AUTO-MATICALLY REACHES OUT TO TURN THE VIDEO OFF. THE PRESENCE FADES AWAY.
VCR
8
I ALMOST HAVE A HEART ATTACK!
SUDDENLY, THE PHONE RINGS.
WA-AH!
BRRIING
9
IT'S A CALL FROM A FRIEND.
THE FIRST THING HE SAYS IS:
BA-BMP
BA-BMP
BA-BMP
10
"WHY DIDN'T YOU SAY ANY-THING WHEN YOU PICKED UP?"
11
HE CALLED ME ONCE, AND I PICKED UP, BUT ALL HE COULD HEAR WAS STATIC. SO HE CALLED AGAIN. THAT WAS RIGHT WHEN I WAS UNDER PARALYSIS. THE PHONE HADN'T RUNG THE FIRST TIME, OBVIOUSLY... I STILL THINK IT WAS "THE VISITOR" WHO HAD INTERCEPTED THE CALL...
12

WILL THERE BE AN EPISODE 2?!

KNIFE-EDGE SUDDEN DEATH!!

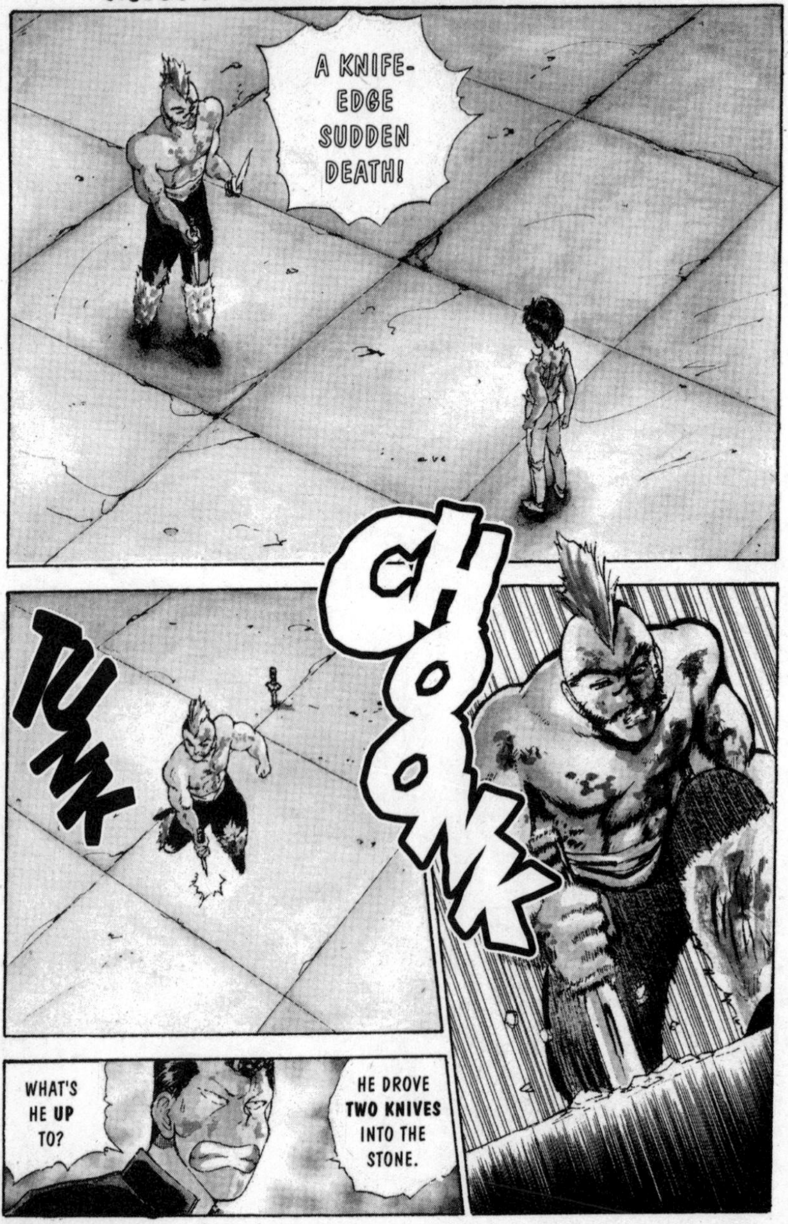

A KNIFE-EDGE SUDDEN DEATH!
CHOONK
TUNK
HE DROVE TWO KNIVES INTO THE STONE.
WHAT'S HE UP TO?

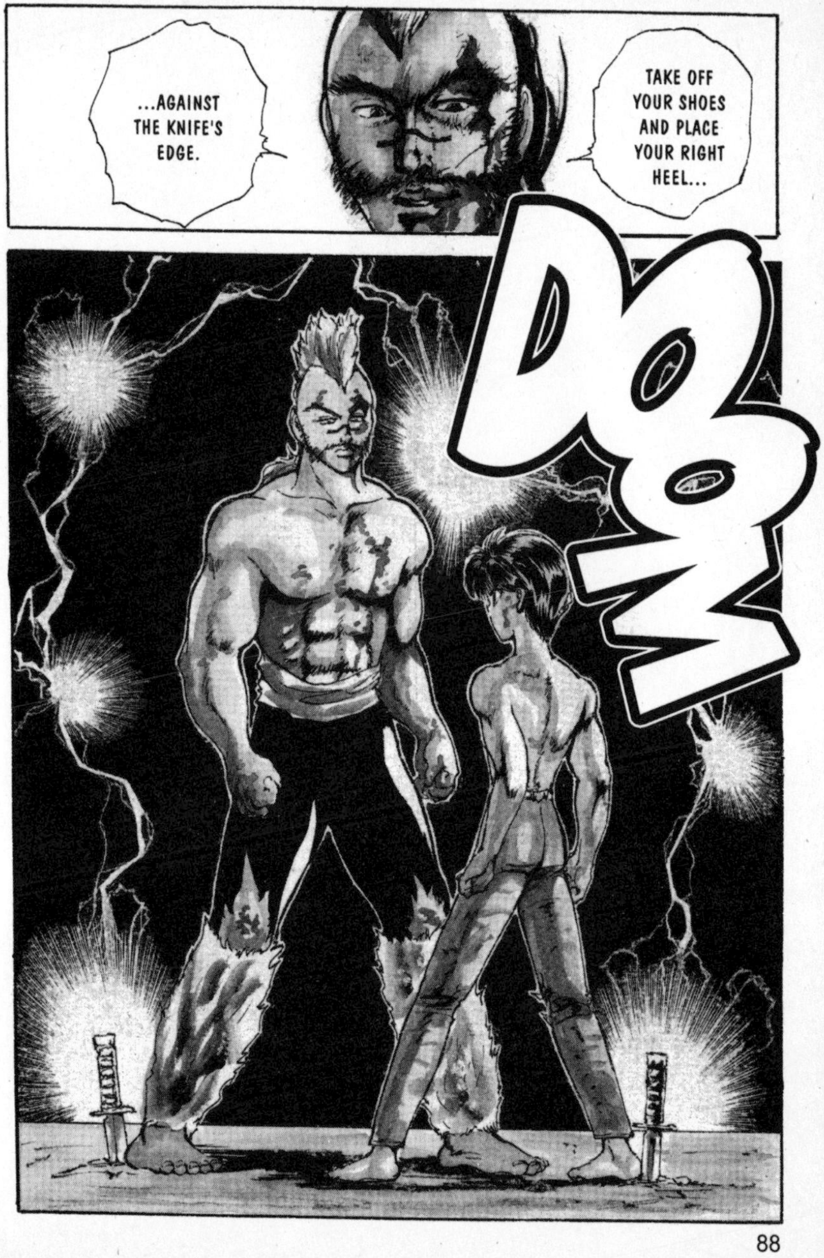
TAKE OFF YOUR SHOES AND PLACE YOUR RIGHT HEEL...
...AGAINST THE KNIFE'S EDGE.
DOOM

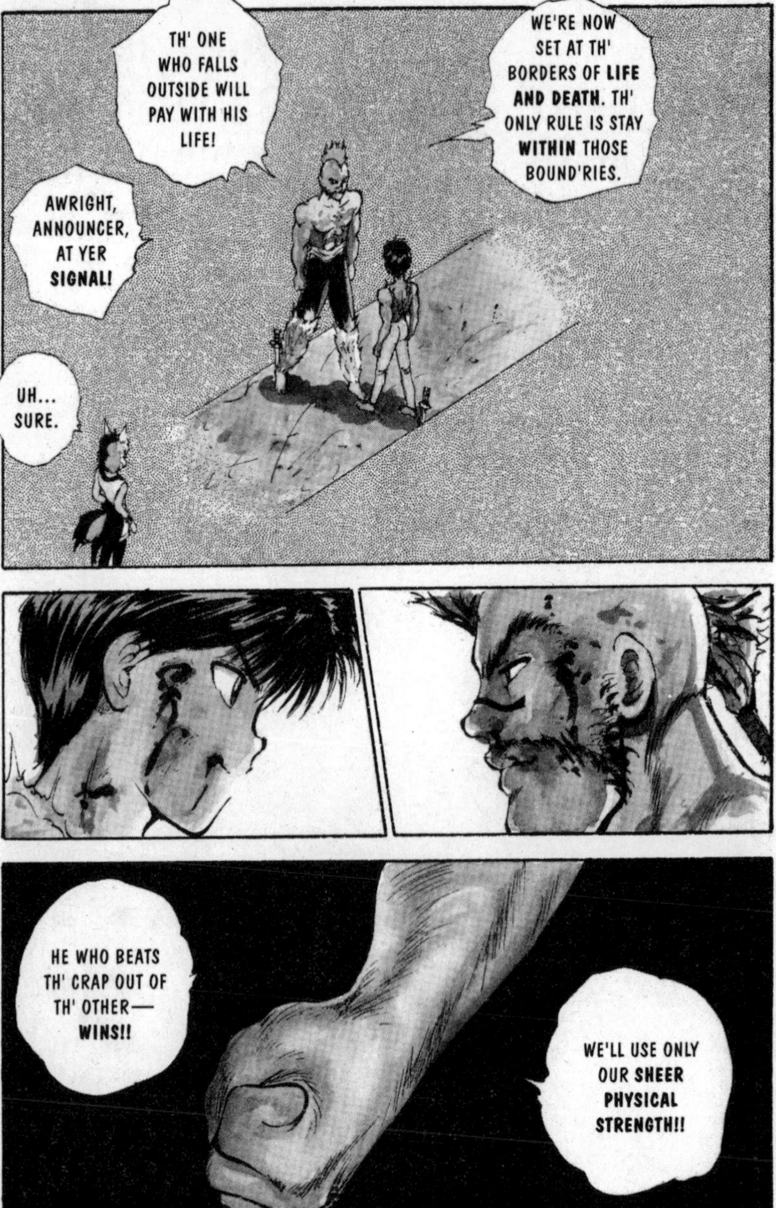
WE'RE NOW SET AT TH' BORDERS OF **LIFE AND DEATH**. TH' ONLY RULE IS STAY **WITHIN** THOSE BOUND'RIES.
TH' ONE WHO FALLS OUTSIDE WILL PAY WITH HIS LIFE!
AWRIGHT, ANNOUNCER, AT YER **SIGNAL!**
UH... SURE.
WE'LL USE ONLY OUR **SHEER PHYSICAL STRENGTH!!**
HE WHO BEATS TH' CRAP OUT OF TH' OTHER— **WINS!!**

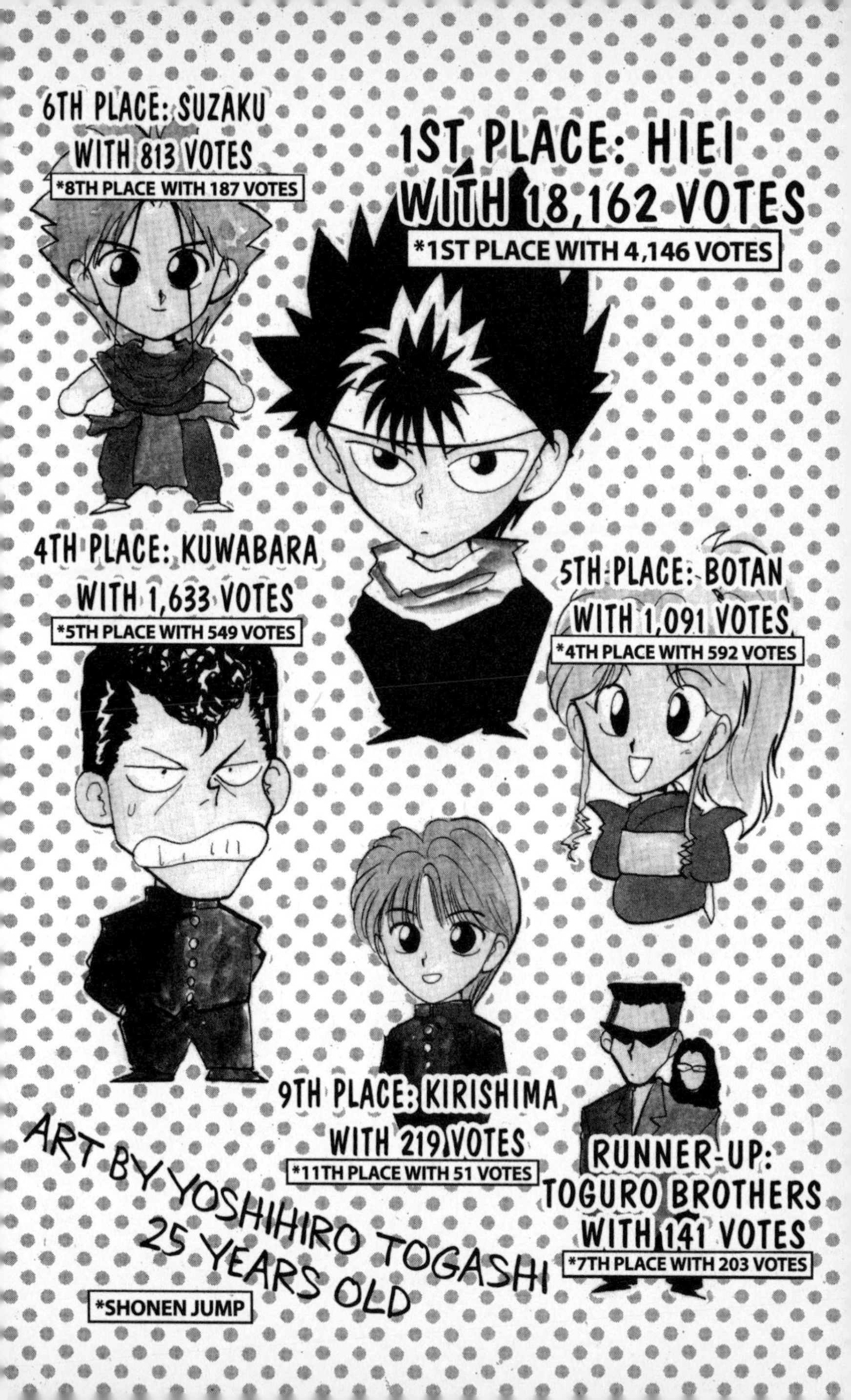
1ST PLACE: HIEI
WITH 18,162 VOTES
*1ST PLACE WITH 4,146 VOTES
6TH PLACE: SUZAKU
WITH 813 VOTES
*8TH PLACE WITH 187 VOTES
5TH PLACE: BOTAN
WITH 1,091 VOTES
*4TH PLACE WITH 592 VOTES
4TH PLACE: KUWABARA
WITH 1,633 VOTES
*5TH PLACE WITH 549 VOTES
RUNNER-UP:
TOGURO BROTHERS
WITH 141 VOTES
*7TH PLACE WITH 203 VOTES
9TH PLACE: KIRISHIMA
WITH 219 VOTES
*11TH PLACE WITH 51 VOTES
ART BY YOSHIHIRO TOGASHI
25 YEARS OLD
*SHONEN JUMP

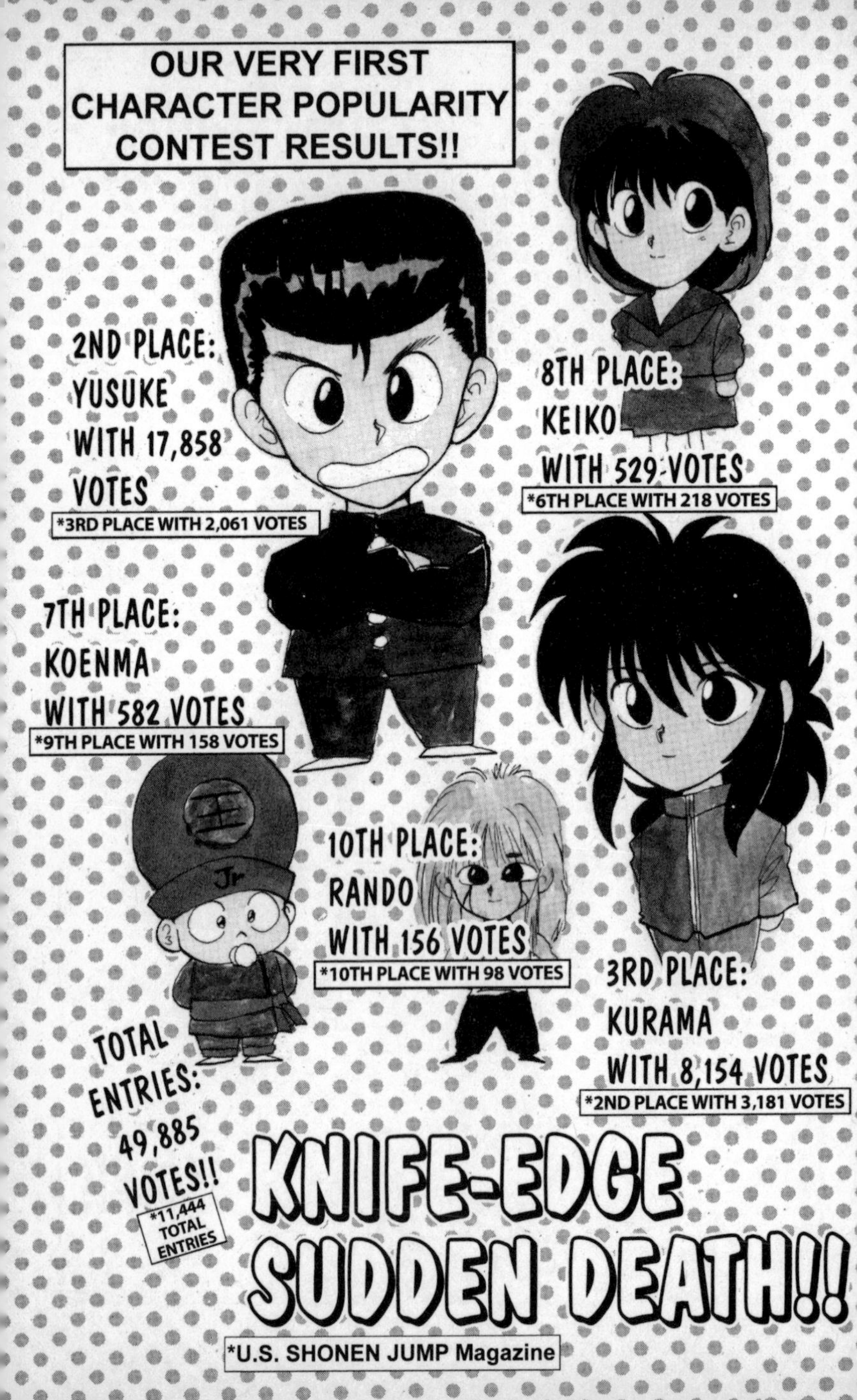
OUR VERY FIRST CHARACTER POPULARITY CONTEST RESULTS!!
2ND PLACE: YUSUKE WITH 17,858 VOTES
*3RD PLACE WITH 2,061 VOTES
8TH PLACE: KEIKO WITH 529 VOTES
*6TH PLACE WITH 218 VOTES
7TH PLACE: KOENMA WITH 582 VOTES
*9TH PLACE WITH 158 VOTES
Jr
10TH PLACE: RANDO WITH 156 VOTES
*10TH PLACE WITH 98 VOTES
3RD PLACE: KURAMA WITH 8,154 VOTES
*2ND PLACE WITH 3,181 VOTES
TOTAL ENTRIES: 49,885 VOTES!!
*11,444 TOTAL ENTRIES
KNIFE-EDGE SUDDEN DEATH!!
*U.S. SHONEN JUMP Magazine

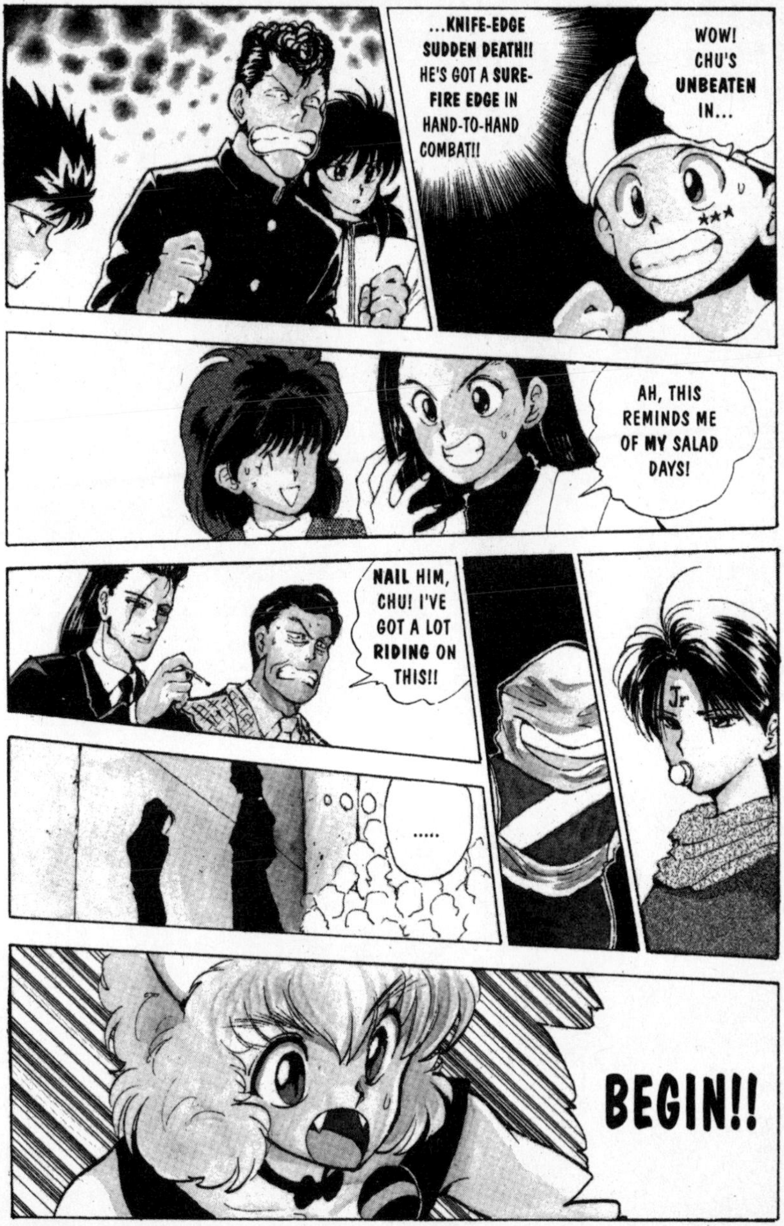
WOW! CHU'S UNBEATEN IN...
...KNIFE-EDGE SUDDEN DEATH!! HE'S GOT A SURE-FIRE EDGE IN HAND-TO-HAND COMBAT!!
AH, THIS REMINDS ME OF MY SALAD DAYS!
Jr
NAIL HIM, CHU! I'VE GOT A LOT RIDING ON THIS!!
.....
BEGIN!!

READ THIS WAY

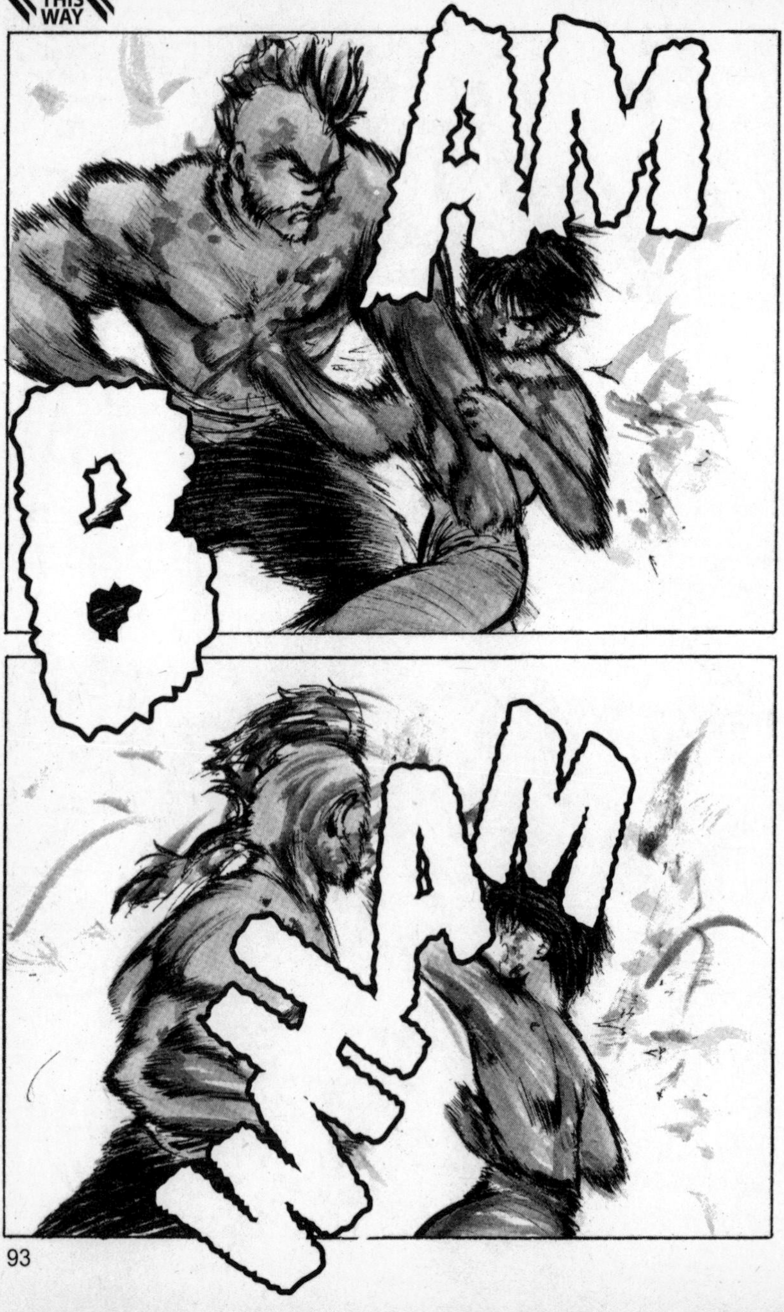
BAM
WHAM

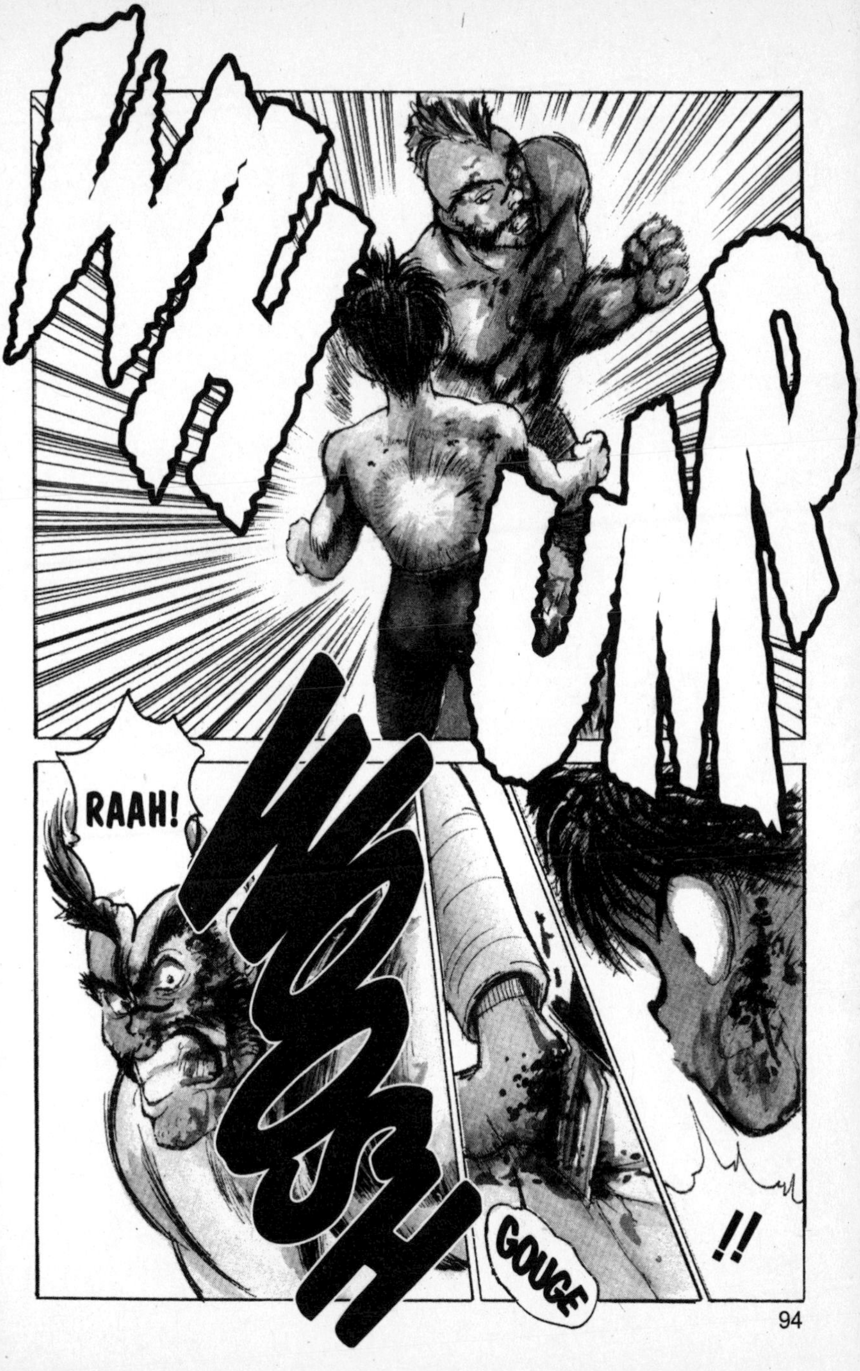
RAAH!
WHOOSH!
GOUGE
!!

READ THIS WAY

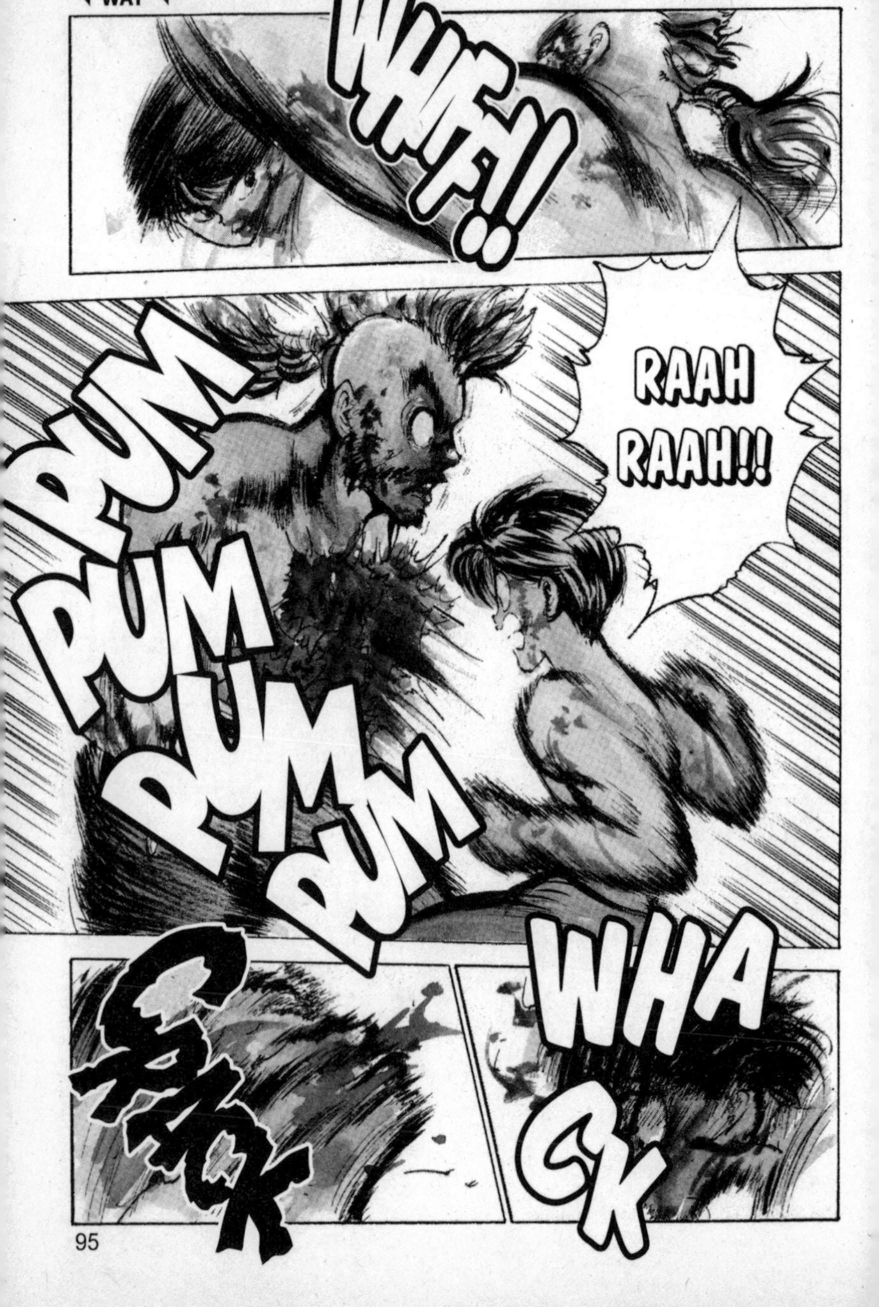

WHIFF!!
RAAH RAAH!!
PUM PUM PUM PUM
WHACK
CRACK

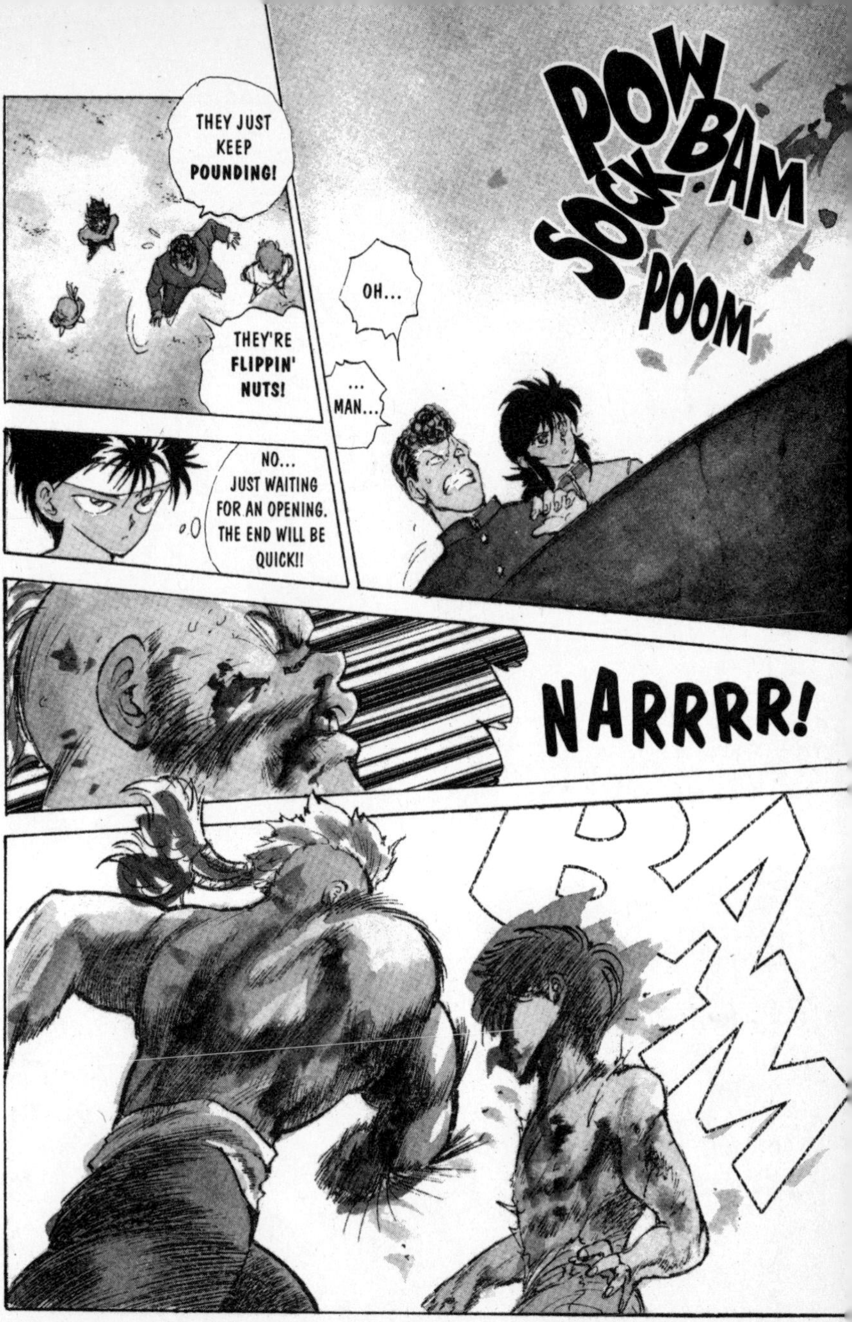
POW
BAM
SOCK
POOM
OH...
...
MAN...
THEY JUST KEEP POUNDING!
THEY'RE FLIPPIN' NUTS!
NO... JUST WAITING FOR AN OPENING. THE END WILL BE QUICK!!
NARRRR!
BAM

READ THIS WAY

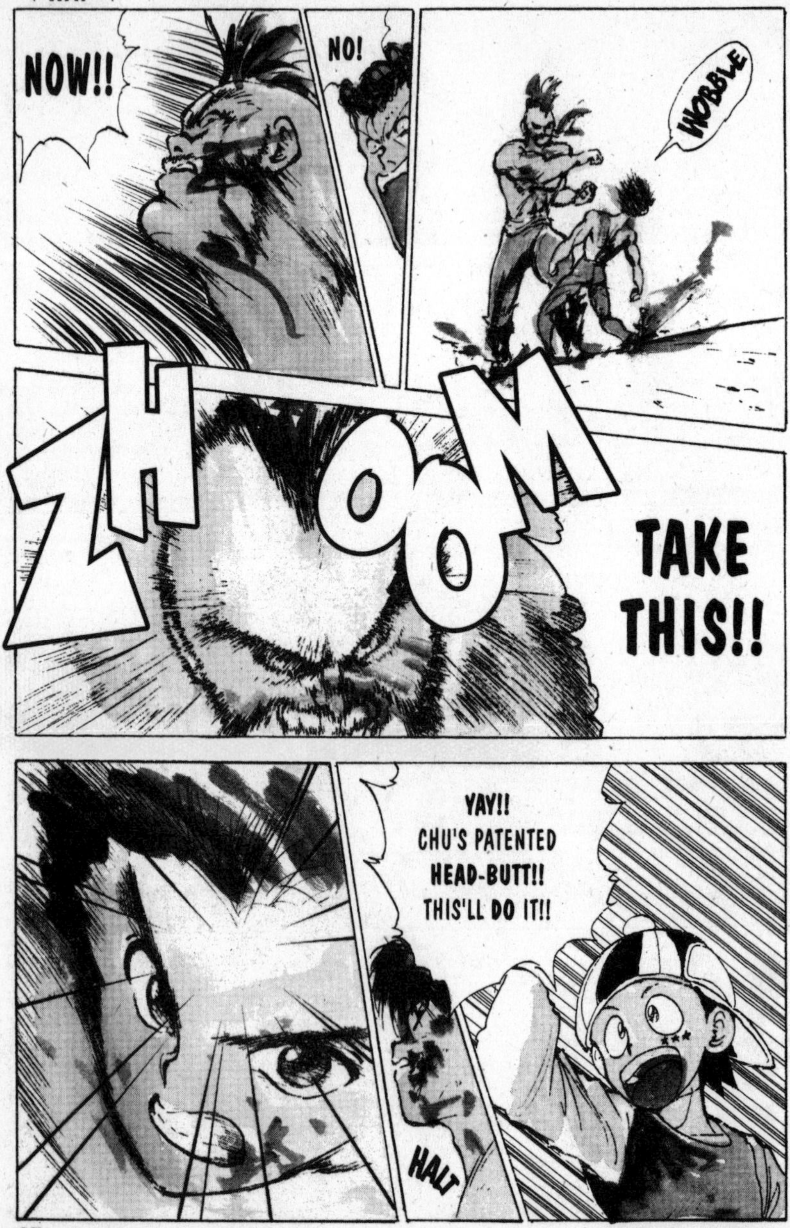
WOBBLE
NO!
NOW!!
ZHOOM
TAKE THIS!!
YAY!! CHU'S PATENTED HEAD-BUTT!! THIS'LL DO IT!!
HALT

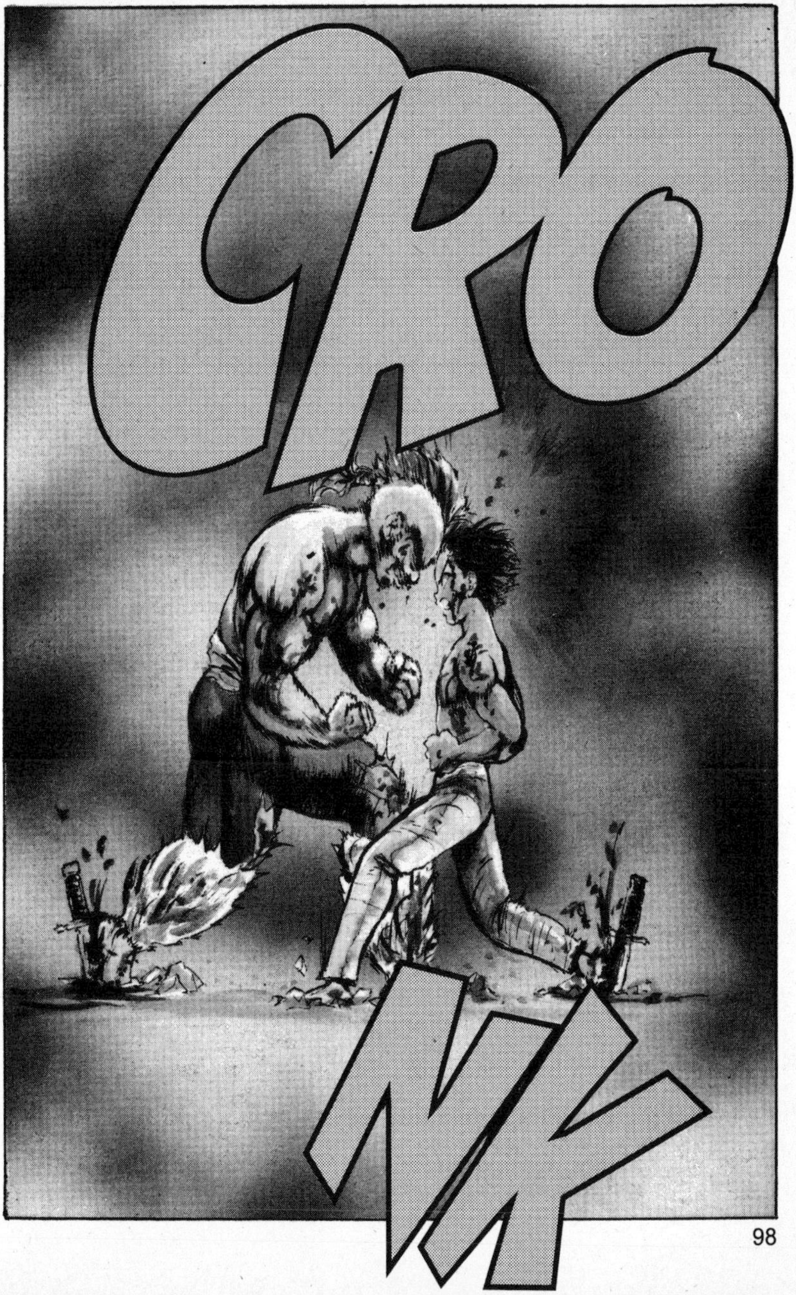
CRO
NK

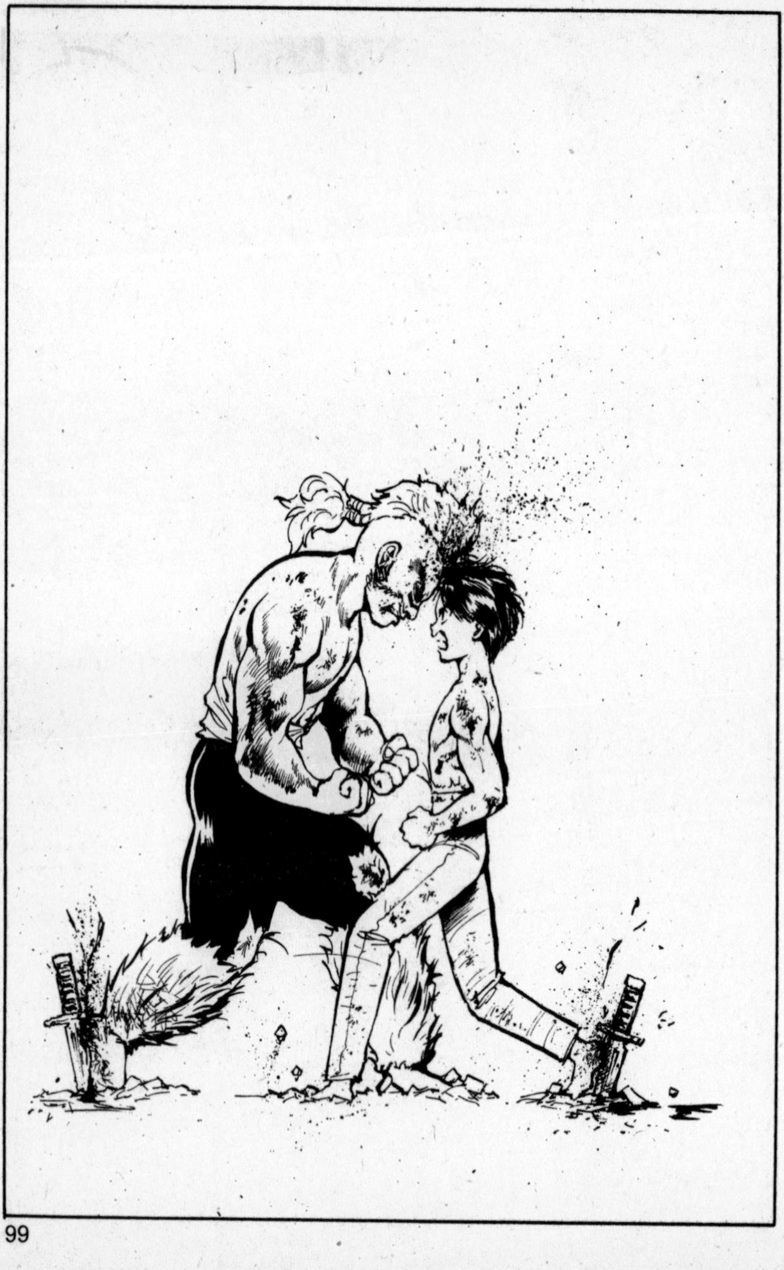

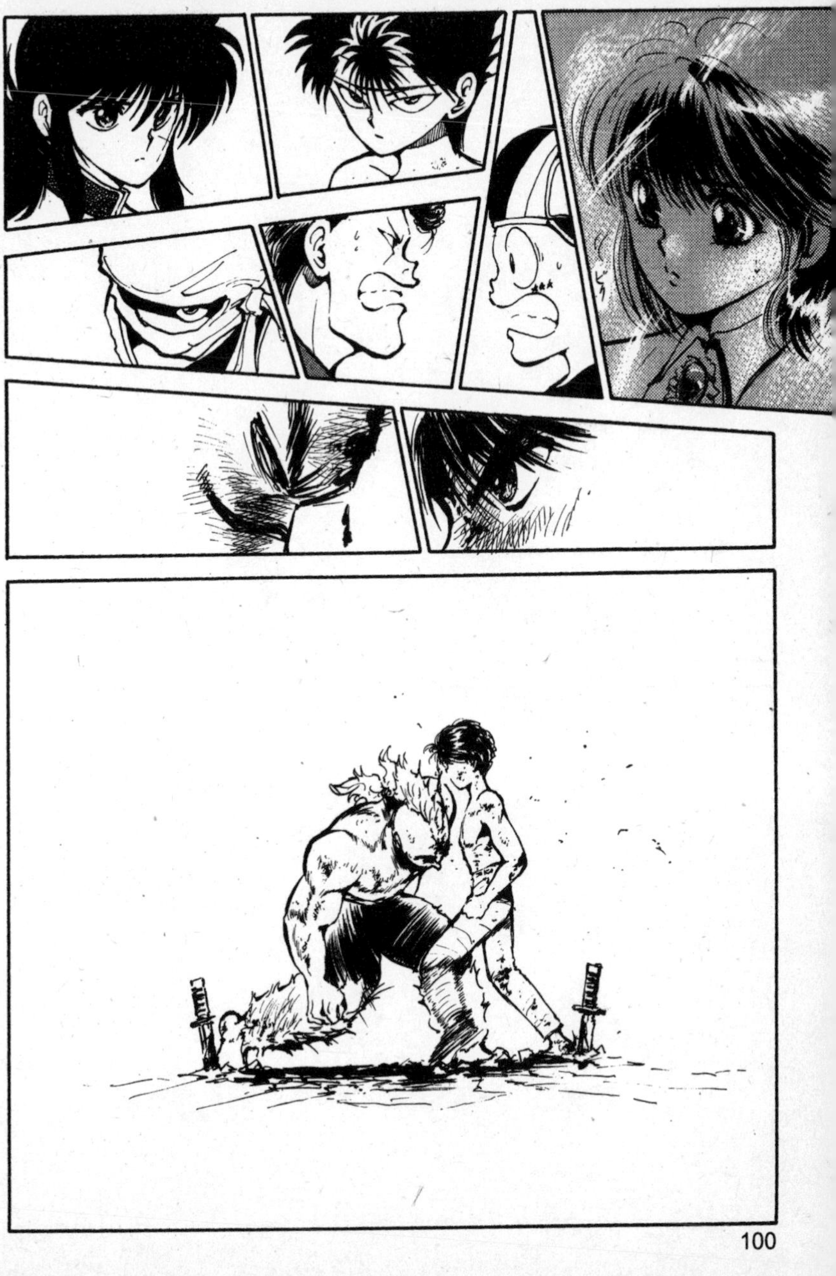
ピク

READ THIS WAY

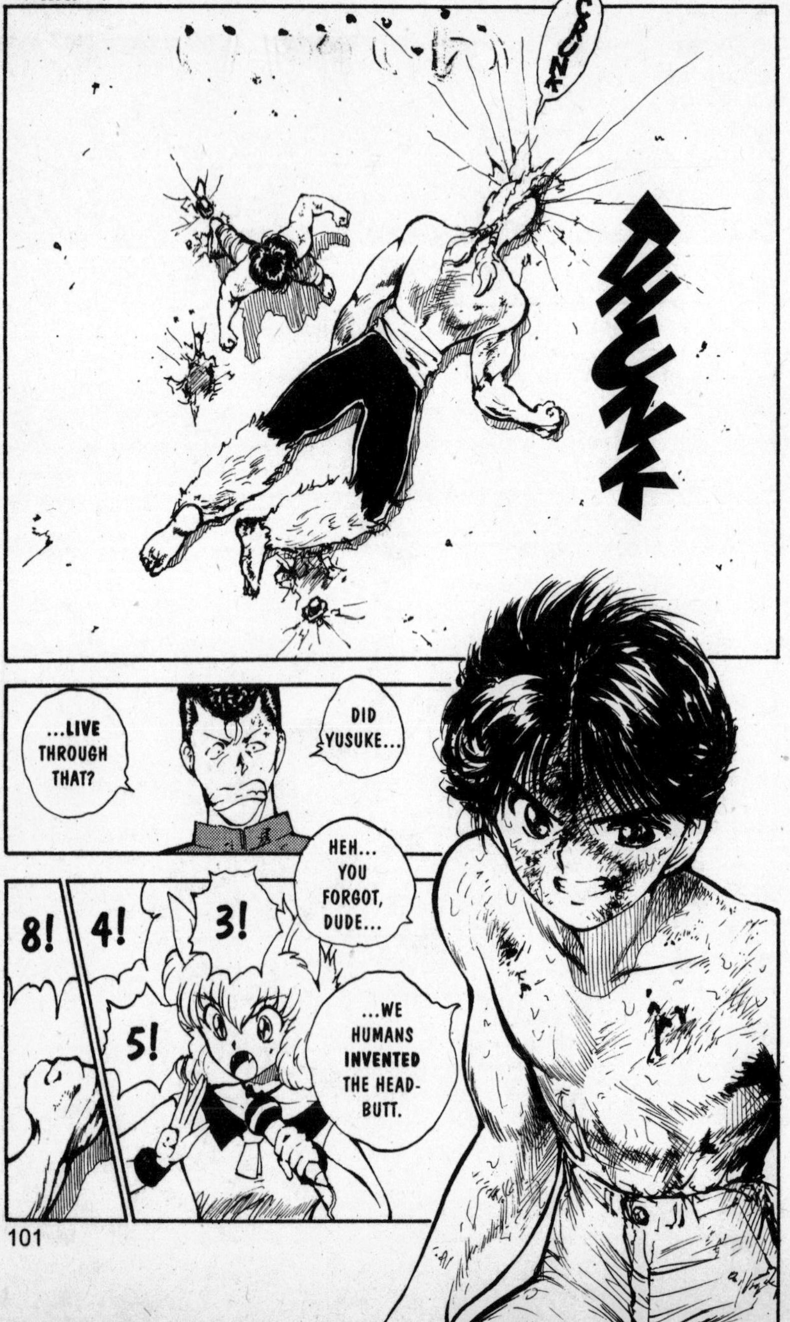
CRUNK
THUNK
DID YUSUKE...
...LIVE THROUGH THAT?
HEH... YOU FORGOT, DUDE...
...WE HUMANS INVENTED THE HEAD-BUTT.
3!
4!
5!
8!

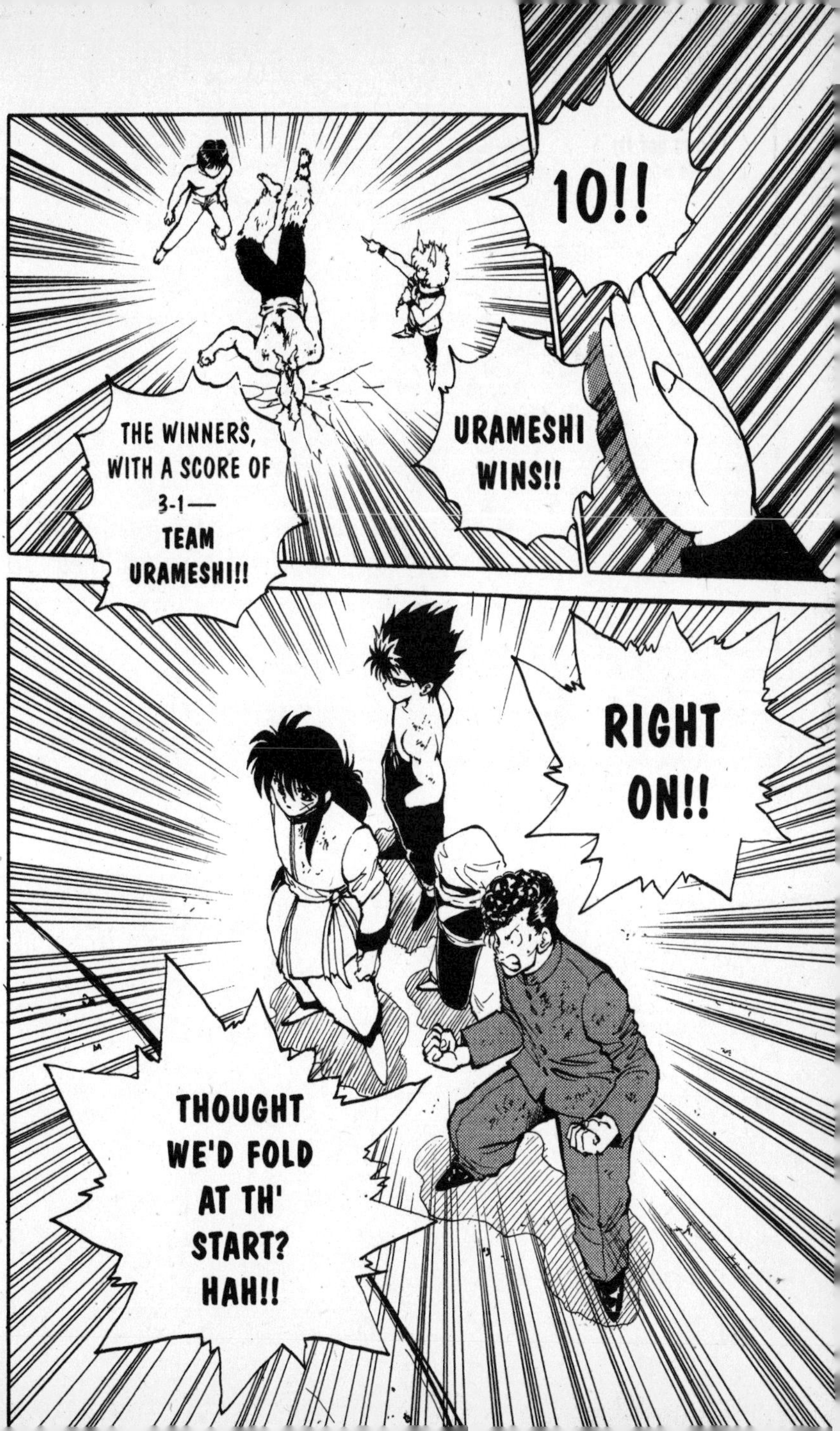
10!!
URAMESHI WINS!!
THE WINNERS, WITH A SCORE OF 3-1— TEAM URAMESHI!!
RIGHT ON!!
THOUGHT WE'D FOLD AT TH' START? HAH!!

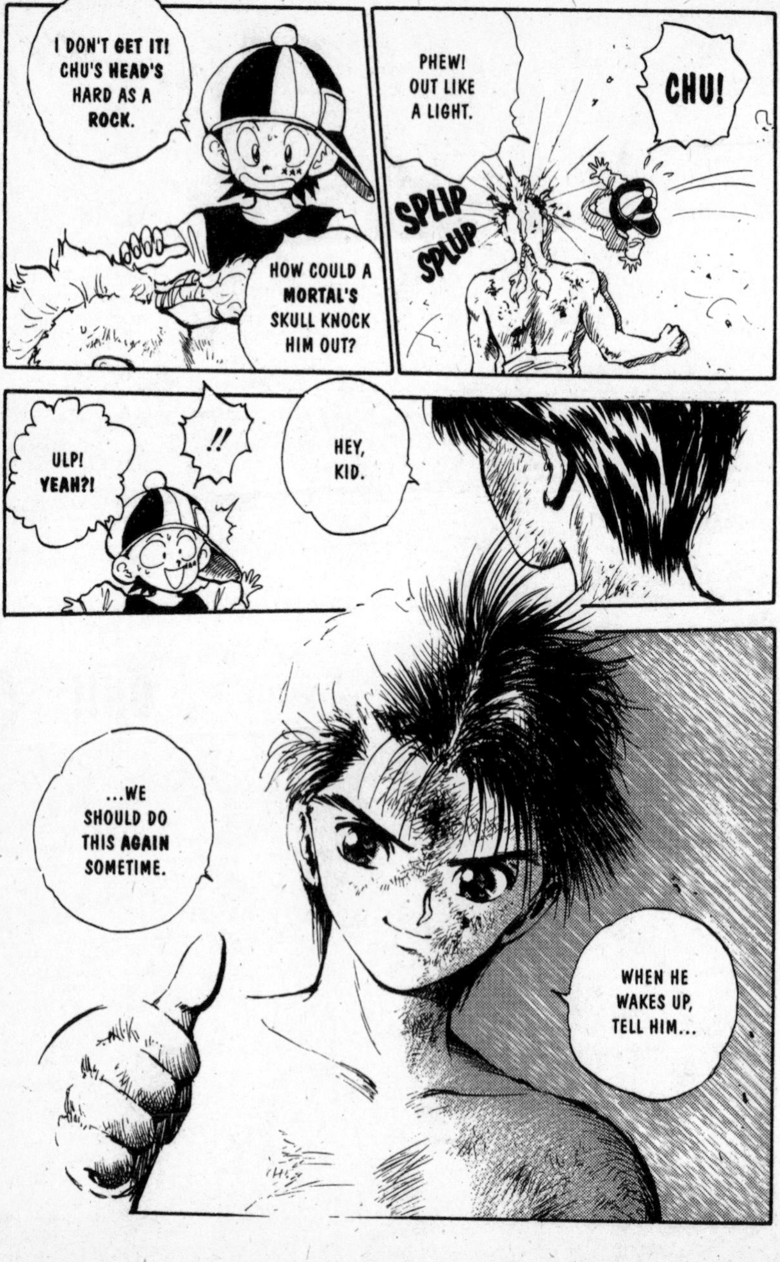
CHU!
PHEW! OUT LIKE A LIGHT.
SPLIP SPLUP
I DON'T GET IT! CHU'S HEAD'S HARD AS A ROCK.
HOW COULD A MORTAL'S SKULL KNOCK HIM OUT?
HEY, KID.
!!
ULP! YEAH?!
WHEN HE WAKES UP, TELL HIM...
...WE SHOULD DO THIS AGAIN SOMETIME.

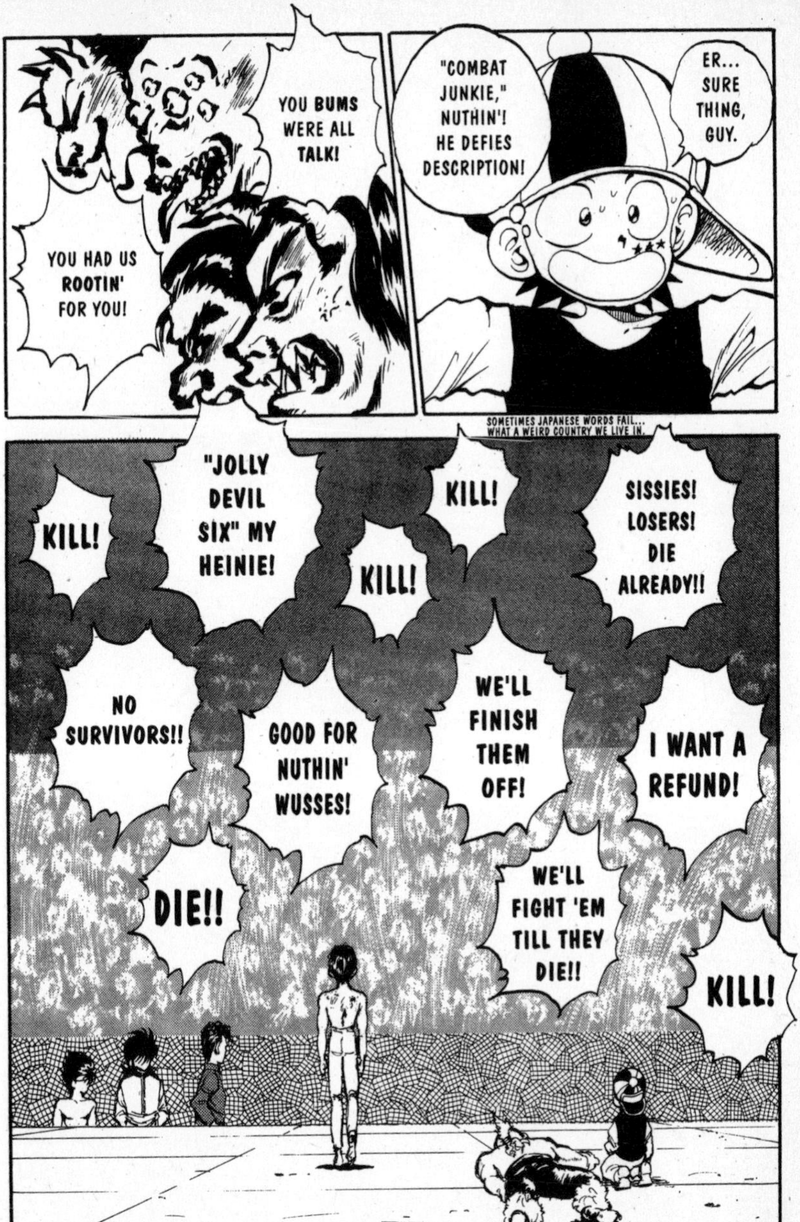

ER... SURE THING, GUY.
"COMBAT JUNKIE," NUTHIN'! HE DEFIES DESCRIPTION!
SOMETIMES JAPANESE WORDS FAIL... WHAT A WEIRD COUNTRY WE LIVE IN.
YOU BUMS WERE ALL TALK!
YOU HAD US ROOTIN' FOR YOU!
SISSIES! LOSERS! DIE ALREADY!!
KILL!
KILL!
"JOLLY DEVIL SIX" MY HEINIE!
KILL!
I WANT A REFUND!
WE'LL FINISH THEM OFF!
GOOD FOR NUTHIN' WUSSES!
NO SURVIVORS!!
KILL!
WE'LL FIGHT 'EM TILL THEY DIE!!
DIE!!

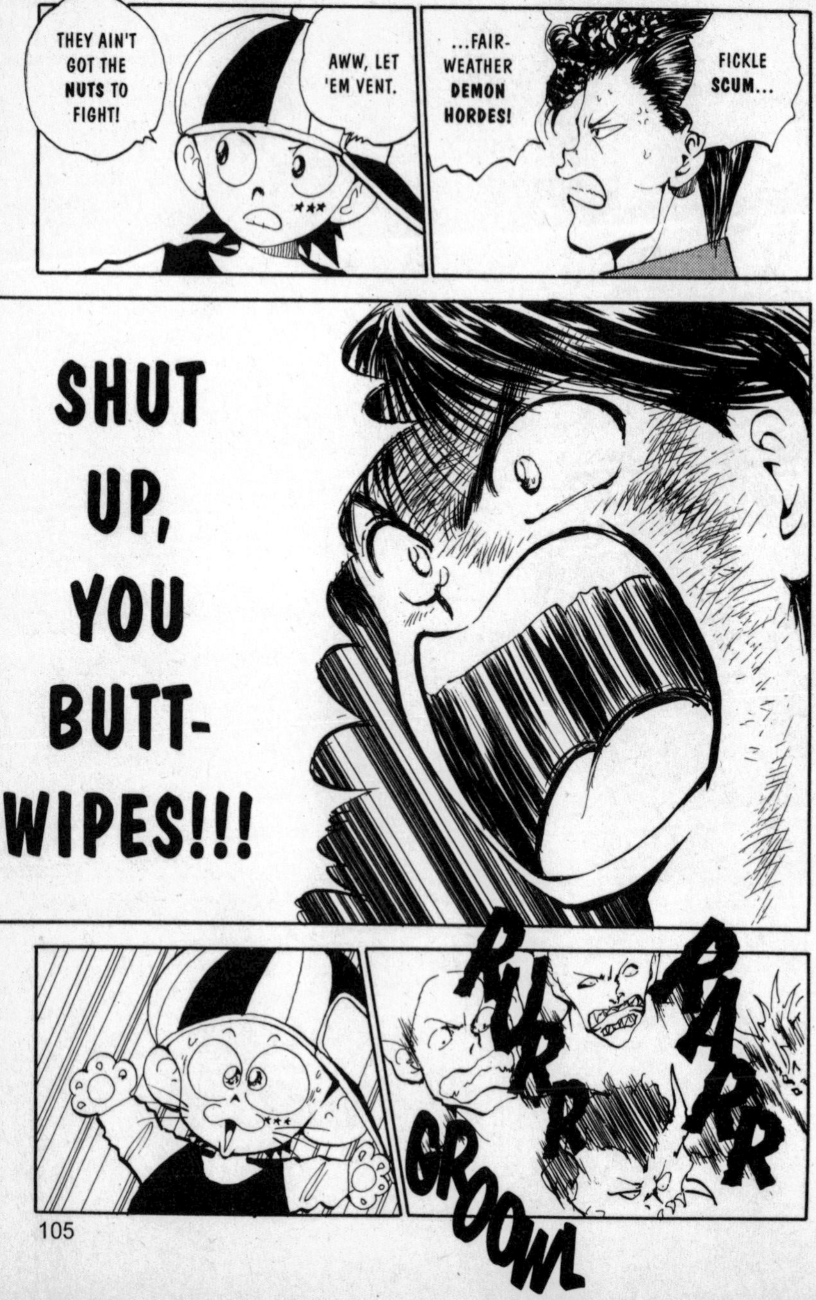
FICKLE SCUM...
...FAIR-WEATHER DEMON HORDES!
AWW, LET 'EM VENT.
THEY AIN'T GOT THE NUTS TO FIGHT!
SHUT UP, YOU BUTT-WIPES!!!
RARRR
RURRR
GROOWL

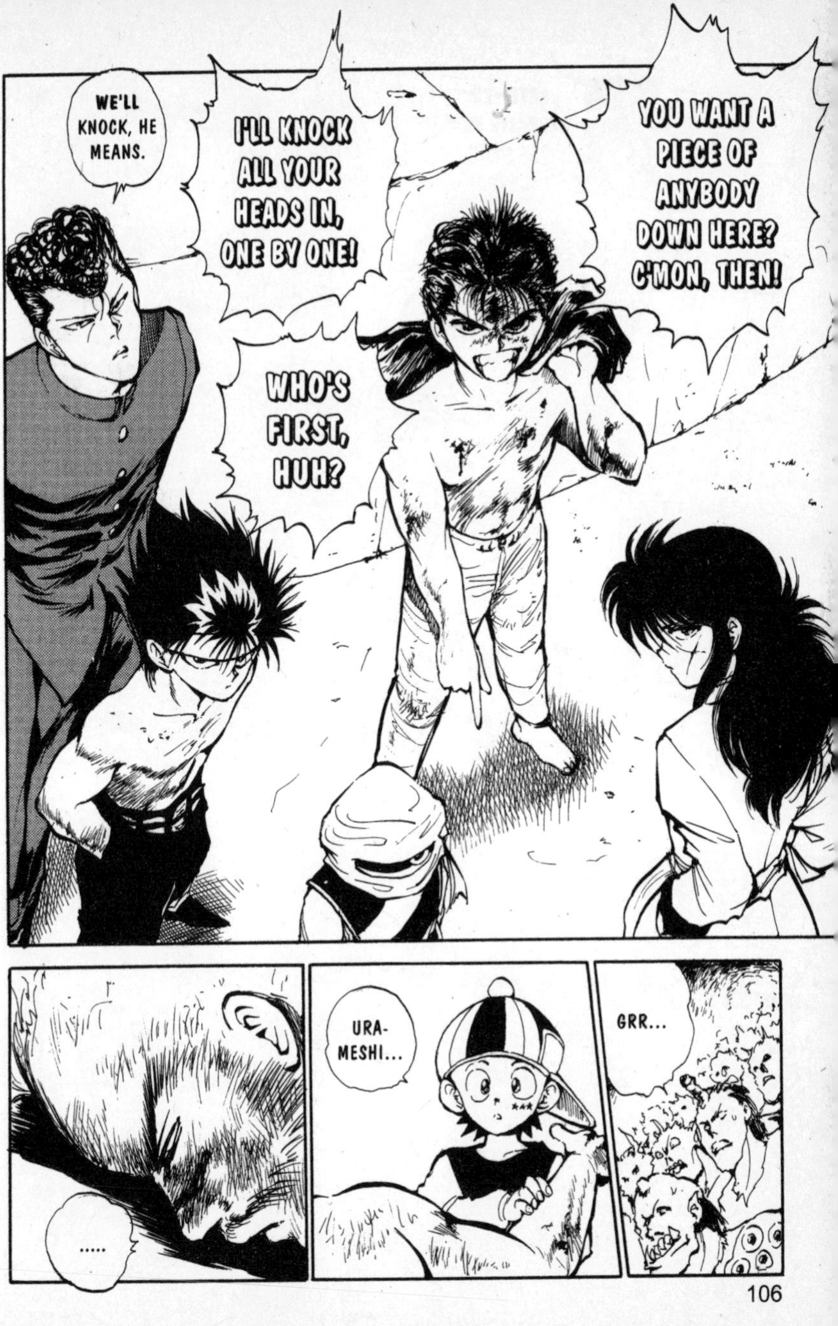
YOU WANT A PIECE OF ANYBODY DOWN HERE? C'MON, THEN!
WHO'S FIRST, HUH?
I'LL KNOCK ALL YOUR HEADS IN, ONE BY ONE!
WE'LL KNOCK, HE MEANS.
GRR...
URA-MESHI...
.....

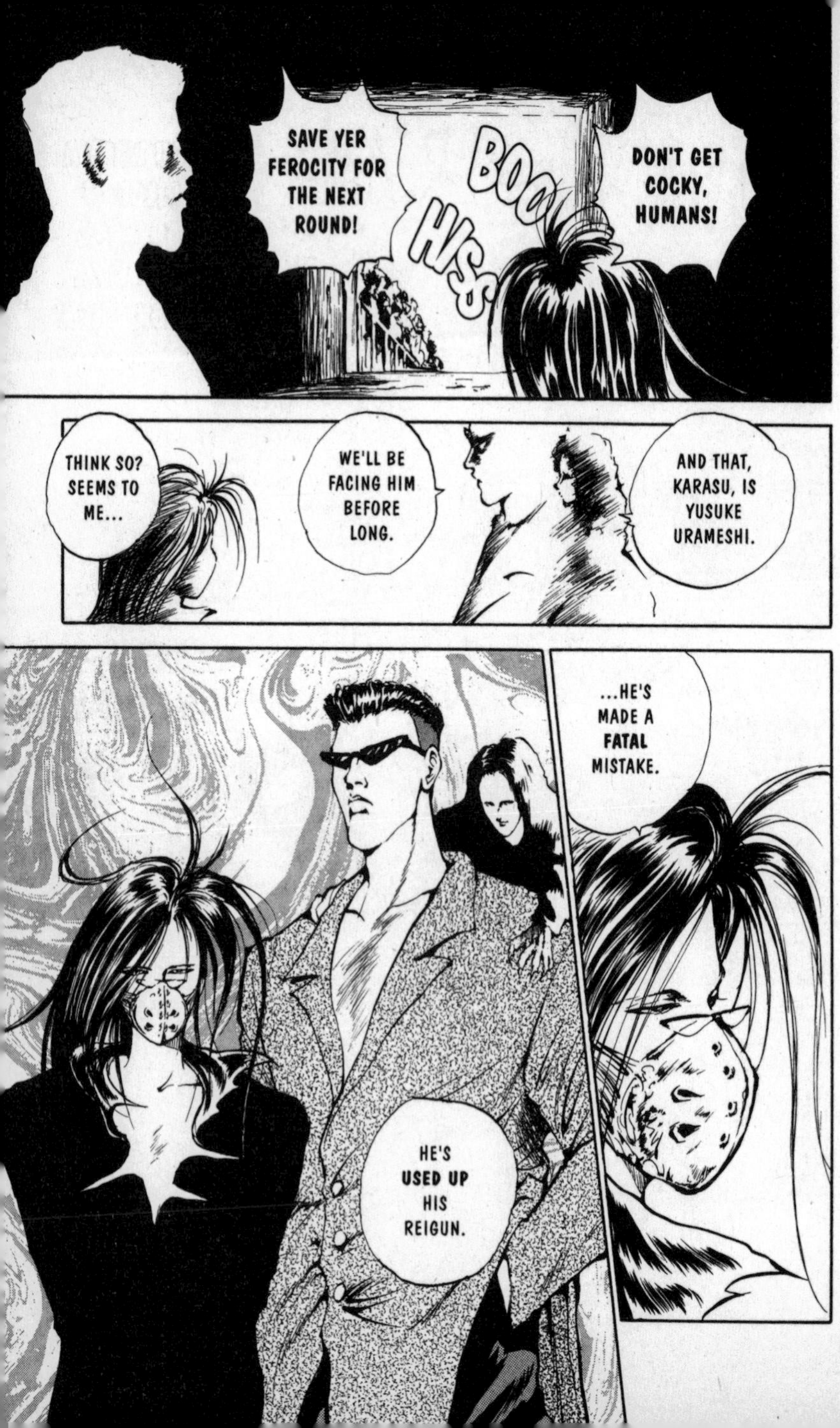
DON'T GET COCKY, HUMANS!
BOO
HISS
SAVE YER FEROCITY FOR THE NEXT ROUND!
AND THAT, KARASU, IS YUSUKE URAMESHI.
WE'LL BE FACING HIM BEFORE LONG.
THINK SO? SEEMS TO ME...
...HE'S MADE A **FATAL** MISTAKE.
HE'S USED UP HIS REIGUN.

I HAD A WEIRD DREAM.

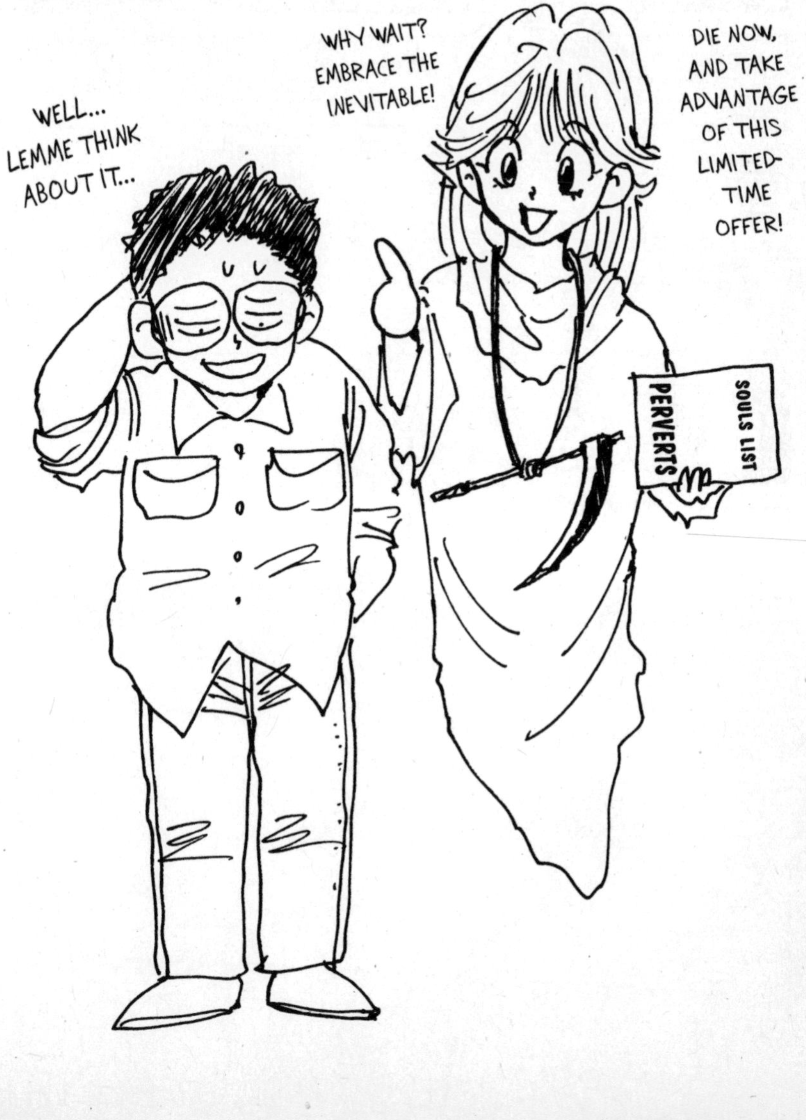
DIE NOW, AND TAKE ADVANTAGE OF THIS LIMITED-TIME OFFER!
WHY WAIT? EMBRACE THE INEVITABLE!
WELL... LEMME THINK ABOUT IT...
SOULS LIST
PERVERTS

THE TOP EIGHT LINE-UP!!

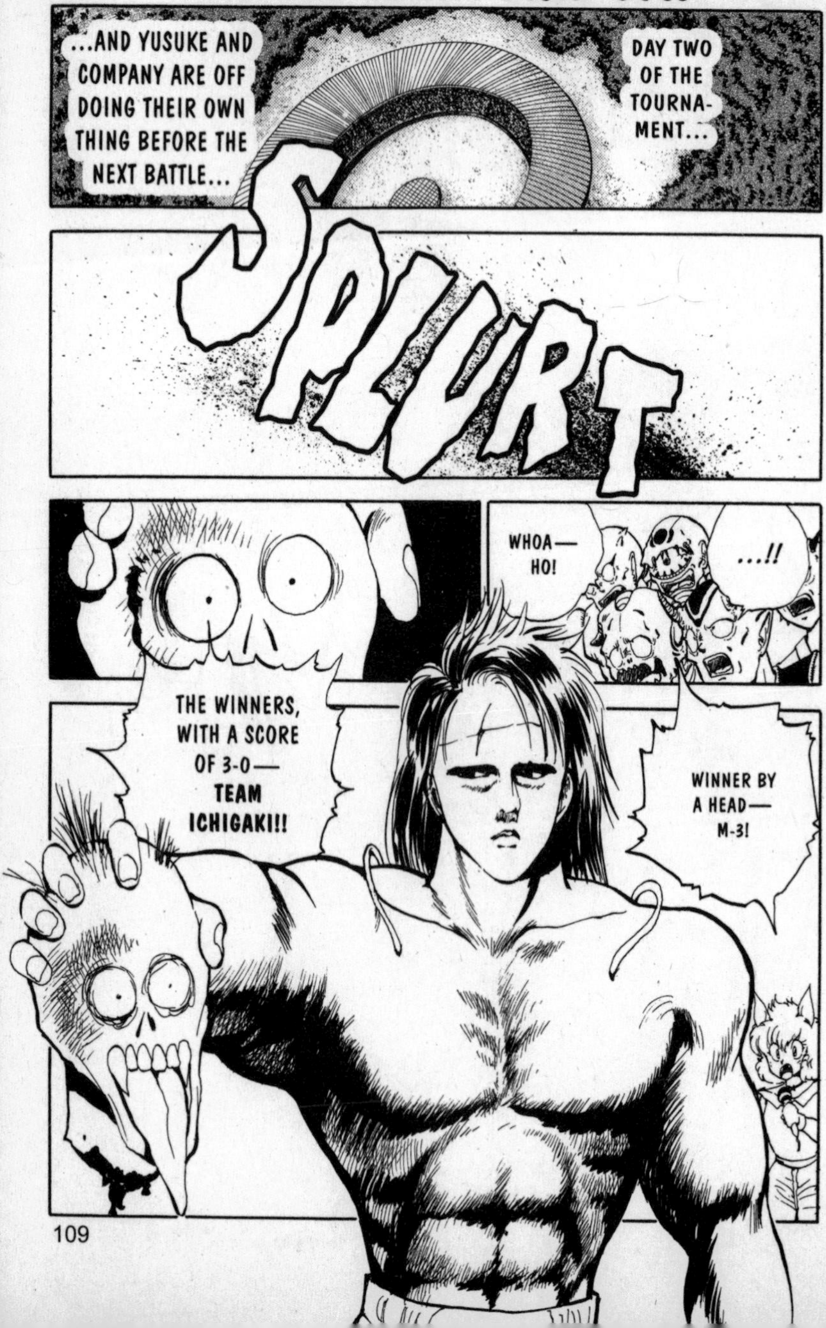
DAY TWO OF THE TOURNA- MENT...
...AND YUSUKE AND COMPANY ARE OFF DOING THEIR OWN THING BEFORE THE NEXT BATTLE...
SPLURT
...!!
WHOA— HO!
WINNER BY A HEAD— M-3!
THE WINNERS, WITH A SCORE OF 3-0— **TEAM ICHIGAKI!!**

THE TOP EIGHT LINE-UP!!

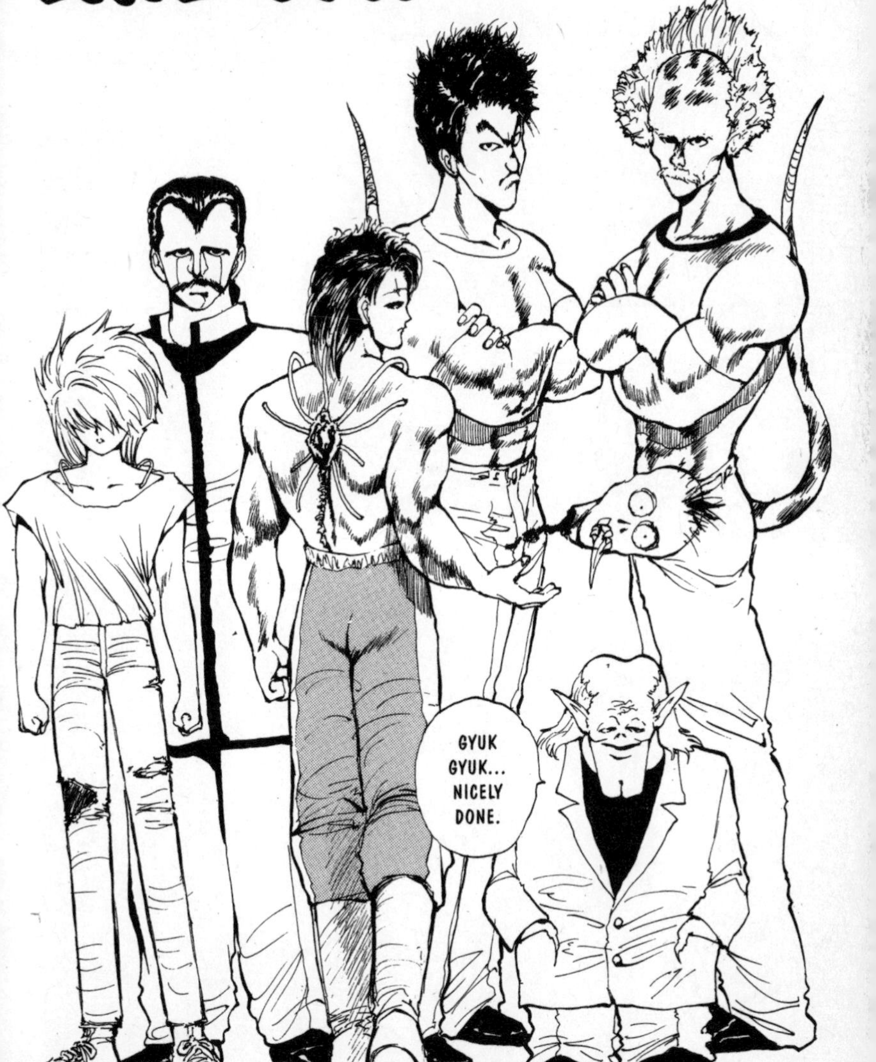
GYUK GYUK... NICELY DONE.

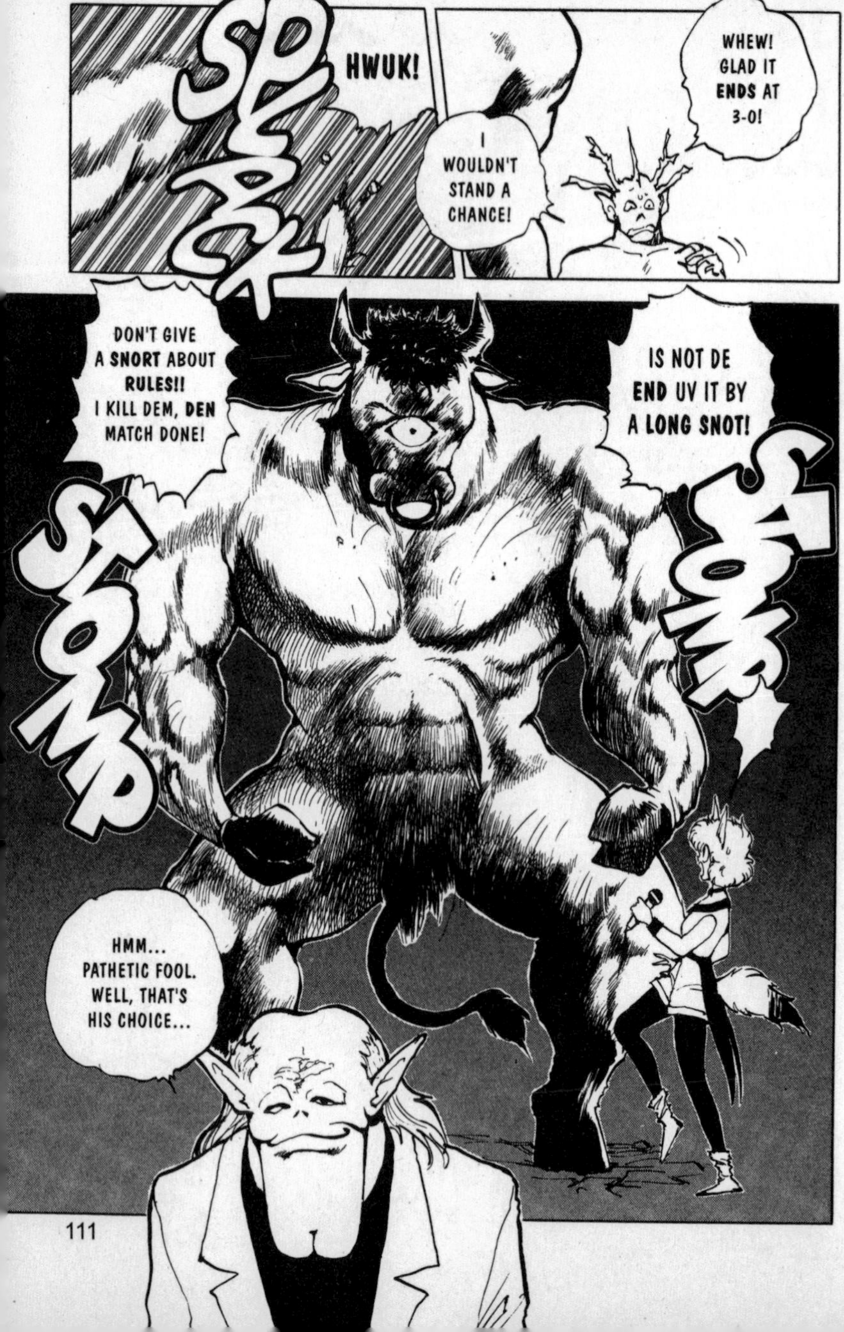
WHEW! GLAD IT ENDS AT 3-0!
I WOULDN'T STAND A CHANCE!
HWUK!
SPLACK
IS NOT DE END UV IT BY A LONG SNOT!
DON'T GIVE A SNORT ABOUT RULES!! I KILL DEM, DEN MATCH DONE!
STOMP
STOMP
HMM... PATHETIC FOOL. WELL, THAT'S HIS CHOICE...

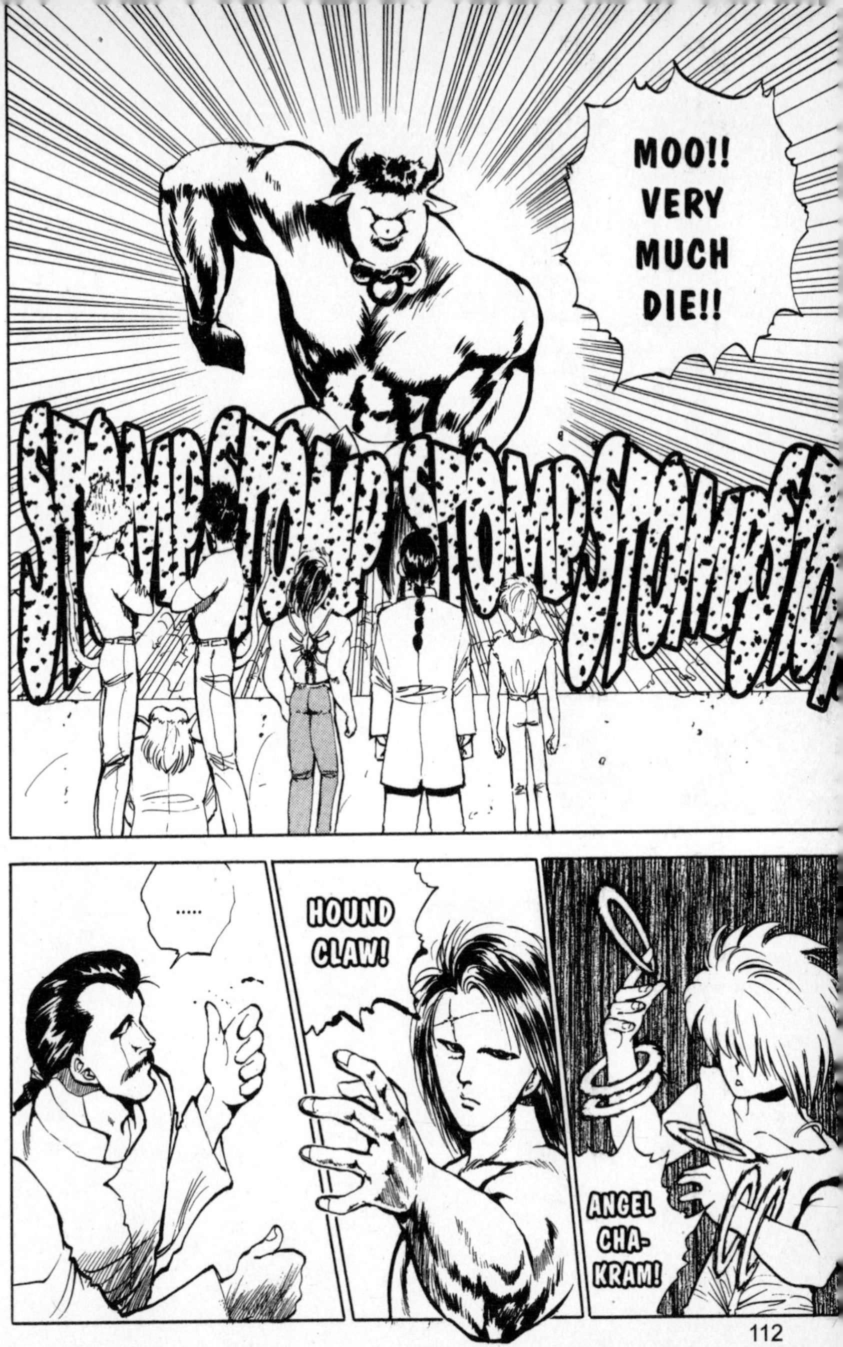
MOO!! VERY MUCH DIE!!
STOMP STOMP STOMP STOMP
ANGEL CHA-KRAM!
HOUND CLAW!
......

READ THIS WAY

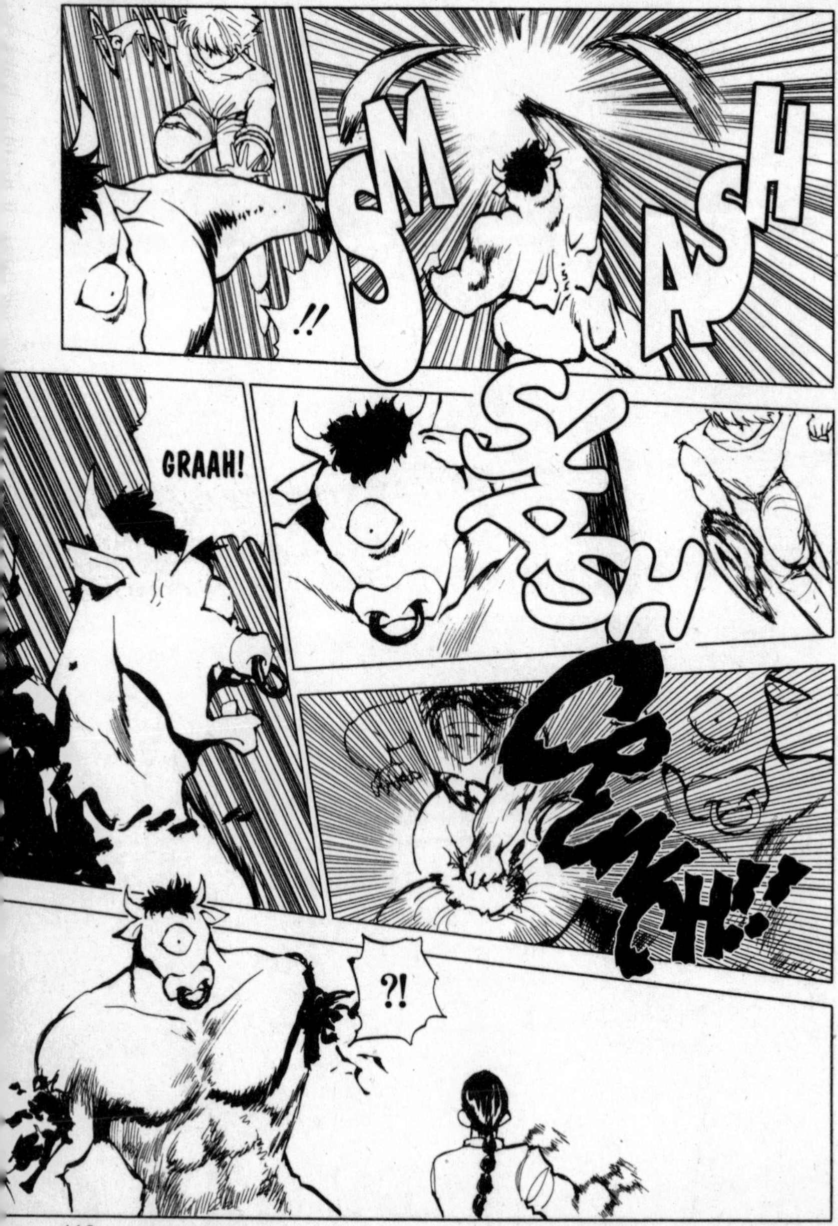
SMASH
!!
SLASH
CRUNCH!!
GRAAH!
?!

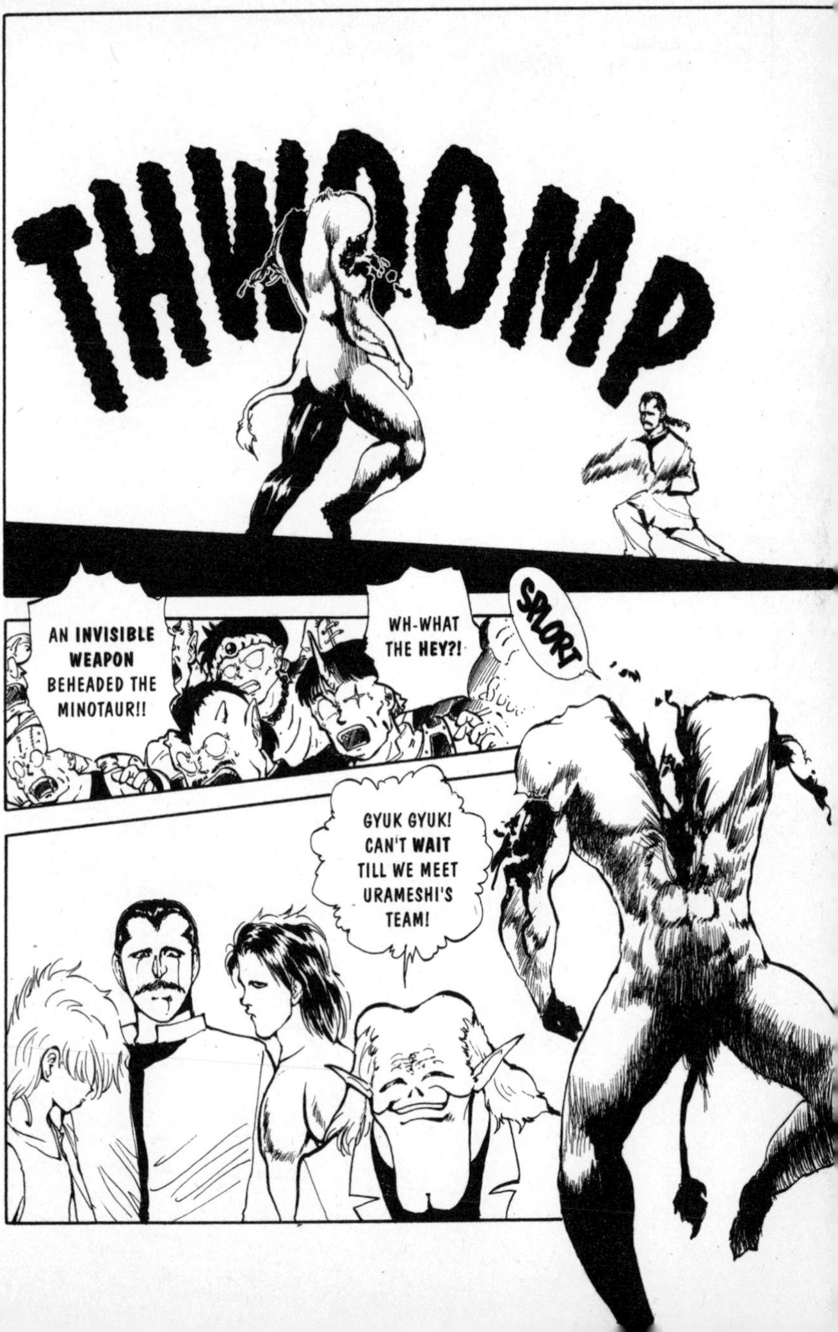
THWOOMP
SPLORT
WH-WHAT THE HEY?!
AN INVISIBLE WEAPON BEHEADED THE MINOTAUR!!
GYUK GYUK! CAN'T WAIT TILL WE MEET URAMESHI'S TEAM!

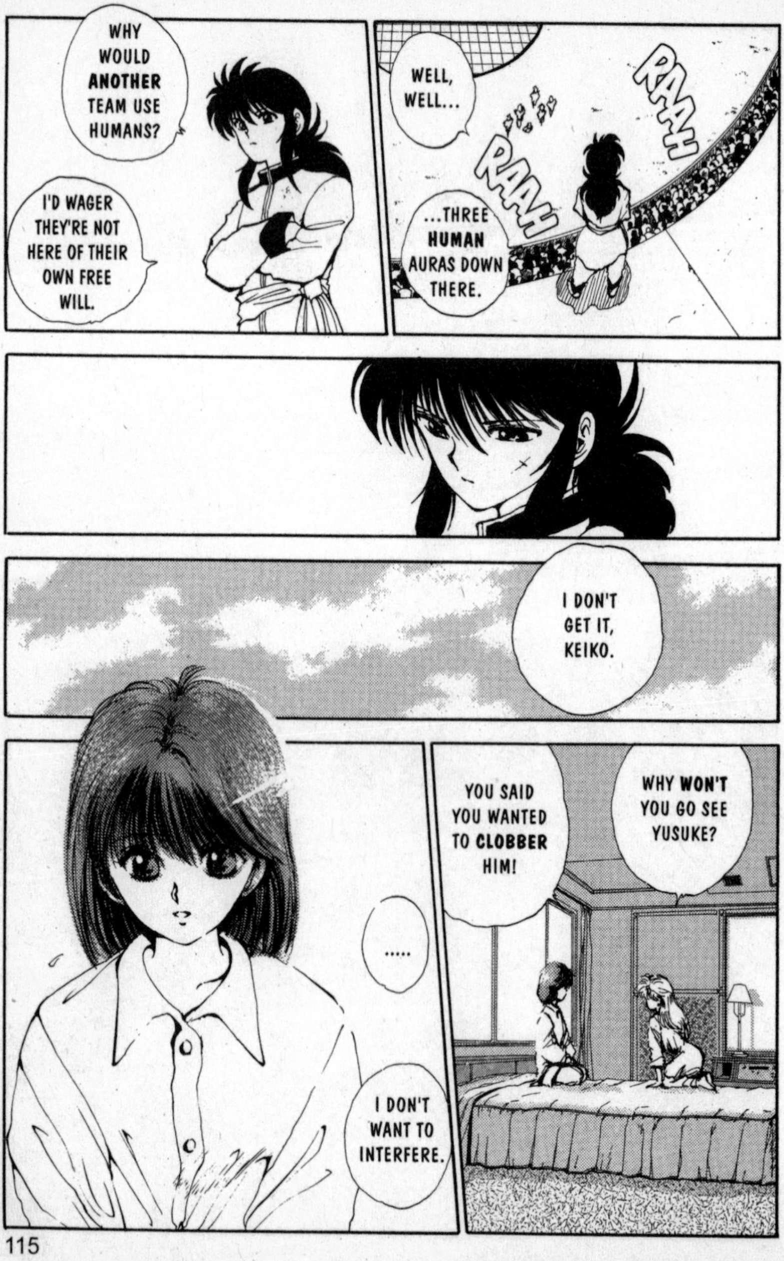
WELL, WELL...
RAAH
RAAH
...THREE HUMAN AURAS DOWN THERE.
WHY WOULD ANOTHER TEAM USE HUMANS?
I'D WAGER THEY'RE NOT HERE OF THEIR OWN FREE WILL.
I DON'T GET IT, KEIKO.
WHY WON'T YOU GO SEE YUSUKE?
YOU SAID YOU WANTED TO CLOBBER HIM!
.....
I DON'T WANT TO INTERFERE.

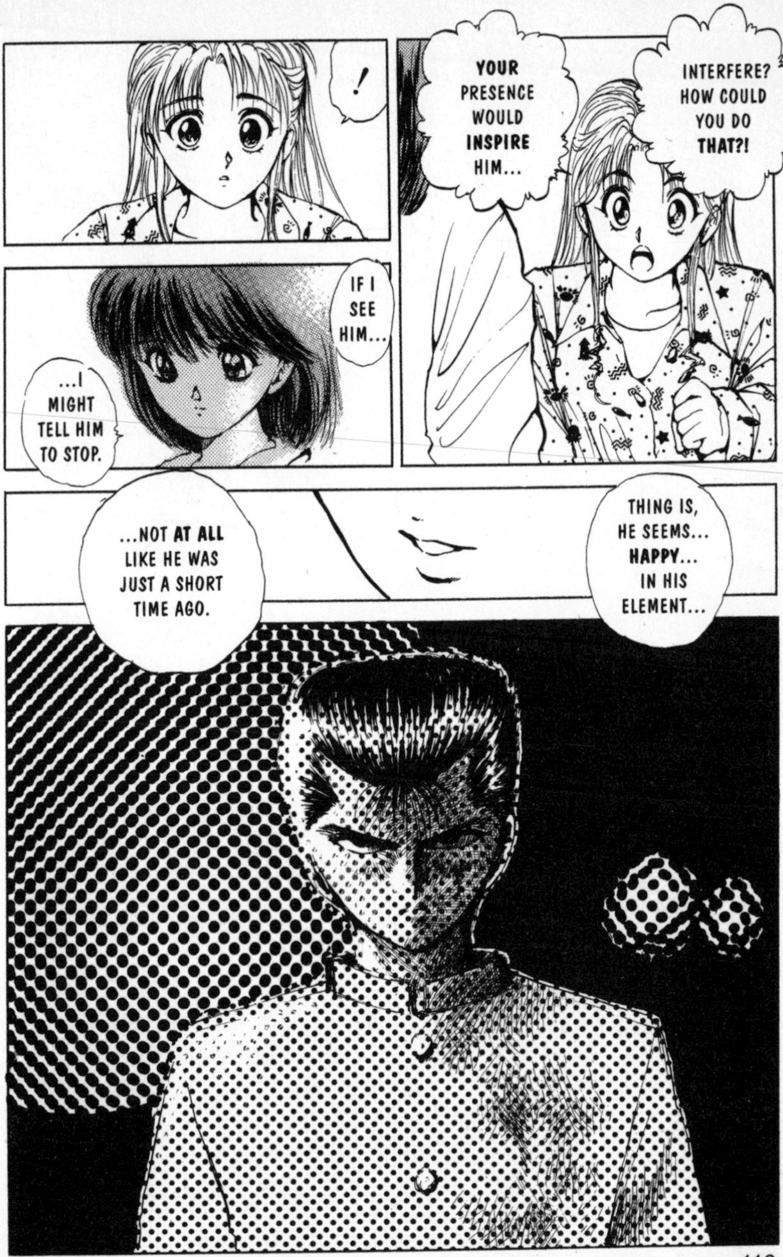

INTERFERE? HOW COULD YOU DO THAT?!
YOUR PRESENCE WOULD INSPIRE HIM...
!
IF I SEE HIM...
...I MIGHT TELL HIM TO STOP.
THING IS, HE SEEMS... HAPPY... IN HIS ELEMENT...
...NOT AT ALL LIKE HE WAS JUST A SHORT TIME AGO.

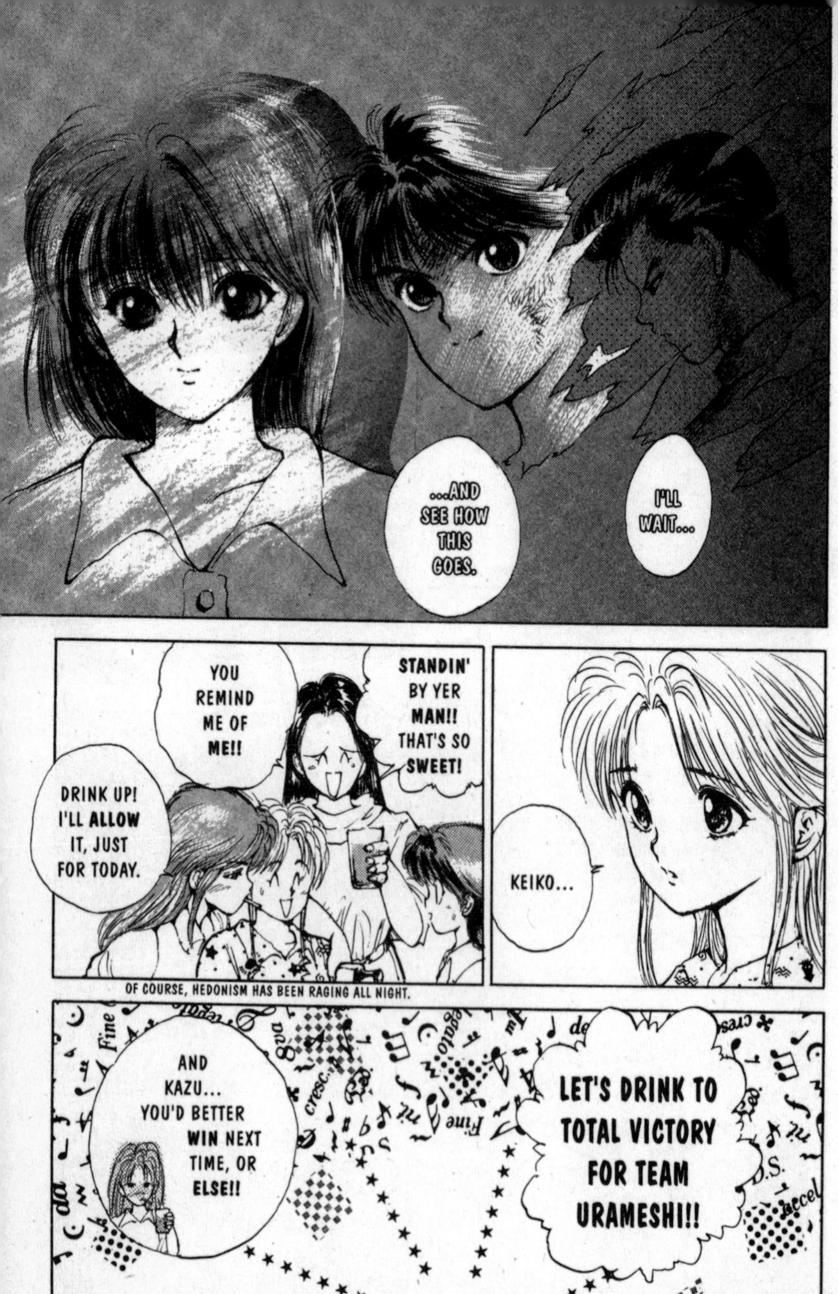
I'LL WAIT...
...AND SEE HOW THIS GOES.
KEIKO...
STANDIN' BY YER MAN!! THAT'S SO SWEET!
YOU REMIND ME OF ME!!
DRINK UP! I'LL ALLOW IT, JUST FOR TODAY.
OF COURSE, HEDONISM HAS BEEN RAGING ALL NIGHT.
LET'S DRINK TO TOTAL VICTORY FOR TEAM URAMESHI!!!
AND KAZU... YOU'D BETTER WIN NEXT TIME, OR ELSE!!

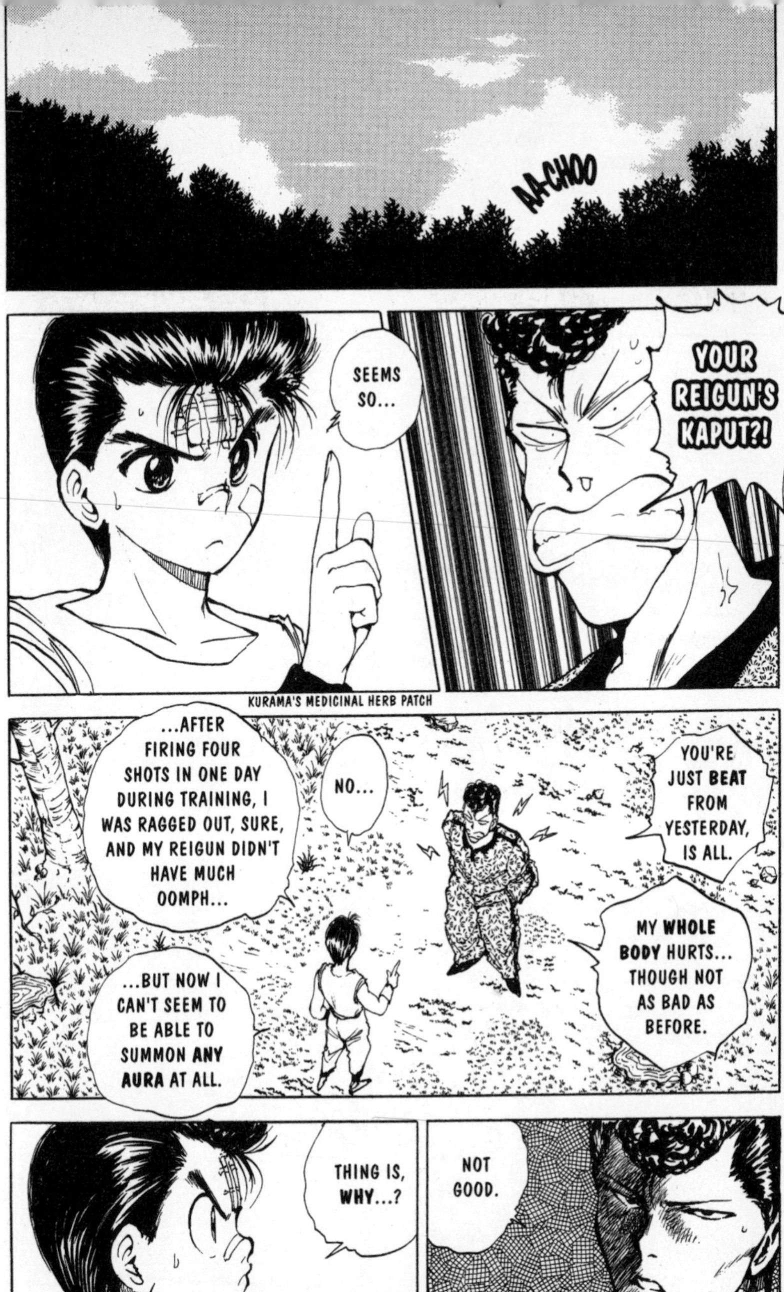
AA-CHOO
YOUR REIGUN'S KAPUT?!
SEEMS SO...
KURAMA'S MEDICINAL HERB PATCH
YOU'RE JUST BEAT FROM YESTERDAY, IS ALL.
NO...
MY WHOLE BODY HURTS... THOUGH NOT AS BAD AS BEFORE.
...AFTER FIRING FOUR SHOTS IN ONE DAY DURING TRAINING, I WAS RAGGED OUT, SURE, AND MY REIGUN DIDN'T HAVE MUCH OOMPH...
...BUT NOW I CAN'T SEEM TO BE ABLE TO SUMMON ANY AURA AT ALL.
NOT GOOD.
THING IS, WHY...?

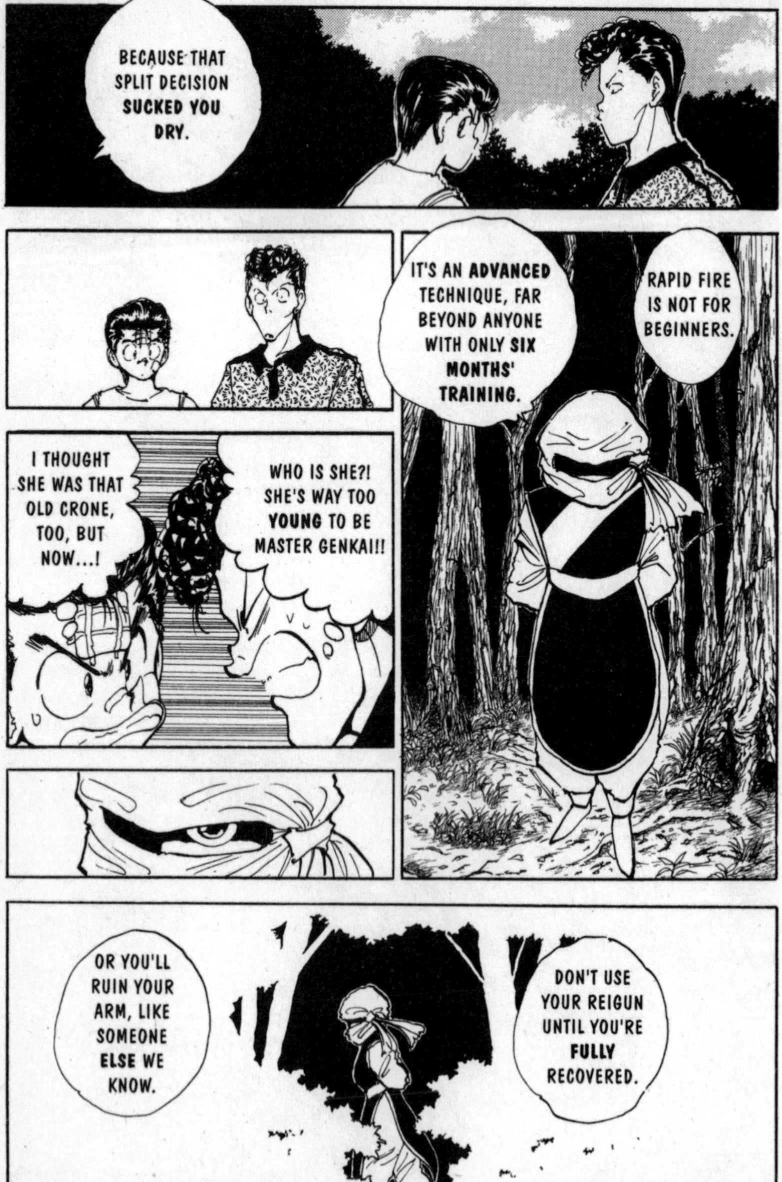
BECAUSE THAT SPLIT DECISION SUCKED YOU DRY.
RAPID FIRE IS NOT FOR BEGINNERS.
IT'S AN ADVANCED TECHNIQUE, FAR BEYOND ANYONE WITH ONLY SIX MONTHS' TRAINING.
WHO IS SHE?! SHE'S WAY TOO YOUNG TO BE MASTER GENKAI!!
I THOUGHT SHE WAS THAT OLD CRONE, TOO, BUT NOW...!
DON'T USE YOUR REIGUN UNTIL YOU'RE FULLY RECOVERED.
OR YOU'LL RUIN YOUR ARM, LIKE SOMEONE ELSE WE KNOW.

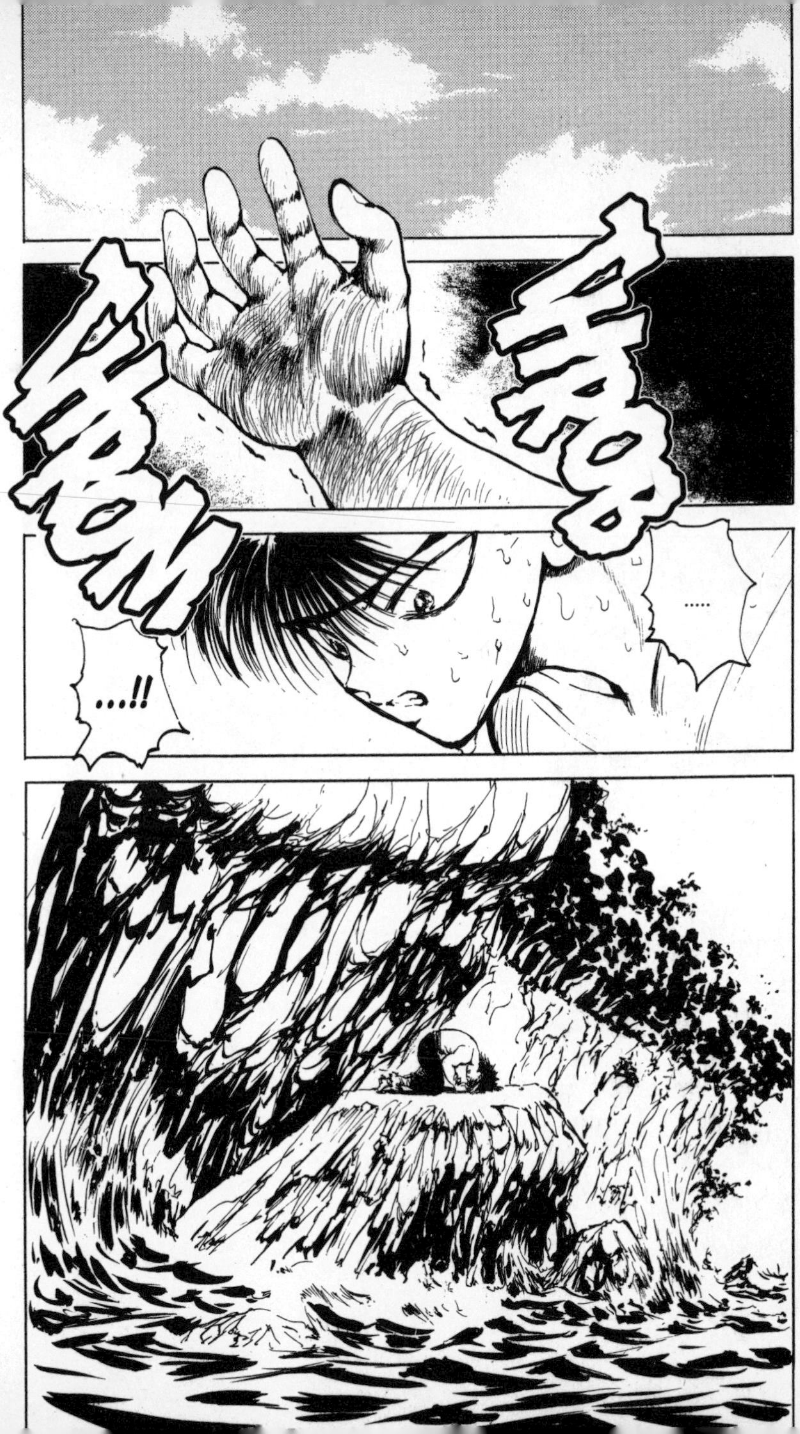
THROB
THROB
.....
...!!

READ THIS WAY

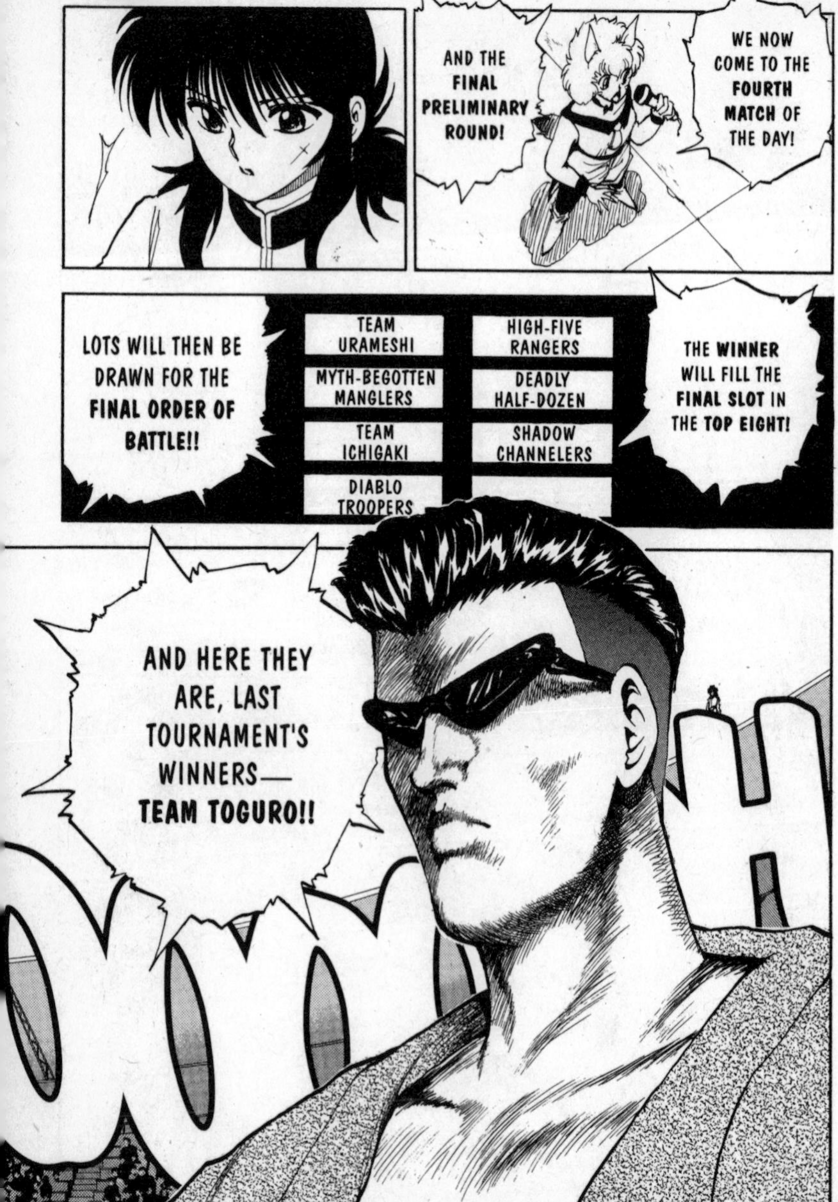
WE NOW COME TO THE FOURTH MATCH OF THE DAY!
AND THE FINAL PRELIMINARY ROUND!
THE WINNER WILL FILL THE FINAL SLOT IN THE TOP EIGHT!
HIGH-FIVE RANGERS
DEADLY HALF-DOZEN
SHADOW CHANNELERS
TEAM URAMESHI
MYTH-BEGOTTEN MANGLERS
TEAM ICHIGAKI
DIABLO TROOPERS
LOTS WILL THEN BE DRAWN FOR THE FINAL ORDER OF BATTLE!!
AND HERE THEY ARE, LAST TOURNAMENT'S WINNERS— TEAM TOGURO!!

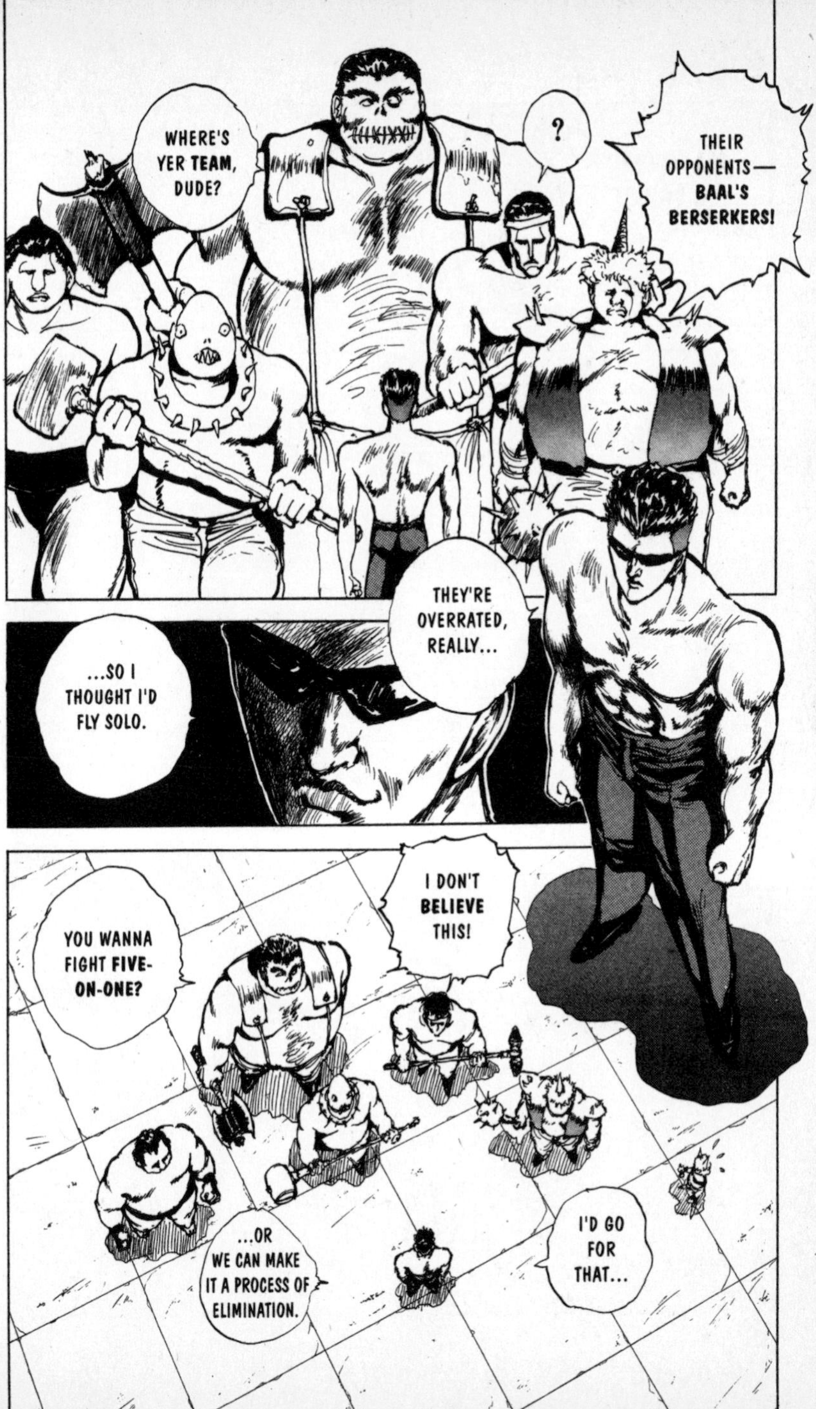
THEIR OPPONENTS— BAAL'S BERSERKERS!
?
WHERE'S YER TEAM, DUDE?
THEY'RE OVERRATED, REALLY...
...SO I THOUGHT I'D FLY SOLO.
I DON'T BELIEVE THIS!
YOU WANNA FIGHT FIVE-ON-ONE?
...OR WE CAN MAKE IT A PROCESS OF ELIMINATION.
I'D GO FOR THAT...

READ THIS WAY

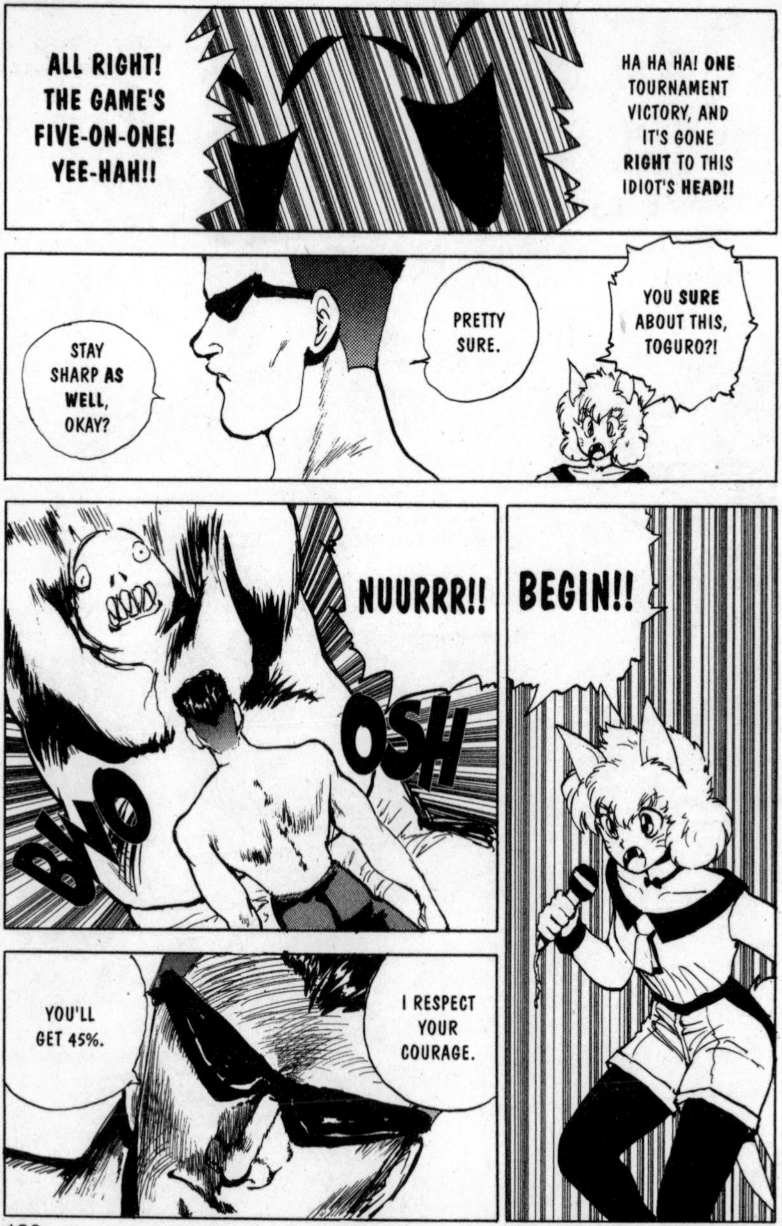
HA HA HA! ONE TOURNAMENT VICTORY, AND IT'S GONE RIGHT TO THIS IDIOT'S HEAD!!
ALL RIGHT! THE GAME'S FIVE-ON-ONE! YEE-HAH!!
YOU SURE ABOUT THIS, TOGURO?!
PRETTY SURE.
STAY SHARP AS WELL, OKAY?
BEGIN!!
NUURRR!!
BWOOSH
I RESPECT YOUR COURAGE.
YOU'LL GET 45%.

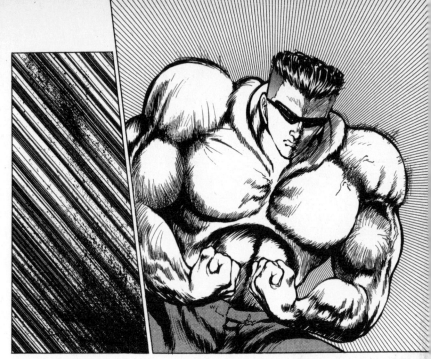

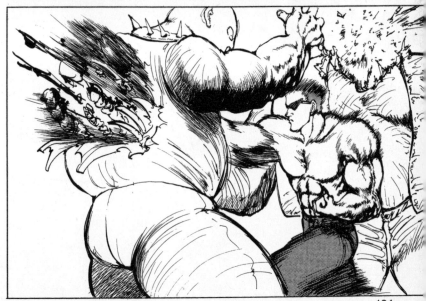

124

READ THIS WAY

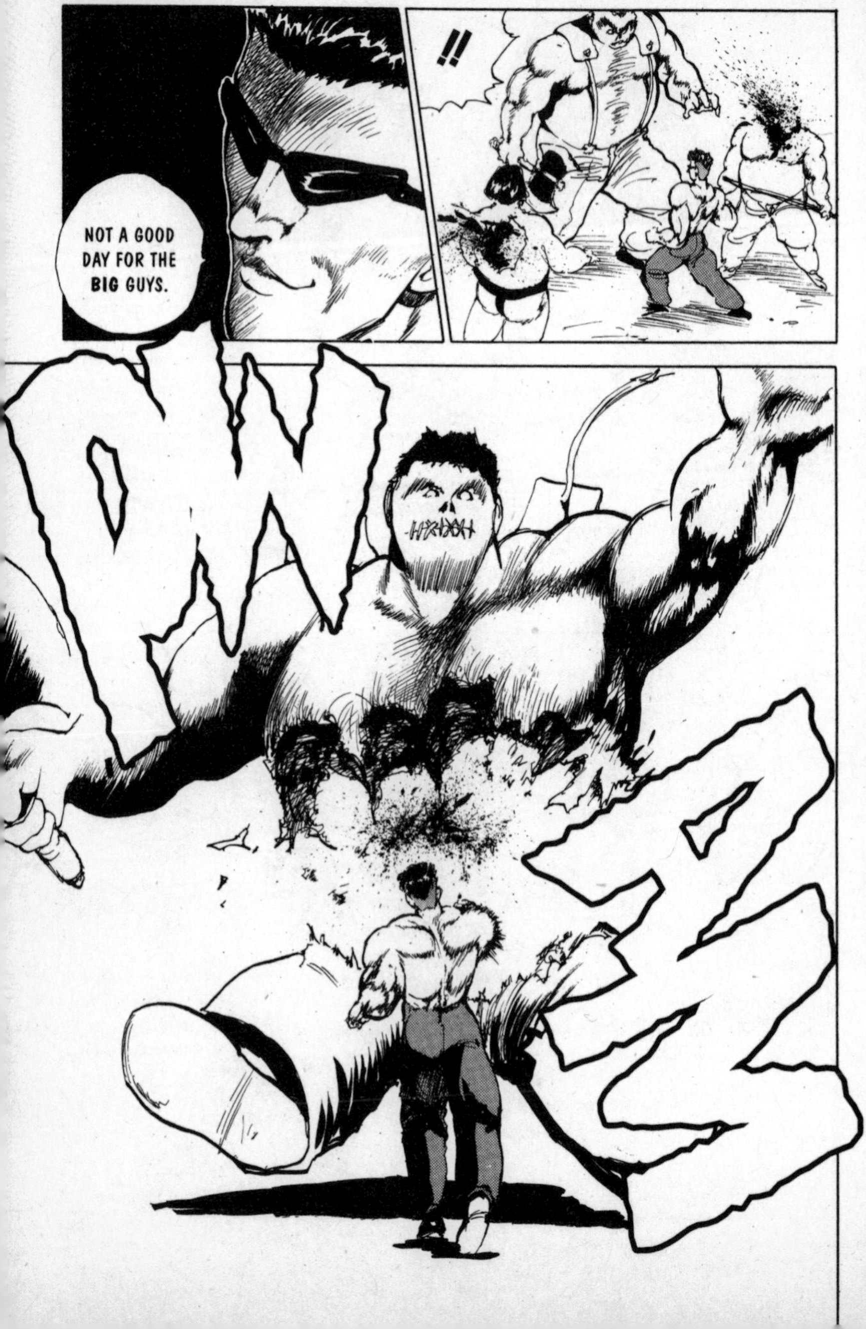
!!
NOT A GOOD DAY FOR THE BIG GUYS.

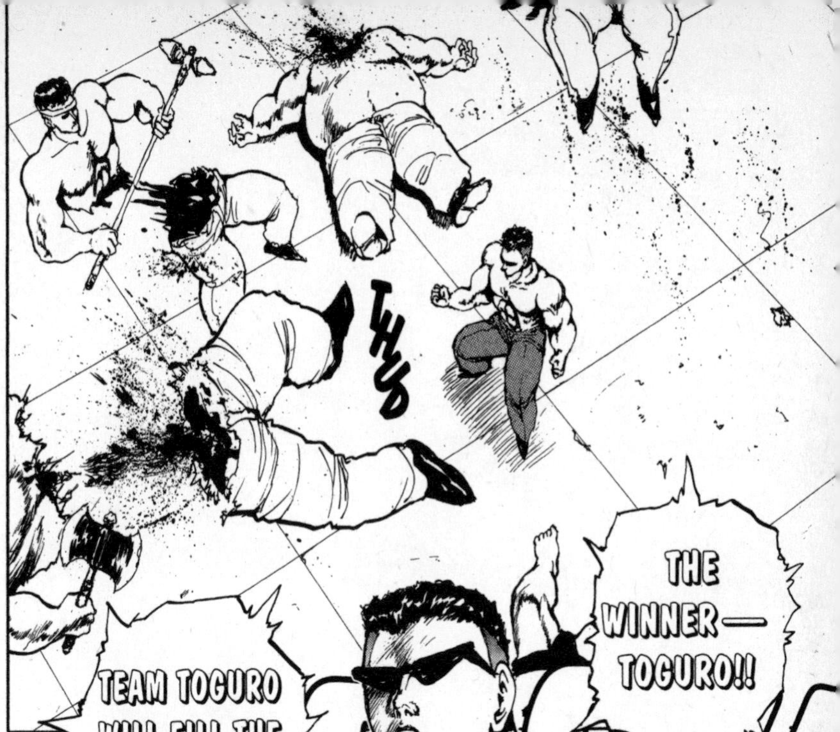
THUD
THE WINNER— TOGURO!!
TEAM TOGURO WILL FILL THE EIGHTH SLOT!!

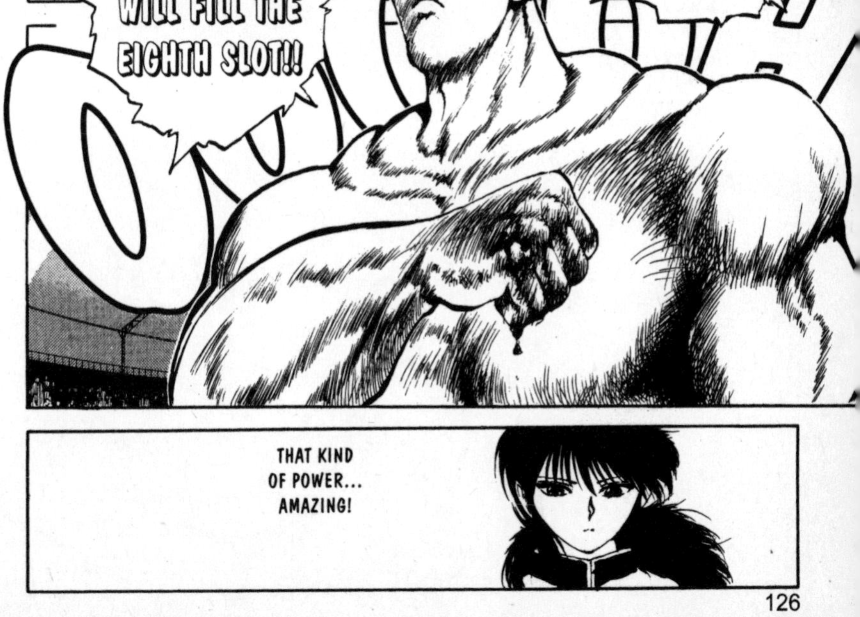
THAT KIND OF POWER... AMAZING!

READ THIS WAY

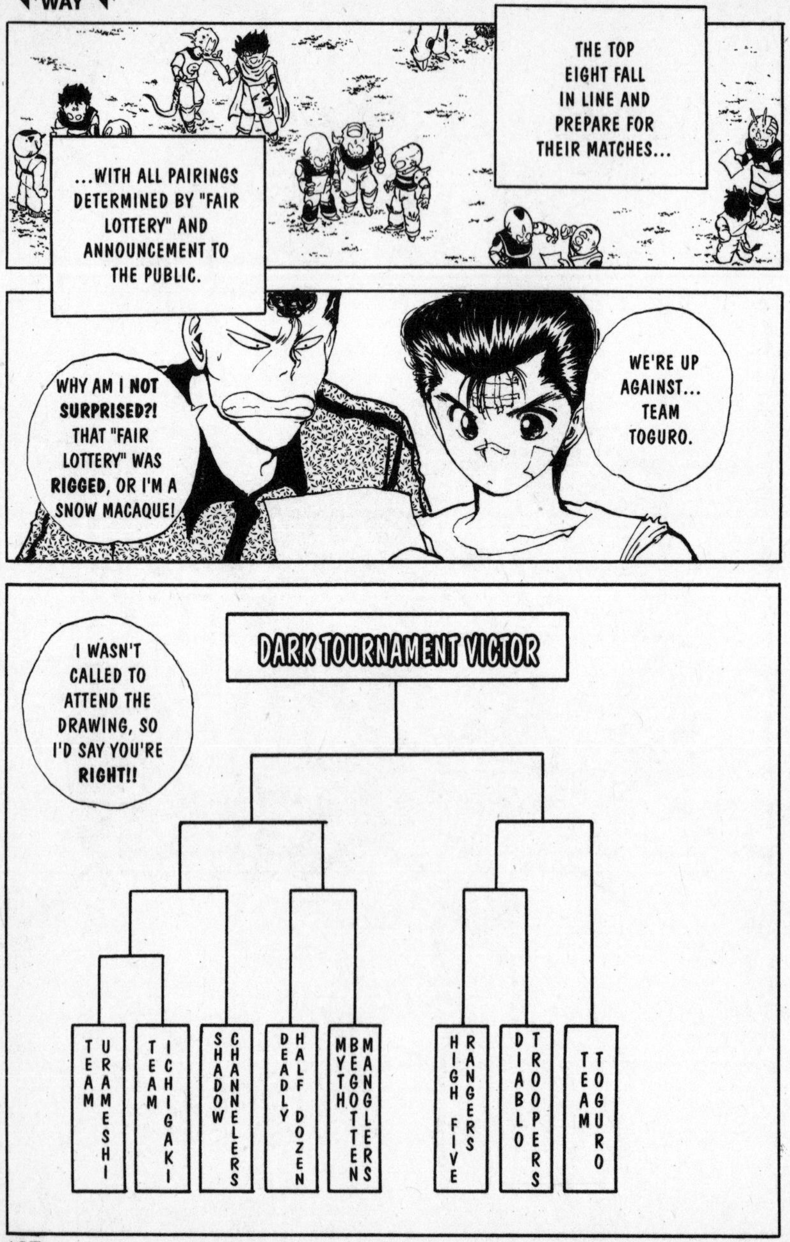

THE TOP EIGHT FALL IN LINE AND PREPARE FOR THEIR MATCHES...
...WITH ALL PAIRINGS DETERMINED BY "FAIR LOTTERY" AND ANNOUNCEMENT TO THE PUBLIC.
WE'RE UP AGAINST... TEAM TOGURO.
WHY AM I **NOT SURPRISED?!** THAT "FAIR LOTTERY" WAS **RIGGED**, OR I'M A SNOW MACAQUE!
I WASN'T CALLED TO ATTEND THE DRAWING, SO I'D SAY YOU'RE **RIGHT!!**
DARK TOURNAMENT VICTOR
TEAM URAMESHI
TEAM ICHIGAKI
SHADOW CHANNELERS
DEADLY HALF DOZEN
MYTHBEGOTTEN MANGLERS
HIGH FIVE RANGERS
DIABLO TROOPERS
TEAM TOGURO

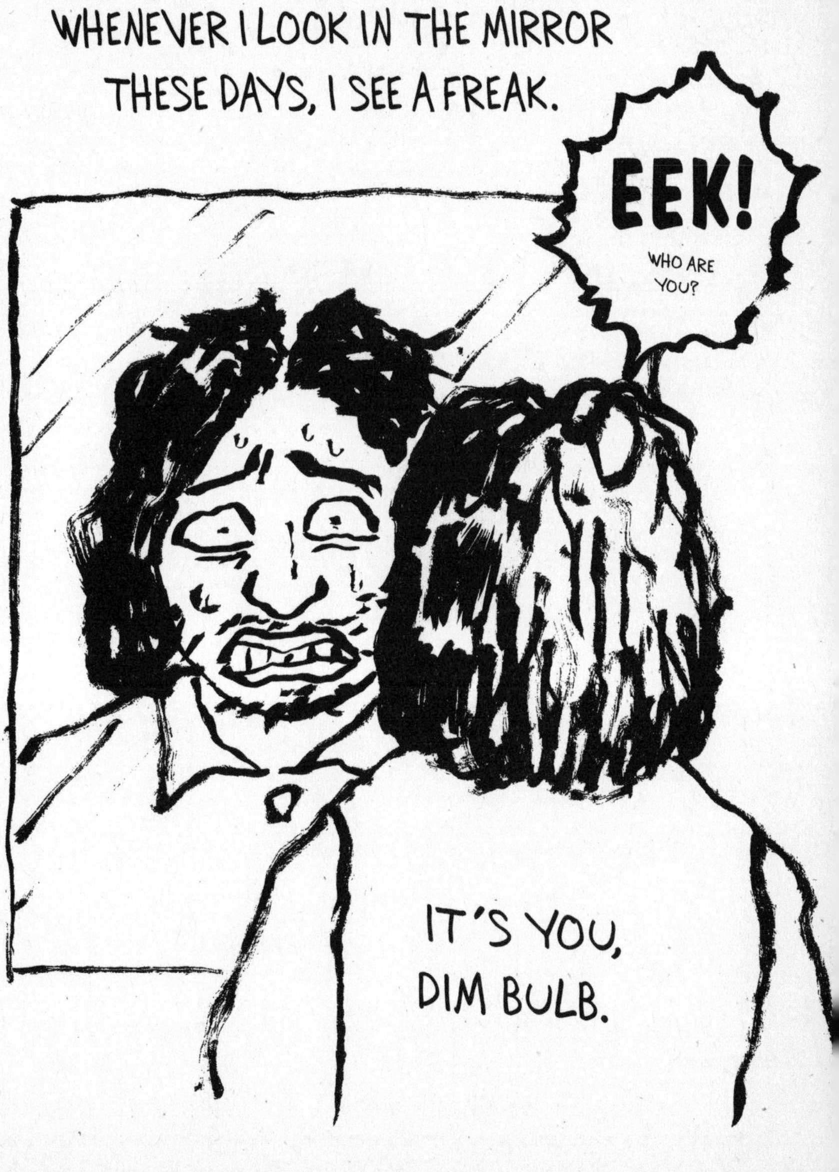
WHENEVER I LOOK IN THE MIRROR THESE DAYS, I SEE A FREAK.
EEK!
WHO ARE YOU?
IT'S YOU, DIM BULB.

THE SECOND ROUND BEGINS!!

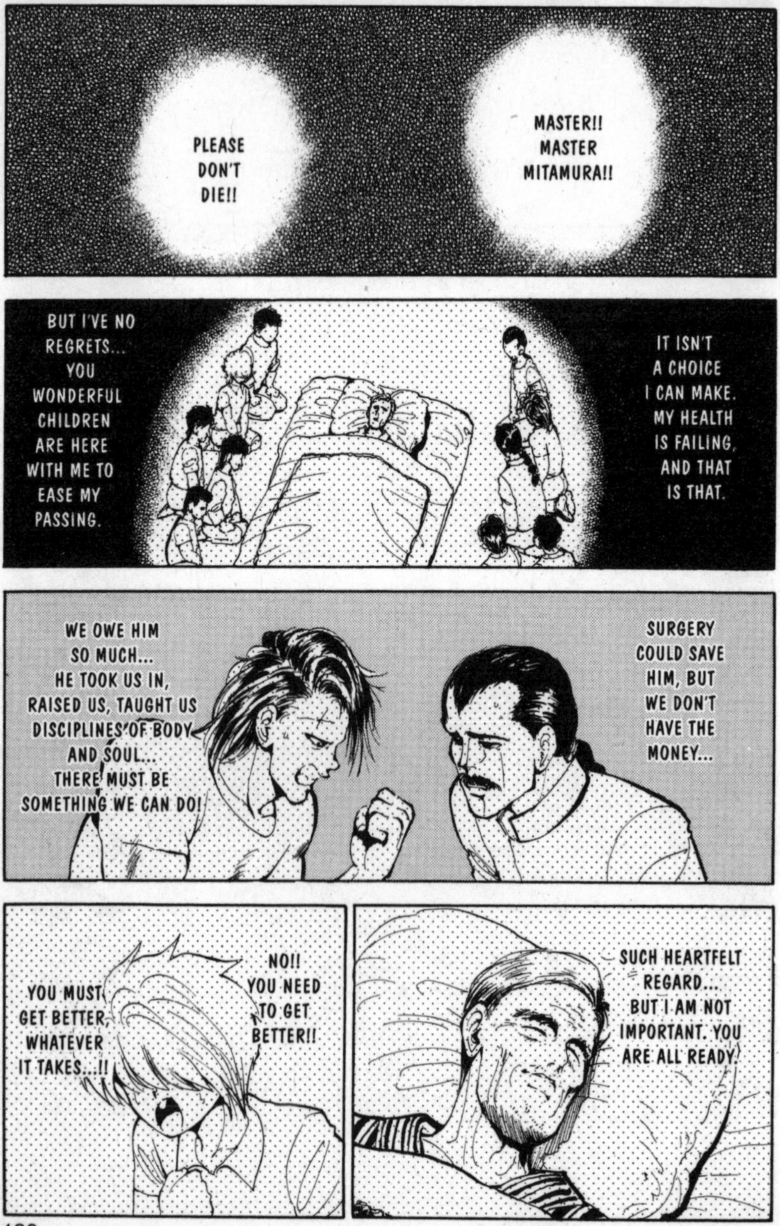
MASTER!! MASTER MITAMURA!!
PLEASE DON'T DIE!!
IT ISN'T A CHOICE I CAN MAKE. MY HEALTH IS FAILING, AND THAT IS THAT.
BUT I'VE NO REGRETS... YOU WONDERFUL CHILDREN ARE HERE WITH ME TO EASE MY PASSING.
SURGERY COULD SAVE HIM, BUT WE DON'T HAVE THE MONEY...
WE OWE HIM SO MUCH... HE TOOK US IN, RAISED US, TAUGHT US DISCIPLINES OF BODY AND SOUL... THERE MUST BE SOMETHING WE CAN DO!
SUCH HEARTFELT REGARD... BUT I AM NOT IMPORTANT. YOU ARE ALL READY.
NO!! YOU NEED TO GET BETTER!!
YOU MUST GET BETTER, WHATEVER IT TAKES...!!

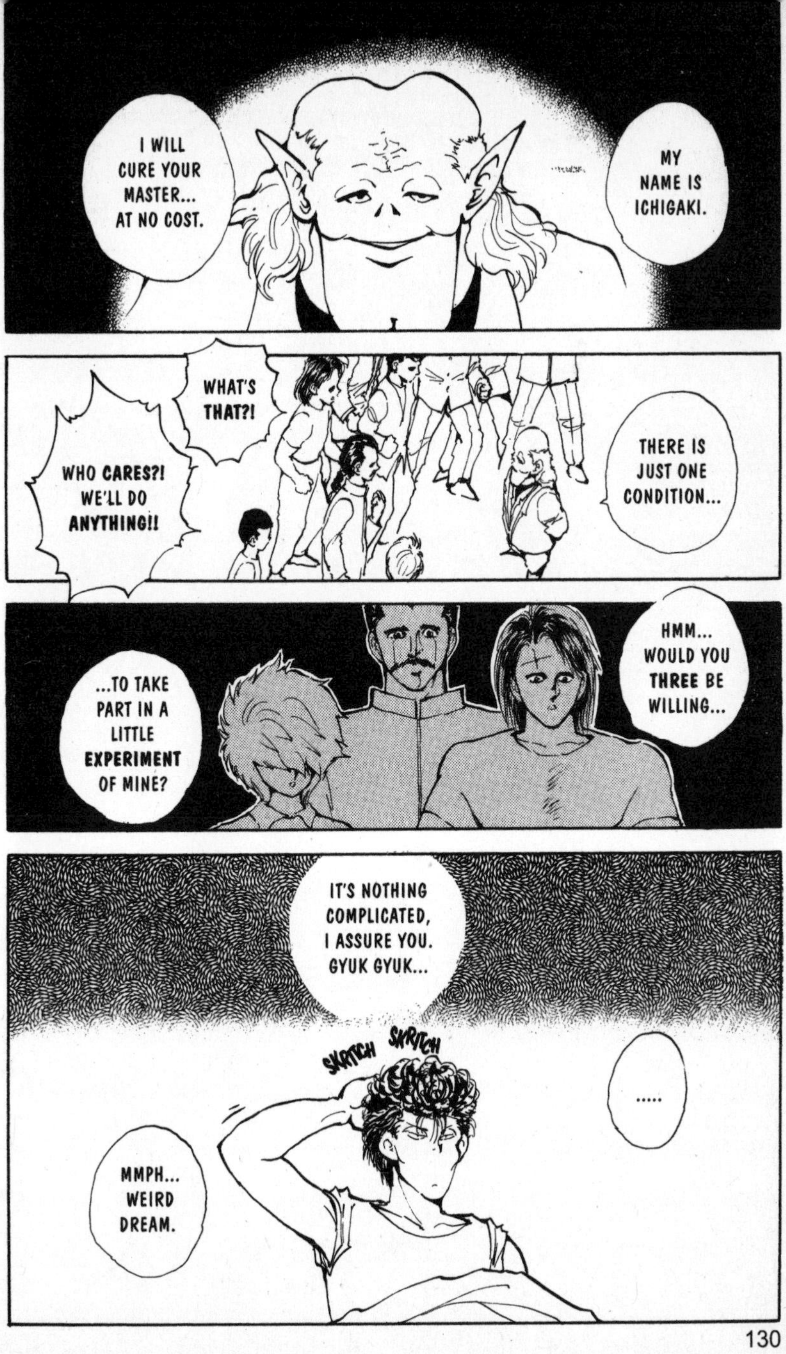
MY NAME IS ICHIGAKI.
I WILL CURE YOUR MASTER... AT NO COST.
THERE IS JUST ONE CONDITION...
WHAT'S THAT?!
WHO CARES?! WE'LL DO ANYTHING!!
HMM... WOULD YOU THREE BE WILLING...
...TO TAKE PART IN A LITTLE EXPERIMENT OF MINE?
IT'S NOTHING COMPLICATED, I ASSURE YOU. GYUK GYUK...
.....
SKRITCH SKRITCH
MMPH... WEIRD DREAM.

READ THIS WAY

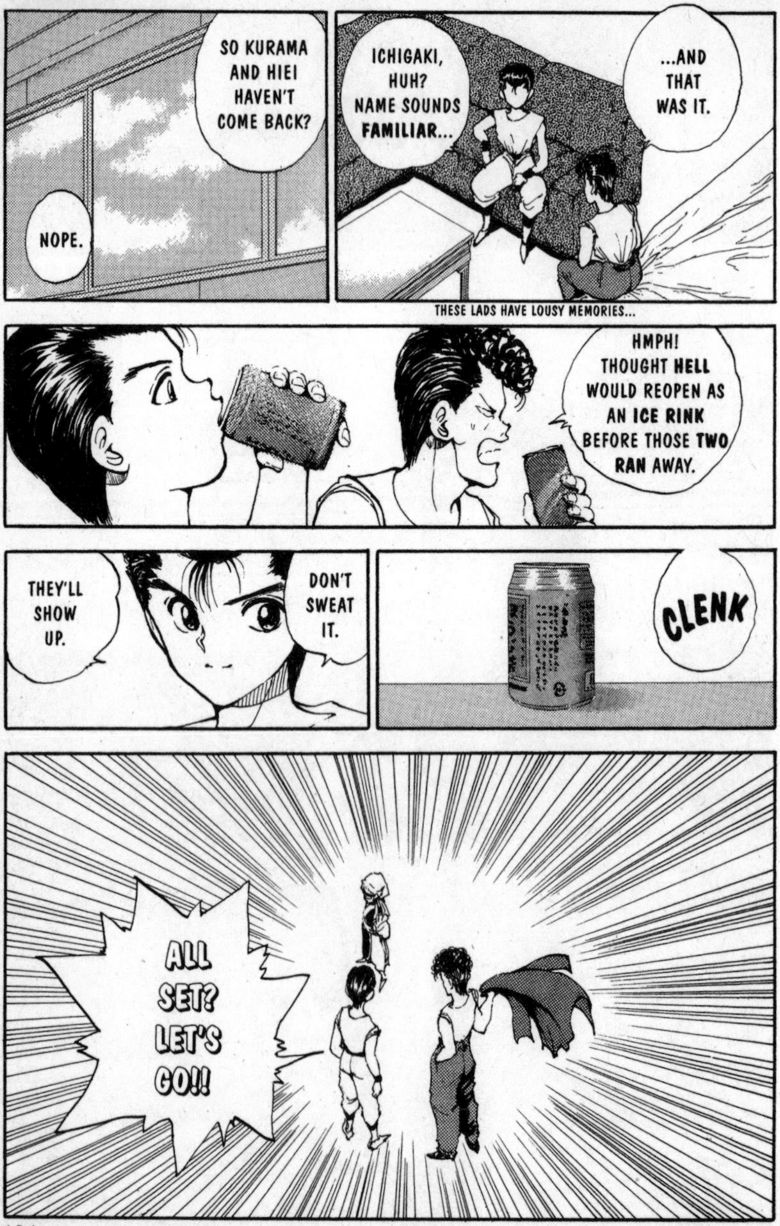

...AND THAT WAS IT.
ICHIGAKI, HUH? NAME SOUNDS FAMILIAR...
SO KURAMA AND HIEI HAVEN'T COME BACK?
NOPE.
THESE LADS HAVE LOUSY MEMORIES...
HMPH! THOUGHT HELL WOULD REOPEN AS AN ICE RINK BEFORE THOSE TWO RAN AWAY.
CLENK
DON'T SWEAT IT.
THEY'LL SHOW UP.
ALL SET? LET'S GO!!

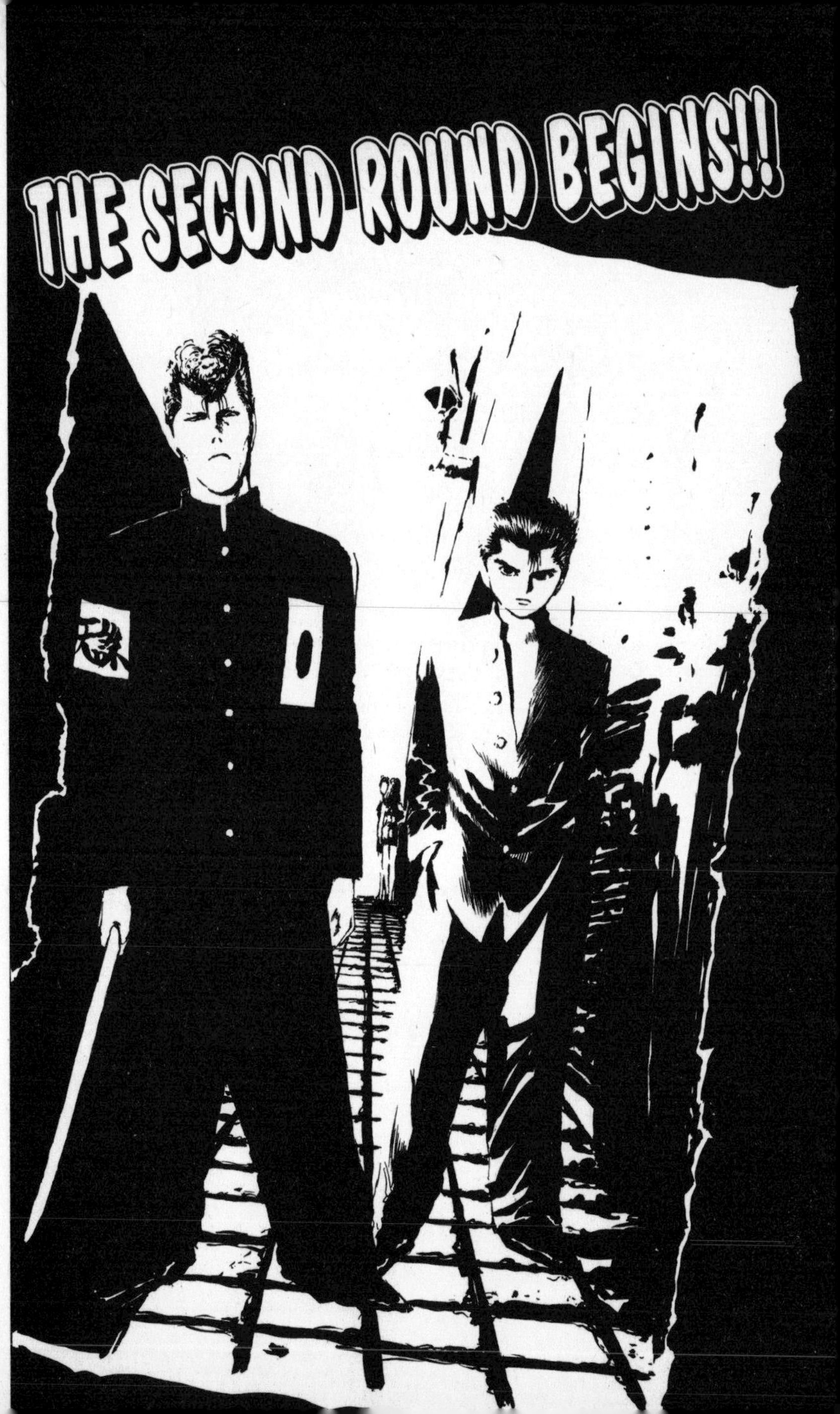
THE SECOND ROUND BEGINS!!

READ THIS WAY

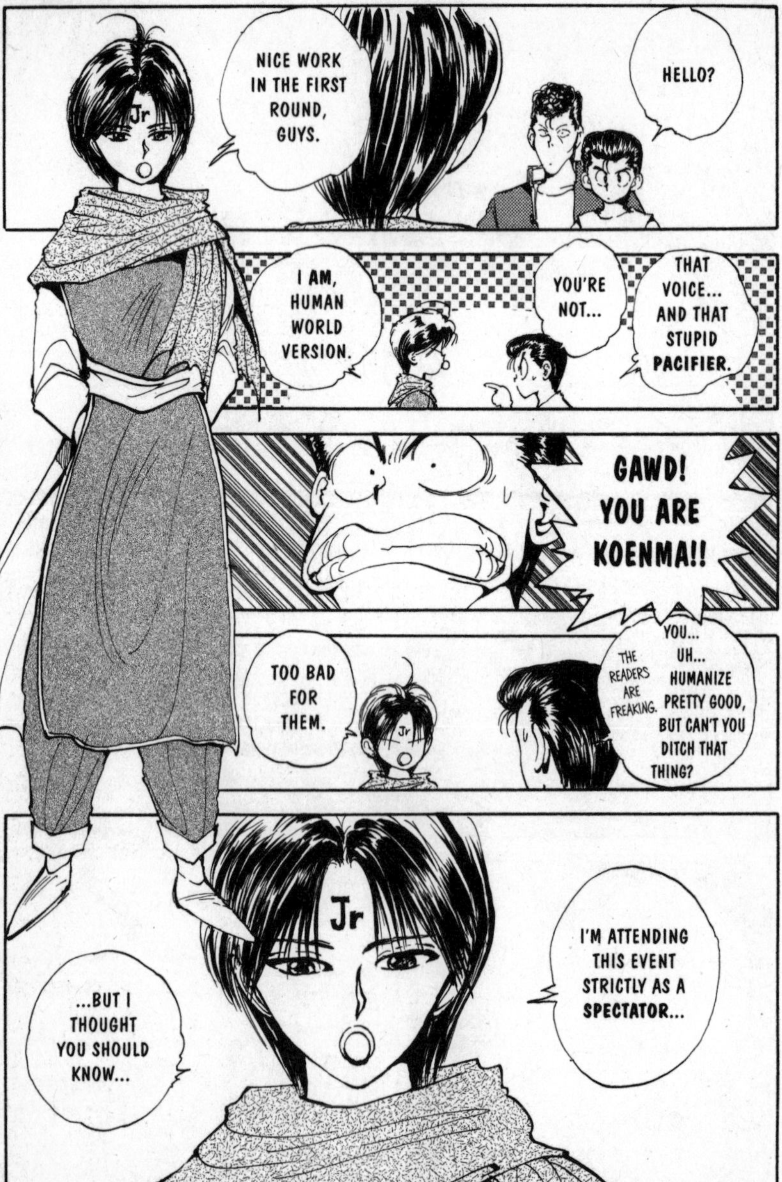
HELLO?
NICE WORK IN THE FIRST ROUND, GUYS.
THAT VOICE... AND THAT STUPID PACIFIER.
YOU'RE NOT...
I AM, HUMAN WORLD VERSION.
GAWD! YOU ARE KOENMA!!
YOU... UH... HUMANIZE PRETTY GOOD, BUT CAN'T YOU DITCH THAT THING?
THE READERS ARE FREAKING.
TOO BAD FOR THEM.
I'M ATTENDING THIS EVENT STRICTLY AS A SPECTATOR...
...BUT I THOUGHT YOU SHOULD KNOW...

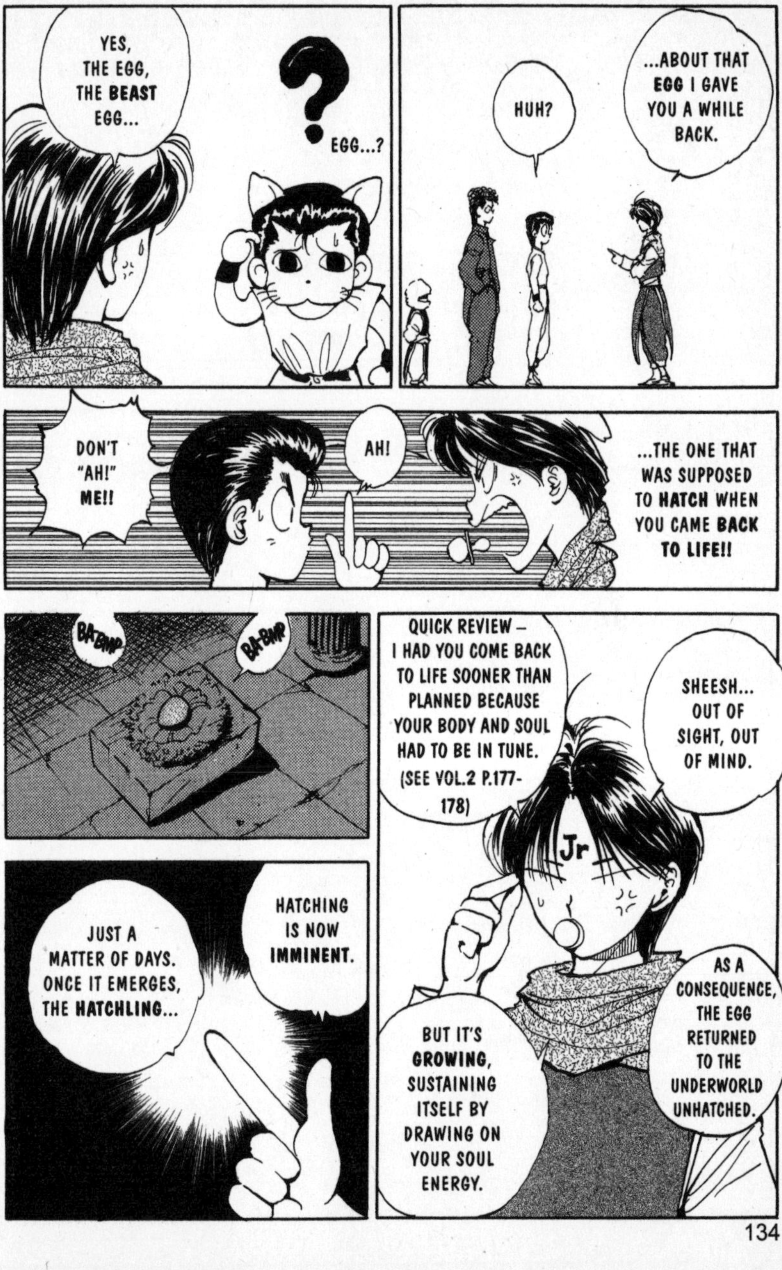
...ABOUT THAT EGG I GAVE YOU A WHILE BACK.
HUH?
YES, THE EGG, THE BEAST EGG...
EGG...?
...THE ONE THAT WAS SUPPOSED TO HATCH WHEN YOU CAME BACK TO LIFE!!
AH!
DON'T "AH!" ME!!
SHEESH... OUT OF SIGHT, OUT OF MIND.
QUICK REVIEW – I HAD YOU COME BACK TO LIFE SOONER THAN PLANNED BECAUSE YOUR BODY AND SOUL HAD TO BE IN TUNE. (SEE VOL.2 P.177-178)
Jr
AS A CONSEQUENCE, THE EGG RETURNED TO THE UNDERWORLD UNHATCHED.
BUT IT'S GROWING, SUSTAINING ITSELF BY DRAWING ON YOUR SOUL ENERGY.
BA-BMP
BA-BMP
HATCHING IS NOW IMMINENT.
JUST A MATTER OF DAYS. ONCE IT EMERGES, THE HATCHLING...

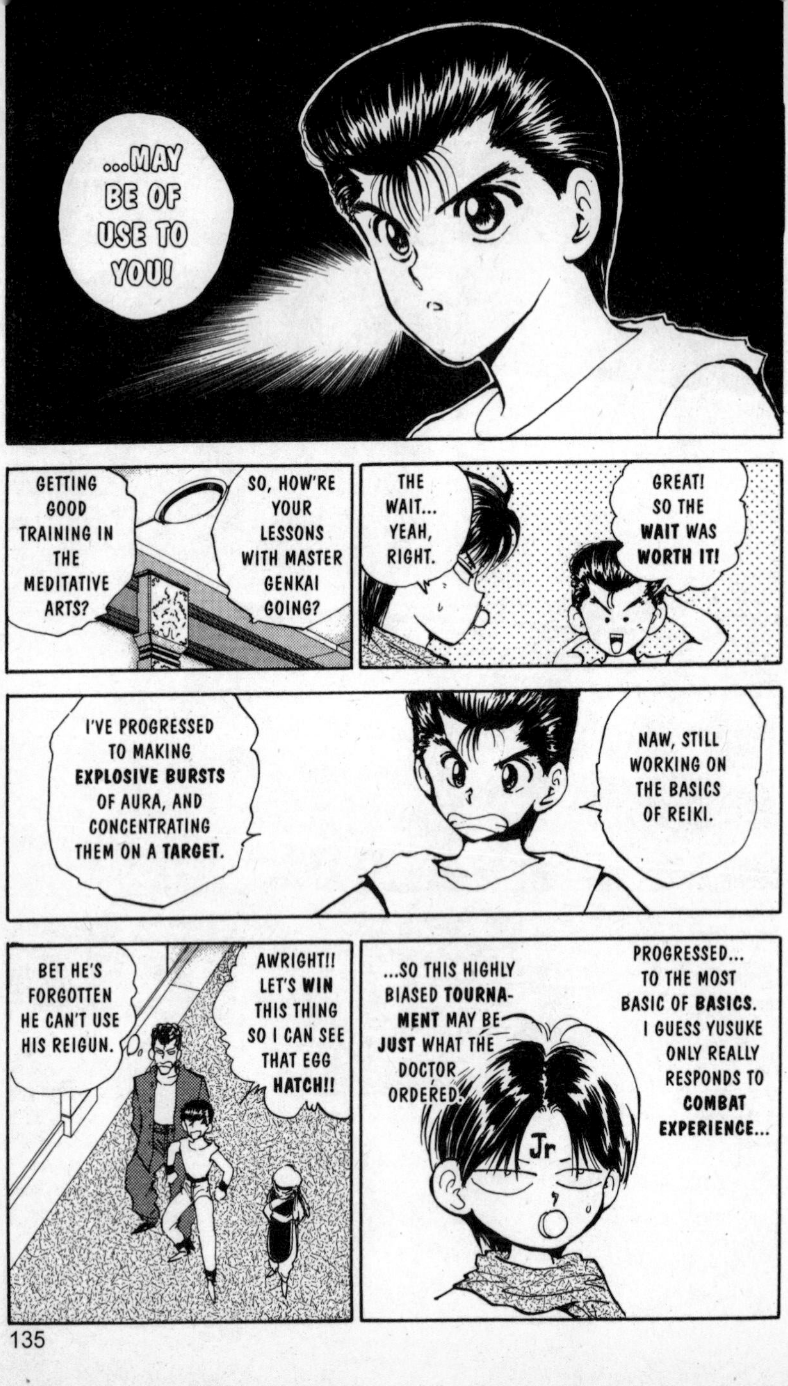

...MAY BE OF USE TO YOU!
GREAT! SO THE WAIT WAS WORTH IT!
THE WAIT... YEAH, RIGHT.
SO, HOW'RE YOUR LESSONS WITH MASTER GENKAI GOING?
GETTING GOOD TRAINING IN THE MEDITATIVE ARTS?
NAW, STILL WORKING ON THE BASICS OF REIKI.
I'VE PROGRESSED TO MAKING EXPLOSIVE BURSTS OF AURA, AND CONCENTRATING THEM ON A TARGET.
PROGRESSED... TO THE MOST BASIC OF BASICS. I GUESS YUSUKE ONLY REALLY RESPONDS TO COMBAT EXPERIENCE...
...SO THIS HIGHLY BIASED TOURNAMENT MAY BE JUST WHAT THE DOCTOR ORDERED.
Jr
AWRIGHT!! LET'S WIN THIS THING SO I CAN SEE THAT EGG HATCH!!
BET HE'S FORGOTTEN HE CAN'T USE HIS REIGUN.

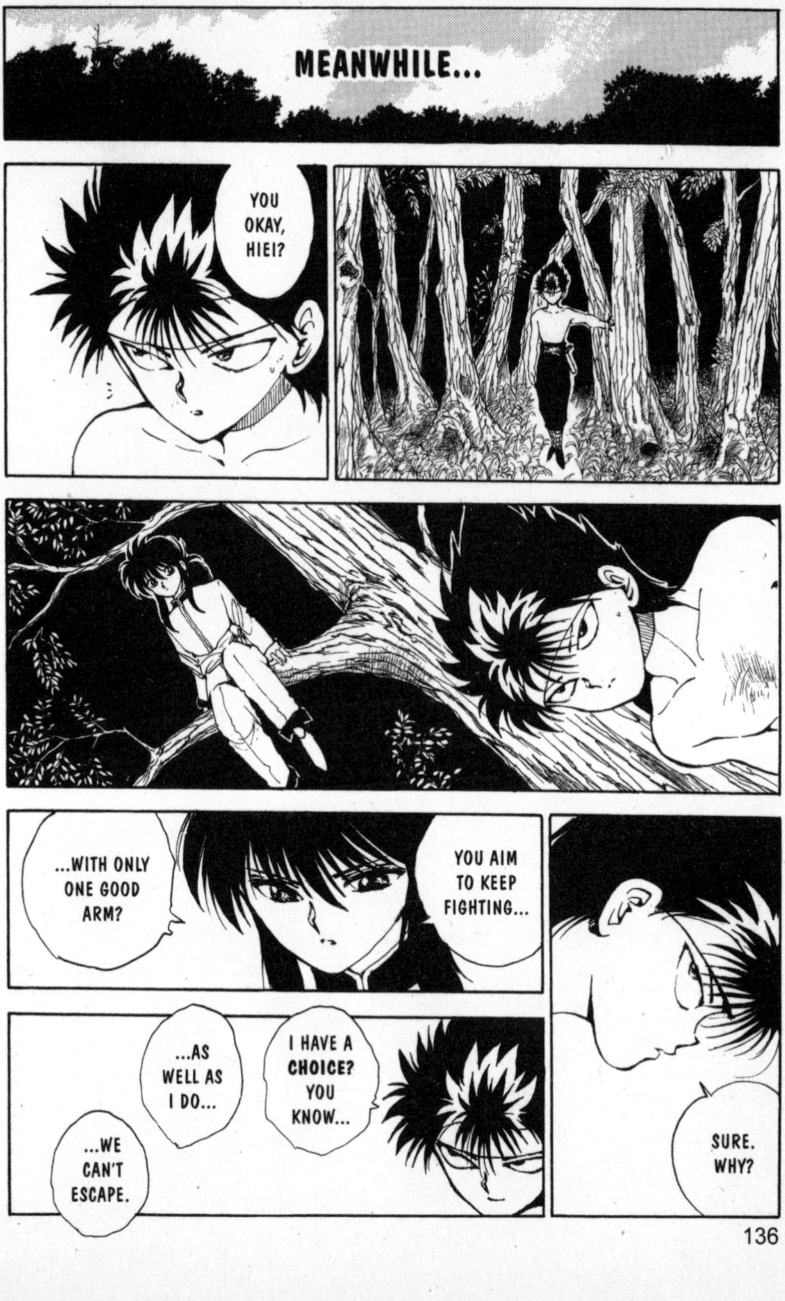
MEANWHILE...
YOU OKAY, HIEI?
SURE. WHY?
YOU AIM TO KEEP FIGHTING...
...WITH ONLY ONE GOOD ARM?
I HAVE A CHOICE? YOU KNOW...
...AS WELL AS I DO...
...WE CAN'T ESCAPE.

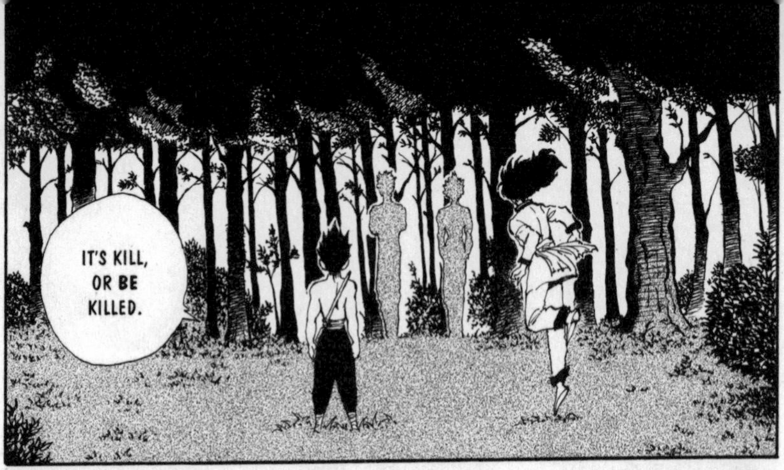
IT'S KILL, OR BE KILLED.

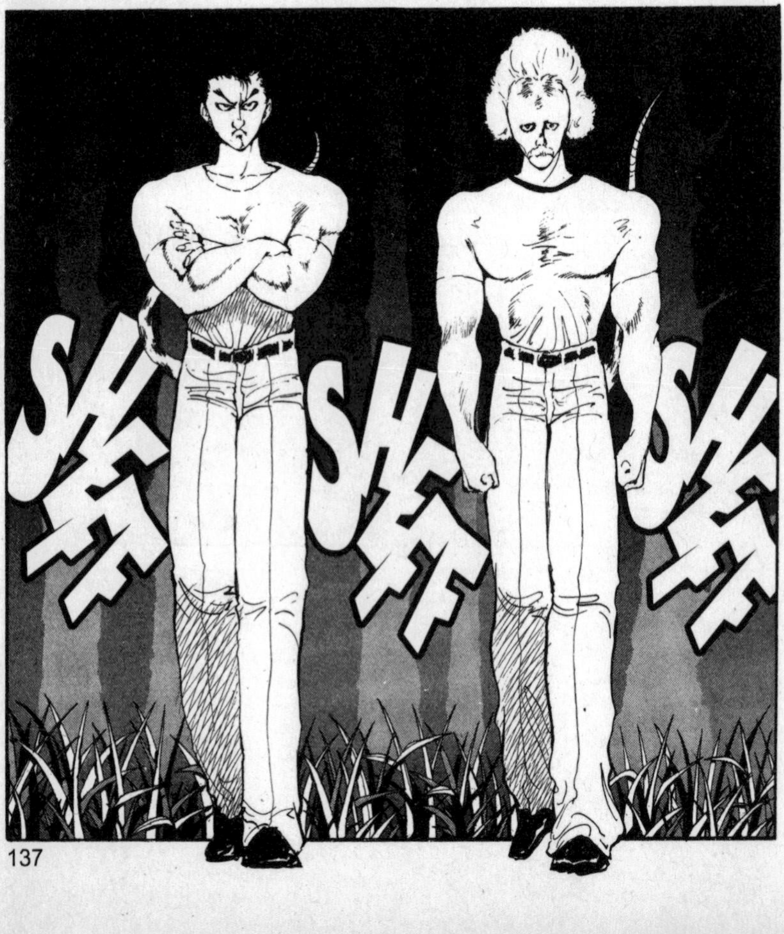
SHFF
SHFF
SHFF

HEY! WHAT'S GOIN' ON?
THOSE TEAMS AIN'T COMPLETE!
RAAAH
RAAAH
RAAAH
RAAAH
THOSE GUYS, THEY'RE...
...RIGHT OUTTA MY DREAM!!
IT'S TIME!! BOTH TEAMS, STEP FORWARD!!

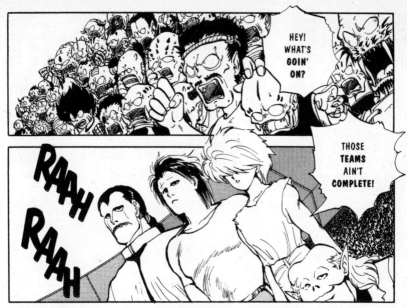

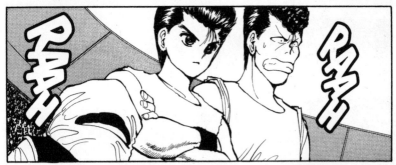

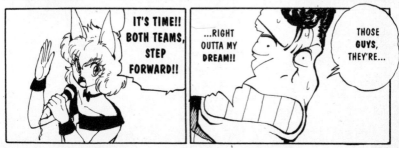

READ THIS WAY

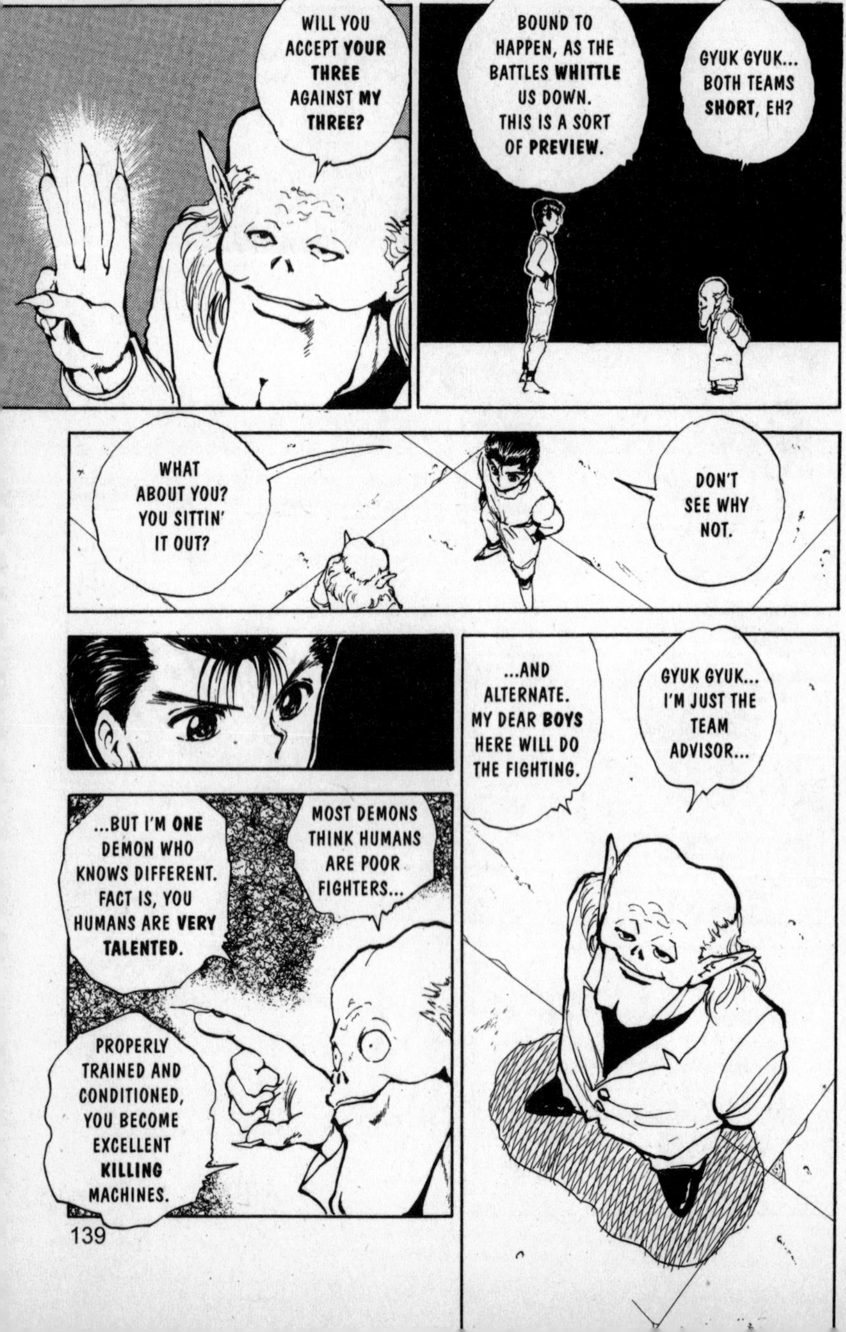
GYUK GYUK... BOTH TEAMS SHORT, EH?
BOUND TO HAPPEN, AS THE BATTLES WHITTLE US DOWN. THIS IS A SORT OF PREVIEW.
WILL YOU ACCEPT YOUR THREE AGAINST MY THREE?
DON'T SEE WHY NOT.
WHAT ABOUT YOU? YOU SITTIN' IT OUT?
GYUK GYUK... I'M JUST THE TEAM ADVISOR...
...AND ALTERNATE. MY DEAR BOYS HERE WILL DO THE FIGHTING.
MOST DEMONS THINK HUMANS ARE POOR FIGHTERS...
...BUT I'M ONE DEMON WHO KNOWS DIFFERENT. FACT IS, YOU HUMANS ARE VERY TALENTED.
PROPERLY TRAINED AND CONDITIONED, YOU BECOME EXCELLENT KILLING MACHINES.

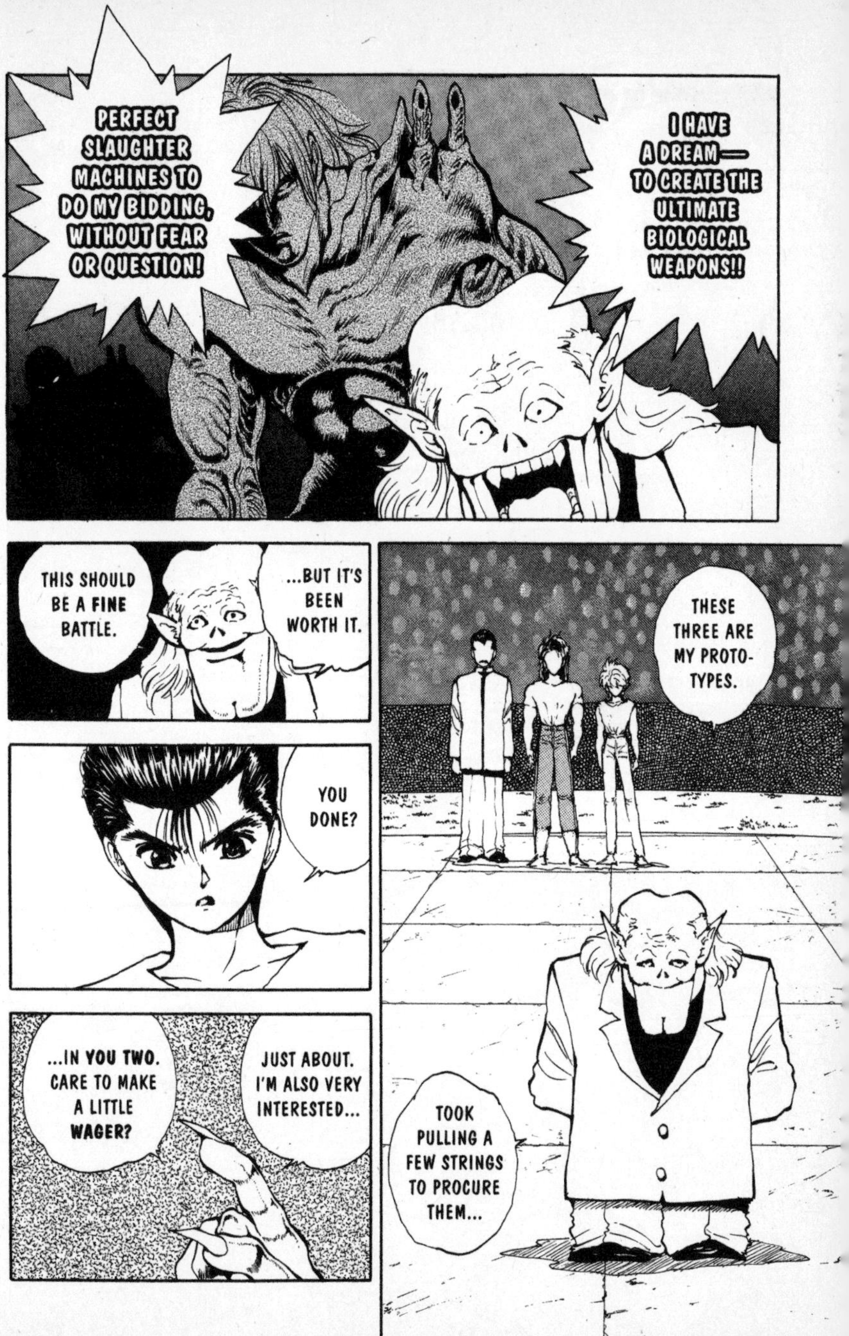
I HAVE A DREAM— TO CREATE THE ULTIMATE BIOLOGICAL WEAPONS!!
PERFECT SLAUGHTER MACHINES TO DO MY BIDDING, WITHOUT FEAR OR QUESTION!
THESE THREE ARE MY PROTO-TYPES.
TOOK PULLING A FEW STRINGS TO PROCURE THEM...
...BUT IT'S BEEN WORTH IT.
THIS SHOULD BE A FINE BATTLE.
YOU DONE?
JUST ABOUT. I'M ALSO VERY INTERESTED...
...IN YOU TWO. CARE TO MAKE A LITTLE WAGER?

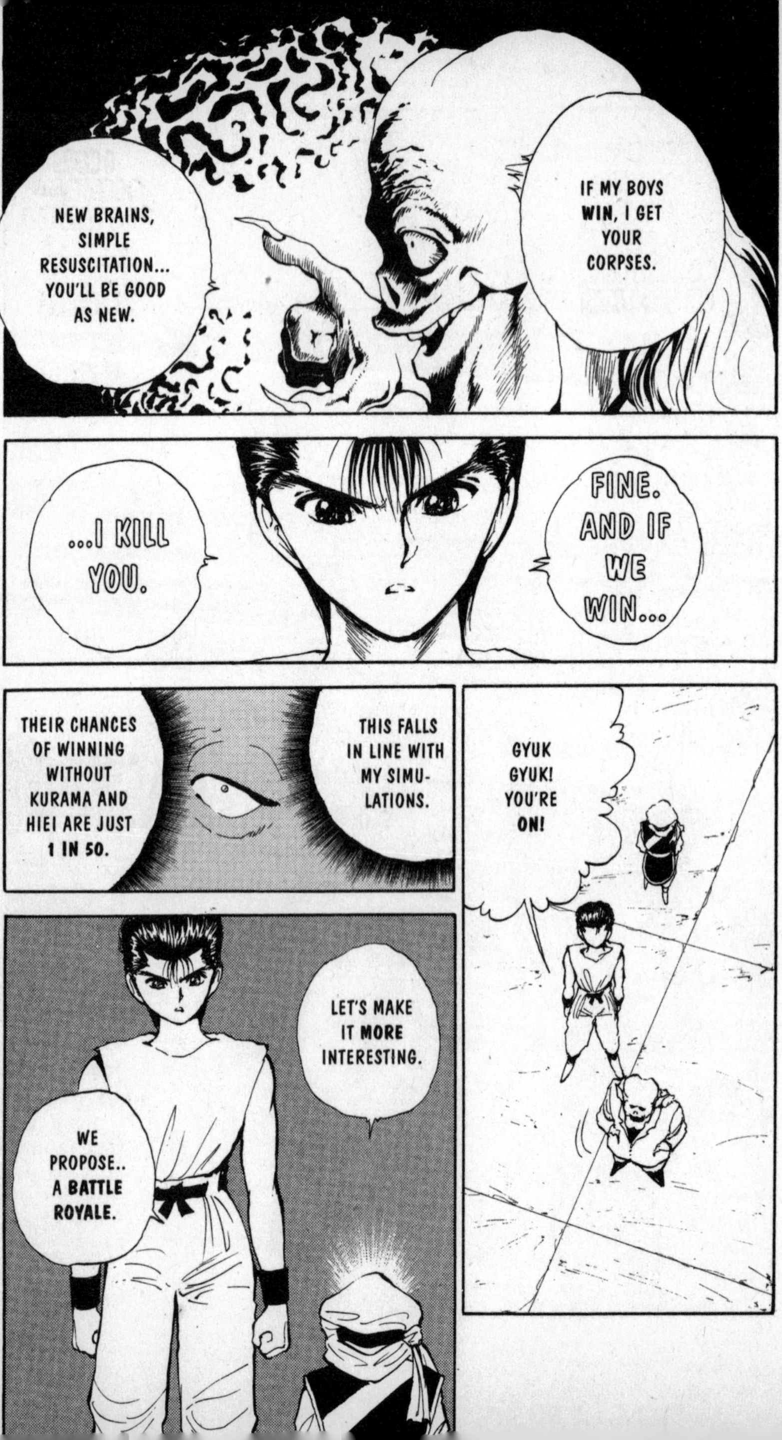
IF MY BOYS WIN, I GET YOUR CORPSES.
NEW BRAINS, SIMPLE RESUSCITATION... YOU'LL BE GOOD AS NEW.
FINE. AND IF WE WIN...
...I KILL YOU.
GYUK GYUK! YOU'RE ON!
THIS FALLS IN LINE WITH MY SIMU-LATIONS.
THEIR CHANCES OF WINNING WITHOUT KURAMA AND HIEI ARE JUST 1 IN 50.
LET'S MAKE IT MORE INTERESTING.
WE PROPOSE.. A BATTLE ROYALE.

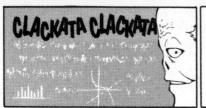

CLACKATA CLACKATA
DING
CHANCE OF VICTORY: 99.95%
GYUK GYUK! WE ACCEPT!
WHY NOT?! THEY'VE JUST DUG THEIR OWN GRAVES!!
INDIVIDUALLY, MY BOYS ARE FORMIDABLE! WORKING AS A TEAM, THEY'RE 1,020 TIMES MORE POWERFUL! TEAM YUSUKE IS DOOMED!!

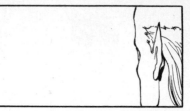

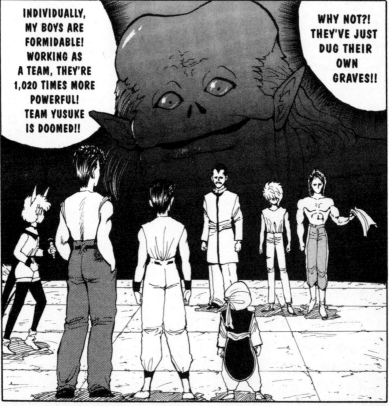

READ THIS WAY

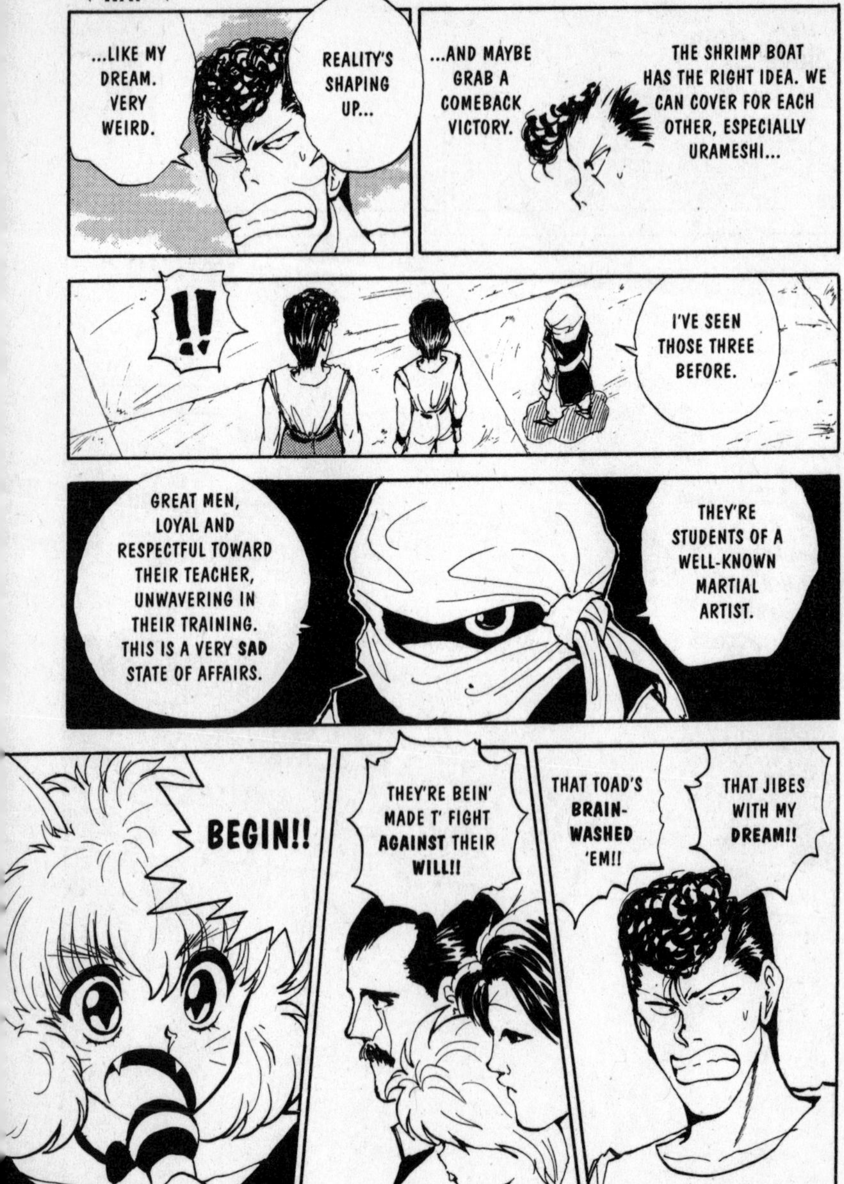

THE SHRIMP BOAT HAS THE RIGHT IDEA. WE CAN COVER FOR EACH OTHER, ESPECIALLY URAMESHI...
...AND MAYBE GRAB A COMEBACK VICTORY.
REALITY'S SHAPING UP...
...LIKE MY DREAM. VERY WEIRD.
I'VE SEEN THOSE THREE BEFORE.
!!
THEY'RE STUDENTS OF A WELL-KNOWN MARTIAL ARTIST.
GREAT MEN, LOYAL AND RESPECTFUL TOWARD THEIR TEACHER, UNWAVERING IN THEIR TRAINING. THIS IS A VERY SAD STATE OF AFFAIRS.
THAT JIBES WITH MY DREAM!!
THAT TOAD'S BRAIN-WASHED 'EM!!
THEY'RE BEIN' MADE T' FIGHT AGAINST THEIR WILL!!
BEGIN!!

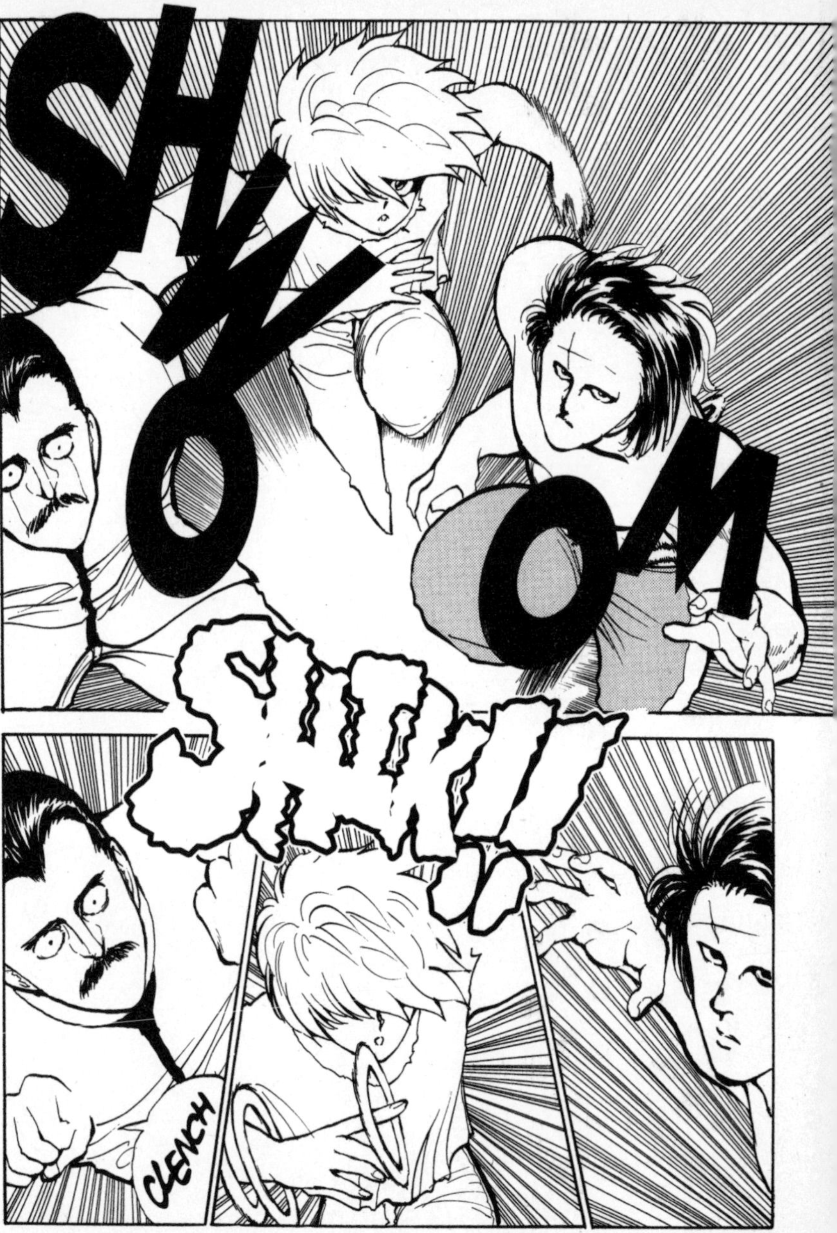
SHWOOM
SHAK!!
CLENCH

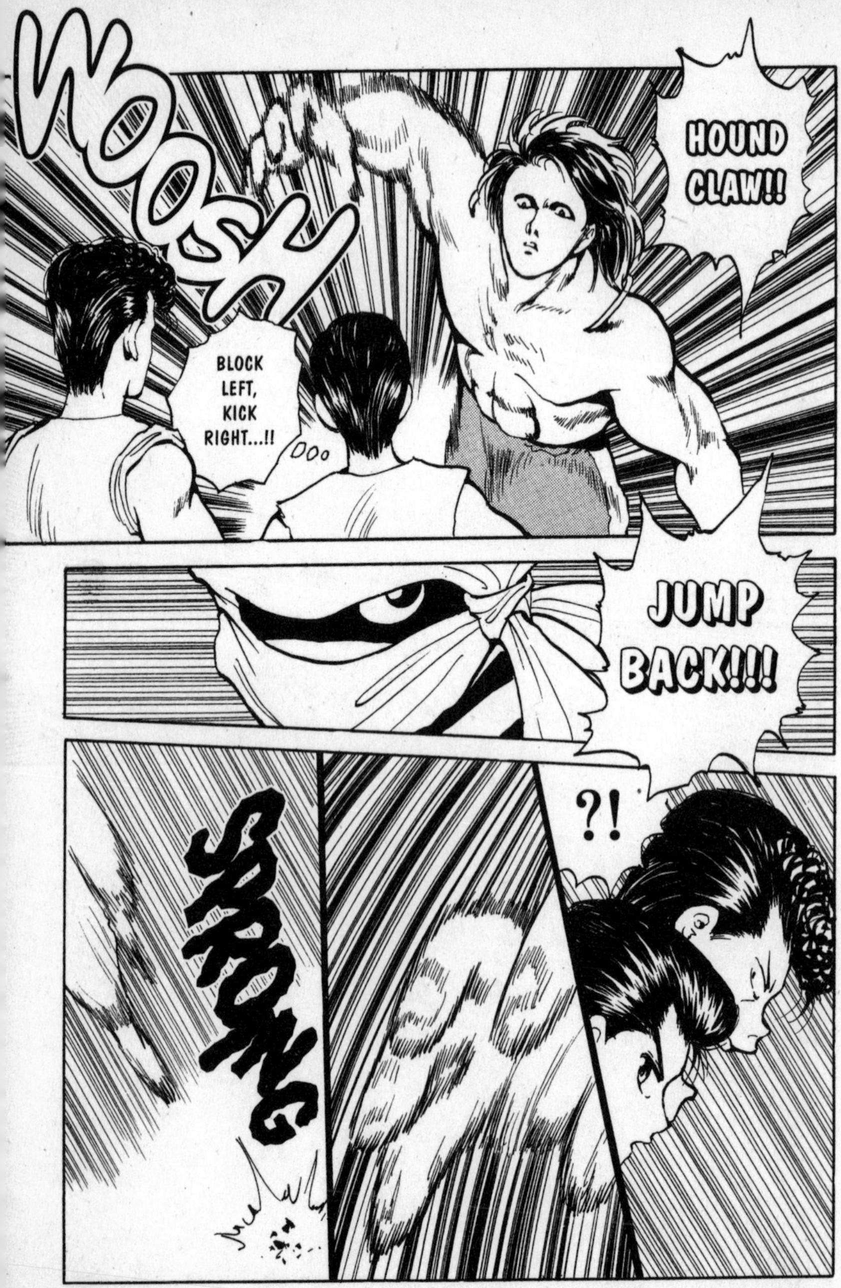
HOUND CLAW!!
WOOSH
BLOCK LEFT, KICK RIGHT...!!
Ooo
JUMP BACK!!!
?!
SKRONG

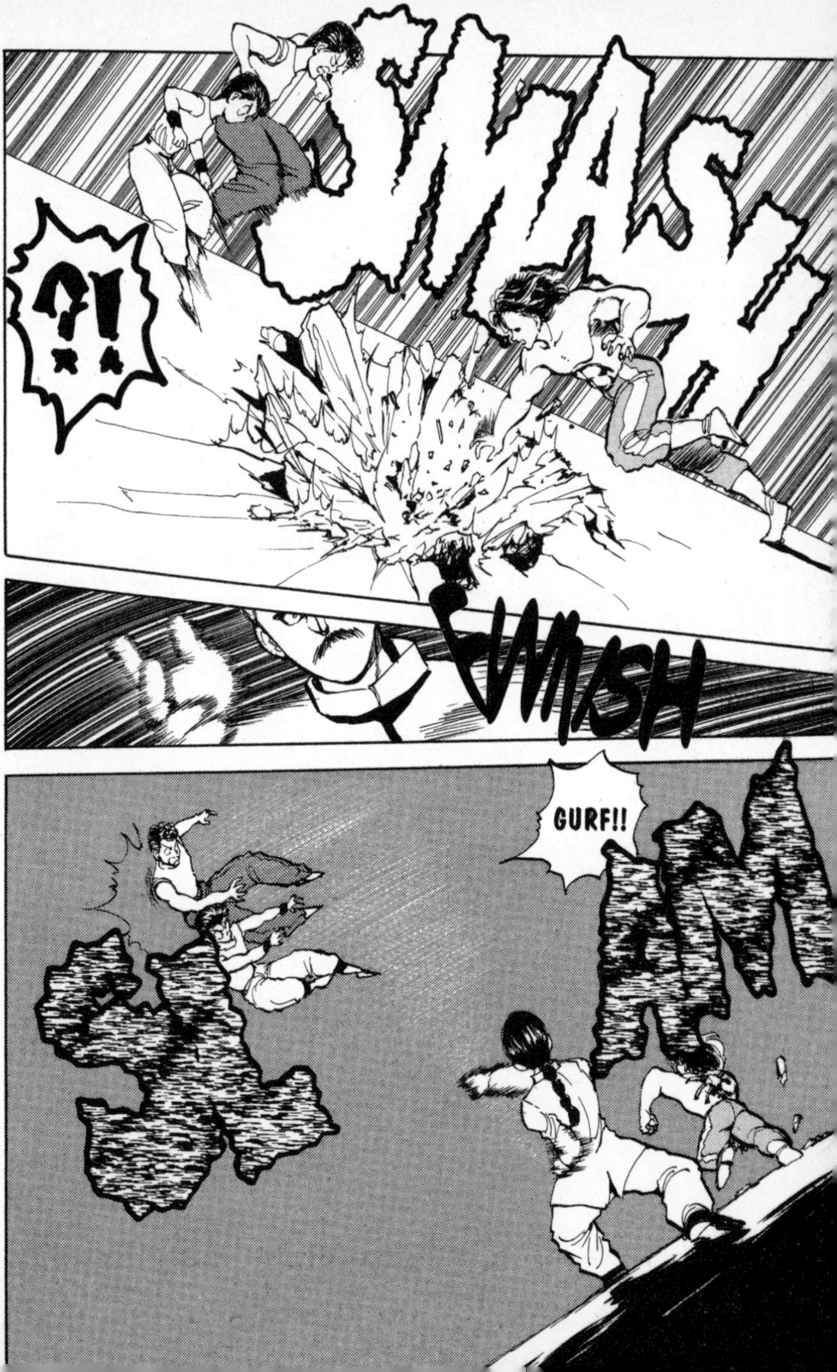
?!
GURF!!

READ THIS WAY

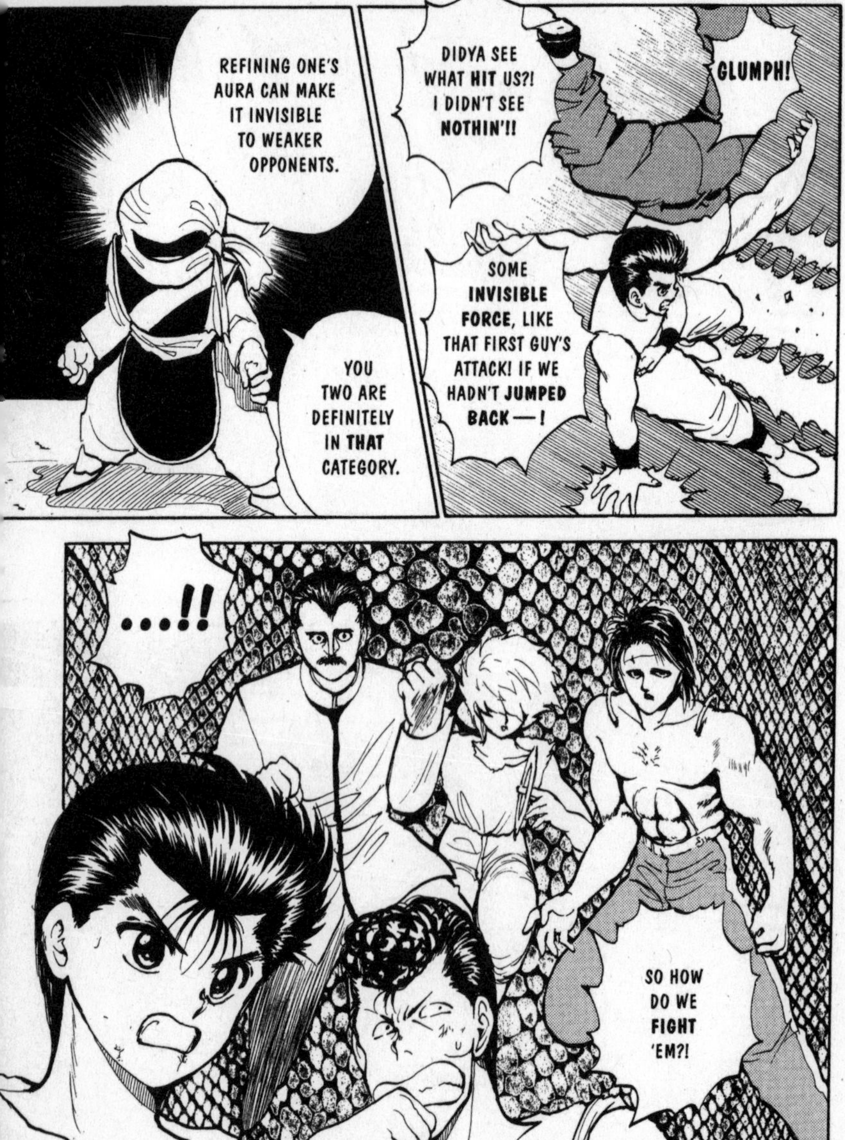
GLUMPH!
DIDYA SEE WHAT HIT US?! I DIDN'T SEE NOTHIN'!!
SOME INVISIBLE FORCE, LIKE THAT FIRST GUY'S ATTACK! IF WE HADN'T JUMPED BACK—!
REFINING ONE'S AURA CAN MAKE IT INVISIBLE TO WEAKER OPPONENTS.
YOU TWO ARE DEFINITELY IN THAT CATEGORY.
...!!
SO HOW DO WE FIGHT 'EM?!

TEST YOUR COLORING TALENT!

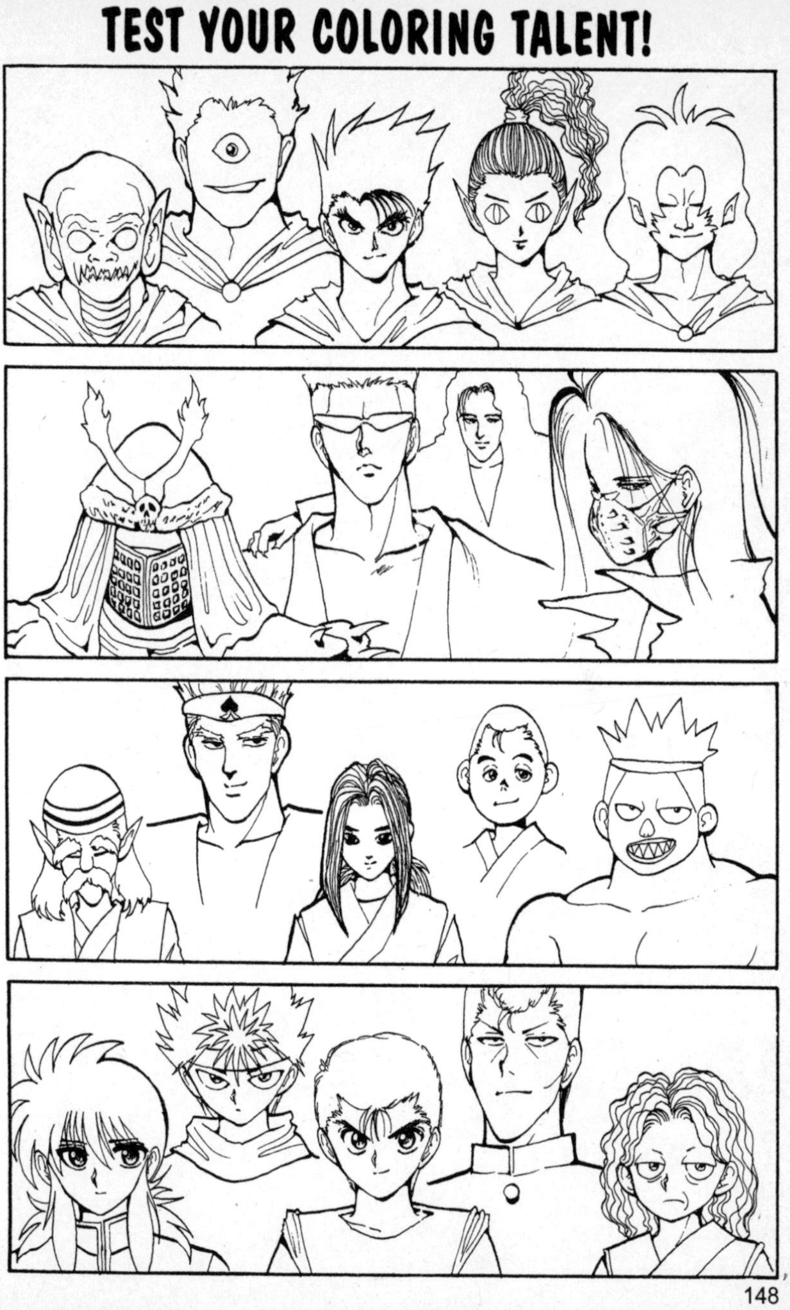

THE DESPICABLE BLOOD-SLAVER NODE!!

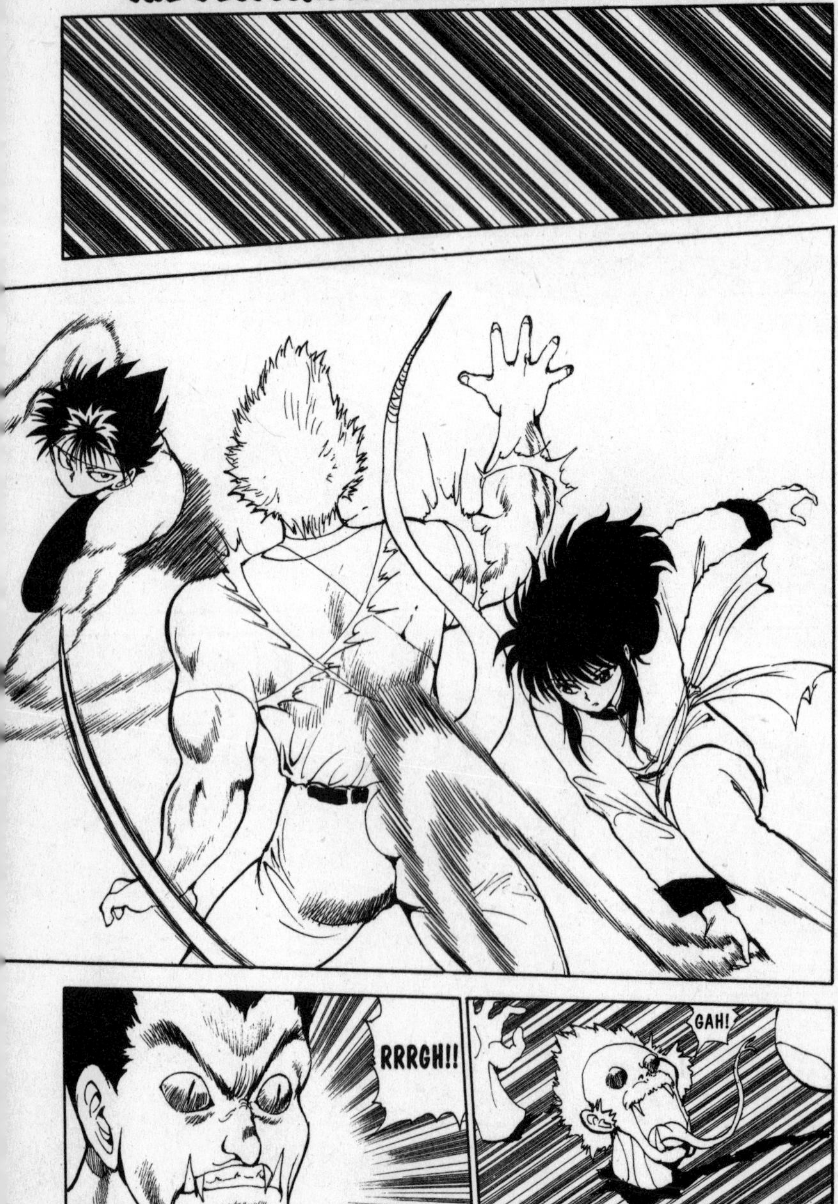
GAH!
RRRGH!!

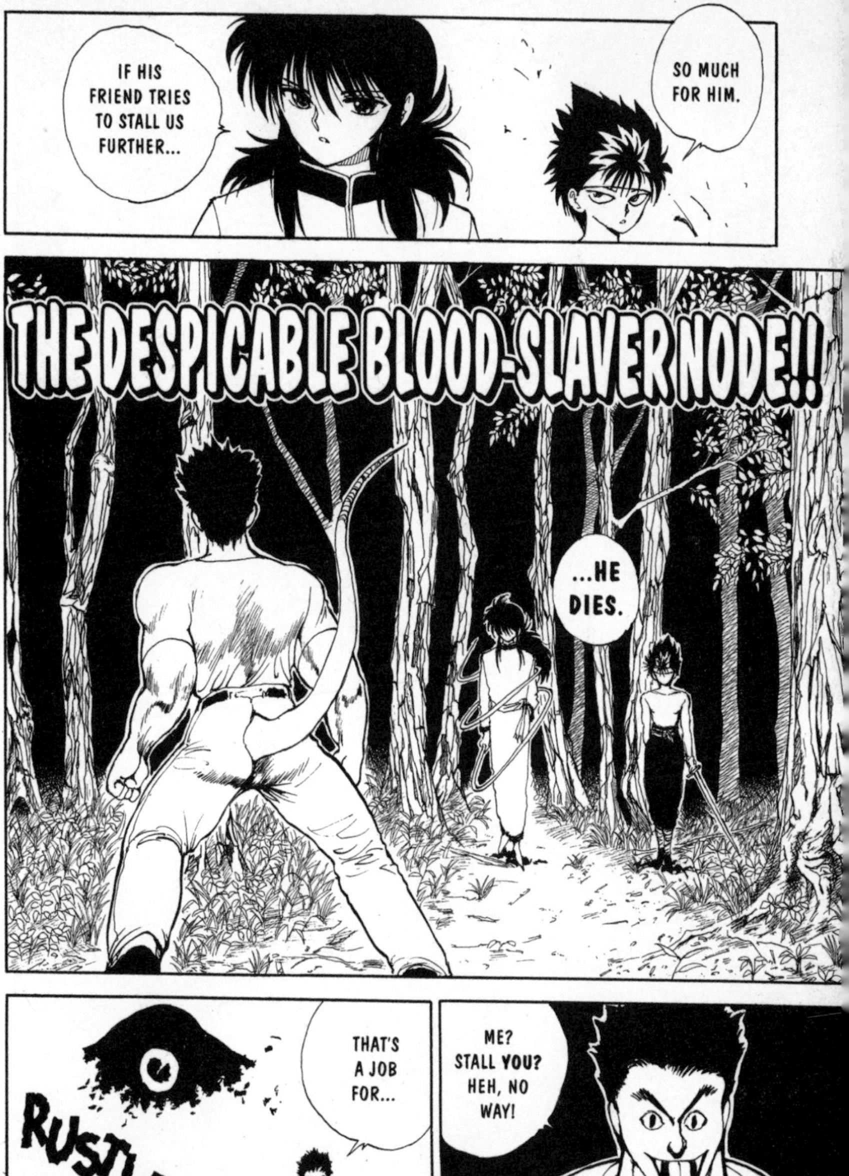
SO MUCH FOR HIM.
IF HIS FRIEND TRIES TO STALL US FURTHER...
THE DESPICABLE BLOOD-SLAVER NODE!!
...HE DIES.
ME? STALL YOU? HEH, NO WAY!
THAT'S A JOB FOR...
RUSTLE

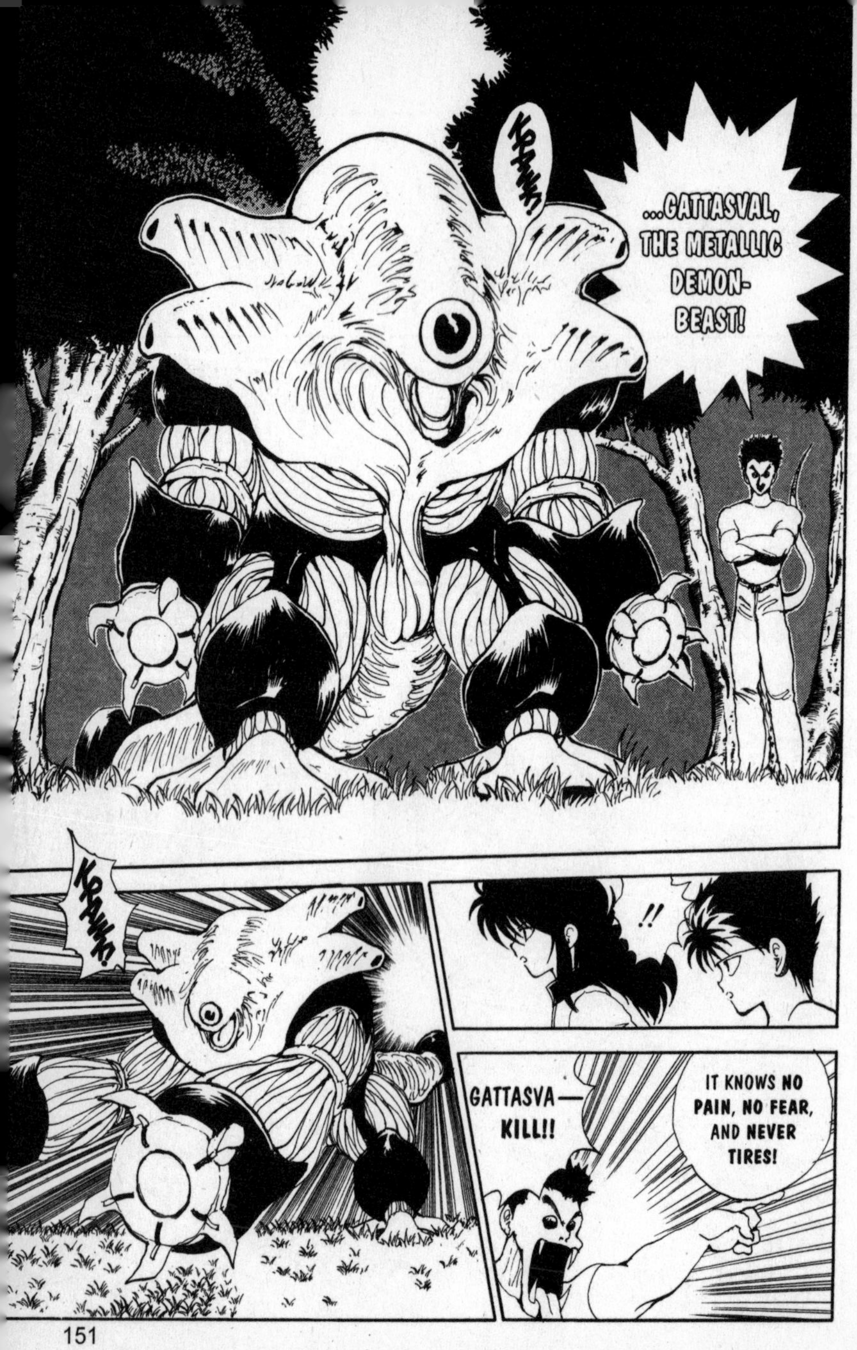
...GATTASVAL, THE METALLIC DEMON-BEAST!
KRAWK!
!!
IT KNOWS NO PAIN, NO FEAR, AND NEVER TIRES!
GATTASVA— KILL!!
KRAWK!

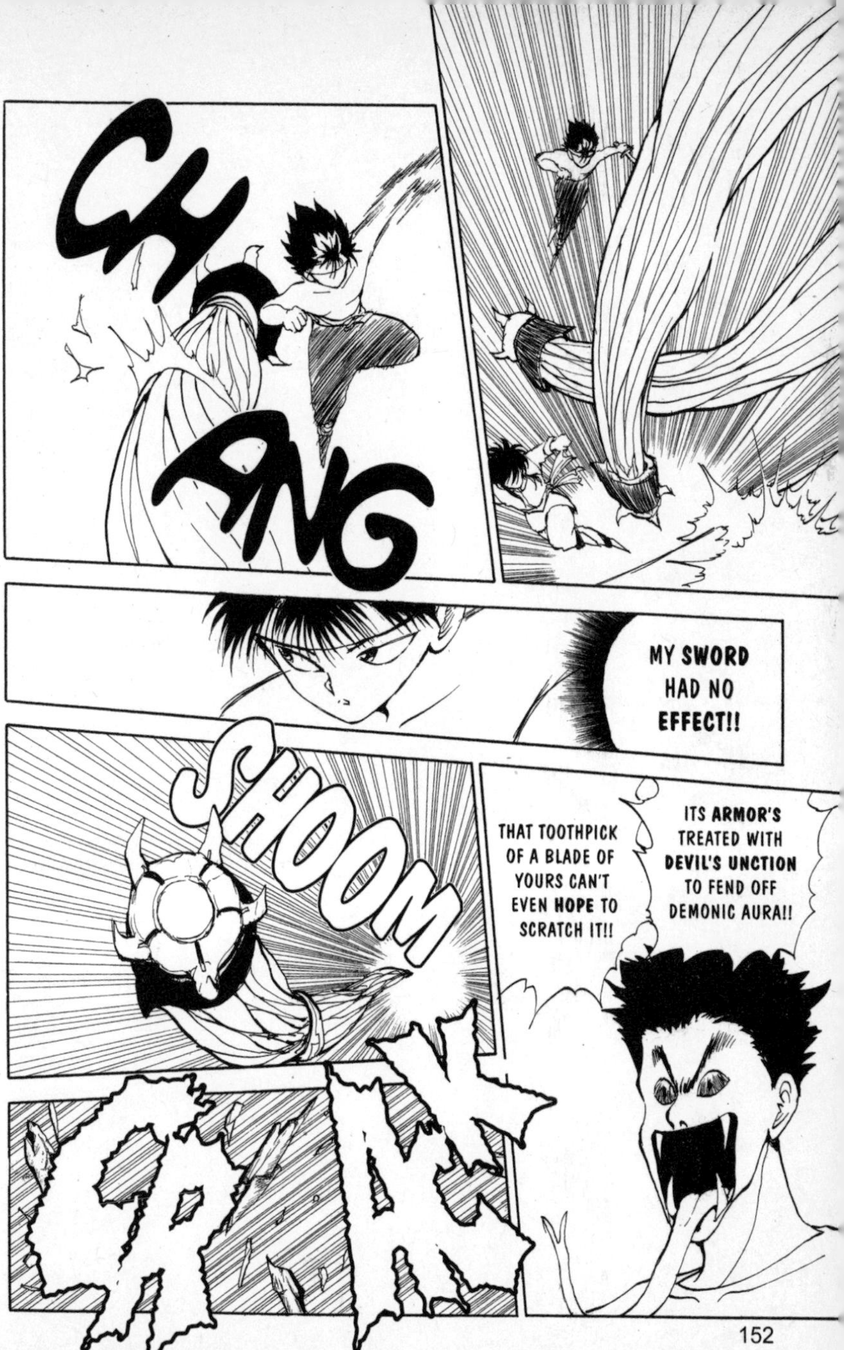
CHANG
MY SWORD HAD NO EFFECT!!
ITS ARMOR'S TREATED WITH DEVIL'S UNCTION TO FEND OFF DEMONIC AURA!!
THAT TOOTHPICK OF A BLADE OF YOURS CAN'T EVEN HOPE TO SCRATCH IT!!
SHOOM
CRAK

READ THIS WAY

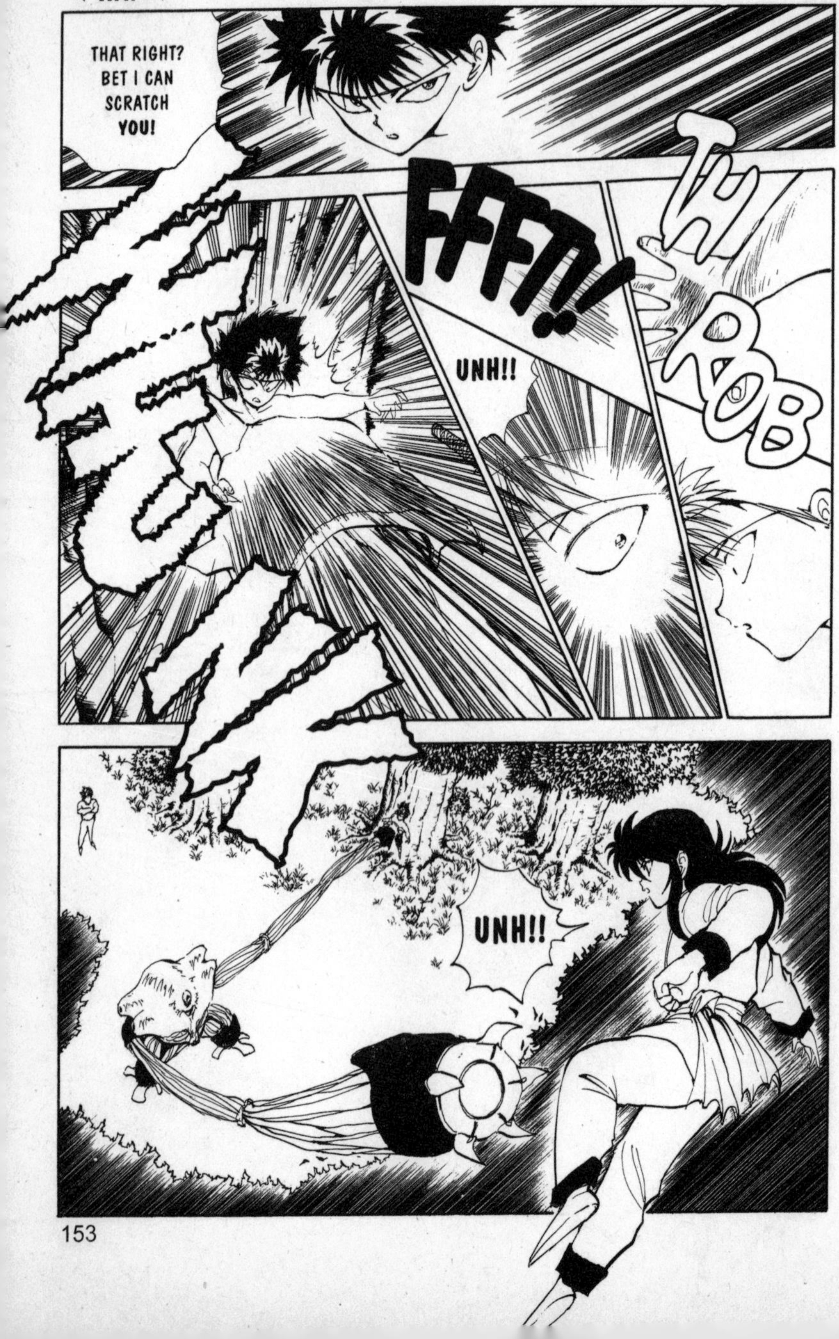

THAT RIGHT? BET I CAN SCRATCH YOU!
TH ROB
FFFT!!
UNH!!
UNH!!

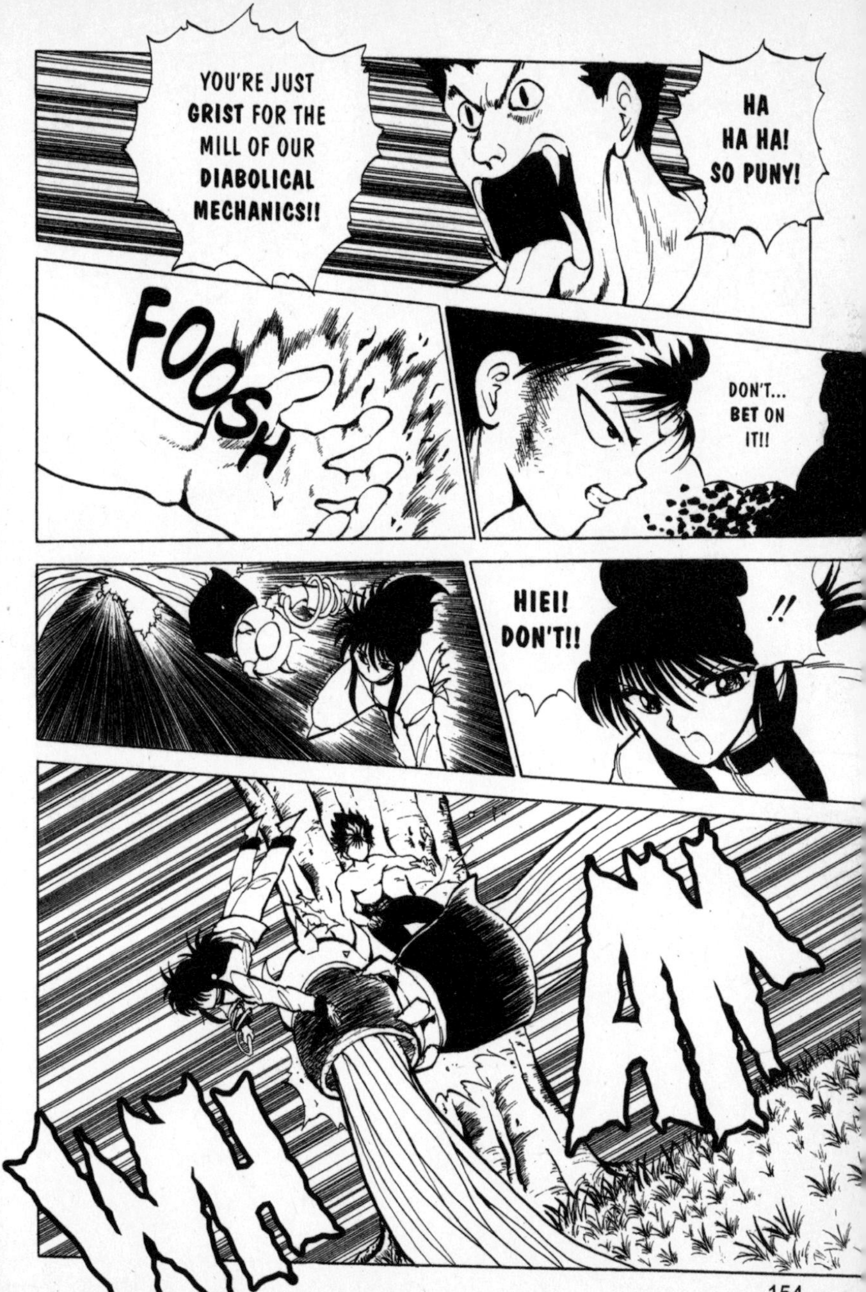
HA HA HA! SO PUNY!
YOU'RE JUST GRIST FOR THE MILL OF OUR DIABOLICAL MECHANICS!!
DON'T... BET ON IT!!
FOOSH
!!
HIEI! DON'T!!

READ THIS WAY

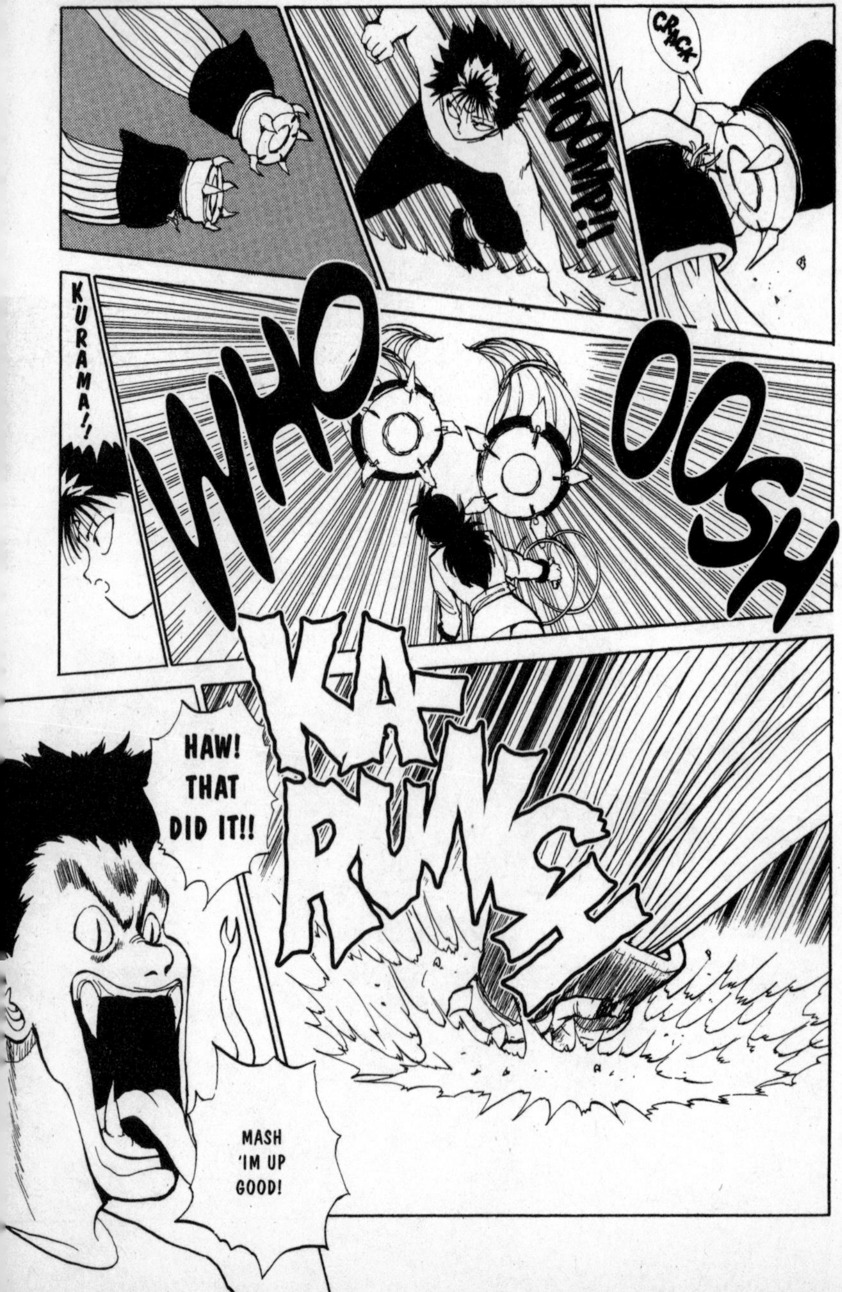
CRACK
WHOOMP!!
WHOOOSH
KURAMA!!
KA RUMP
HAW! THAT DID IT!!
MASH 'IM UP GOOD!

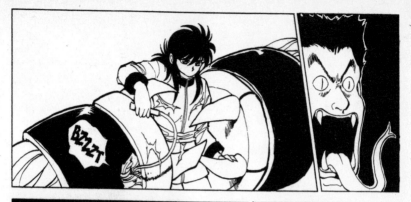

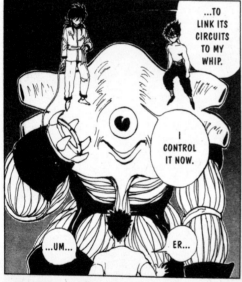

BZZZT
N-NO...
...HOW COULD HE...?
IT SHOULD'VE BEEN DESIGNED TO FEEL PAIN.
IT MIGHT'VE RECOILED BEFORE I HAD ENOUGH TIME...
...TO LINK ITS CIRCUITS TO MY WHIP.
I CONTROL IT NOW.
ER...
...UM...
YOUR CHOICE!
SUB-MISSION OR DEATH?

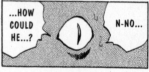

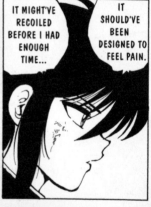

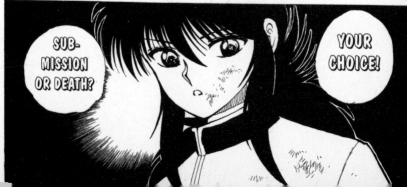

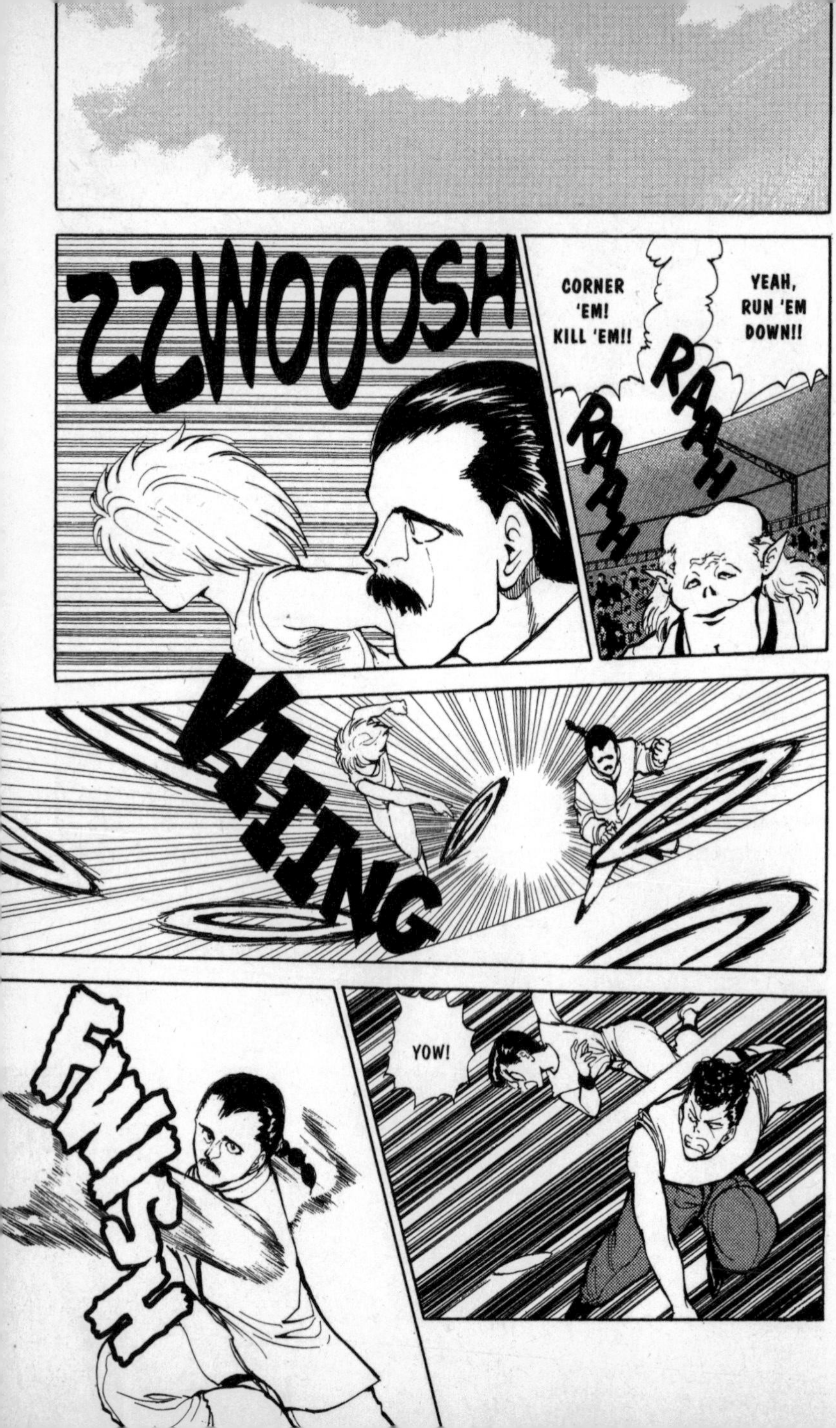
YEAH, RUN 'EM DOWN!!
CORNER 'EM! KILL 'EM!!
RAAH
RAAH
ZZWOOOSH
VHING
YOW!
FWISH

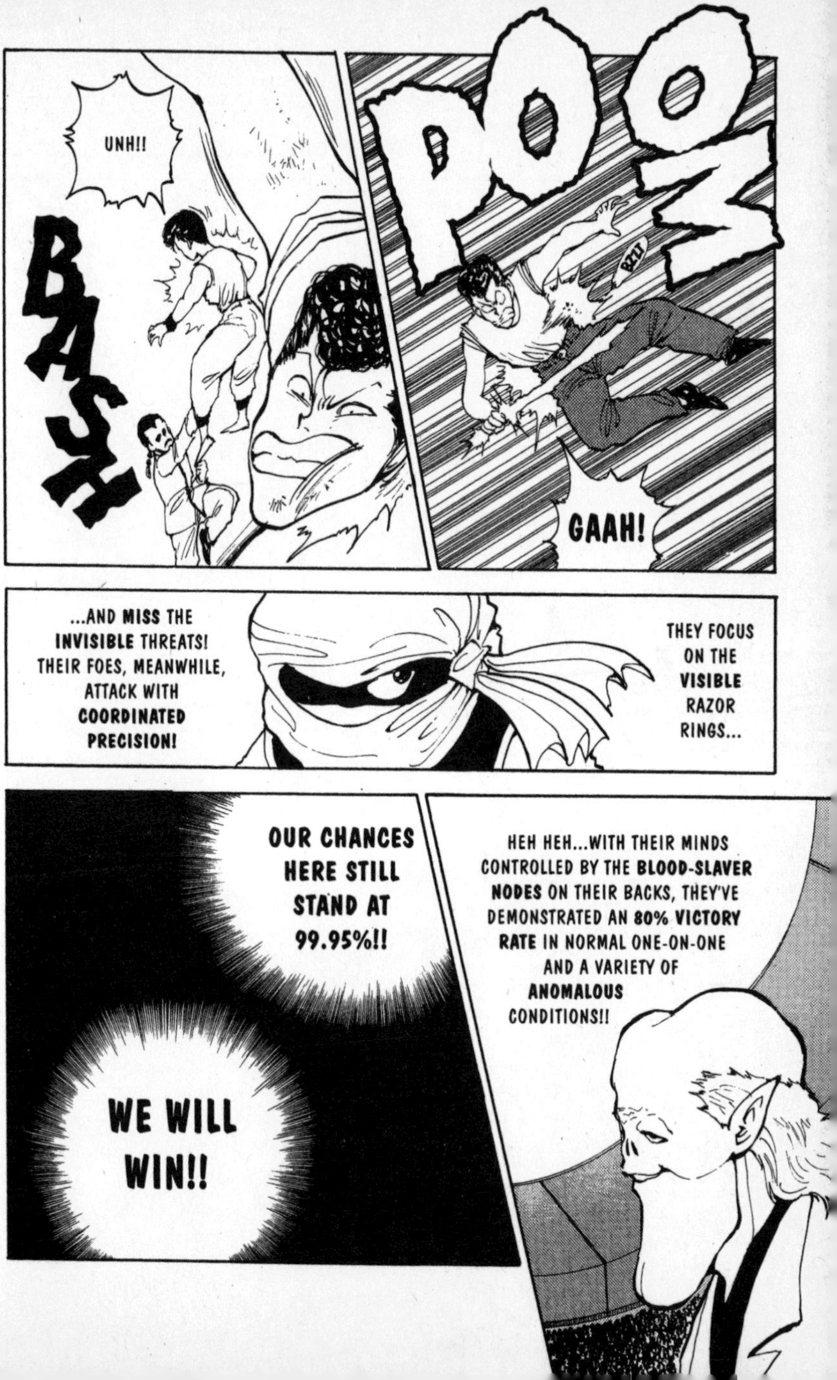
DOOM
GAAH!
UNH!!
BASH
THEY FOCUS ON THE VISIBLE RAZOR RINGS...
...AND MISS THE INVISIBLE THREATS! THEIR FOES, MEANWHILE, ATTACK WITH COORDINATED PRECISION!
HEH HEH...WITH THEIR MINDS CONTROLLED BY THE BLOOD-SLAVER NODES ON THEIR BACKS, THEY'VE DEMONSTRATED AN 80% VICTORY RATE IN NORMAL ONE-ON-ONE AND A VARIETY OF ANOMALOUS CONDITIONS!!
OUR CHANCES HERE STILL STAND AT 99.95%!!
WE WILL WIN!!

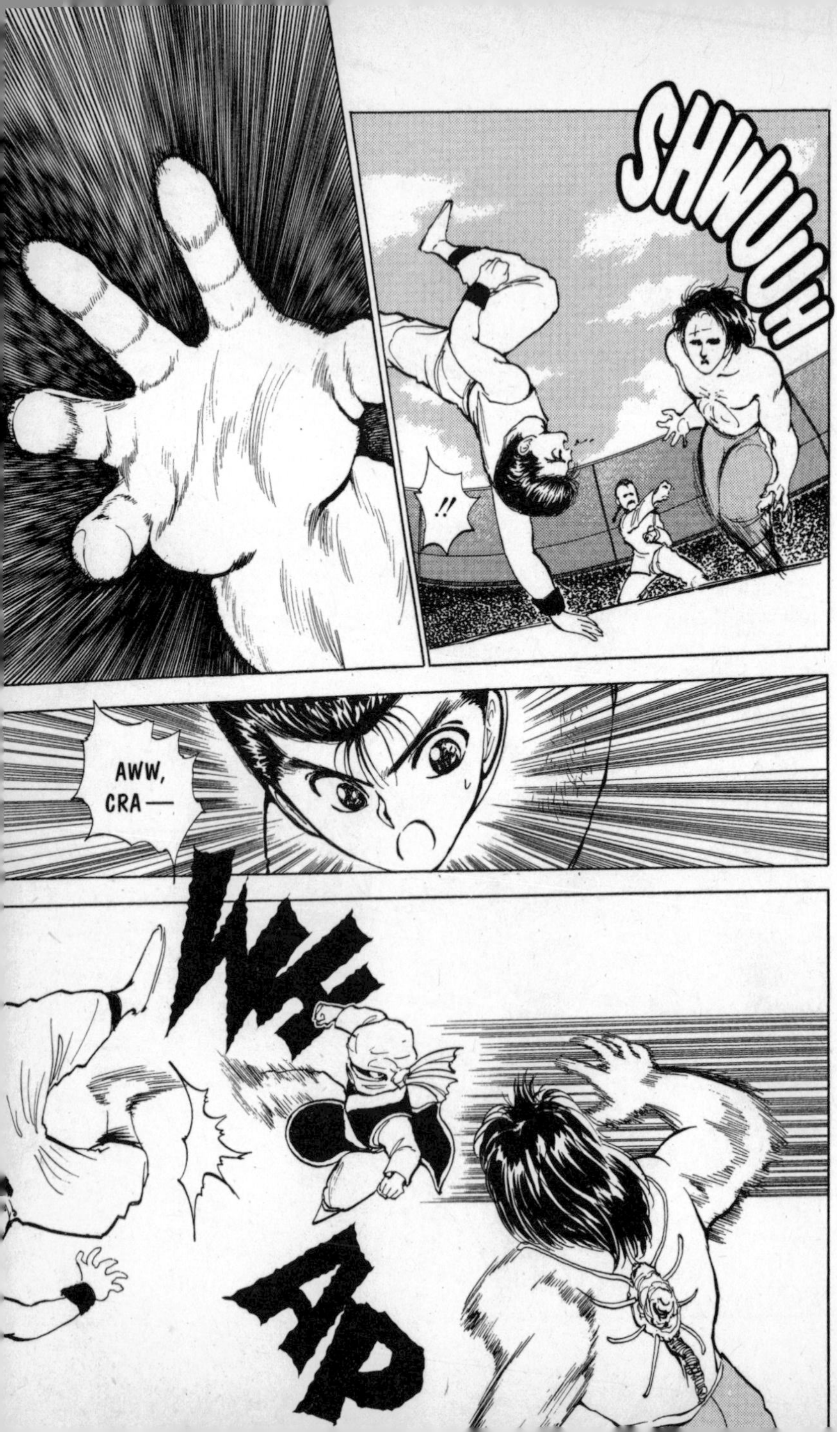
SHWUUCH!
!!
AWW, CRA—
WHAP

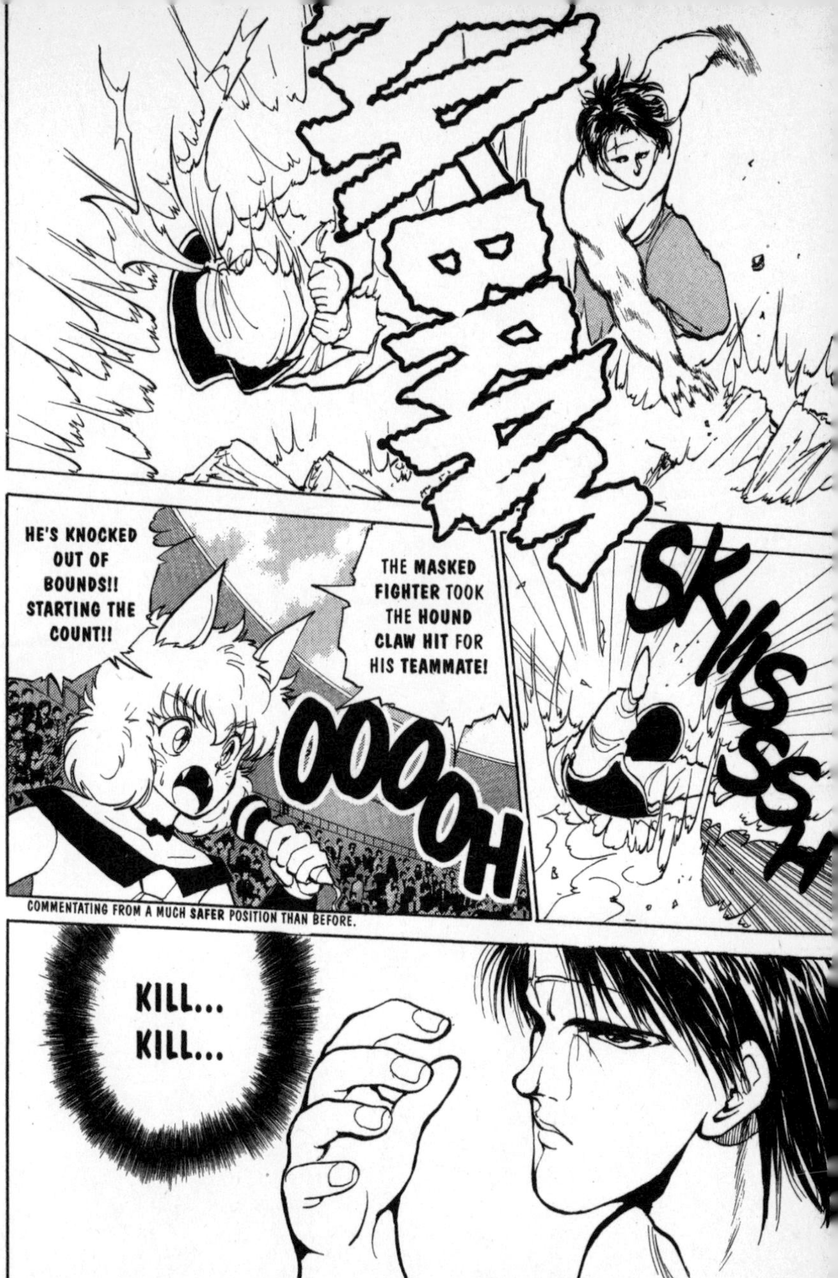
BAM
SKIIISSSH
THE MASKED FIGHTER TOOK THE HOUND CLAW HIT FOR HIS TEAMMATE!
HE'S KNOCKED OUT OF BOUNDS!! STARTING THE COUNT!!
OOOOOH
COMMENTATING FROM A MUCH SAFER POSITION THAN BEFORE.
KILL... KILL...

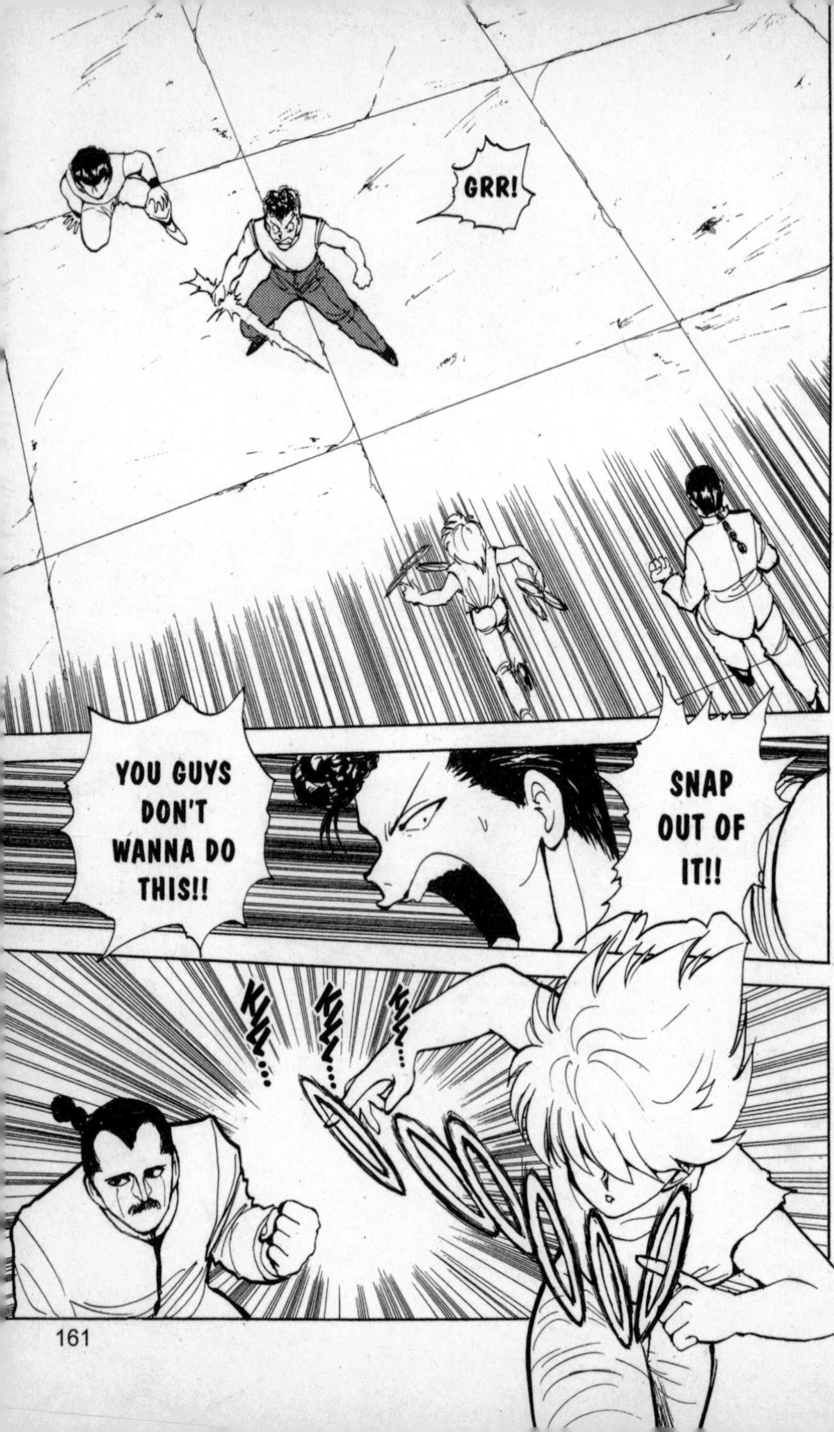
GRR!
SNAP OUT OF IT!!
YOU GUYS DON'T WANNA DO THIS!!
KILL...
KILL...
KILL...

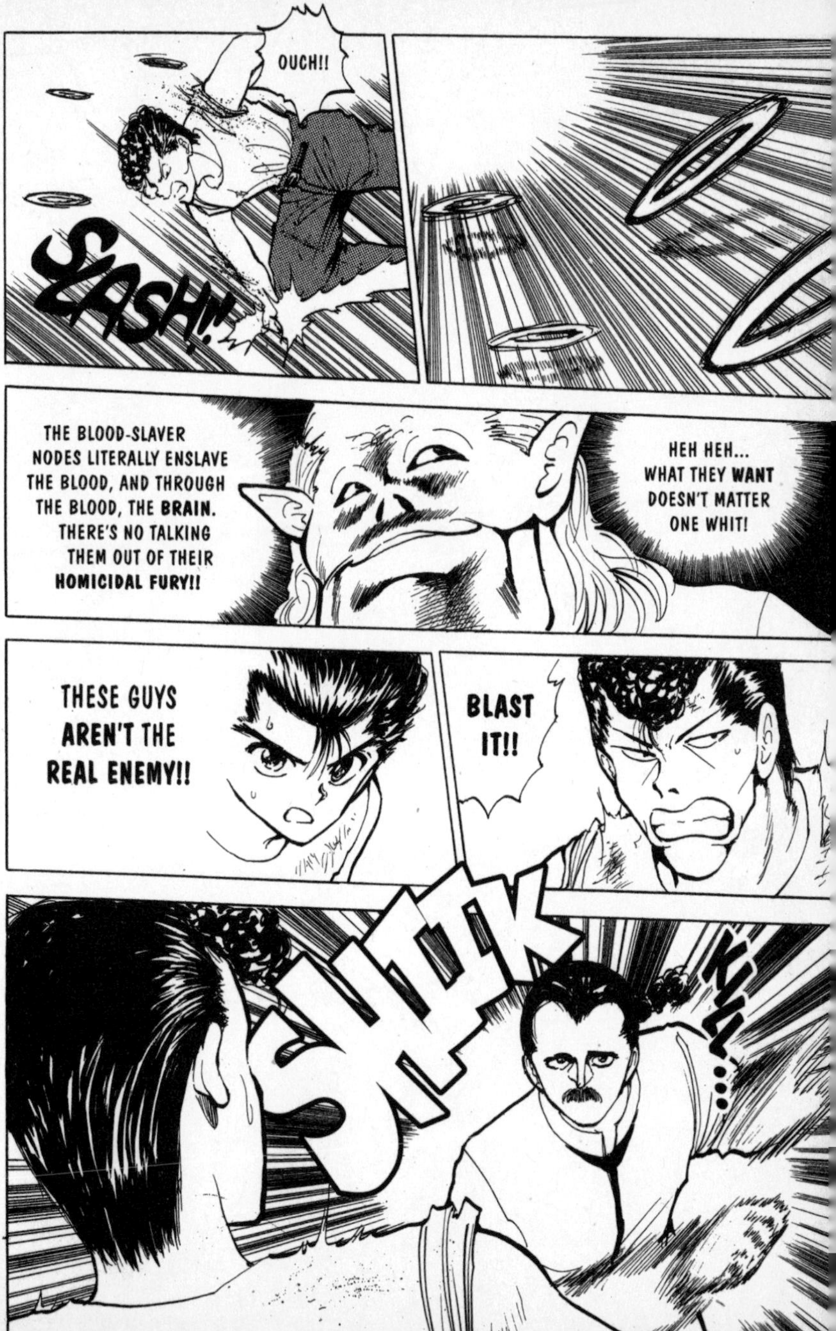
OUCH!!
SLASH!!
HEH HEH... WHAT THEY **WANT** DOESN'T MATTER ONE WHIT!
THE BLOOD-SLAVER NODES LITERALLY ENSLAVE THE BLOOD, AND THROUGH THE BLOOD, THE **BRAIN**. THERE'S NO TALKING THEM OUT OF THEIR **HOMICIDAL FURY!!**
BLAST IT!!
THESE GUYS **AREN'T** THE **REAL ENEMY!!**
KILL...

READ THIS WAY

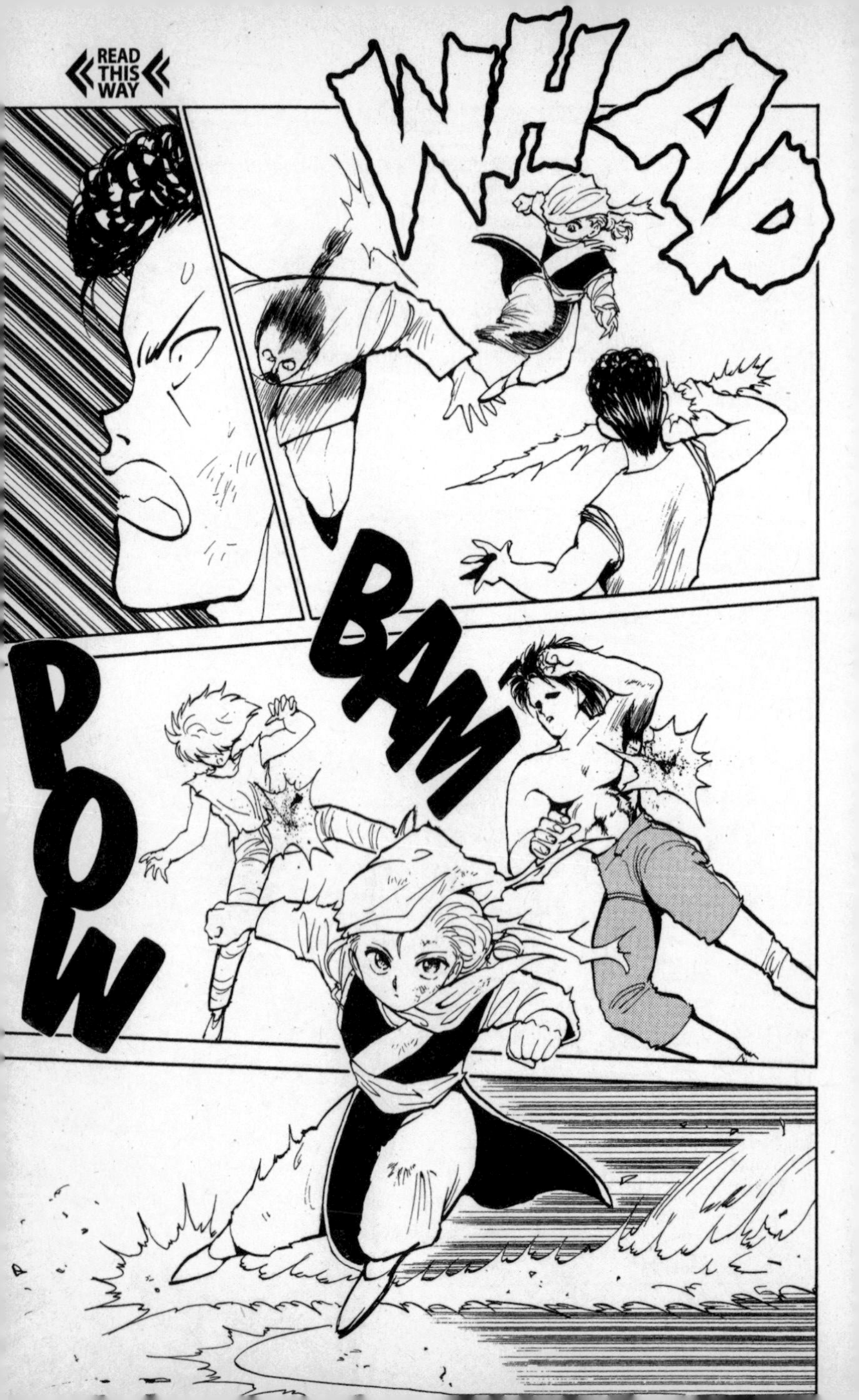
WHAD
BAM
POW

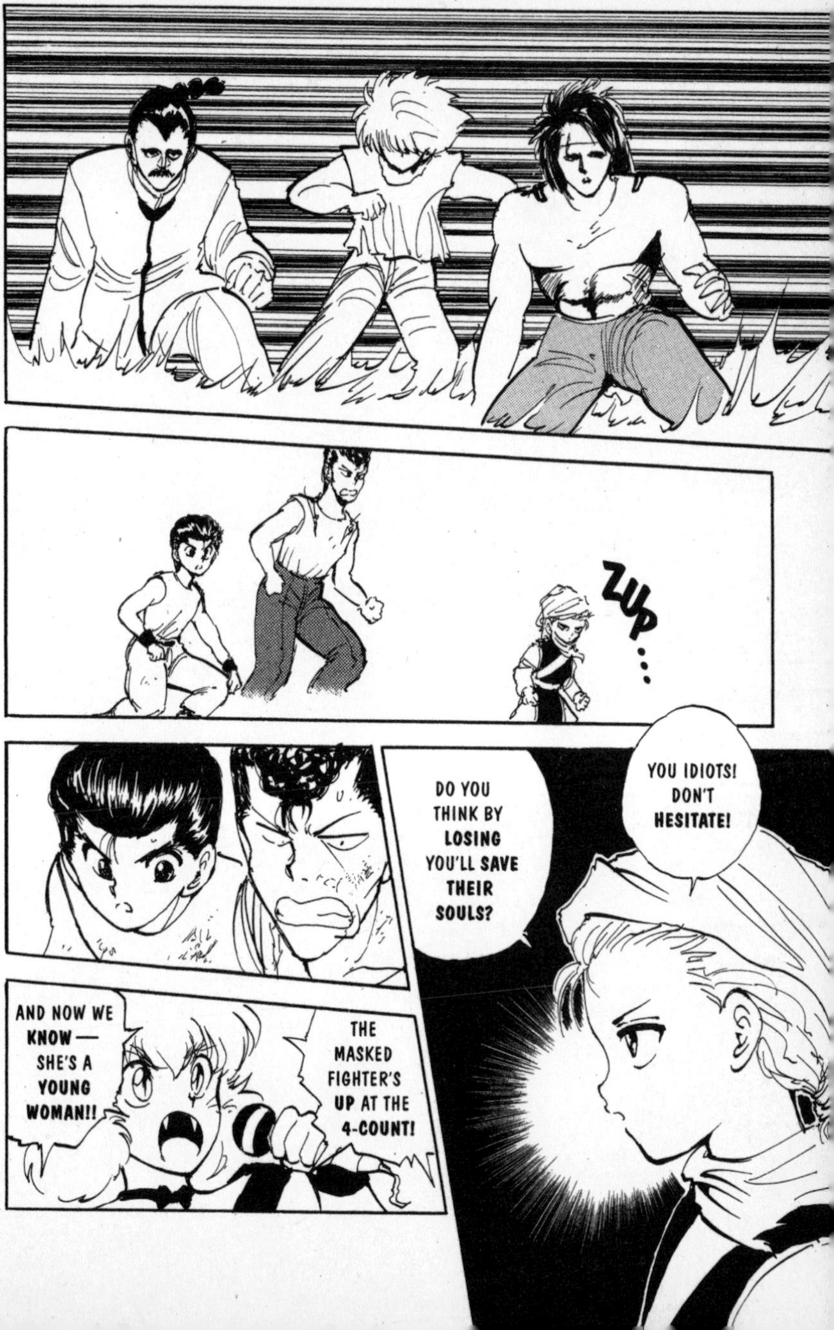
ZUP...
YOU IDIOTS! DON'T HESITATE!
DO YOU THINK BY LOSING YOU'LL SAVE THEIR SOULS?
THE MASKED FIGHTER'S UP AT THE 4-COUNT!
AND NOW WE KNOW— SHE'S A YOUNG WOMAN!!

READ THIS WAY

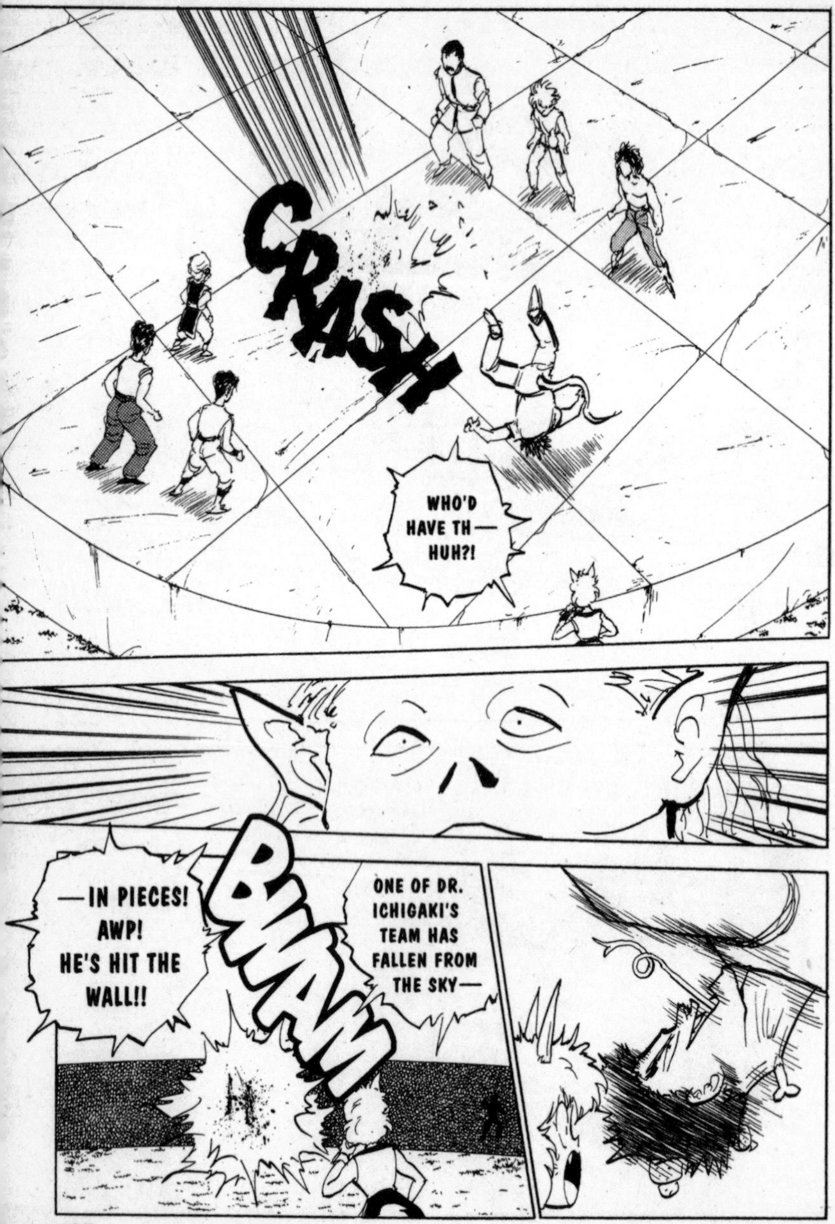
CRASH
WHO'D HAVE TH— HUH?!
ONE OF DR. ICHIGAKI'S TEAM HAS FALLEN FROM THE SKY—
BWAM
—IN PIECES! AWP! HE'S HIT THE WALL!!

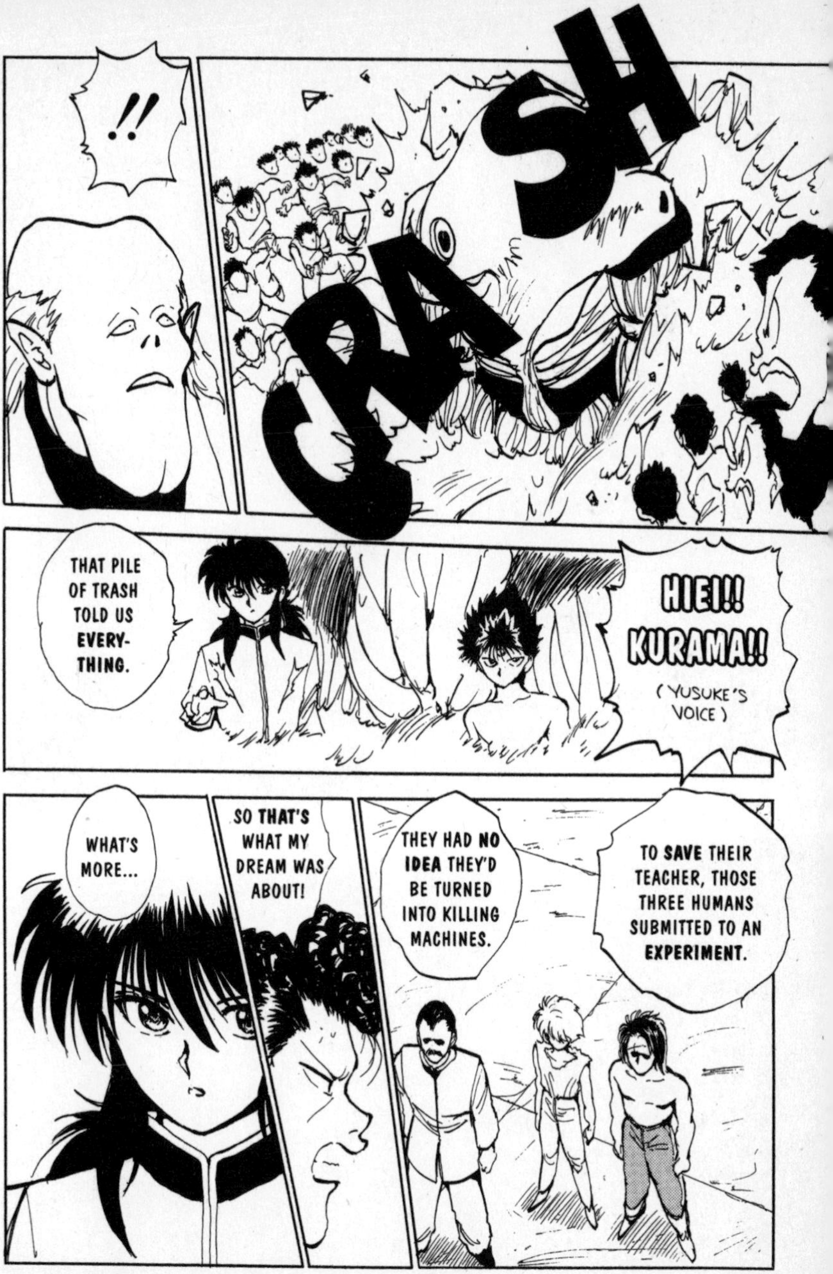
CRASH
!!
HIEI!! KURAMA!!
(YUSUKE'S VOICE)
THAT PILE OF TRASH TOLD US EVERYTHING.
TO SAVE THEIR TEACHER, THOSE THREE HUMANS SUBMITTED TO AN EXPERIMENT.
THEY HAD NO IDEA THEY'D BE TURNED INTO KILLING MACHINES.
SO THAT'S WHAT MY DREAM WAS ABOUT!
WHAT'S MORE...

READ THIS WAY

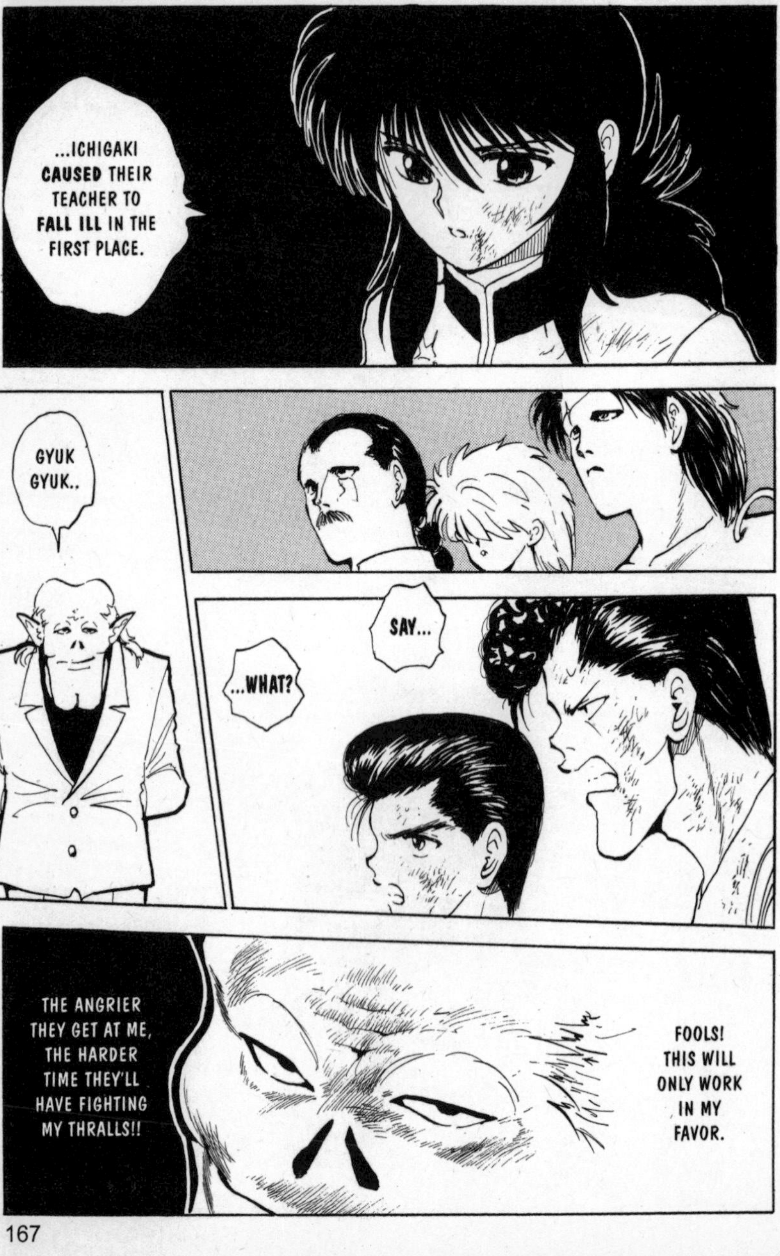

...ICHIGAKI CAUSED THEIR TEACHER TO FALL ILL IN THE FIRST PLACE.
SAY...
...WHAT?
GYUK GYUK..
FOOLS! THIS WILL ONLY WORK IN MY FAVOR.
THE ANGRIER THEY GET AT ME, THE HARDER TIME THEY'LL HAVE FIGHTING MY THRALLS!!

SORRY - I USED TO DO THESE.

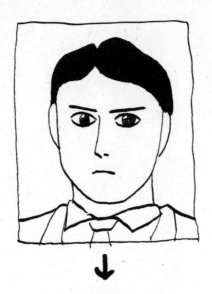

FAMOUS PERSON'S PICTURE IN A TEXTBOOK.

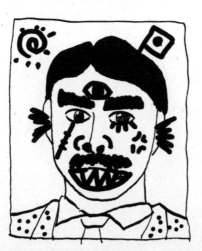

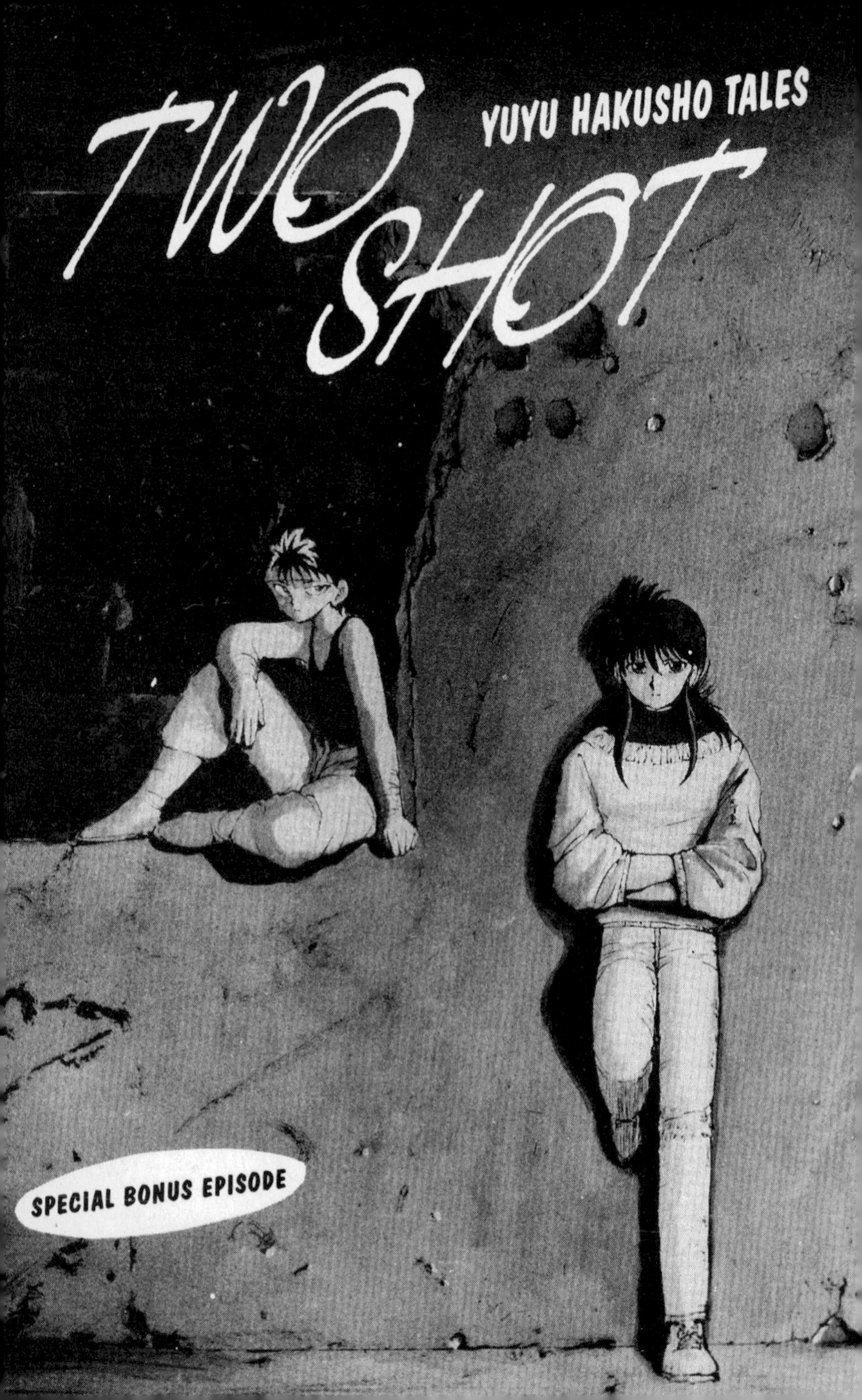
TWO SHOT
YUYU HAKUSHO TALES
SPECIAL BONUS EPISODE

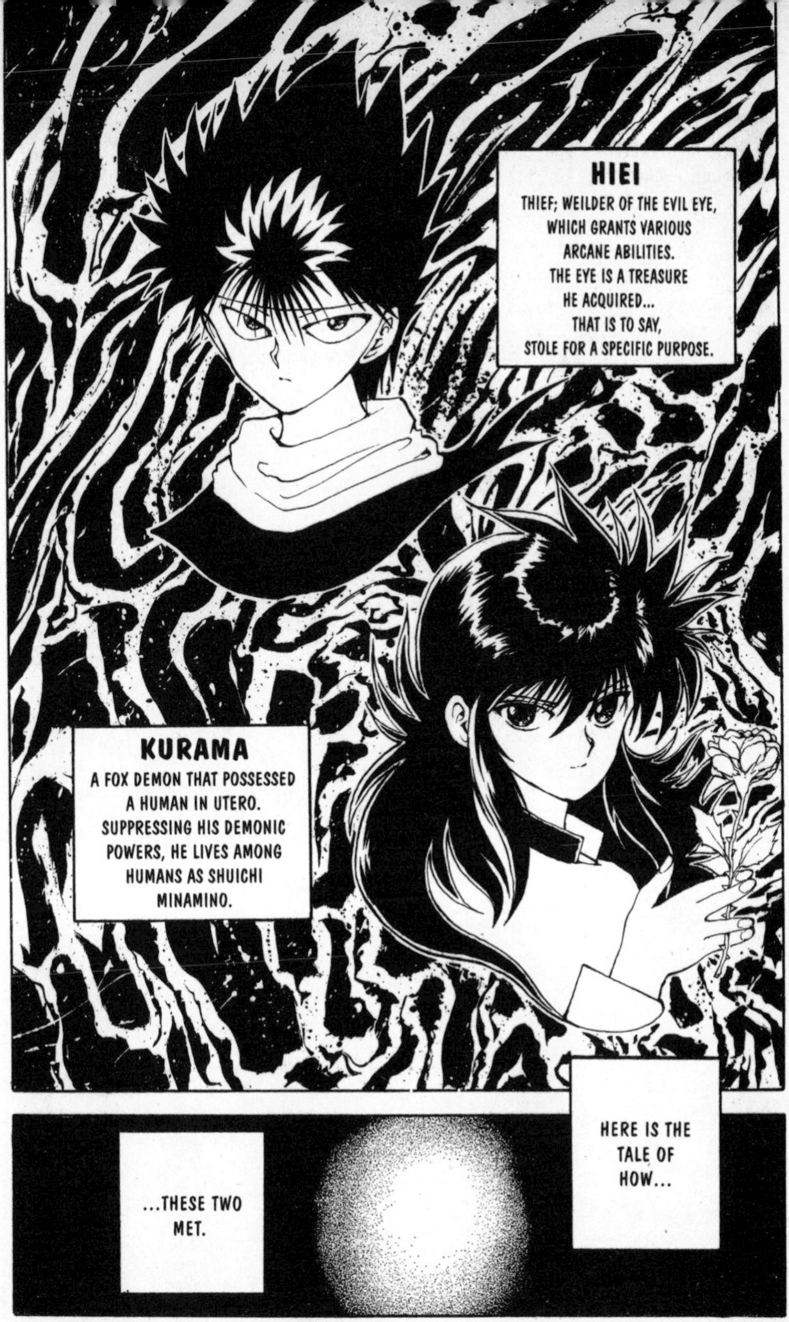
HIEI
THIEF; WEILDER OF THE EVIL EYE, WHICH GRANTS VARIOUS ARCANE ABILITIES. THE EYE IS A TREASURE HE ACQUIRED... THAT IS TO SAY, STOLE FOR A SPECIFIC PURPOSE.
KURAMA
A FOX DEMON THAT POSSESSED A HUMAN IN UTERO. SUPPRESSING HIS DEMONIC POWERS, HE LIVES AMONG HUMANS AS SHUICHI MINAMINO.
HERE IS THE TALE OF HOW...
...THESE TWO MET.

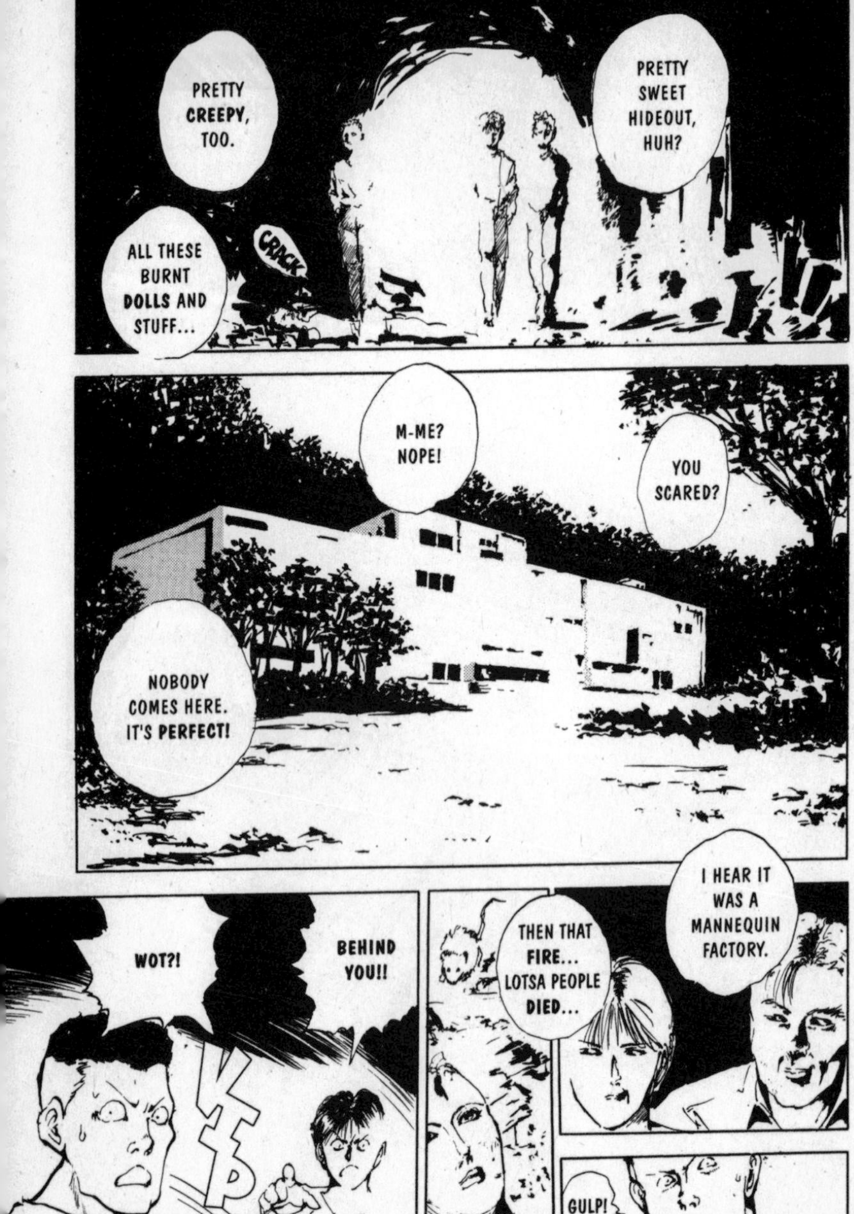
PRETTY SWEET HIDEOUT, HUH?
PRETTY CREEPY, TOO.
CRACK
ALL THESE BURNT DOLLS AND STUFF...
YOU SCARED?
M-ME? NOPE!
NOBODY COMES HERE. IT'S PERFECT!
I HEAR IT WAS A MANNEQUIN FACTORY.
GULP!
THEN THAT FIRE... LOTSA PEOPLE DIED...
BEHIND YOU!!
WOT?!

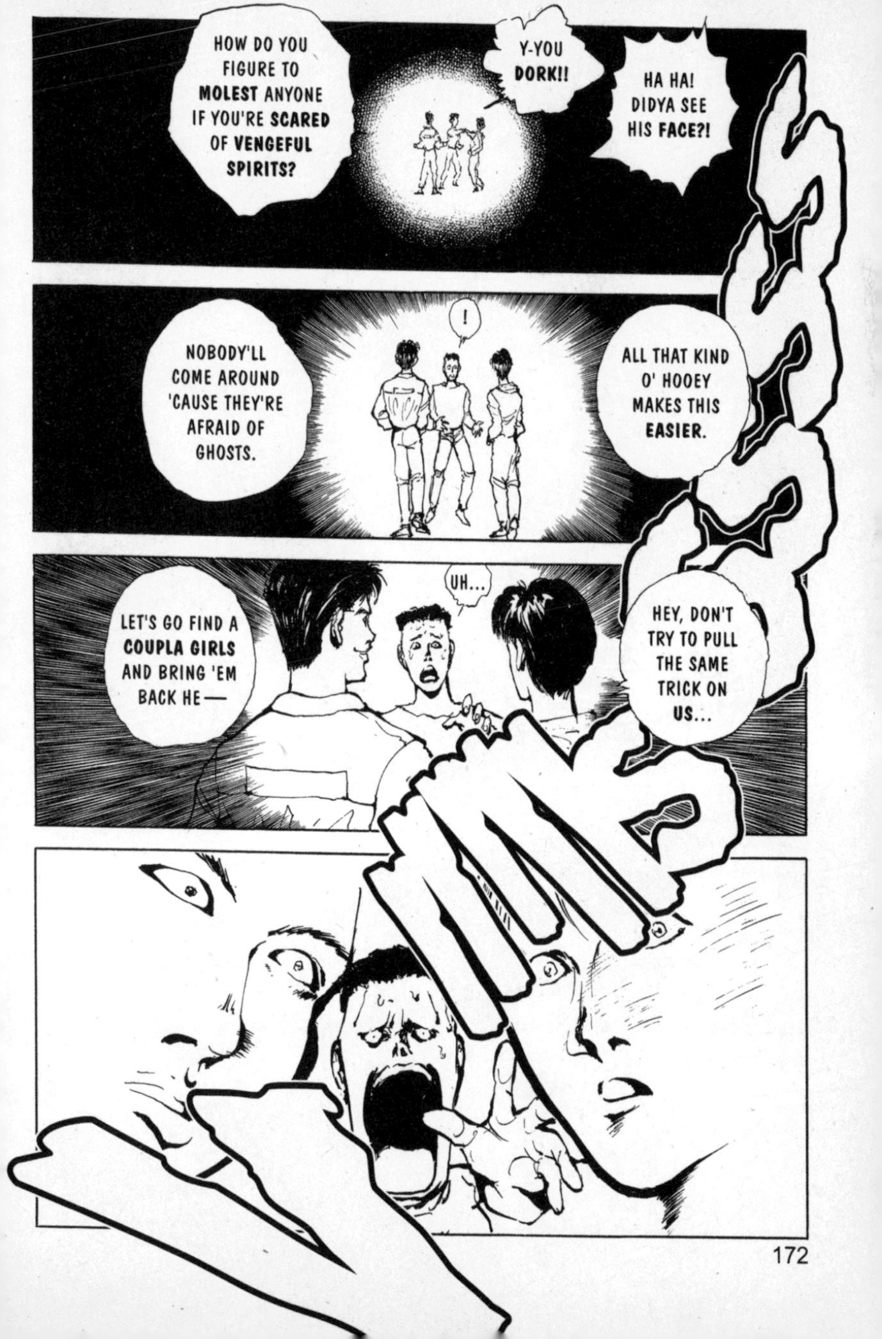
HA HA! DIDYA SEE HIS FACE?!
Y-YOU DORK!!
HOW DO YOU FIGURE TO MOLEST ANYONE IF YOU'RE SCARED OF VENGEFUL SPIRITS?
ALL THAT KIND O' HOOEY MAKES THIS EASIER.
!
NOBODY'LL COME AROUND 'CAUSE THEY'RE AFRAID OF GHOSTS.
HEY, DON'T TRY TO PULL THE SAME TRICK ON US...
UH...
LET'S GO FIND A COUPLA GIRLS AND BRING 'EM BACK HE—

READ THIS WAY

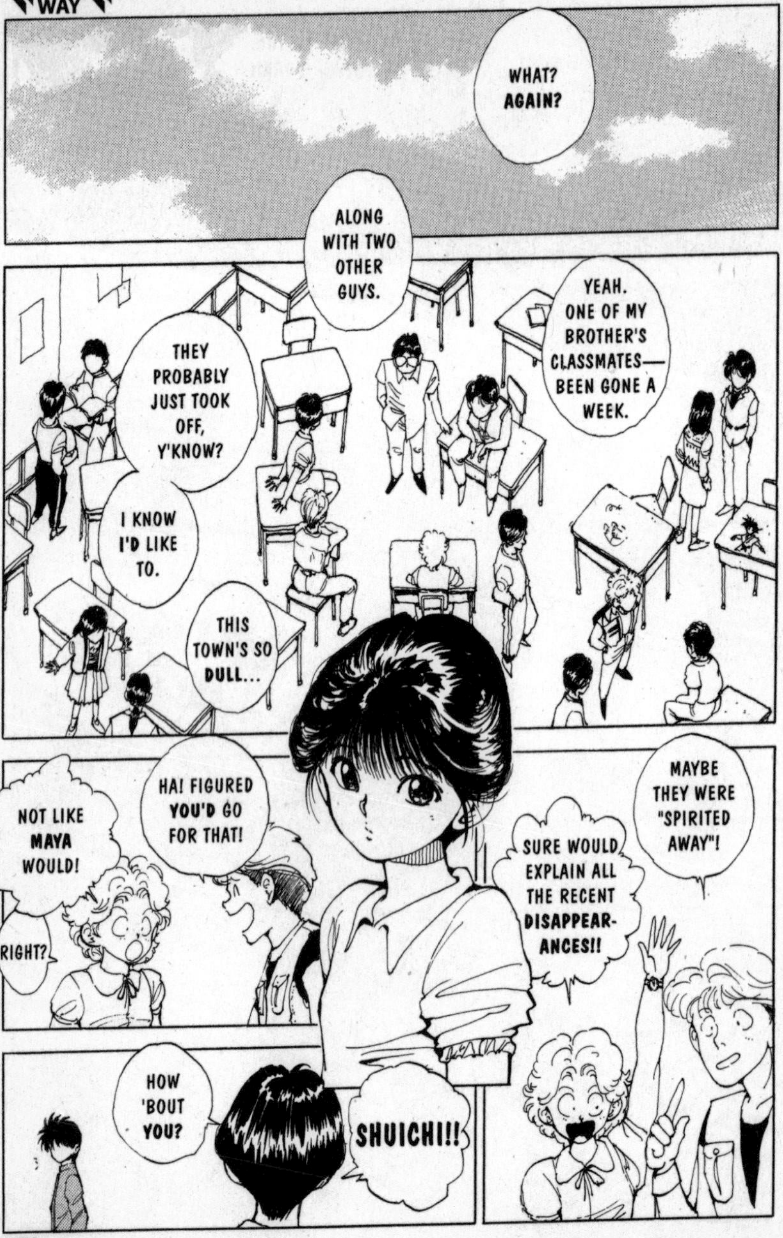
WHAT? AGAIN?
ALONG WITH TWO OTHER GUYS.
YEAH. ONE OF MY BROTHER'S CLASSMATES— BEEN GONE A WEEK.
THEY PROBABLY JUST TOOK OFF, Y'KNOW?
I KNOW I'D LIKE TO.
THIS TOWN'S SO DULL...
MAYBE THEY WERE "SPIRITED AWAY"!
SURE WOULD EXPLAIN ALL THE RECENT DISAPPEAR-ANCES!!
HA! FIGURED YOU'D GO FOR THAT!
NOT LIKE MAYA WOULD!
RIGHT?
SHUICHI!!
HOW 'BOUT YOU?

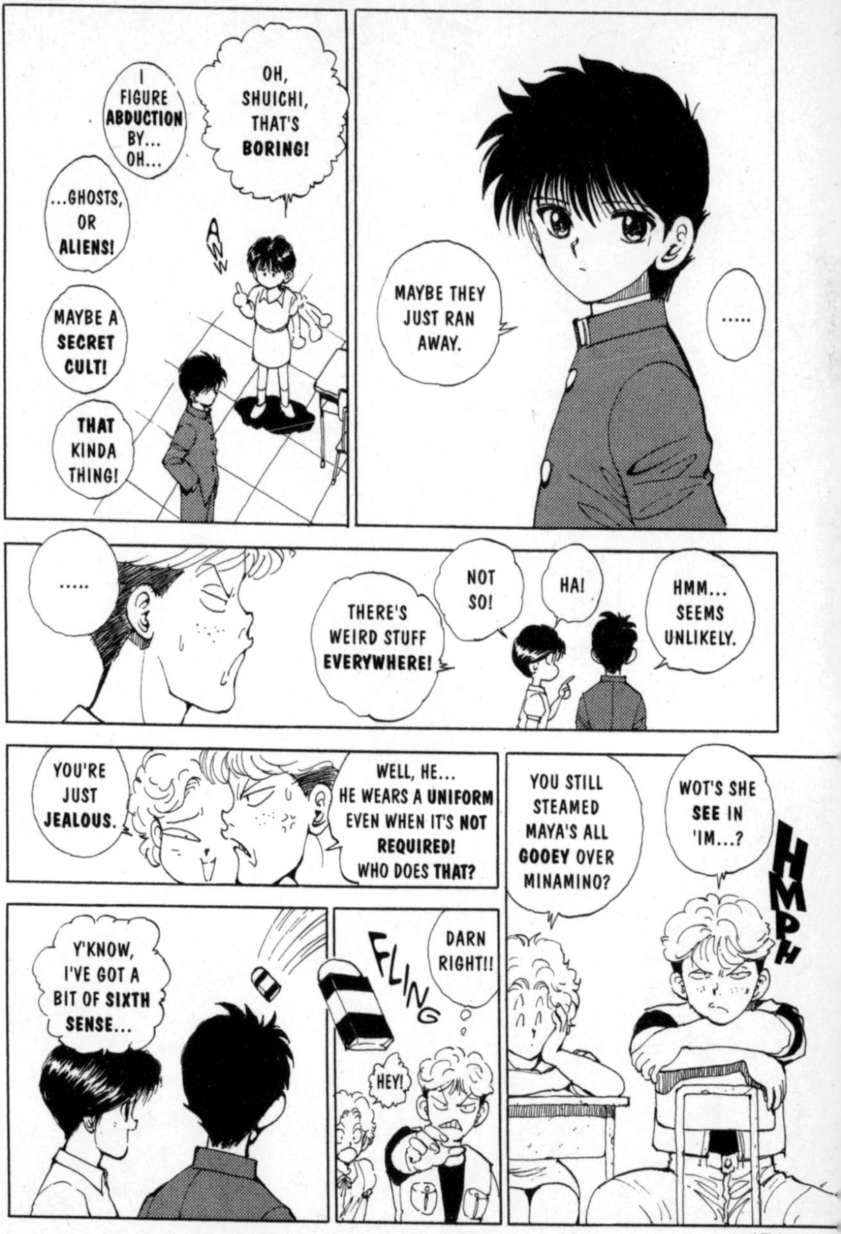
.....
MAYBE THEY JUST RAN AWAY.
OH, SHUICHI, THAT'S BORING!
I FIGURE ABDUCTION BY... OH...
...GHOSTS, OR ALIENS!
AWW
MAYBE A SECRET CULT!
THAT KINDA THING!
HMM... SEEMS UNLIKELY.
HA!
NOT SO!
THERE'S WEIRD STUFF EVERYWHERE!
.....
WOT'S SHE SEE IN 'IM...?
HMPH
YOU STILL STEAMED MAYA'S ALL GOOEY OVER MINAMINO?
WELL, HE... HE WEARS A UNIFORM EVEN WHEN IT'S NOT REQUIRED! WHO DOES THAT?
YOU'RE JUST JEALOUS.
DARN RIGHT!!
FLING
HEY!
Y'KNOW, I'VE GOT A BIT OF SIXTH SENSE...

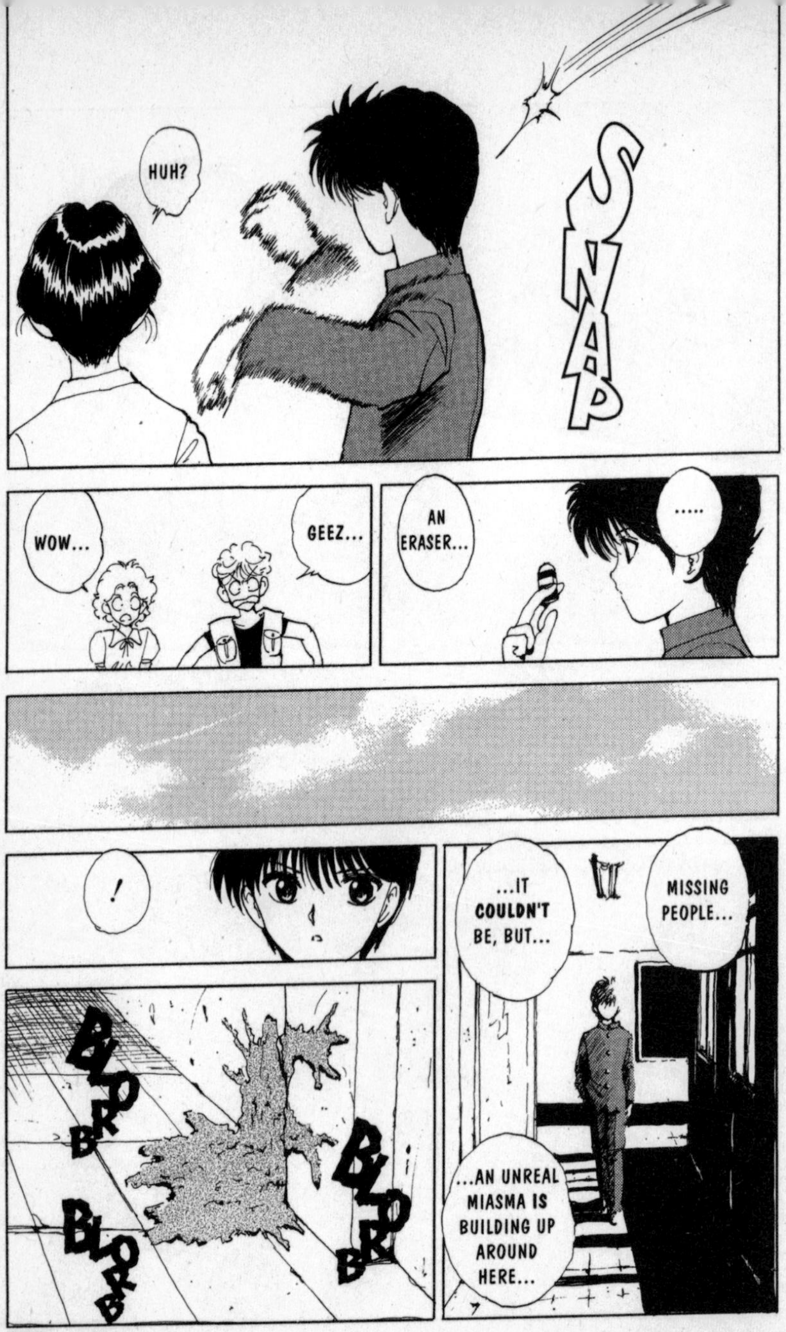
SNAP
HUH?
.....
AN ERASER...
GEEZ...
WOW...
MISSING PEOPLE...
...IT COULDN'T BE, BUT...
...AN UNREAL MIASMA IS BUILDING UP AROUND HERE...
!
BLORB
BLORB
BLORB

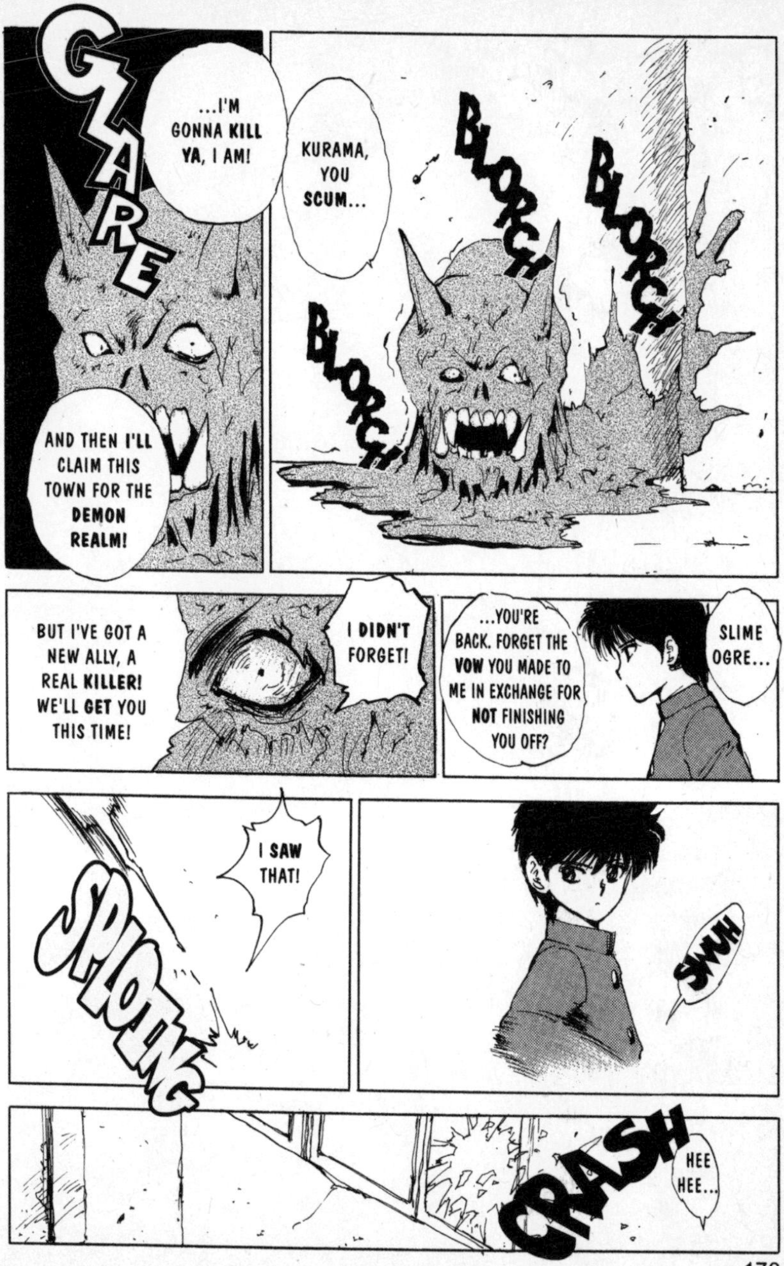
KURAMA, YOU SCUM...
BLORCH
BLORCH
BLORCH
GLARE
...I'M GONNA KILL YA, I AM!
AND THEN I'LL CLAIM THIS TOWN FOR THE DEMON REALM!
SLIME OGRE...
...YOU'RE BACK. FORGET THE VOW YOU MADE TO ME IN EXCHANGE FOR NOT FINISHING YOU OFF?
I DIDN'T FORGET!
BUT I'VE GOT A NEW ALLY, A REAL KILLER! WE'LL GET YOU THIS TIME!
SWUH
I SAW THAT!
SPLOING
HEE HEE...
CRASH

READ THIS WAY

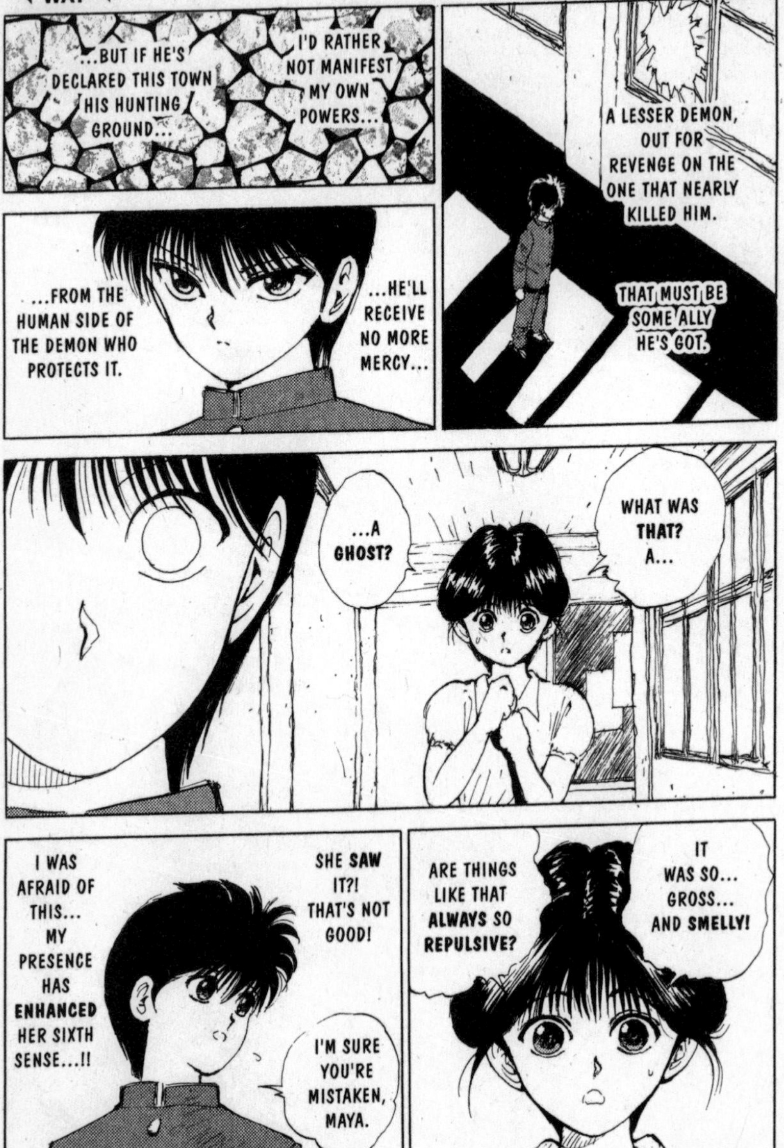

A LESSER DEMON, OUT FOR REVENGE ON THE ONE THAT NEARLY KILLED HIM.
THAT MUST BE SOME ALLY HE'S GOT.
I'D RATHER NOT MANIFEST MY OWN POWERS...
...BUT IF HE'S DECLARED THIS TOWN HIS HUNTING GROUND...
...HE'LL RECEIVE NO MORE MERCY...
...FROM THE HUMAN SIDE OF THE DEMON WHO PROTECTS IT.
WHAT WAS THAT? A...
...A GHOST?
IT WAS SO... GROSS... AND SMELLY!
ARE THINGS LIKE THAT ALWAYS SO REPULSIVE?
SHE SAW IT?! THAT'S NOT GOOD!
I WAS AFRAID OF THIS... MY PRESENCE HAS ENHANCED HER SIXTH SENSE...!!
I'M SURE YOU'RE MISTAKEN, MAYA.

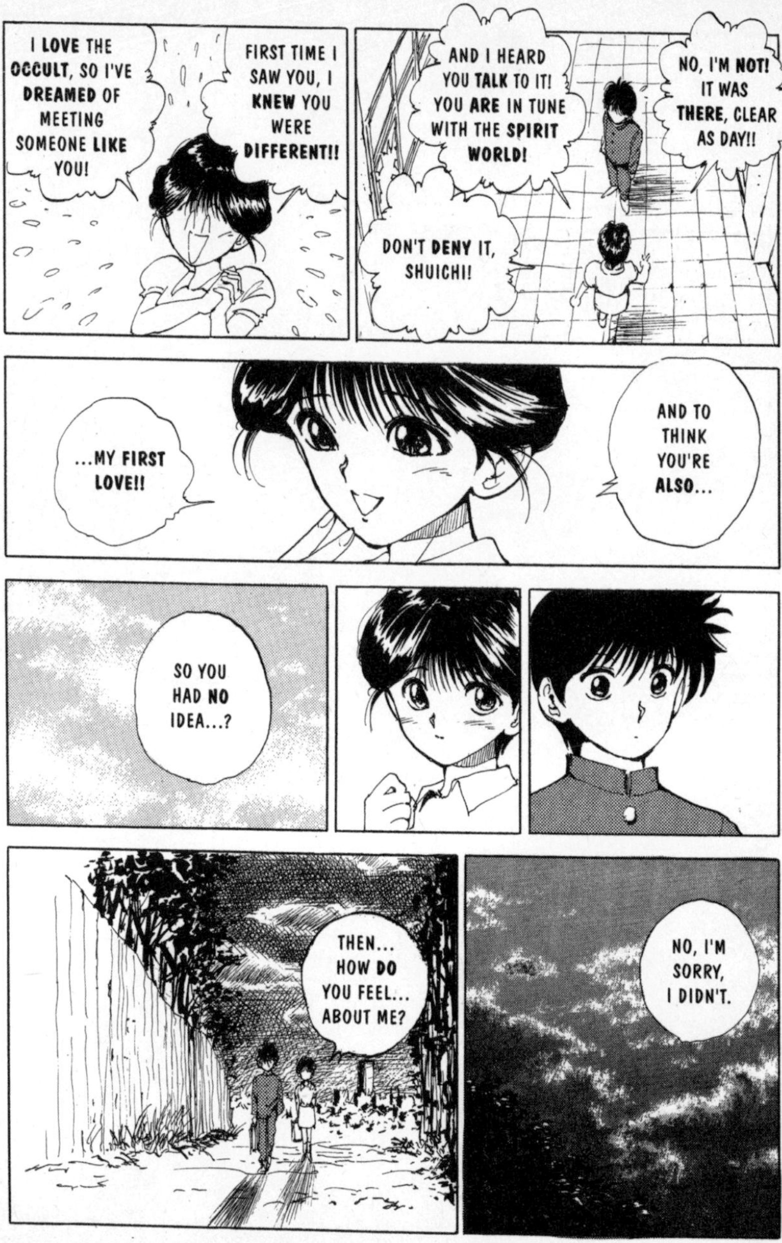
NO, I'M NOT! IT WAS THERE, CLEAR AS DAY!!
AND I HEARD YOU TALK TO IT! YOU ARE IN TUNE WITH THE SPIRIT WORLD!
DON'T DENY IT, SHUICHI!
FIRST TIME I SAW YOU, I KNEW YOU WERE DIFFERENT!!
I LOVE THE OCCULT, SO I'VE DREAMED OF MEETING SOMEONE LIKE YOU!
AND TO THINK YOU'RE ALSO...
...MY FIRST LOVE!!
SO YOU HAD NO IDEA...?
NO, I'M SORRY, I DIDN'T.
THEN... HOW DO YOU FEEL... ABOUT ME?

READ THIS WAY

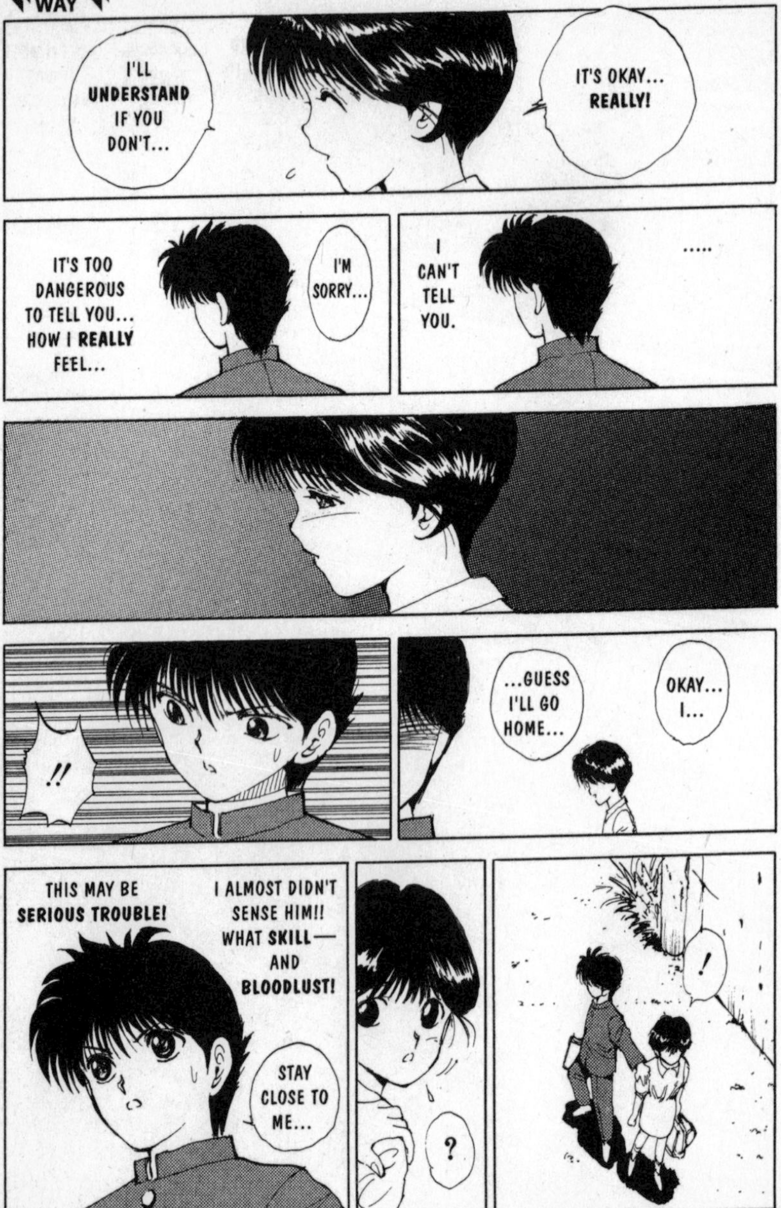
IT'S OKAY... REALLY!
I'LL UNDERSTAND IF YOU DON'T...
.....
I CAN'T TELL YOU.
I'M SORRY...
IT'S TOO DANGEROUS TO TELL YOU... HOW I REALLY FEEL...
OKAY... I...
...GUESS I'LL GO HOME...
!!
!
?
I ALMOST DIDN'T SENSE HIM!! WHAT SKILL— AND BLOODLUST!
THIS MAY BE SERIOUS TROUBLE!
STAY CLOSE TO ME...

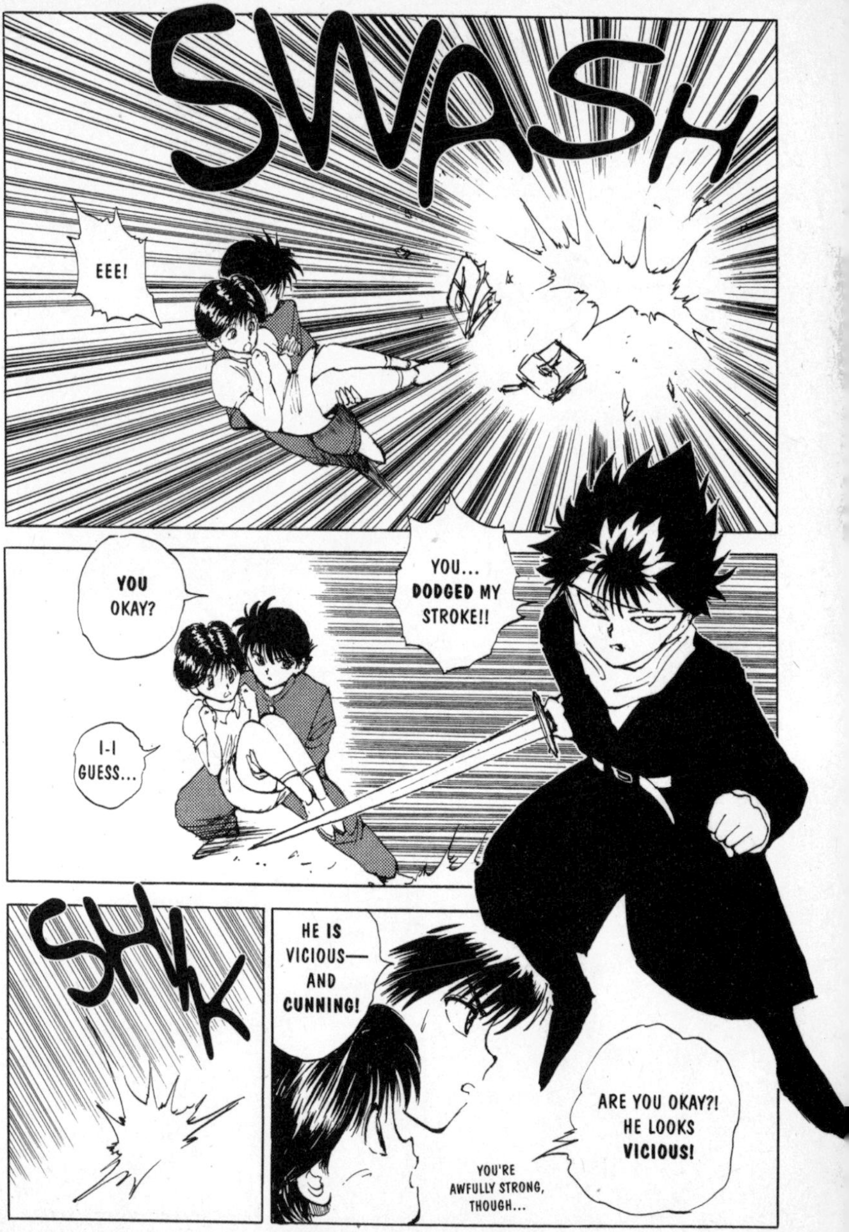
SWASH
EEE!
YOU... DODGED MY STROKE!!
YOU OKAY?
I-I GUESS...
HE IS VICIOUS—AND CUNNING!
ARE YOU OKAY?! HE LOOKS VICIOUS!
YOU'RE AWFULLY STRONG, THOUGH...
SHK

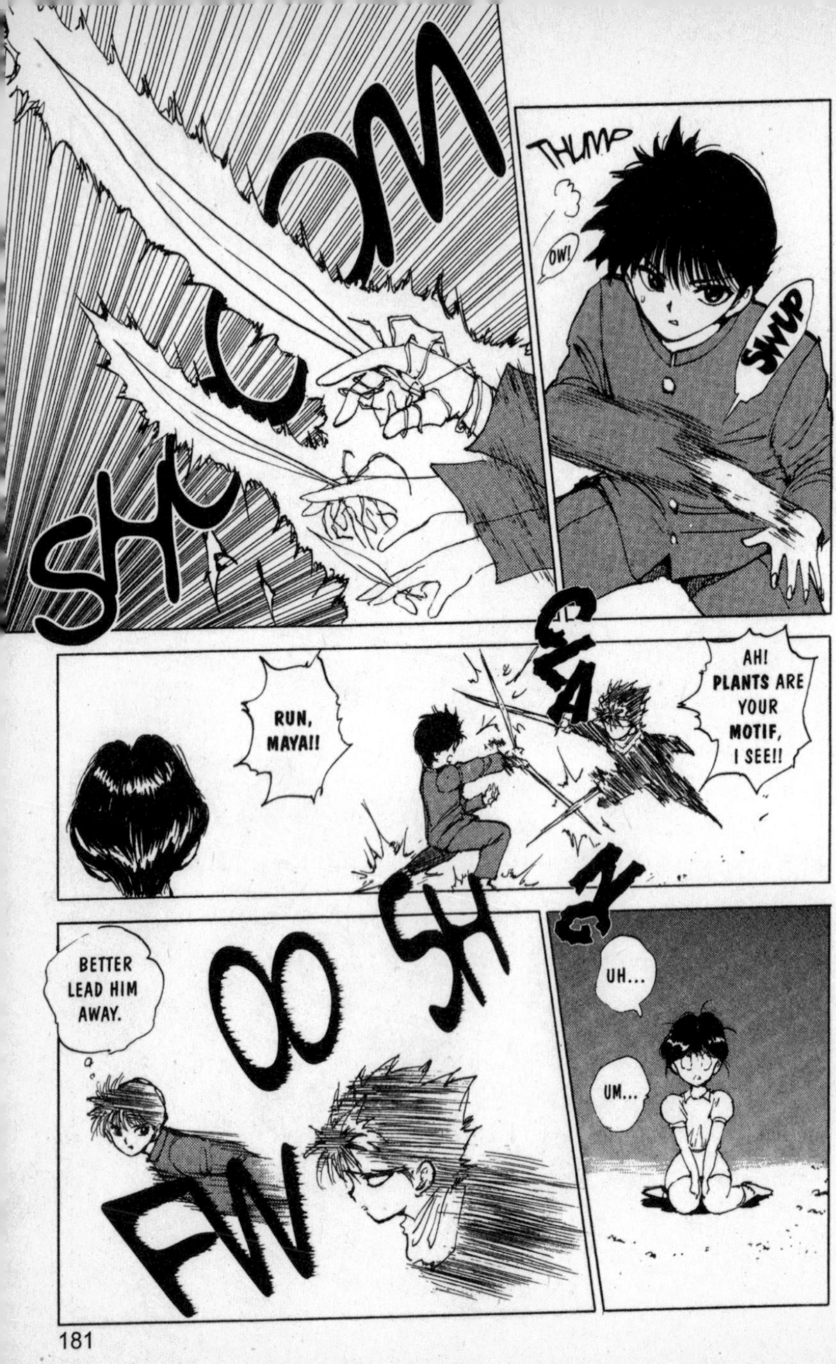
THUMP
OW!
SWUP
AH! PLANTS ARE YOUR MOTIF, I SEE!!
CLANG
RUN, MAYA!!
UH...
UM...
BETTER LEAD HIM AWAY.
FWOOSH

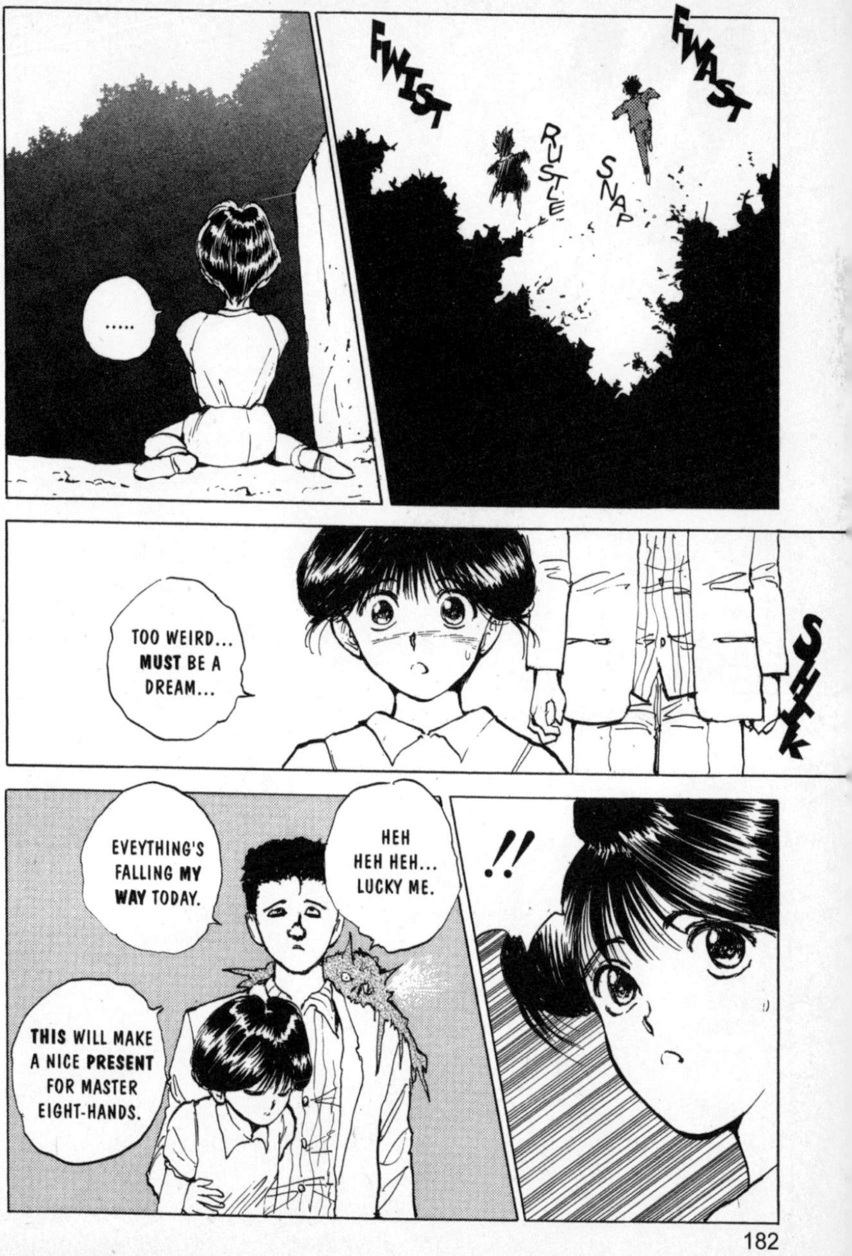
FWAST
SNAP
RUSTLE
FWIST
......
TOO WEIRD... MUST BE A DREAM...
!!
HEH HEH HEH... LUCKY ME.
EVEYTHING'S FALLING MY WAY TODAY.
THIS WILL MAKE A NICE PRESENT FOR MASTER EIGHT-HANDS.

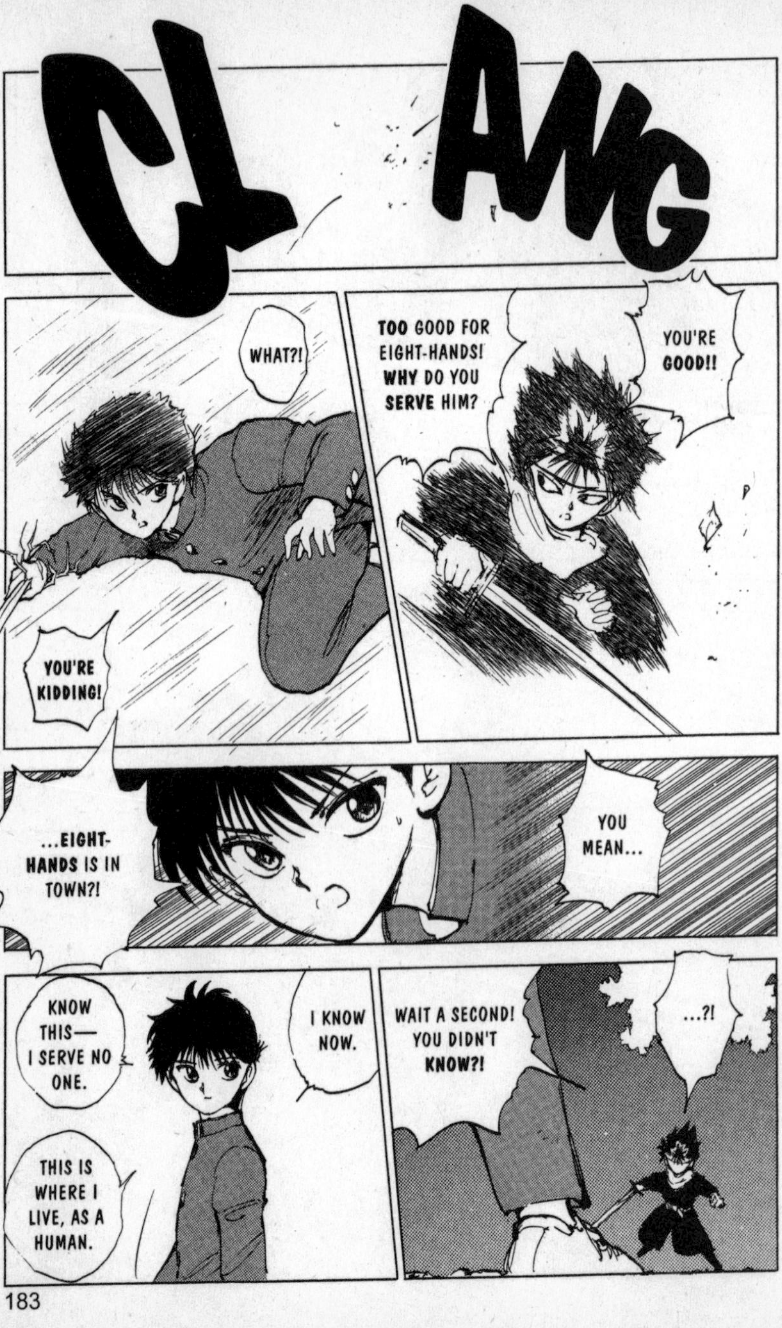
CLANG
YOU'RE GOOD!!
TOO GOOD FOR EIGHT-HANDS! WHY DO YOU SERVE HIM?
WHAT?!
YOU'RE KIDDING!
YOU MEAN...
...EIGHT-HANDS IS IN TOWN?!
...?!
WAIT A SECOND! YOU DIDN'T KNOW?!
I KNOW NOW.
KNOW THIS— I SERVE NO ONE.
THIS IS WHERE I LIVE, AS A HUMAN.

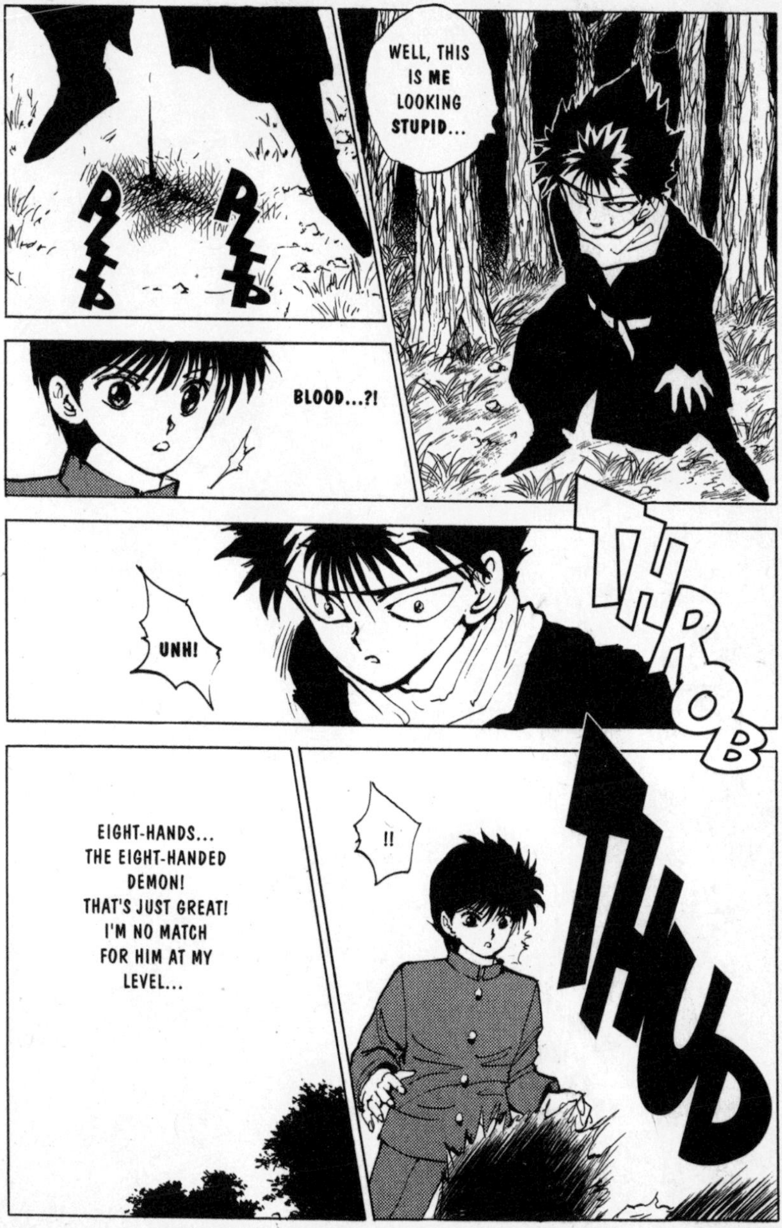

WELL, THIS IS ME LOOKING STUPID...
BLOOD...?!
UNH!
THROB
!!
THUD
EIGHT-HANDS... THE EIGHT-HANDED DEMON! THAT'S JUST GREAT! I'M NO MATCH FOR HIM AT MY LEVEL...

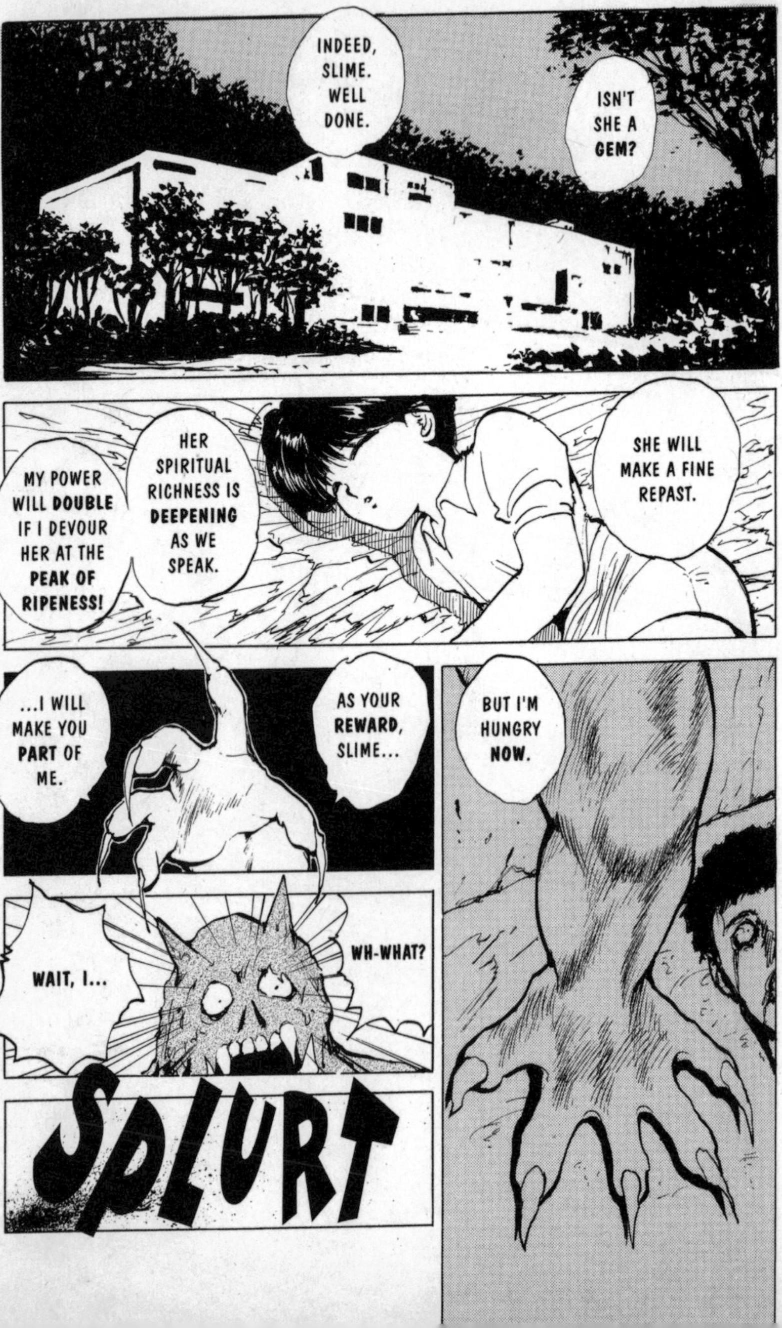
ISN'T SHE A GEM?
INDEED, SLIME. WELL DONE.
SHE WILL MAKE A FINE REPAST.
HER SPIRITUAL RICHNESS IS DEEPENING AS WE SPEAK.
MY POWER WILL DOUBLE IF I DEVOUR HER AT THE PEAK OF RIPENESS!
BUT I'M HUNGRY NOW.
AS YOUR REWARD, SLIME...
...I WILL MAKE YOU PART OF ME.
WH-WHAT?
WAIT, I...
SPLURT

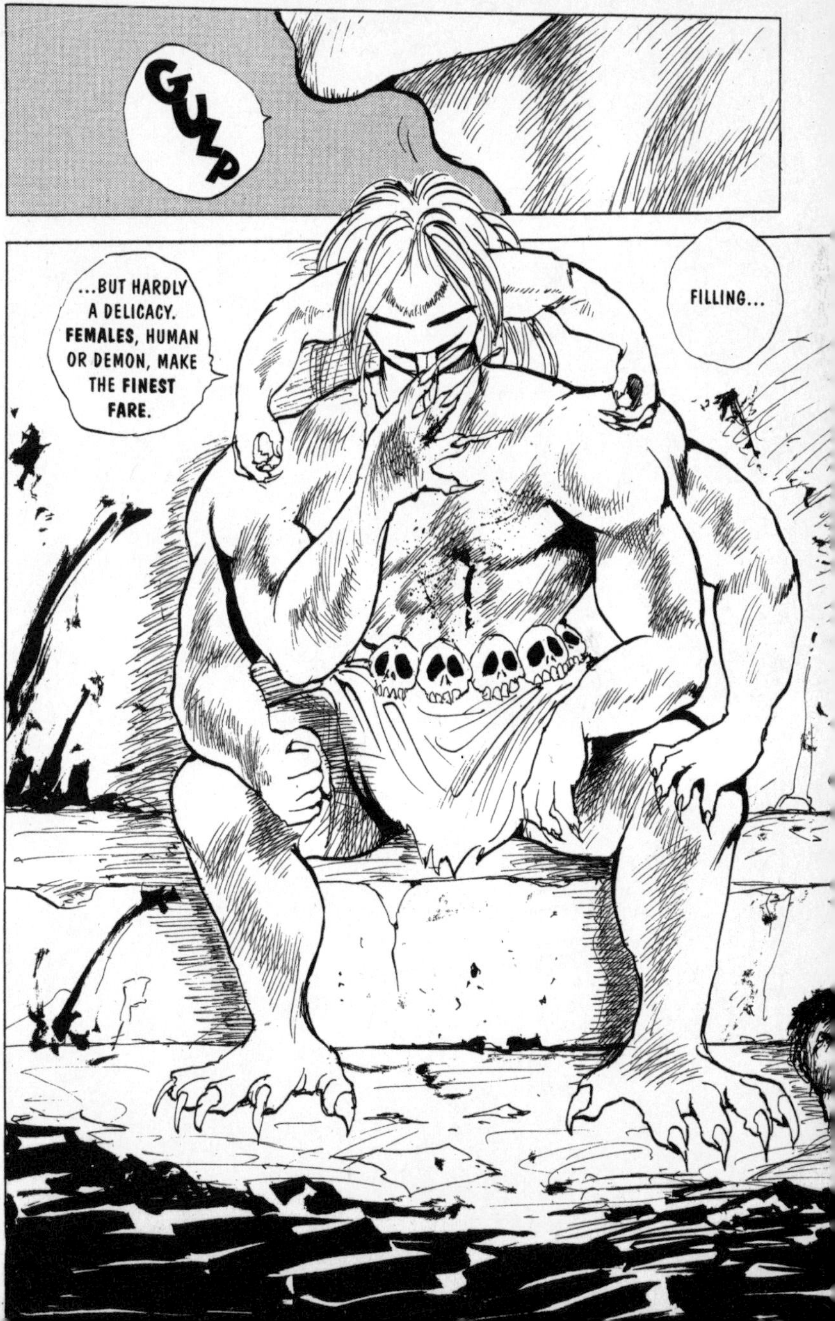
GULP
FILLING...
...BUT HARDLY A DELICACY. FEMALES, HUMAN OR DEMON, MAKE THE FINEST FARE.

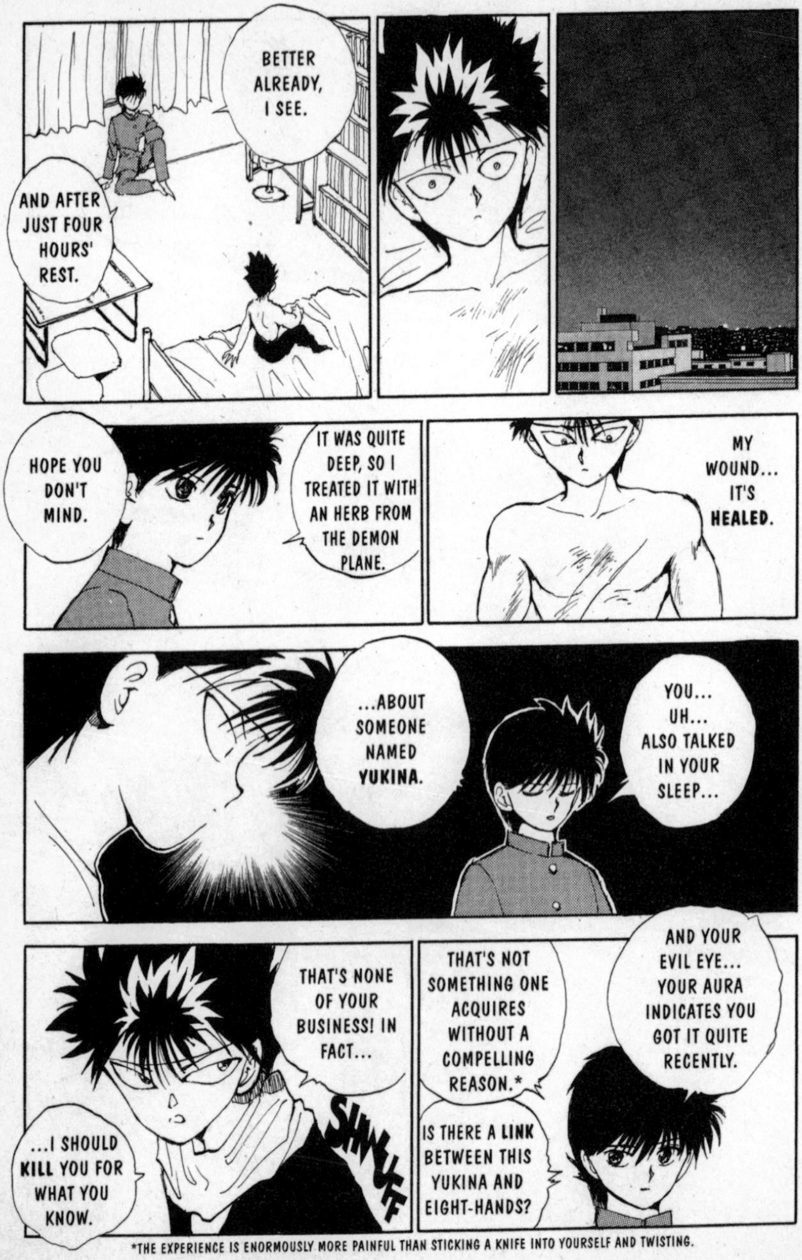
BETTER ALREADY, I SEE.
AND AFTER JUST FOUR HOURS' REST.
MY WOUND... IT'S **HEALED.**
IT WAS QUITE DEEP, SO I TREATED IT WITH AN HERB FROM THE DEMON PLANE.
HOPE YOU DON'T MIND.
YOU... UH... ALSO TALKED IN YOUR SLEEP...
...ABOUT SOMEONE NAMED **YUKINA.**
AND YOUR EVIL EYE... YOUR AURA INDICATES YOU GOT IT QUITE RECENTLY.
THAT'S NOT SOMETHING ONE ACQUIRES WITHOUT A COMPELLING REASON.*
IS THERE A **LINK** BETWEEN THIS YUKINA AND EIGHT-HANDS?
THAT'S NONE OF YOUR BUSINESS! IN FACT...
SHWUFF
...I SHOULD **KILL** YOU FOR WHAT YOU KNOW.

*THE EXPERIENCE IS ENORMOUSLY MORE PAINFUL THAN STICKING A KNIFE INTO YOURSELF AND TWISTING.

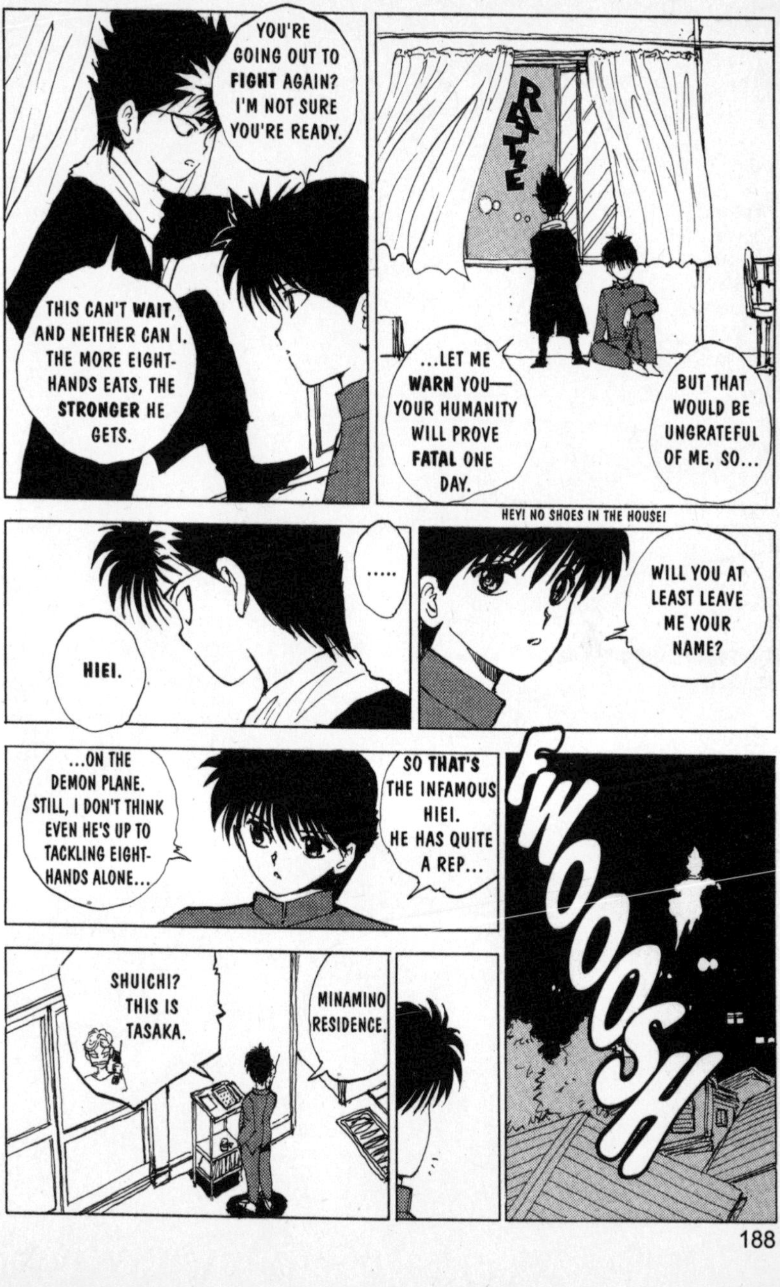
RATTLE
BUT THAT WOULD BE UNGRATEFUL OF ME, SO...
...LET ME WARN YOU— YOUR HUMANITY WILL PROVE FATAL ONE DAY.
HEY! NO SHOES IN THE HOUSE!
YOU'RE GOING OUT TO FIGHT AGAIN? I'M NOT SURE YOU'RE READY.
THIS CAN'T WAIT, AND NEITHER CAN I. THE MORE EIGHT-HANDS EATS, THE STRONGER HE GETS.
WILL YOU AT LEAST LEAVE ME YOUR NAME?
.....
HIEI.
FWOOOSH
SO THAT'S THE INFAMOUS HIEI. HE HAS QUITE A REP...
...ON THE DEMON PLANE. STILL, I DON'T THINK EVEN HE'S UP TO TACKLING EIGHT-HANDS ALONE...
MINAMINO RESIDENCE.
SHUICHI? THIS IS TASAKA.

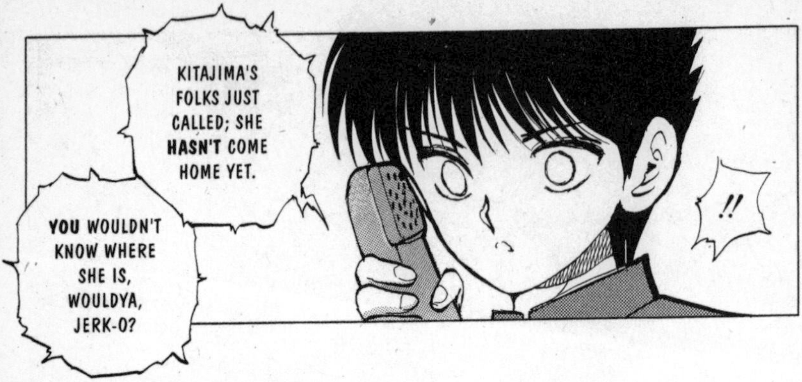
KITAJIMA'S FOLKS JUST CALLED; SHE **HASN'T** COME HOME YET.
YOU WOULDN'T KNOW WHERE SHE IS, WOULDYA, JERK-O?
!!

THE WORST-CASE SCENARIO — IT'S HAPPENED...

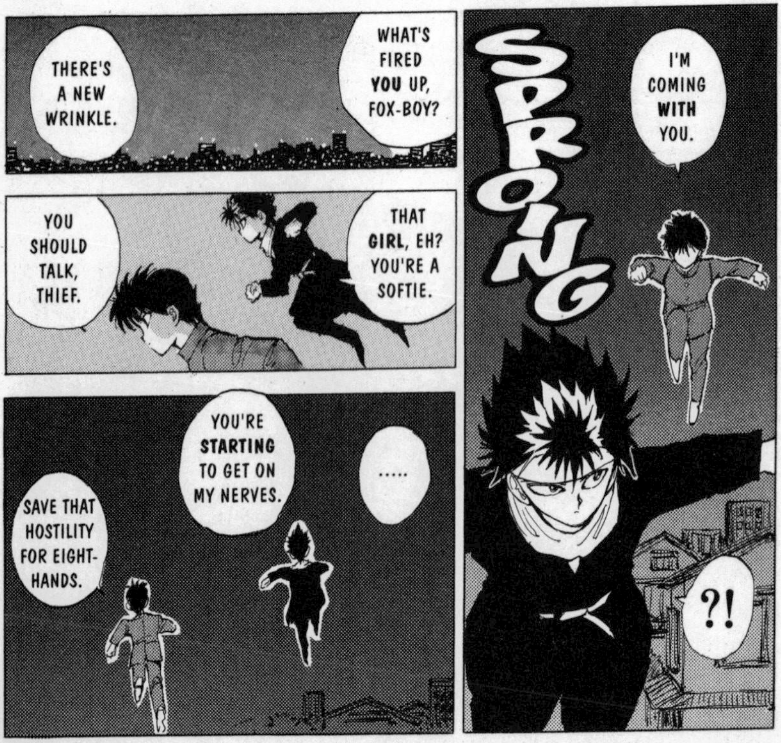
I'M COMING **WITH** YOU.
SPRONG
?!
WHAT'S FIRED **YOU** UP, FOX-BOY?
THERE'S A NEW WRINKLE.
THAT **GIRL**, EH? YOU'RE A SOFTIE.
YOU SHOULD TALK, THIEF.
.....
YOU'RE **STARTING** TO GET ON MY NERVES.
SAVE THAT HOSTILITY FOR EIGHT-HANDS.

A BURNT-OUT FACTORY...
...JUST THE PLACE...
...FOR THIRD-RATE DEMON TRASH TO HANG OUT.
MAYA...!!
.....
SO GLAD YOU DISAPPROVE.

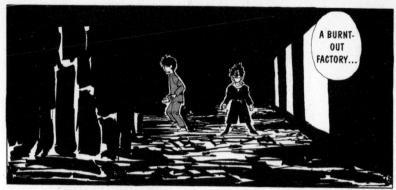

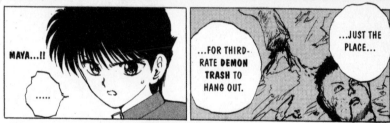

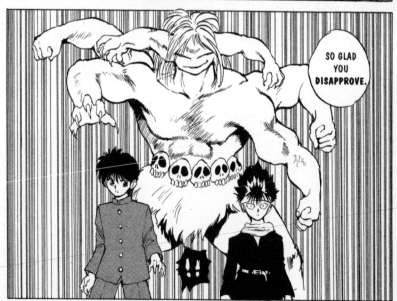

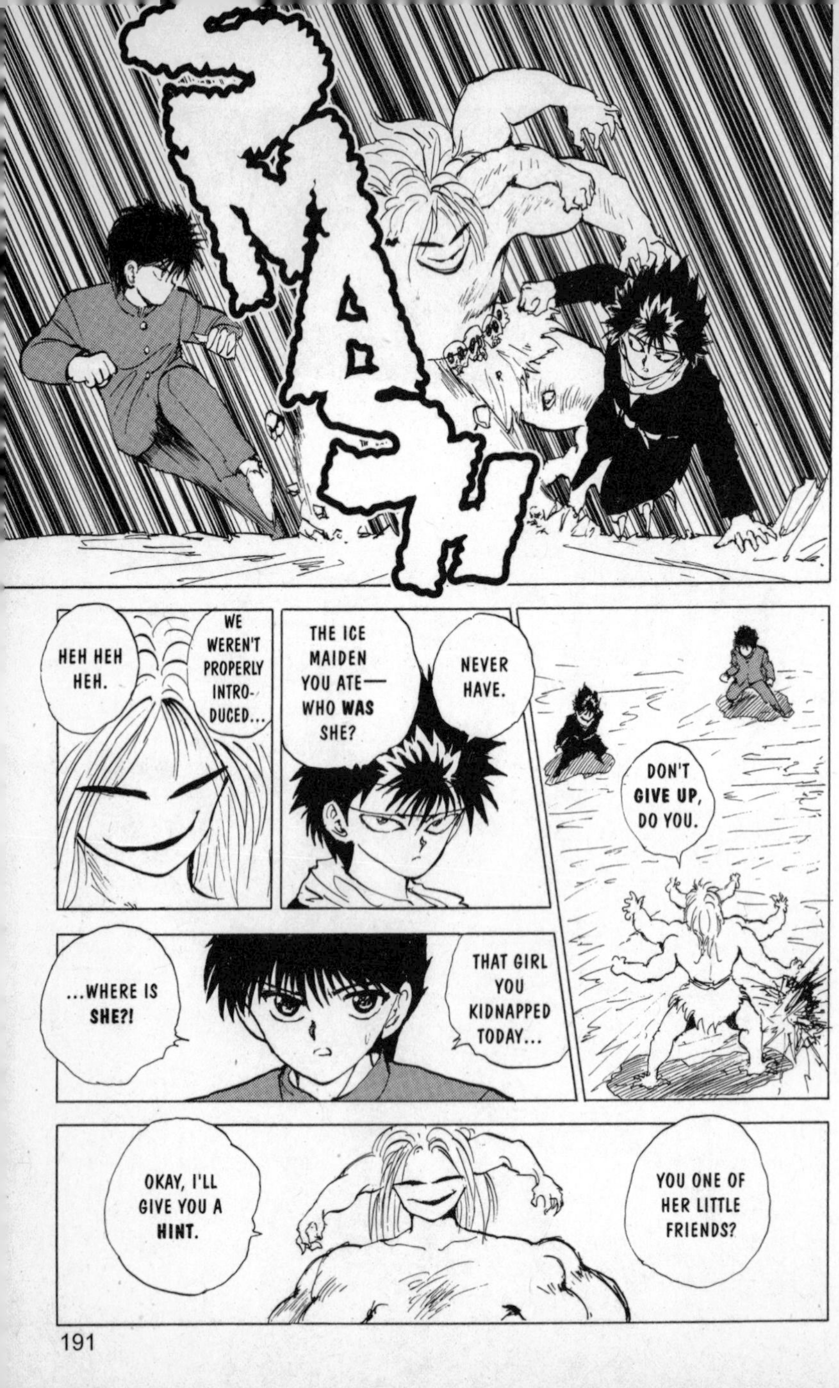
DON'T GIVE UP, DO YOU.
NEVER HAVE.
THE ICE MAIDEN YOU ATE— WHO WAS SHE?
WE WEREN'T PROPERLY INTRO-DUCED...
HEH HEH HEH.
THAT GIRL YOU KIDNAPPED TODAY...
...WHERE IS SHE?!
YOU ONE OF HER LITTLE FRIENDS?
OKAY, I'LL GIVE YOU A HINT.

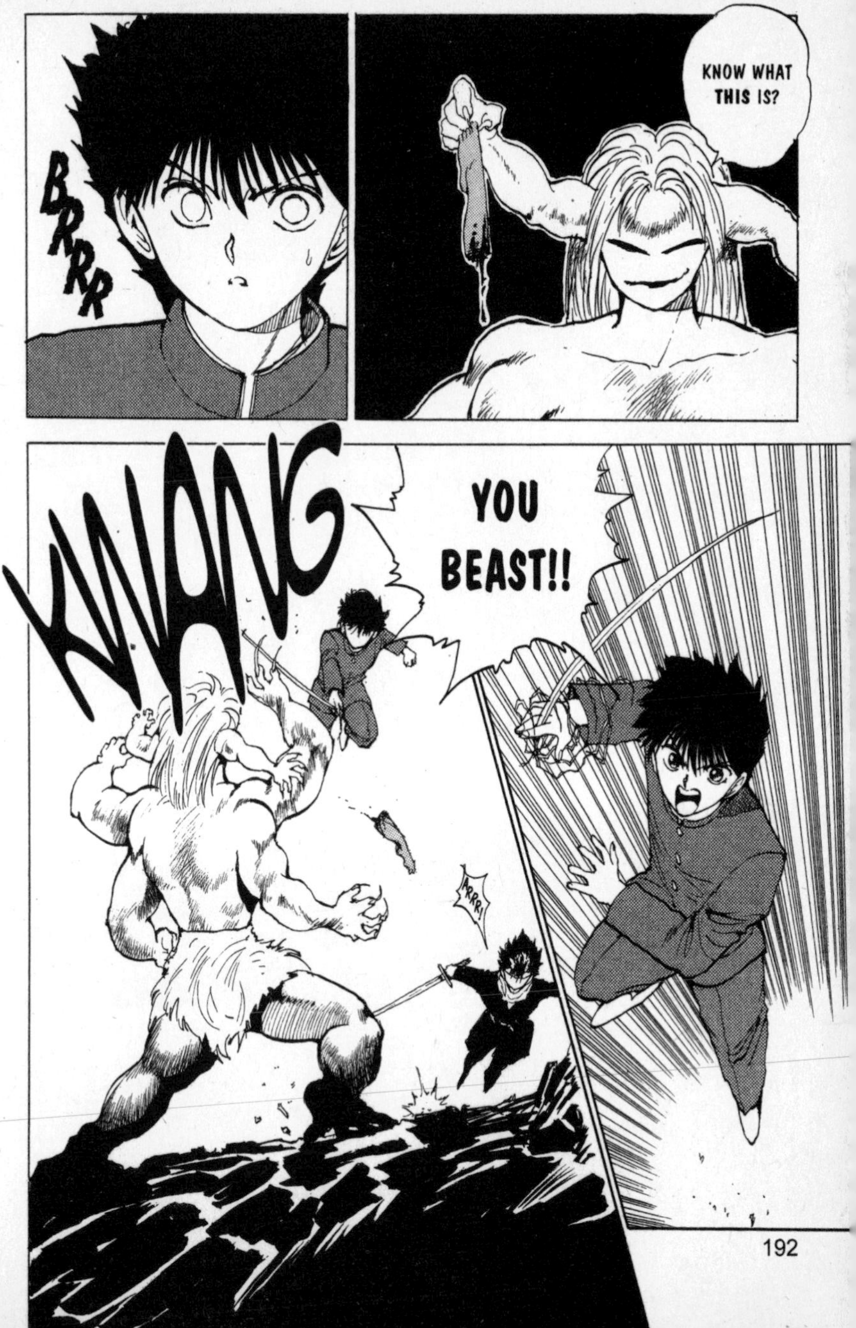
KNOW WHAT THIS IS?
BRRRR
YOU BEAST!!
KWANG
ARRR!

READ THIS WAY

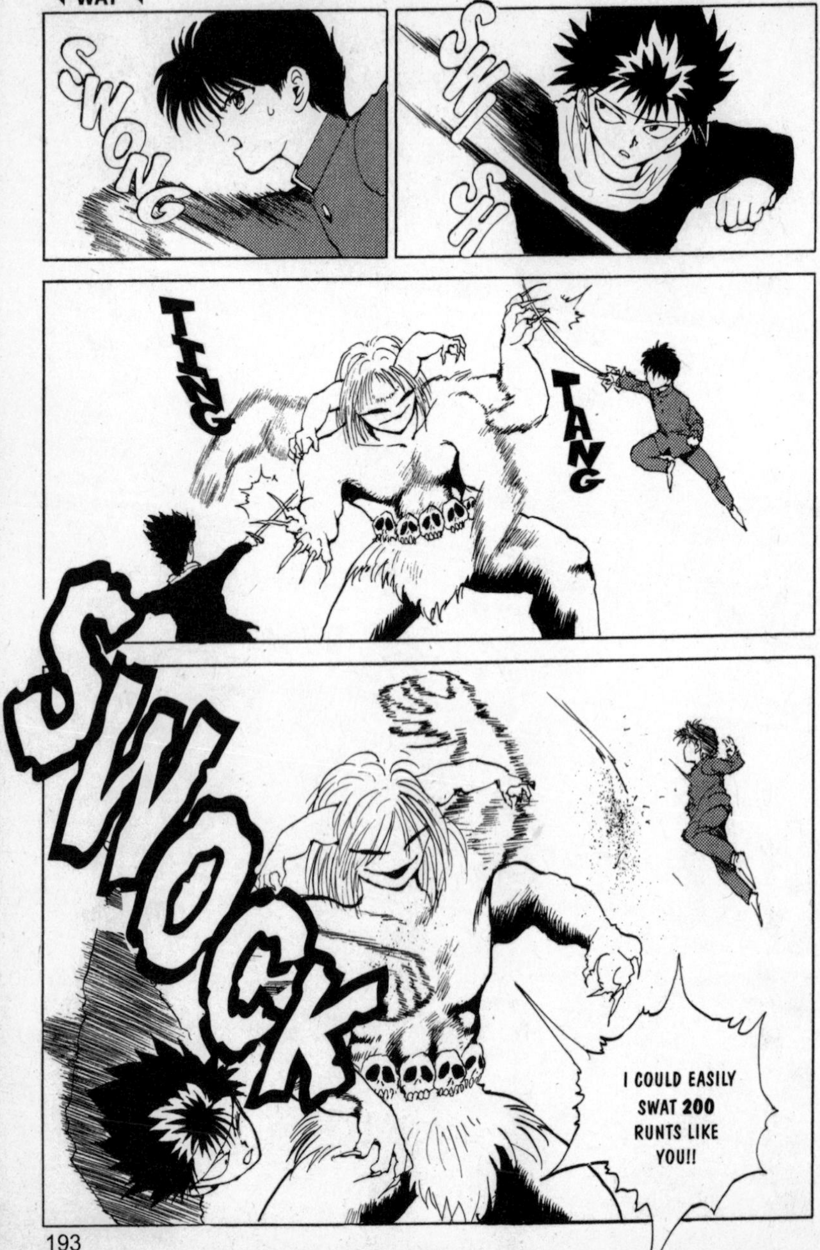
SWISH
SWONG
TING
TANG
SWOCK
I COULD EASILY SWAT 200 RUNTS LIKE YOU!!

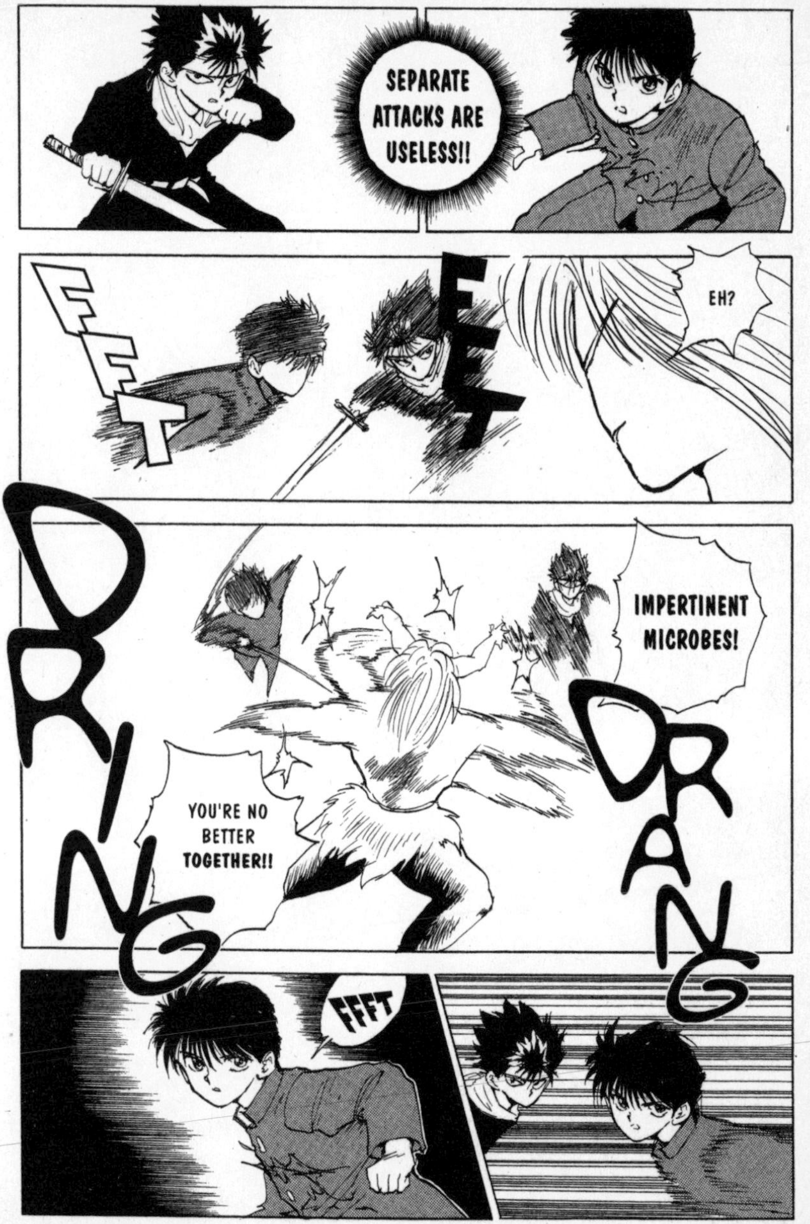
SEPARATE ATTACKS ARE USELESS!!
EH?
FFFT
FFFT
IMPERTINENT MICROBES!
DRANG
YOU'RE NO BETTER TOGETHER!!
DRING
FFFT

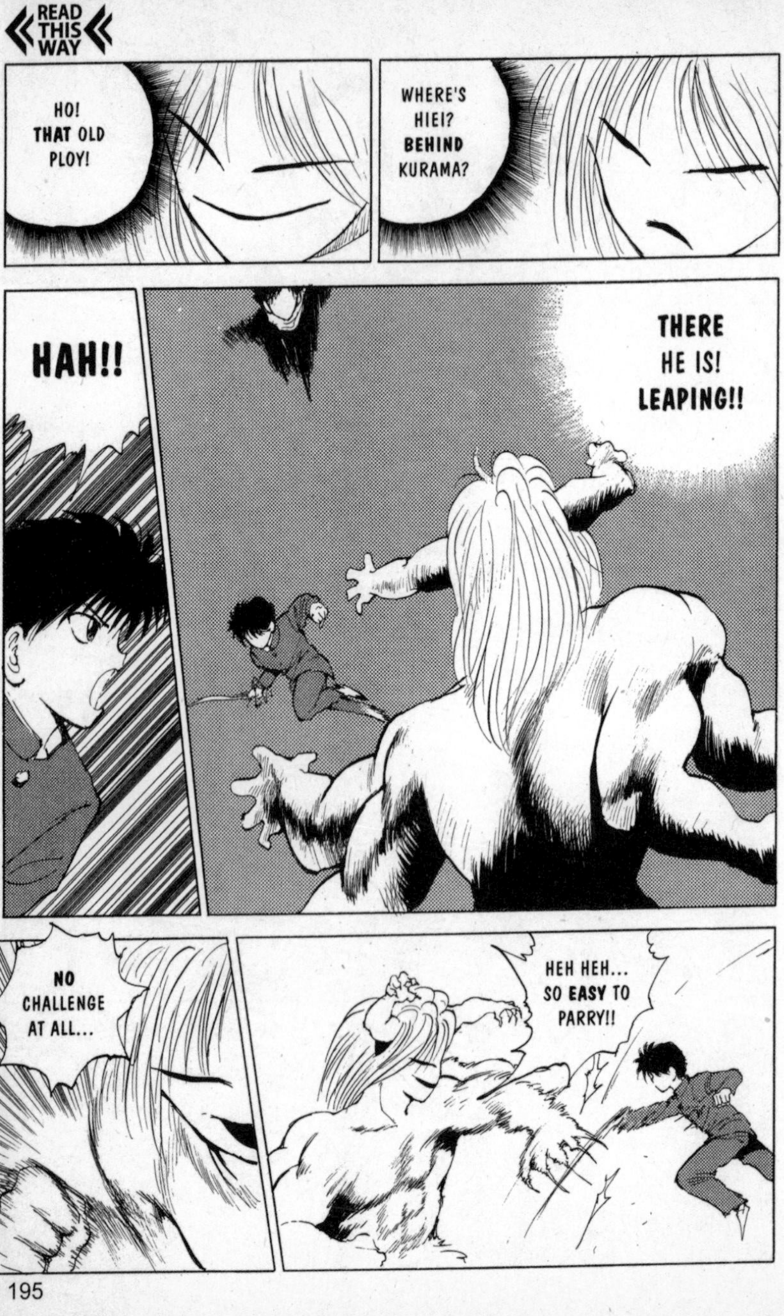
READ THIS WAY
WHERE'S HIEI? BEHIND KURAMA?
HO! THAT OLD PLOY!
THERE HE IS! LEAPING!!
HAH!!
HEH HEH... SO EASY TO PARRY!!
NO CHALLENGE AT ALL...

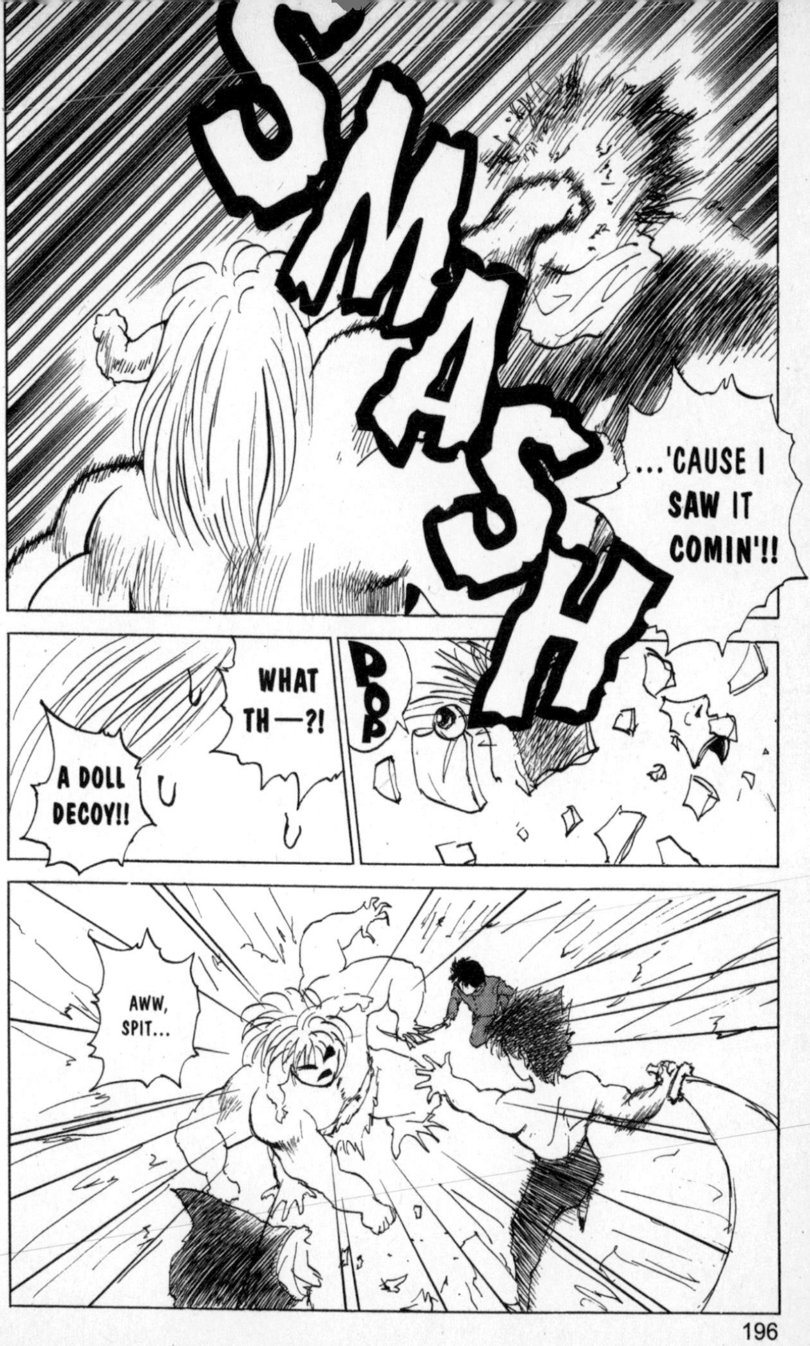
SMASH
...'CAUSE I SAW IT COMIN'!!
POP
WHAT TH—?!
A DOLL DECOY!!
AWW, SPIT...

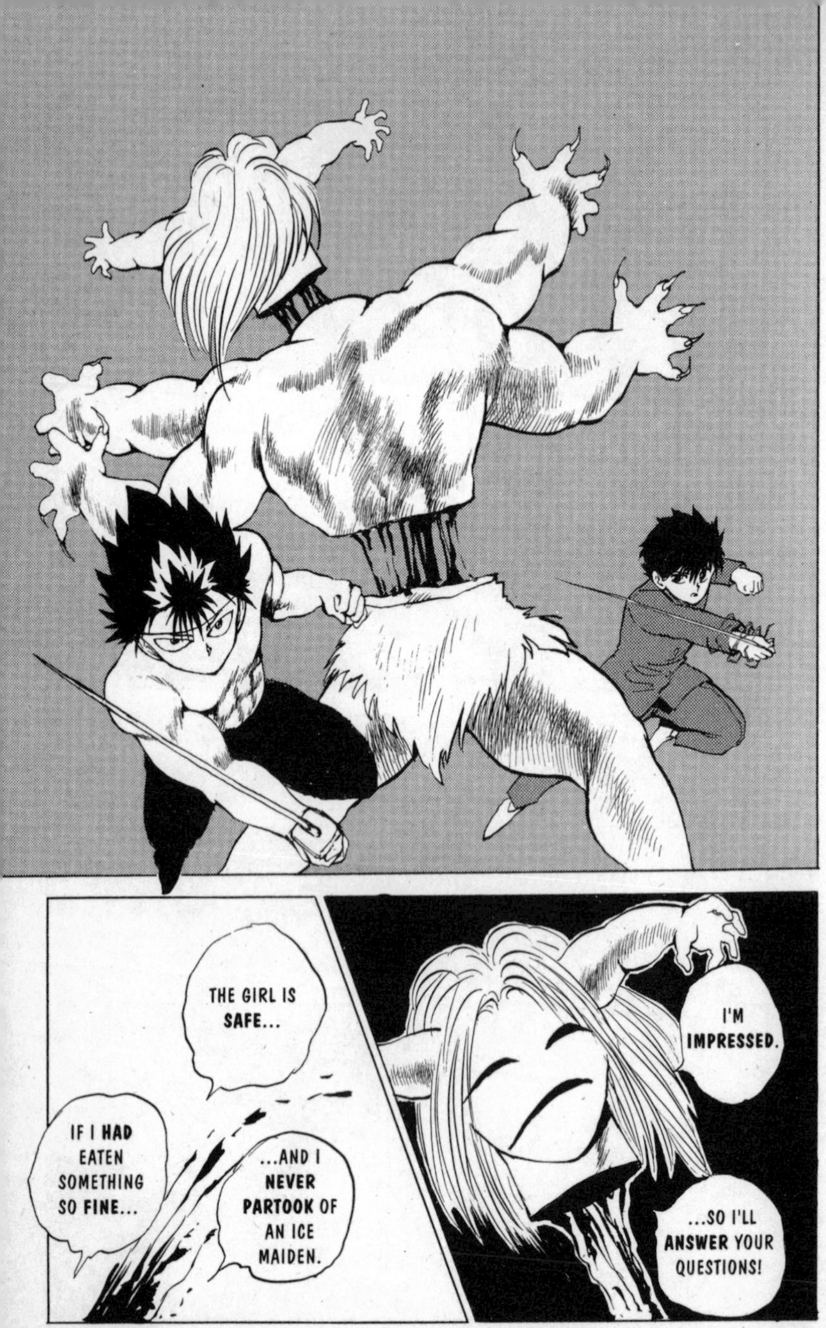
I'M IMPRESSED.
...SO I'LL ANSWER YOUR QUESTIONS!
THE GIRL IS SAFE...
...AND I NEVER PARTOOK OF AN ICE MAIDEN.
IF I HAD EATEN SOMETHING SO FINE...

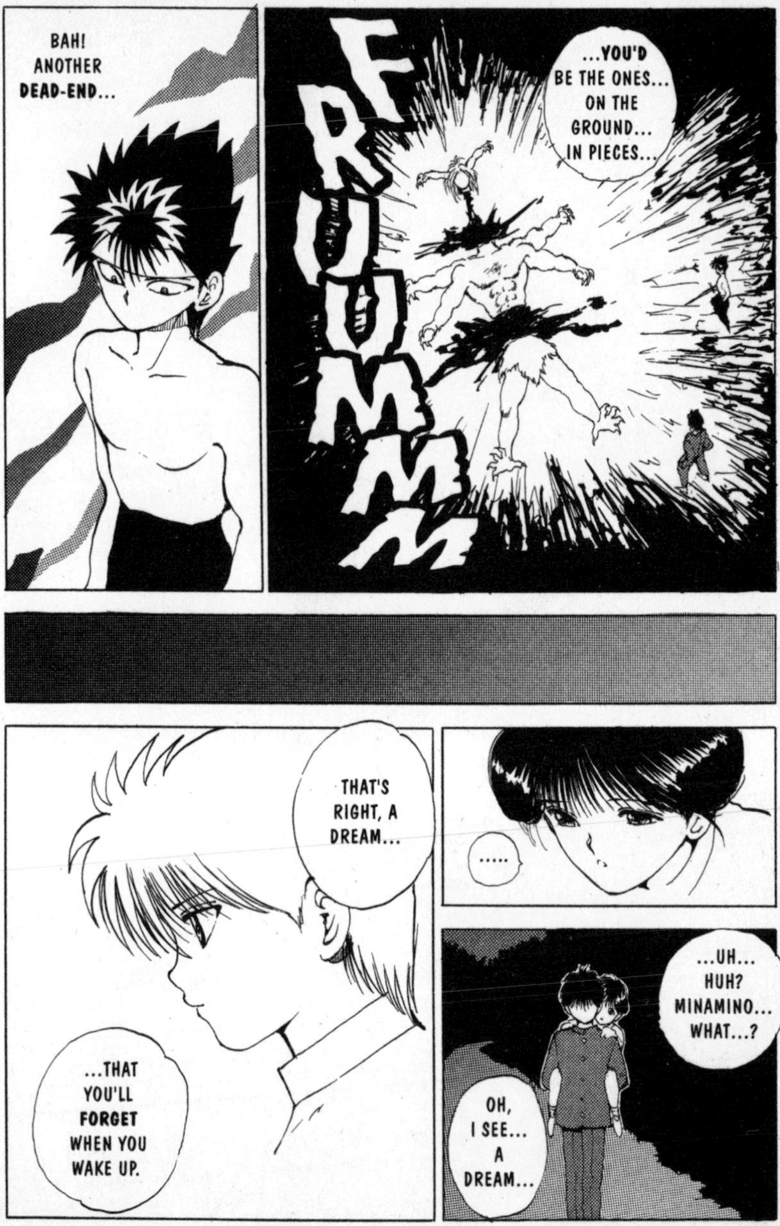
FRUUMMMM
...YOU'D BE THE ONES... ON THE GROUND... IN PIECES...
BAH! ANOTHER DEAD-END...
.....
...UH... HUH? MINAMINO... WHAT...?
OH, I SEE... A DREAM...
THAT'S RIGHT, A DREAM...
...THAT YOU'LL FORGET WHEN YOU WAKE UP.

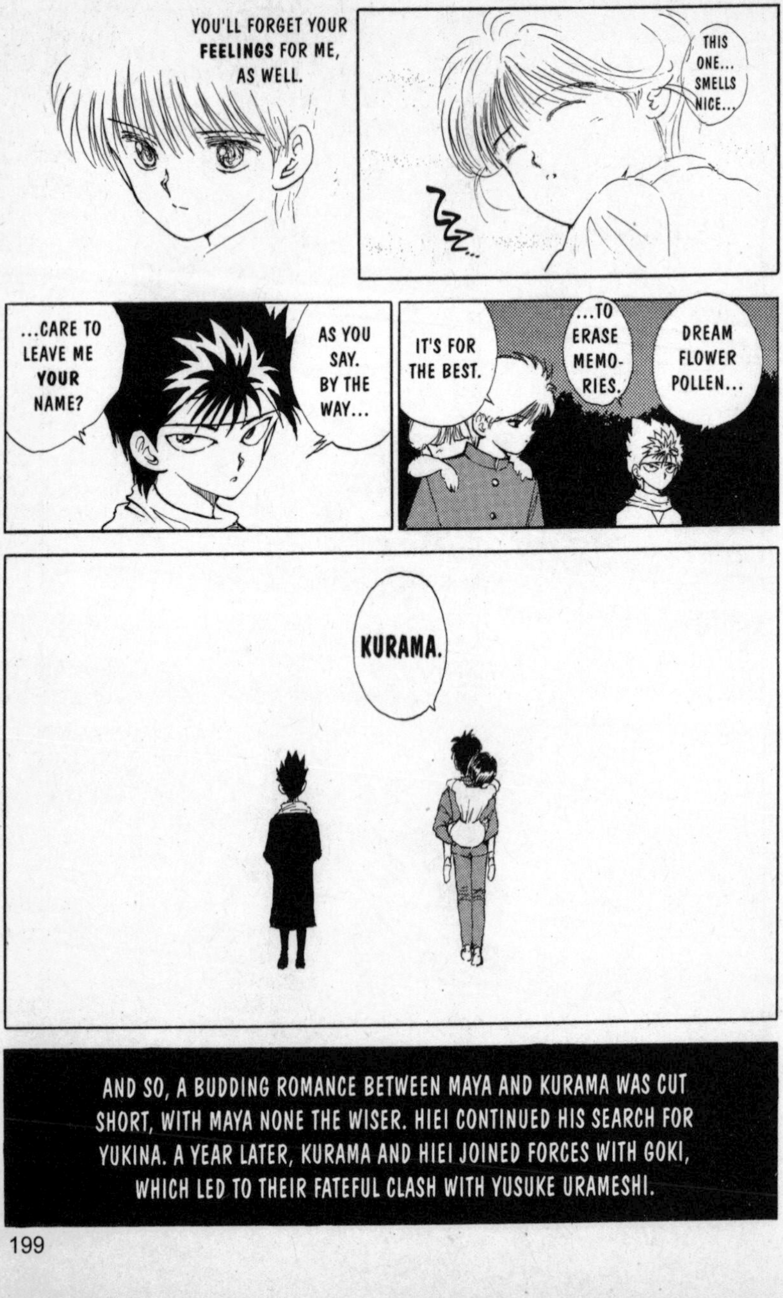
THIS ONE... SMELLS NICE...
ZZZ...
YOU'LL FORGET YOUR FEELINGS FOR ME, AS WELL.
DREAM FLOWER POLLEN...
...TO ERASE MEMORIES.
IT'S FOR THE BEST.
AS YOU SAY. BY THE WAY...
...CARE TO LEAVE ME YOUR NAME?
KURAMA.

AND SO, A BUDDING ROMANCE BETWEEN MAYA AND KURAMA WAS CUT SHORT, WITH MAYA NONE THE WISER. HIEI CONTINUED HIS SEARCH FOR YUKINA. A YEAR LATER, KURAMA AND HIEI JOINED FORCES WITH GOKI, WHICH LED TO THEIR FATEFUL CLASH WITH YUSUKE URAMESHI.

COMING NEXT VOLUME...

Dr. Ichigaki's evil ploy is in gear—he's installed nodes in the martial arts students' bodies, and they're acting like his subservient pawns in the latest episode of the Dark Tournament! It's been a bumpy ride for Team Urameshi, but the fight isn't over yet as the Underworld isn't showing signs of running short on their supply of diabolical creatures to prevent Team Urameshi from winning the tournament.

Coming October 2005

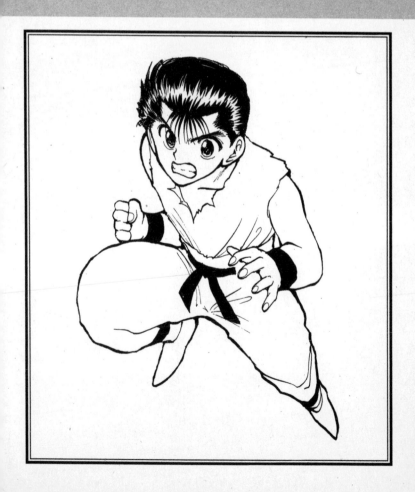

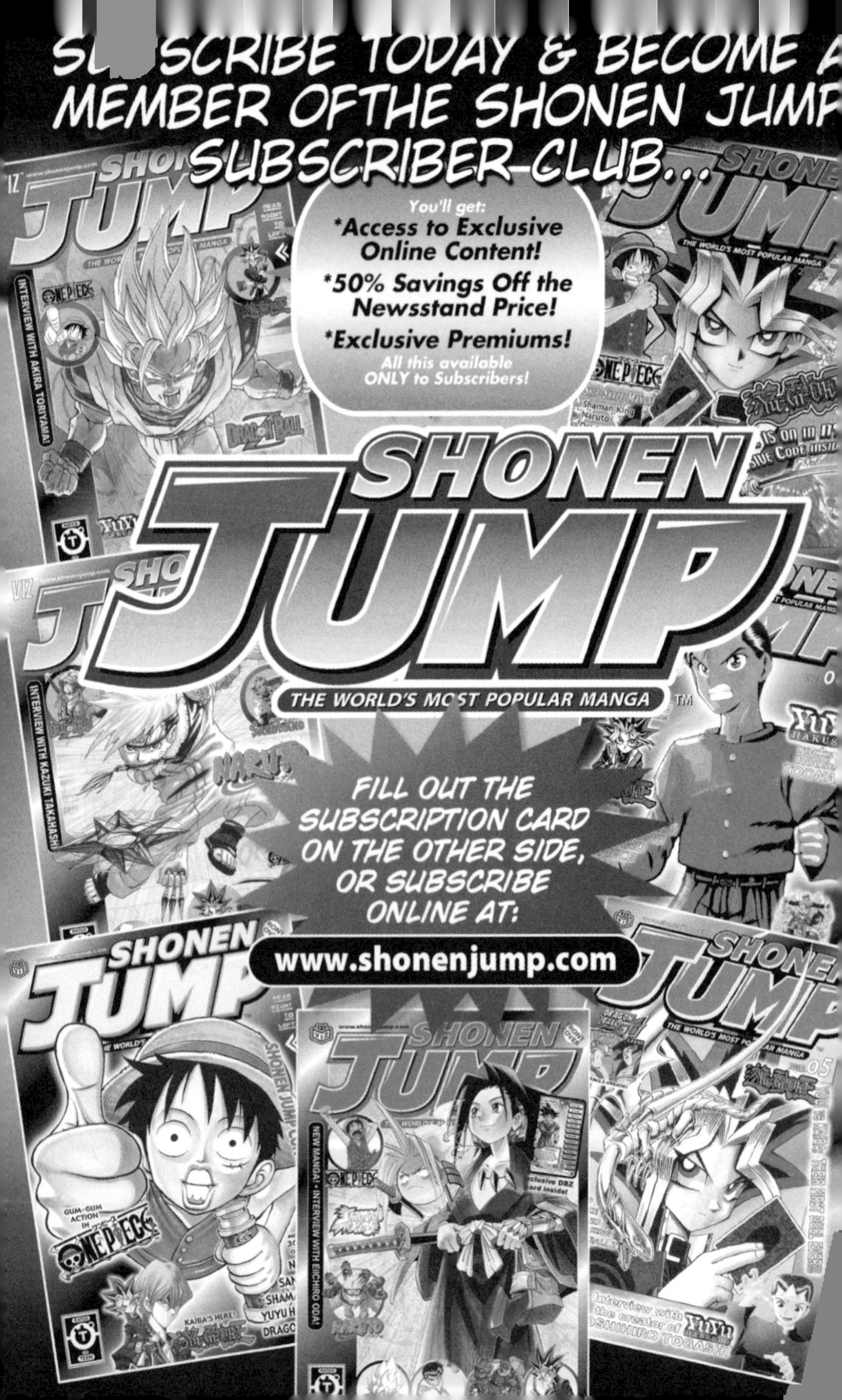
SUBSCRIBE TODAY & BECOME A MEMBER OFTHE SHONEN JUMP SUBSCRIBER CLUB...
You'll get:
*Access to Exclusive Online Content!
*50% Savings Off the Newsstand Price!
*Exclusive Premiums!
All this available ONLY to Subscribers!
SHONEN JUMP
THE WORLD'S MOST POPULAR MANGA
FILL OUT THE SUBSCRIPTION CARD ON THE OTHER SIDE, OR SUBSCRIBE ONLINE AT:
www.shonenjump.com

Save 50% off the newsstand price!

SHONEN JUMP
THE WORLD'S MOST POPULAR MANGA

SUBSCRIBE TODAY and SAVE 50% OFF the cover price PLUS enjoy all the benefits of the SHONEN JUMP SUBSCRIBER CLUB, exclusive online content & special premiums ONLY AVAILABLE to SUBSCRIBERS!

☑ **YES!** Please enter my 1 year subscription (12 issues) to *SHONEN JUMP* at the INCREDIBLY LOW SUBSCRIPTION RATE of $29.95 and sign me up for the SHONEN JUMP Subscriber Club!

Only $29.95!

NAME

ADDRESS

CITY   STATE   ZIP

E-MAIL ADDRESS

☐ MY CHECK IS ENCLOSED   ☐ BILL ME LATER

CREDIT CARD: ☐ VISA   ☐ MASTERCARD

ACCOUNT #   EXP. DATE

SIGNATURE

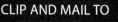

CLIP AND MAIL TO →

SHONEN JUMP
Subscriptions Service Dept.
P.O. Box 515
Mount Morris, IL 61054-0515

Make checks payable to: **SHONEN JUMP.**
Canada add US $12. No foreign orders. Allow 6-8 weeks for delivery.

P5SJGN   YU-GI-OH! © 1996 by KAZUKI TAKAHASHI / SHUEISHA Inc.

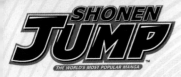

COMPLETE OUR SURVEY AND LET US KNOW WHAT YOU THINK!

☐ Please do NOT send me information about VIZ and SHONEN JUMP products, news and events, special offers, or other information.

☐ Please do NOT send me information from VIZ's trusted business partners.

Name: _____

Address: _____

City: _____ State: _____ Zip: _____

E-mail: _____

☐ Male ☐ Female   Date of Birth (mm/dd/yyyy): ___ / ___ / ___   (Under 13? Parental consent required)

❶ Do you purchase SHONEN JUMP Magazine?

☐ Yes   ☐ No (if no, skip the next two questions)

If **YES**, do you subscribe?
☐ Yes   ☐ No

If **NO**, how often do you purchase SHONEN JUMP Magazine?

☐ 1-3 issues a year

☐ 4-6 issues a year

☐ more than 7 issues a year

❷ Which SHONEN JUMP Graphic Novel did you purchase? (please check one)

☐ Beet the Vandel Buster   ☐ Bleach   ☐ Dragon Ball
☐ Dragon Ball Z   ☐ Dr. Slump   ☐ Eyeshield 21
☐ Hikaru no Go   ☐ Hunter x Hunter   ☐ I"s
☐ Knights of the Zodiac   ☐ Legendz   ☐ Naruto
☐ One Piece   ☐ Rurouni Kenshin   ☐ Shaman King
☐ The Prince of Tennis   ☐ Ultimate Muscle   ☐ Whistle!
☐ Yu-Gi-Oh!   ☐ Yu-Gi-Oh!: Duelist   ☐ YuYu Hakusho
☐ Other _____

Will you purchase subsequent volumes?
☐ Yes   ☐ No

❸ How did you learn about this title? (check all that apply)

☐ Favorite title   ☐ Advertisement   ☐ Article
☐ Gift   ☐ Read excerpt in SHONEN JUMP Magazine
☐ Recommendation   ☐ Special offer   ☐ Through TV animation
☐ Website   ☐ Other _____

4 Of the titles that are serialized in SHONEN JUMP Magazine, have you purchased the Graphic Novels?

☐ Yes   ☐ No

If **YES**, which ones have you purchased? (ch...)

☐ Dragon Ball Z   ☐ Hikaru no G...   ☐ ...Piece
☐ Shaman King   ☐ Yu-Gi-Oh!   ☐ ...

If **YES**, what were your reasons for purchasing? (please pick up to 3)

☐ A favorite title   ☐ A favorite creator/artist   ☐ I want to read it in one go
☐ I want to read it over and over again   ☐ There are extras that aren't in the magazine
☐ The quality of printing is better than the magazine   ☐ Recommendation
☐ Special offer   ☐ Other

If **NO**, why did/would you not purchase it?

☐ I'm happy just reading it in the magazine   ☐ It's not worth buying the graphic novel
☐ All the manga pages are in black and white unlike the magazine
☐ There are other graphic novels that I prefer   ☐ There are too many to collect for each title
☐ It's too small   ☐ Other _____

5 Of the titles NOT serialized in the Magazine, which ones have you purchased?
(check all that apply)

☐ Beet the Vandel Buster   ☐ Bleach   ☐ Dragon Ball   ☐ Dr. Slump
☐ Eyeshield 21   ☐ Hunter x Hunter   ☐ I"s   ☐ Knights of the Zodiac
☐ Legendz   ☐ The Prince of Tennis   ☐ Rurouni Kenshin   ☐ Whistle!
☐ Yu-Gi-Oh!: Duelist   ☐ None   ☐ Other _____

If you did purchase any of the above, what were your reasons for purchase?

☐ A favorite title   ☐ A favorite creator/artist
☐ Read a preview in SHONEN JUMP Magazine and wanted to read the rest of the story
☐ Recommendation   ☐ Other

Will you purchase subsequent volumes?

☐ Yes   ☐ No

6 What race/ethnicity do you consider yourself? (please check one)

☐ Asian/Pacific Islander   ☐ Black/African American   ☐ Hispanic/Latino
☐ Native American/Alaskan Native   ☐ White/Caucasian   ☐ Other

THANK YOU! Please send the completed form to:

VIZ Survey
42 Catharine St.
Poughkeepsie, NY 12601

All information provided will be used for internal purposes only. We promise not to sell or otherwise divulge your information.

NO PURCHASE NECESSARY. Requests not in compliance with all terms of this form will not be acknowledged or returned. All submissions are subject to verification and become the property of VIZ, LLC. Fraudulent submission, including use of multiple addresses or P.O. boxes to obtain additional VIZ information or offers may result in prosecution. VIZ reserves the right to withdraw or modify any terms of this form. Void where prohibited, taxed, or restricted by law. VIZ will not be liable for lost, misdirected, mutilated, illegible, incomplete or postage-due mail. © 2003 VIZ, LLC. All Rights Reserved. VIZ, LLC, property titles, characters, names and plots therein under license to VIZ, LLC. All Rights Reserved.

KU-482-778